The New Sabin

Entries 15804-17945

The New Sabin;

Books Described by Joseph Sabin and His

Successors, Now Described Again on the

Basis of Examination of Originals,

and Fully Indexed by Title, Subject,

Joint Authors, and Institutions and Agencies.

by

Lawrence S. Thompson

Entries 15804-17945

Volume VII

The Whitston Publishing Company

Troy, New York

1980

To Henry Raup Wagner

(1862-1957)

PREFACE

The titles represented in this volume of *The New Sabin* deal with the Trans-Mississippi West, with a few exceptions, and include the microfiche editions in a collection issued by the Lost Cause Press. It is a continuation of the second volume, in which nearly all the titles in Wagner-Camp are included. As the collection grows, subsequent volumes of *The New Sabin* will be devoted to it.

Here, along with the Wagner-Camp titles in the second volume, is a library of cornerstone works on the history of the Old West. Many others are in the first six volumes of *The New Sabin* particularly the first and the fifth, and the student of western American history should use the cumulative index to the first five volumes to supplement the present one. With the tenth volume and each subsequent fifth volume there will be new cumulative indexes.

What has been included thus far on the West is not, nor is it intended to be, a definitive collection. The history of the individual western states and regions and of single aspects of western history such as the fur trade, mining, Indians, Mormons, or the cattle industry can be covered comprehensively only in detailed subject bibliographies or catalogues of special collections. Here, and in subsequent volumes to be devoted to the Trans-Mississippi West, a strong effort will be made to include basic nineteenth and early twentieth century titles. The specialized bibliographer must cover the enormous production of western historians in the last seventy-five years.

A few titles appear not to be related directly to the history of the West. In nearly every instance there are significant portions which relate to western history and are so identified in the subject index. Further, the history of the Southwest, Old and New, is closely related to that of the Old South. By the same token, the Ohio Valley states were way-stations for western pioneers. The Mormons are an egregious example. Hence we have here some titles in which the emphasis is on the Trans-Allegheny West. Even the sixth volume of *The New Sabin,* primarily on Kentucky history, contains several items of considerable interest for western history. Texas, New Mexico, and Wyoming were heavily populated by gun-toting Kentuckians who did not care to face justice in the New Commonwealth. A good proportion of professional men and political leaders of the Old West were graduates of Transylvania University in Lexington. And printing was introduced to Saxon California by buckskin-clad Kentuckians.

Lawrence S. Thompson
Lexington, Kentucky
December, 1979

15804 Abbott, Carlisle Stewart, b. 1828.
         Recollections of a California pioneer, by Carlisle
       S. Abbott. New York, The Neale publishing company,
       1917.
         285 p.   front. (port.)   19½ cm.

15805 Abbott, John Stevens Cabot, 1805-1877.
         ... Christopher Carson. Familiarly known as Kit
       Carson. By John S. C. Abbott. With illustrations
       by Eleanor Greatorex. New York, Dodd & Mead, 1875.
         x, 348 p.   illus.   19 cm.

15806 Abernethy, George.
         Circular to the Oregon emigrants... Dated at
       Oregon City, this 22d of April, 1847. [n.p., n.d.]
         Broadside.   29½ x 21½ cm.
         Incipit: It being my duty, as Superintendent of
       Indian affairs... "to give such instructions and
       directions to Emigrants to this Territory... by
       observance of which, they will be most likely to ob-
       tain and promote peace and friendship between them
       and the Indian tribes..."

15807 Abney, A   H
         Life and adventures of L. D. Lafferty; being a
       true biography of one of the most remarkable men of
       the great Southwest, from an adventurous boyhood
       in Arkansas, through a protracted life of almost
       unparalleled sufferings and hairbreadth escapes upon
       the frontier of Texas... By A. H. Abney...
       New York, H. S. Goodspeed & co. [1875]
         219 p. incl. front., plates, ports.   19 cm.

15808 [Account of the discovery of gold in California;
       in the biography of James W. Marshall]
       (In National Cyclopedia of American Biography,
       vol. V, p. 146)

15809 Ackley, Richard Thomas, 1832-1881.
         Across the plains in 1858, by Richard Thomas Ackley

of Camden, New Jersey. Salt Lake City, Utah State
Historical Society, 1941. (In Utah historical
quarterly, v. 9, nos. 3, 4, July, October 1941,
p. 190-228)

15810 Adam, George.
    The dreadful sufferings and thrilling adventures
of an overland party of emigrants to California,
their terrible conflicts with savage tribes of
Indians!! and Mexican bands of robbers!!! with
marriage, funeral, and other interesting ceremonies
and customs of Indian life in the far West.
Compiled from the journal of Mr. George Adam,
one of the adventurers, by Prof. Wm. Beschke.
St. Louis, Mo., Barclay & co., 1850.
    x, [13]-71, [1] p. incl. front., illus., pl.
23½ cm.

15811 Adams, Mrs. Emma Hildreth.
    To and fro, up and down in southern California,
Oregon, and Washington territory, with sketches in
Arizona, New Mexico and British Columbia. By
Emma H. Adams... Cincinnati, Chicago [etc.]
Cranston & Stowe [c1888]
    1 p.l., 608 p.   front., illus.   21 cm.

15812 Adams, Ephraim, 1818-
    The Iowa band. New and rev. ed. By Rev. Ephraim
Adams, D. D. Boston, Chicago, The Pilgrim press
[1902]
    xx, 240 p. incl. illus., map.   front., pl.,
port.   19½ cm.
    "Introduction to first edition, by Rev. William
Barrows", dated May, 1870. "Introduction to the
second edition by Rev. James L. Hill."

15813 Adams, Ephraim D
    British interests and activities in Texas, 1838-
1846. Baltimore, 1910.
    8, 267 p.   22 cm.   (The Albert Shaw lectures
on diplomatic history, 1909)

15814 Adams, John Quincy, pres. U.S., 1767-1848.
    Speech of John Quincy Adams, of Massachusetts,
upon the right of the people, men and women, to
petition; on the freedom of speech and of debate
in the House of Representatives of the United States
on the resolutions of seven state legislatures,

and the petitions of more than one hundred thousand
petitioners, relating to the annexation of Texas
to this Union. Delivered in the House of Representatives of the United States, in fragments of the
morning hour, from the 16th of June to the 7th of
July, 1838, inclusive. Washington, Printed by Gales
and Seaton, 1838.
131 p.   24½ cm.

15815   [Adams, William L   ]
A melodrame entitled "Treason, stratagems, and
spoils," in five acts, by Breakspear. Portland, Ore.,
1852.
32 p.   illus.   25½ cm.

15816   Adams, William L
Oregon as it is; its present and future, by a
resident for twenty-five years, being a reply to
inquirers. Portland, Ore., "Bulletin" steam book
and job printing rooms, 1873.
61 p.   20½ cm.

15817   Adamson, Archibald R   1839-
North Platte and its associations. By Archibald
R. Adamson... North Platte, Neb., The Evening
telegraph [c1910]
3 p.l., 241, [3] p.   front. (port.)   illus.
19 cm.

15818   Additon, Lucia H   Faxon.
Twenty eventful years of the Oregon Woman's
Christian temperance union, 1880-1900. Statistical,
historical and biographical. Portraits of prominent
pioneer workers. [By] Lucia H. Faxon Additon...
Portland, Or., Gotshall printing company, 1904.
xv, 112 p.   pl., ports.   19 cm.

15819   Adney, Edwin Tappan, 1868-1950.
The Klondike stampede, by Tappan Adney. New York,
Harper, 1900.
xii, 470 p.   illus., maps (1 double)   21 cm.

15820   Adsit, Mrs. C   D
New education in California. Repr. by permission
from "Education", Boston, Mass. Milwaukee, 1889.
15 p.   23½ cm.

15821 Agee, George W
       Rube Burrow, king of outlaws, and his band of
       train robbers. An accurate and faithful history
       of their exploits and adventures. By G. W. Agee...
       [Cincinnati, O., Printed by C. J. Krehbiel & co.,
       c1890]
       x, 194 p.   front., plates, ports.   20 cm.

15822 Aguilar Arevalo, Roberto, 1901-1966.
       Crónicas de ayer. Cuenca, Núcleo del Azuay,
       Casa de la Cultura Ecuatoriana, 1969.
       140 p.   port.   23 cm.

15823 Aiken, Charles S   comp.
       California today: San Francisco, its metropolis;
       a concise statement concerning the state that faces
       the Orient, and the city by the Golden Gate...
       San Francisco, 1903.
       192 p.   pl.   18 cm.
       Issued by the California Promotion Committee of
       San Francisco.

15824 Aimard, Gustave, 1818-1883.
       The Indian scout. A story of the Aztec city. By
       Gustave Aimard... London, Ward and Lock, 1861.
       vi, 429 p.   16 cm.
       Preface signed: L. W. [i.e. Lascelles Wraxall];
       a translation of "L'éclaireur"; sequel to "The
       prairie flower".

15825 Aimard, Gustave, 1818-1883.
       The pirates of the prairies; by Gustave Aimard...
       Rev. and ,ed. by Percy B. St. John. New York,
       J. W. Lovell company [1887]
       vi, [7]-127 p.   18½ cm.   (On cover: Lovell's
       library, no. 1011)
       Sequel: The trapper's daughter.

15826 Aimard, Gustave, 1818-1883.
       The tiger-slayer; a tale of the Indian desert,
       by Gustave Aimard... London, for the proprietors,
       1865.
       4 p.l., 339 p.   16½ cm.
       Preface signed: Lascelles Wraxall; a translation
       of "La grande flibuste"; sequel: The gold-seekers.

15827 Aimard, Gustave, 1818-1883.
       The trappers of Arkansas. A narrative. By

4

Gustave Aimard... Rev. and ed. by Percy B. St. John.
New York, J. W. Lovell company [1887]
   128 p.   18½ cm.   (On cover: Lovell's library,
no. 1045)
   Sequel: "The border rifles."

15828 Ainsworth, Danforth Hurlburt, 1828-
   Recollections of a civil engineer; experiences
in New York, Iowa, Nebraska, Dakota, Illinois,
Missouri, Minnesota and Colorado. [By] D. H.
Ainsworth. Newton, Ia., 1901.
   1 p.l., 192 p.   21 cm.

15829 Alderson, Matt W
   Bozeman, a guide to its places of recreation and
a synopsis of its superior natural adventages,
industries and opportunities... Bozeman, Montana
[n.d.]
   54 p.   map.   15 cm.

15830 Aldrich, Vernice M
   The Columbia River Historical Expedition.
[Bismarck, N.D., State Historical Society of North
Dakota, 1926]
   49-50 p.   illus.   25 cm.
   In North Dakota historical quarterly, v. 1, no. 1,
Oct. 1926.

15831 Aldridge, Reginald.
   Ranch notes in Kansas, Colorado, the Indian
territory and northern Texas. By Reginald Aldridge...
London, Longmans, Green, and co., 1884.
   3 p.l., 227 p.   front., plates.   19 cm.
   American edition (New York, D. Appleton and company)
has title: Life on a range; ranch notes in Kansas,
Colorado, the Indian territory, and northern Texas.

15832 Allen, Miss A   J
   Thrilling adventures, travels and explorations
of Doctor Elijah White, among the Rocky Mountains
and in the far west, with incidents of two sea
voyages via Sandwich Islands around Cape Horn...
New York, 1859.
   430 p.   front. (port.)   20½ cm.
   Published in 1848 and 1850 under title: Ten
years in Oregon.

15833   [Allen, George] 1792-1883.
        An appeal to the people of Massachusetts, on the
        Texas question. [2d ed.] Boston, C. C. Little &
        J. Brown, 1844.
        20 p.   22½ cm.

15834   [Allen, George] 1792-1883.
        The complaint of Mexico, and conspiracy against
        liberty. Boston, J. W. Alden, 1843.
        44 p.   24 cm.
        Appendix: Letter from Daniel Webster to Waddy
        Thompson (p. [33]-44)

15835   Allen, Joel Asaph, 1838-1921.
        ... The American bisons, living and extinct. By
        J. A. Allen... With twelve plates and a map.
        Cambridge, University press [etc.] 1876.
        3 p.l., [v]-ix, 246 p.   illus., XII pl. (part
        fold.) fold. map.   29½ cm.   (Memoirs of the
        Museum of comparative zoology at Harvard college...
        vol. IV, no. 10)
        "Published by permission of N. S. Shaler, director
        of the Kentucky geological survey." Issued also
        as "Kentucky. Geological survey, 1873-1891.
        Memoirs... v. 1, pt. 2."

15836   Allen, John Taylor.
        Early pioneer days in Texas. [Dallas, 1918]
        267 p.   illus., port.   21 cm.

15837   Allen, W   W
        California gold book; first nugget, its discovery
        and discoverers, and some of the results proceeding
        therefrom; by W. W. Allen and R. B. Avery. San
        Francisco and Chicago, Donohue & Henneberry,
        printers, 1893.
        1 p.l., iii, [2]-439 p.   front., pl.   20 cm.

15838   Allen, William Alonzo, 1848-
        Adventures with Indians and game, or, Twenty years
        in the Rocky mountains, by Dr. William A. Allen...
        Chicago, A. W. Bowen & co., 1903.
        302 p. incl. front. (port.)   plates.   23 cm.

15839   Allen, William Alonzo, 1848-
        The sheep eaters, by W. A. Allen, D.D.S. New York,
        The Shakespeare press, 1913.
        78 p.   front. (port.) plates.   19½ cm.

15840 [Allen, William M   ]
      Five years in the West; or, How an inexperienced
      young man finds his occupation. With reminiscences
      and sketches of real life. By a Texas preacher.
      Nashville, Tenn., Southern Methodist publishing
      house, 1884.
      211 p.   19 cm.

15841 Alley, B   F
      Linn County, Oregon, descriptive and resources, its
      cities and towns... Albany, Ore., Electric power
      print. [n.d.]
      112 p.   17 cm.

15842 Allsopp, Fred W
      Twenty years in a newspaper office... consisting
      principally of random sketches of things seen,
      heard and experienced on the "Arkansas gazette".
      Little Rock, Ark., 1907.
      266 p.   illus., port.   19½ cm.

15843 Alta California: embracing notices of the climate,
      soil, and agricultural products of northern Mexico
      and the Pacific seaboard; also, A history of the
      military and naval operations of the United States
      directed against the territories of northern Mexico...
      1846-47. With documents declaratory of the policy
      of the present administration of the national
      government in regard to the annexation of conquered
      territory of this union... by a Captain of volunteers.
      Philadelphia, H. Packer & co., 1847.
      64 p.   18 cm.

15844 Alter, J   Cecil, 1879-
      Father Escalante's map, by J. Cecil Alter. Salt
      Lake City, Utah State Historical Society, 1941.
      (In Utah historical quarterly, v. 9, nos. 1, 2,
      January, April 1941, p. 64-72)
      Map by Bernardo de Miero y Pacheco: between
      p. 65 and p. 66.

15845 Alter, J   Cecil, 1879-   ed.
      The Mormons and the Indians, news items and
      editorials, from the Mormon press, selected and
      arranged by J. Cecil Alter. Salt Lake City, Utah
      State Historical Society, 1944. (In Utah historical
      quarterly, v. 12, nos. 1, 2, January, April, 1944,
      p. 49-68)

7

15846   Alter, J   Cecil, 1879-
        Some useful early Utah Indian references, by
        J. Cecil Alter. Salt Lake City, Utah State
        Historical Society, 1928-29. (In Utah historical
        quarterly, v. 1, no. 1, January 1928, p. 26-32;
        v. 1, no. 2, April 1928, p. 53-56; v. 1, no. 3,
        July 1928, p. 75-86; v. 1, no. 4, p. 18-25;
        v. 2, no. 2, April 1929, p. 46-54)

15847   Alter, J   Cecil, 1879-
        W. A. Ferris in Utah, 1830-1835, by J. Cecil Alter.
        Salt Lake City, Utah State Historical Society, 1941.
        (In Utah historical quarterly, v. 9, no. 1, 2,
        January, April, 1941, p. 81-108)

15848   The American sketch book. A collection of historical
        incidents with descriptions of corresponding
        localities... Ed. by Bella French... [v. 1-3]
        La Crosse, Wis., Sketch book company, 1874-76.
        3 v.   front. (v. 3) plates, ports., fold. maps.
        23 cm. (v. 3: 24 cm.)
        Vol. 3 has imprint: Green Bay, Wis., The American
        sketch book company, 1876.
        Historical and descriptive sketches of towns and
        counties in Wisconsin, together with stories, poems,
        and other miscellaneous matter.
        Announced as a monthly publication, but v. 1
        (1874-75) was issued in 6 nos., v. 2 (1875-76) in 3,
        and v. 3 (1876) in 1. No more volumes were published
        in Wisconsin.
        Publication continued at Austin, Texas, by
        Mrs. Bella French Swisher, 1878-82, under title:
        The American sketch book; an historical and home
        monthly.

15849   Ames, John H
        Lincoln, the capital of Nebraska. A complete
        history of its foundation and growth up to the
        present time, together with a full description of
        all the public state buildings, salt springs, and
        other matters of interest, situated thereat, by
        J. H. Ames... Lincoln, Neb., State journal power
        press print, 1870.
        30 p.   25 cm.

15850   Anderson, Alexander Dwight.
        The silver country; or, The great Southwest;
        a review of the mineral and other wealth, the

8

attractions and material development of the former
Kingdom of New Spain, comprising Mexico and the
Mexican cessions to the United States in 1848 and
1853. New York, G. P. Putnam's sons, 1887.
    221 p.   fold. map.   20½ cm.

15851 Anderson, Bernice Gibbs.
       The gentile city of Corinne, by Bernice Gibbs
Anderson. Salt Lake City, Utah State Historical
Society, 1941. (In Utah historical quarterly,
v. 9, nos. 3, 4, July, October 1941, p. 141-144)

15852 Anderson, Charles.
       A paper [Texas, before, and on the eve of the
rebellion] read before the Cincinnati society of
ex-army and navy officers, Jan. 3d, 1884.
Cincinnati, 1884.
    51 p.   20 cm.

15853 Anderson, J   J
       Did the Louisiana purchase extend to the Pacific
ocean? and, Our title to Oregon. New York, 1881.
    8 p.   map.   21 cm.

15854 [Anderson, Mrs. Mabel Washbourne]
       Life of General Stand Watie, the only Indian
brigadier general of the Confederate army and the
last general to surrender. [Pryor, Okl., Mayes
county republican, c1915]
    58 p.   illus. (incl. ports.)   22 cm.

15855 [Angel, Myron] ed.
       History of Nevada. With illustrations and bio-
graphical sketches of its prominent men and pioneers.
Oakland, Cal., Thompson & West, 1881.
    xiv, [15]-680 p.   illus., plates (part double)
ports.   30½ cm.

15856 Angel, Myron.
       ... La Nevada orientale; géographie, resources,
climat et état social; rapport addressé au comité
local pour l'Exposition de Paris, par Myron Angel.
I. éd. de cinq cents exemplaires. Paris, Impr.
générale de C. Lahure, 1867.
    2 p.l., 164 p.   17½ cm.
    English and French.
    At head of title: Exposition universelle de 1867.
États-Unis d'Amérique.

15857   Ansted, David T[homas] 1814-1880.
         The gold-seeker's manual. By David T. Ansted...
         London, J. Van Voorst, 1849.
         2 p.l., 172 p.   17½ cm.

15858   Anti-monopoly Association of the Pacific Coast.
         A history of the wrongs of Alaska. An appeal to
         the people and press of America... San Francisco,
         1875.
         43 p.   17 cm.

15859   The Anti-Texass [!] legion. Protest of some free men,
         states and presses against the Texass [!] rebellion,
         against the laws of nature and of nations...
         Albany, Sold at the Patriot office, 1844.
         [60], 74 p.   illus.   19½ cm.
         Originally pub. at Albany, 1843, under title
         "The legion of liberty." The 10th edition, New
         York, 1847, with above title, has "Advertisement"
         preface signed: J.R.A. [i.e. Julius Rubens Ames?]
         Ascribed also to Benjamin Lundy. cf. Cushing,
         Anonyms. 1889. p. 37.

15860   Appeal by the people of the state of Texas, of the
         territory between the Nueces river and the Rio Grande...
         to the president, to Congress, and to the country,
         for protection against incursions of the savages
         of the state of Cohahuila, Mexico... Corpus Christi,
         Texas, 1878.
         40 p.   20 cm.

15861   Applegate, Jesse A   1835-1919.
         Recollections of my boyhood, by Jesse Applegate,
         Oregon pioneer of 1843. Roseburg, Or., Press of
         Review publishing co., 1914.
         99 p.   21 cm.

15862   Appler, Augustus C
         The guerrillas of the West; or, The life, character
         and daring exploits of the Younger brothers; with
         a sketch of the life of Henry W. Younger, father
         of the Younger brothers... The war record of
         Quantrell... also a sketch of the life of the
         James boys... By Augustus C. Appler... St. Louis,
         Eureka publishing company, 1876.
         iv, 5-208 p.   4 pl. (incl. front.)   21½ cm.

15863 Arizona (Ter.) Legislative assembly.
       Memorial and affidavits showing outrages perpetrated
       by the Apache Indians, in the territory of Arizona,
       for the years 1869 and 1870. Pub. by authority of
       the legislature of the territory of Arizona. San
       Francisco, Francis & Valentine, printers, 1871.
       32 p.   22½ cm.

15864 Arkansas. History Commission.
       Bibliography of historical and literary writings
       of Arkansans. [Little Rock, 1912]
       73-87 p.   23 cm.   (In its Bulletin of information,
       no. 4, 1912)

15865 Arkansas. History Commission.
       The Kie Oldham papers. [Little Rock, 1913]
       107-173 p.   23 cm.   (Bulletin of information,
       no. 5, 1913)

15866 Arkansas. History Commission.
       The L. C. Gulley collection of state papers.
       [Little Rock, 1912]
       17-52 p.   23½ cm.   (In Bulletin of information,
       no. 2, 1912)

15867 Arkansas. Mining, Manufacturing & Agricultural Bureau.
       [Information regarding the state of Arkansas
       and the varied advantages which it offers to
       intending settlers] [Little Rock, 1890]
       31 p.   fold. map.   18 cm.

15868 Armes, George Augustus, 1844-1919.
       Ups and downs of an army officer. By Col. George
       A. Armes, U.S.A. Washington, D.C., 1900.
       xix, 784 p.   front. (port.) illus. (incl. ports.,
       facsims.)   22½ cm.

15869 Armstrong, A   N
       Oregon: comprising a brief history and full
       description of the territories of Oregon and
       Washington... together with remarks upon the
       social position, productions, resources and
       prospects of the country, a dissertation upon the
       climate, and a full description of the Indian
       tribes of the Pacific slope... Interspersed with
       incidents of travel and adventure. By A. N.
       Armstrong... Chicago, C. Scott & co., 1857.
       vi, [7]-147 p.   19½ cm.

11

15870 Armstrong, Benjamin G   1820-
        Early life among the Indians. Reminiscences from
        the life of Benj. G. Armstrong. Treaties of 1835,
        1837, 1842, and 1854. Habits and customs of the
        red men... Incidents, biographical sketches, battles,
        &c. Dictated to and written by Thos. P. Wentworth...
        Ashland, Wis., Press of A. W. Bowron, 1892.
        266 p. incl. front., illus., port.   plates.
        20½ cm.

15871 Art work of the state of Arkansas. Racine, Wis.,
        The Harney Photogravure Co., 1905.
        2 p.l., 2-21 numb. l.   1 illus., 63 pl.
        35 x 28½ cm.
        Text by George B. Rose.
        On cover: Art work, state of Arkansas. Theodore
        Roosevelt. To our President on the occasion of his
        visit to Little Rock, October 25, 1905.

15872 Art work of Utah. Chicago, W. H. Parish, 1896.
        1 v. (unpaged)   illus. 35 cm.
        "Published in twelve parts."

15873 Asbury, Henry, 1810-1896.
        Reminiscences of Quincy, Illinois, containing
        historical events, anecdotes, matters concerning
        old settlers and old times, etc., by Henry Asbury.
        Quincy, Ill., D. Wilcox & sons, printers, 1882.
        224 p. incl. front.   23½ cm.
        Cover-title: History of Quincy, old times and
        old stories.

15874 Atherton, Mrs. Gertrude Franklin (Horn) 1857-1948.
        California; an intimate history, by Gertrude
        Atherton... New York and London, Harper & brothers,
        1914.
        4 p.l., vii-ix, [1] p., 1 l., 329, [1] p.
        front., illus., plates, ports.   22½ cm.

15875 Atherton, William.
        Narrative of the suffering & defeat of the north-
        western army under General Winchester: massacre
        of the prisoners: sixteen months imprisonment of
        the writer and others with the Indians and British:
        by William Atherton. Frankfort, Ky., Printed for
        the author, by A. G. Hodges, 1842.
        152 p.   16½ cm.

15876 Atkinson, George H
The northwest coast, including Oregon, Washington
and Idaho; a series of articles upon the N.P.R.R.,
in its relations to the basins of the Columbia and
of Puget's sound. First published in the Oregonian.
Portland, 1878.
56 p.   map.   21 cm.

15877 Atkinson, Mrs. Nancy (Bates) comp.
Biography of Rev. G. H. Atkinson... Journal of
sea voyage to Oregon in 1848, and selected addresses
and printed articles, and a particular account of
his church work in the Pacific Northwest, prepared
by Rev. Myron Eells, D.D. Compiled by Nancy Bates
Atkinson. Portland, Or., F. W. Baltes and company,
printers, 1893.
508 p.   illus., pl., 3 port. (incl. front.)
23½ cm.

15878 Atwood, A
The conquerors; historical sketches of the American
settlement of the Oregon country, embracing facts
in the life and work of Rev. Jason Lee... by Rev.
A. Atwood... Cincinnati [etc.] Jennings and Graham
[1907?]
316 p.   front., plates, ports., maps, facsim.
21 cm.
"Published with the indorsement of the officers of
'The Washington State Historical Society, Tacoma,
Washington."

15879 Audubon, John James, 1785-1851.
Audubon and his journals, by Maria R. Audubon,
with zoological and other notes by Elliott Coues...
New York, C. Scribner's sons, 1897.
2 v.   fronts. (v. 1, port.) illus., 13 pl.,
19 port., 12 facsim.   23 cm.

15880 Auerbach, Herbert Samuel, 1882-1945.
Father Escalante's itinerary, by Herbert S.
Auerbach. Salt Lake City, Utah State Historical
Society, 1941. (In Utah historical quarterly, v. 9,
nos. 3, 4, July, October, 1941, p. 109-128)

15881 Auerbach, Herbert Samuel, 1882-1945.
Father Escalante's route (as depicted by Bernardo
de Miera y Pacheco) by Herbert S. Auerbach. Salt
Lake City, Utah State Historical Society, 1941.

(In Utah historical quarterly, v. 9, nos. 1, 2,
January, April 1941, p. 73-80)

15882 Auerbach, Herbert Samuel, 1882-1945.
Old trails, old forts, old trappers and traders
by Herbert S. Auerbach. Salt Lake City, Utah State
Historical Society, 1941. (In Utah historical
quarterly, v. 9, nos. 1, 2, January, April 1941,
p. 12-63)

15883 Auger, Edouard.
Recits d'outre-mer. Paris, 1873.
303 p.   18 cm.

15884 Aughey, Samuel.
Sketches of the physical geography and geology
of Nebraska... Omaha, Daily republican book & job
office, 1880.
2 p.l., 326 p.   20 cm.

15885 Aughey, Samuel.
Superficial deposits of Nebraska. Extracted from
the annual report of the United States geological
and geographical survey of the territories for 1874.
Ed. 2. [Lincoln, Neb., 1875?]
31 p.   21 cm.

15886 Austin, Mrs. Mary Hunter, 1868-1934.
California, the land of the sun, painted by
Sutton Palmer, described by Mary Austin. New York
[1914]
viii, 178 p.   32 col. pl., fold. map.   24 cm.

15887 Austin, Mrs. Mary Hunter, 1868-1934.
The land of little rain, by Mary Austin. Boston
and New York, Houghton, Mifflin and company, 1903.
xi p., 2 l., 280, [2] p.   front., illus.   22 cm.
Illustrated by E. Boyd Smith.

15888 Austin, Stephen Fuller, 1793-1836.
Exposicion al publico sobre los asuntos de Tejas.
Por el C. Estevan F. Austin. Megico, C. C. Sebring,
1835.
32 p.   19½ cm.

15889 Auzias-Turenne, Raymond, 1861-
... Voyage au pays des mines d'or; le Klondike.
Ouvrage contenant quarante illustrations et deux

cartes... Paris, Calmann Lévy, 1899.
3 p.l., 318 p., 1 l. incl. illus., plates, ports.,
fold. maps.   ports.   18½ cm.

15890 Awes, Addison, jr.
Why a rich Yankee did not settle in California.
Boston & San Francisco, Cubery & co., 1900.
2 p.l., 114 p., 1 l.   front., illus., pl.   20 cm.

15891 Ayer, I   Winslow.
Life in the wilds of America, and wonders of the
West in and beyond the bounds of civilization...
By I. Winslow Ayer... Grand Rapids, Mich., The
Central publishing company, 1880.
528 p. incl. front., illus.   22 cm.

15892 Ayers, Nathaniel Monroe, 1846-
Building a new empire, by Nathaniel M. Ayers;
a historical story of the settlement of the wild
West... New York, Chicago [etc.] Broadway publishing
co. [c1910]
211 p.   front. (port.) plates.   20 cm.
Early days in Furnas co., Neb.

B

15893 Babcock, Mrs. Bernie (Smade) 1868-
Yesterday and today in Arkansas; a folio of rare
and interesting pictures from Mrs. Babcock's
collection for Stories and legends of Arkansas.
1st ed. [Little Rock, Ark., Jordon & Foster
printing co., c1917]
[104] p.   illus. (incl. ports.)   25½ cm.
Largely devoted to Little Rock.

15894 Badger, Joseph, 1757-1846.
A memoir of Rev. Joseph Badger; containing an
autobiography, and selections from his private
journal and correspondence. Hudson, O., Sawyer,
Ingersoll and company, 1851.
185 p.   front. (port.)   18½ cm.
A record of missionary work in the Western Reserve.
"Rev. H. N. Day wrote the preface." - Sabin,
vol. XI, p. 579.

15

15895   [Baegert, Jakob] 1717-1772.
        Nachrichten von der Amerikanischen Halbinsel
        Californien: Mit einem zweyfachen Anhang falscher
        Nachrichten. Geschrieben von einem Priester der
        Gesellschaft Jesu, welcher lang darinn diese letztere
        Jahre gelebt hat. Mannheim, Churfürstl. hof- und
        academie Buchdr., 1772.
            8 p.l., 358 p., 1 l.   plates, fold. map.
        17½ x 10 cm.

15896   [Bailey], Florence A[ugusta] (Merriam) "Mrs. Vernon
        Bailey."
            My summer in a Mormon village... Boston and New
        York, Houghton, Mifflin & co., 1894.
            4 p.l., 171 p.   front.   19 cm.

15897   Bailey, Washington, 1831-
            A trip to California in 1853, by Washington
        Bailey. Recollections of a gold seeking trip by ox
        train across the plains and mountains by an old
        Illinois pioneer. [Le Roy, Ill.] Le Roy journal
        printing company, 1915.
            1 p.l., 50 p.   front. (port.)   23 cm.

15898   Baines, Thomas F
            My life in two hemispheres; what was suffered
        for love of country. Third ed. San Francisco, 1889.
            180 p.   18 cm.

15899   Baird, Sarah Elizabeth (Pentland) 1878-
            A traveler's mail bag, descriptive of the paradise
        of the Pacific and California; letters from Mrs.
        John E. Baird, February to August, 1914. Phila-
        delphia, Priv. pub., 1915.
            133 p.   front., plates.   23½ cm.

15900   Baker, Charles S
            Oklahoma. Fidelity to treaty covenants and homes
        for the homeless. Speech in the House of Repre-
        sentatives, May 1, 1886. Washington, 1886.
            14 p.   23 cm.

15901   Baker, De Witt Clinton, 1832-1881.
            A brief history of Texas from its earliest
        settlement. To which is appended the constitution
        of the state. For schools. New York and Chicago,
        A. S. Barnes & co., 1873.
            xi p., 1 l., [15]-200 p.   front., illus., port.

15902   Baldridge, Samuel Coulter, 1829-1898.
        Sketches of the life and times of the Rev. Stephen
        Bliss, A.M., with notices of his co-laborers: Rev.
        Isaac Bennet [and others]... by Rev. Svmuel [!]
        C. Baldridge. Cincinnati, Elm street printing
        company, 1870.
        3 p.l., v-vi p., 1 l., 7-280 p.   16 cm.

15903   Ball, Nicholas.
        The pioneers of '49; a history of the excursion
        of the Society of California pioneers of New England,
        from Boston to the leading cities of the golden
        state, April 10-May 17, 1890, with reminiscences
        and descriptions. Boston, 1891.
        xv, 288 p.   front., illus., pl., ports.   18 cm.

15904   Ballantyne, Robert Michael, 1825-1894.
        The golden dream; or, Adventures in the far West.
        By R. M. Ballantyne... London, J. F. Shaw and co.,
        1861.
        viii, 358 p.   front., plates.   18 cm.

15905   Bancroft, Hubert Howe, 1832-1918.
        ... California pastoral. 1769-1848. San Francisco,
        The History company, 1888.
        vi, 808 p.   23½ cm.   (The works of Hubert Howe
        Bancroft, vol. XXXIV)
        Also pub. separately the same year.
        Bibliography: p. 751-792.

15906   Bancroft, Hubert Howe, 1832-1918.
        Chronicles of the builders of the commonwealth:
        historical character study. San Francisco, 1891-2.
        6 v.   illus.   23 cm.

15907   Bancroft, Hubert Howe, 1832-1918.
        History of Texas and the north Mexican states.
        San Francisco, The History Co., 1890.
        2 v.   maps.   24 cm.
        "Authorities quoted": vol. 1, p. xix-xlviii.
        According to W. A. Morris, in Quarterly of the
        Oregon historical society, v. 4, p. 287-364, these
        volumes were the work of H. L. Oak, J. J. Peatfield,
        and William Nemos.
        Contents: v. 1. 1531-1800. - v. 2 1801-1889.

15908   Bancroft, Hubert Howe, 1832-1918.
        The new Pacific. By Hubert Howe Bancroft.

New York, The Bancroft co., 1900.
iv p., 1 l., 738 p.   front. (map)   22 cm.

15909   Bancroft, Hubert Howe, 1832-1918.
Retrospection, political and personal by Hubert
Howe Bancroft. New York, 1912.
x, 562 p.   port.

15910   Barclay, James W
Mormonism exposed. The other side. An English
view of the case. [n.p.] 1884.
30 p.   21½ cm.
First appeared in The Nineteenth Century, v. 15,
under title: A New View of Mormonism.

15911   Barde, Alexandre.
Histoire des comités de vigilance aux Attakapas,
par Alexandre Barde... Saint-Jean-Baptiste (Louisiane)
Impr. du Meschacébé et de l'Avant-coureur, 1861.
3 p.l., [iii]-vi, [7]-428 p.   18 cm.
Introduction by Eugene Dumez.

15912   Barker, Eugene Campbell.
Organization of the Texas revolution. Reprint
from publications of Southern History Association,
November, 1901. [n.p., n.d.]
26 p.   22 cm.

15913   Barker, Eugene Campbell.
Public opinion in Texas preceding the revolution.
American Historical Association, annual report for
1911. Washington, 1913.
217-228 p.   (Vol. 1)   22 cm.
Bibliographical foot-notes.

15914   Barker, Eugene Campbell.
Some causes of the Texan Declaration of Independence
[faculty address at the celebration of Texas
Independence Day by the students of the University
of Texas, March 2, 1911] [n.p.] 1911.
336-341 p.   22 cm.
Reprinted from the University of Texas record,
v. 10, no. 4.

15915   Barker, Eugene Campbell.
Stephen F. Austin and the independence of Texas.
[n.p., n.d.]
24-64 p.   22 cm.

18

Reprinted from The Quarterly of Texas State
Historical Association, v. 13, no. 4.

15916   Barker, Eugene Campbell.
        The Texan declaration of causes for taking up arms
        against Mexico. [n.p.] 1912.
        173-185 p.   22 cm.
        Reprinted from the Quarterly of the Texas State
        Historical Association, v. 15, no. 3, Jan. 1912.

15917   Barneby, William Henry, 1843-
        Life and labour in the far, far West: being notes
        of a tour in the western states, British Columbia,
        Manitoba, and the Northwest territory. By W. Henry
        Barneby... London, New York [etc.] Cassell & company,
        1884.
        xvi, 432 p.   21½ cm.

15918   Barnes, Charles Merritt.
        Combats and conquests of immortal heroes, sung in
        song and told in story, by Charles Merritt Barnes...
        San Antonio, Tex., Guessaz & Ferlet company, 1910.
        268 p.   col. front., illus. (incl. ports.)
        25½ cm.

15919   Barnes, Demas, 1827-1888.
        From the Atlantic to the Pacific, overland. A
        series of letters by Demas Barnes, describing a trip
        from New York... to San Francisco, thence home, by
        Acapulco, and the isthmus of Panama. New York, D.
        Van Nostrand, 1866.
        136 p.   front. (port.)   19½ cm.

15920   Barnes, William Croft, 1858-1936.
        Western grazing grounds and forest ranges; a
        history of the live-stock industry as conducted on
        the open ranges of the arid West, with particular
        reference to the use now being made of the ranges
        in the national forests, by Will C. Barnes...
        Chicago, The Breeder's gazette, 1913.
        390 p.   col. front., illus., col. plates.   20 cm.
        "List of books consulted": p. 20.

15921   Barra, Ezekiel I
        A tale of two oceans: a new story by an old
        Californian. An account of a voyage from Philadelphia
        to San Francisco around Cape Horn, years 1849-50,
        calling at Rio de Janeiro, Brazil, and at Juan

Fernandez, in the South Pacific. By E. I. Barra.
San Francisco [Press of Eastman & co.] 1893.
198 p.   illus.   23½ cm.

15922 Barreiro, Antonio.
Ojeada sobre Nuevo-México, que da una idea de sus
producciones naturales, y de algunas otras cosas que
se consideran oportunas para mejorar su estado...
[con apéndice] Puebla, J. M. Campos, 1832.
42 p., 2 l., 10 p.   19 cm.

15923 Barrett, Jay A
History and government of Nebraska. Lincoln, Neb.,
1892.
[6], 171 p.   maps.   19 cm.

15924 [Barrows, William] 1815-1891.
The general; or, Twelve nights in the hunters' camp.
A narrative of real life... Boston, Lee and Shepard
[c1869]
2 p.l., iii-iv, 268 p.   front., plates.   17½ cm.
(Added t.-p.: The frontier series)

15925 Barrows, William, 1815-1891.
Oregon, the struggle for possession. 2d ed.
Boston, Houghton, Mifflin, 1884.
viii, 363 p.   double map.   18 cm.   (American
Commonwealths [v.2])
"Authorities": p. [iii]-vi.

15926 Barrows, William, 1815-1891.
The United States of yesterday and of to-morrow.
By William Barrows... Boston, Roberts brothers,
1888.
viii, [9]-432 p.   19 cm.

15927 Barry, Theodore Augustus, 1825-1881.
Men and memories of San Francisco, in the "spring
of '50." By T. A. Barry and B. A. Patten...
San Francisco, A. L. Bancroft & company, 1873.
296 p.   21 cm.

15928 Bartlett, Ichabod S   ed.
History of Wyoming. I. S. Bartlett, ed. ...
Chicago, The S. J. Clarke publishing company, 1918.
3 v.   col. front. (v. 1) illus., ports.
27½ cm.

15929   Bashford, James Whitford, bp., 1849-
         The Oregon missions; the story of how the line was
         run between Canada and the United States, by James W.
         Bashford... New York, Cincinnati, The Abingdon press
         [c1918]
             311 p. incl. front. (map)   19 cm.
             Bibliography: p. 301-304.

15930   Baskin, Robert Newton, 1835-
         Argument against the admission of Utah, and the
         recent message of Governor West to the Utah legis-
         lature. Washington, D.C., 1888.
             22, [4] p.   20 cm.

15931   Baskin, Robert Newton, 1835-
         Reminiscences of early Utah, by R. N. Baskin...
         [Salt Lake City, Tribune-reporter printing co.,c1914]
             3 p.l., 5-252 p.   front., 1 illus., ports.
             23½ cm.

15932   Baskin, Robert Newton, 1835-
         Reply by R. N. Baskin to certain statements, by
         O. F. Whitney in his history of Utah, published in
         1916. [Salt Lake City, Lakeside printing co., 1916?]
             cover-title, 29 p.   3 port.   23 cm.

15933   Bassett, Samuel Clay, 1844-
         Buffalo County, Nebraska, and its people; a record
         of settlement, organization, progress and achievement,
         by Samuel Clay Bassett... Chicago, The S. J. Clarke
         publishing company, 1916.
             2 v.   front., illus., plates, ports., map.   27 cm.

15934   Batchelder, George Alexander.
         A sketch of the history and resources of Dakota
         Territory. By George Alexander Batchelder...
         Yankton, Press steam power printing company, 1870.
             56 p.   front. (map)   22½ cm.
             Author assisted by the History society of Dakota.

15935   Bates, Mrs. D   B
         Incidents on land and water, or Four years on the
         Pacific coast. Being a narrative of the burning of
         the ships Nonantum, Humayoon and Fanchon together with
         many... adventures on sea and land. By Mrs. D. B.
         Bates. Boston, J. French & co., 1858.
             336 p.   front., pl.   18 cm.

15936   Bates, Edmond Franklin, 1851-
            History and reminiscences of Denton County, by
        Ed. F. Bates... Denton, Tex., McNitzky printing
        company [c1918]
            1 p.l., [ix]-vi p., 2 l., 412 p.   front., illus.,
        2 fold pl., ports.   23½ cm.

15937   Bates, Marcus W
            The sugar pine lands of California.   [Duluth, Minn.?
        1897?]
            20 p.   fold. plates.   15 cm.

15938   Battey, Thomas C
            The life and adventures of a Quaker among the
        Indians.   By Thomas C. Battey...   Boston, Lee and
        Shepard, 1903.
            xii, 9-349 p.   front., 7 pl.   19 cm.   (On cover:
        Patriotic series for boys and girls.   [22])
            First edition, 1875.
            "This book is recommended to the public as a truthful
        statement of the customs and habits of the Kiowa
        Indians."

15939   Battle of Lake Pokeguma.   Narrated by an eye-witness.
        St. Paul, Minnesota Historical Society, 1852.
        (In Annals of the Minnesota Historical Society,
        1852, p. 59-61)

15940   Batty, Joseph.
            Over the wilds to California; or, Eight years
        from home.   By Joseph Batty...   Ed. by Rev. John
        Simpson.   Leeds, J. Parrott, 1867.
            2 p.l., 64 p.   16½ cm.

15941   Baughman, Theodore, 1845-
            Baughman, the Oklahoma scout.   Personal reminis-
        cences, by Theodore Baughman...   Chicago & New York,
        Belford, Clarke & co., 1886.
            215 p. incl. front.   11 pl.   18 cm.

15942   Baxley, Henry Willis, 1803-1876.
            What I saw on the west coast of South and North
        America, and at the Hawaiian Islands.   By H. Willis
        Baxley, M.D.   New York, D. Appleton & company, 1865.
            632 p.   front., illus., plates.   25 cm.

15943   Beall, John Bramblett, 1833-1917.
            In barrack and field; poems and sketches of army

life, by Lieut. Col. John B. Beall... Nashville,
Tenn., Dallas, Tex., Smith & Lamar, agents,
Publishing house of the M. E. church, South, 1906.
420 p.   front. (port.)   19 cm.

15944   Beatty, Bessie, 1886-
A political primer for the new voter. Introduction
by William Kent. San Francisco, Whitaker & Tay-Wiggin,
1912.
[5] p.l., [3]-76 p.   18 cm.
Partly reprinted from the San Francisco bulletin.

15945   Beaugrand, Honoré, 1849-1906.
Six mois dans les Montagnes-Rocheuses. Colorado-
Utah-Nouveau-Mexique; par H. Beaugrand... Avec une
préface de Louis Fréchette. Montréal, Granger frères,
1890.
2 p.l., [8]-323 p., 1 l. incl. illus., plates.
front. (fold. map) plates.   23 cm.

15946   Beaumont, William, 1785-1853.
Experiments and observations on the gastric juice,
and the physiology of digestion. By William Beaumont
... Plattsburgh, Printed by F. P. Allen, 1833.
280 p.   illus.   22½ cm.
Based upon observations of the digestive processes
of Alexis St. Martin.

15947   Becker, George Ferdinand.
... Atlas to accompany a monograph on the geology
of the quicksilver deposits of the Pacific slope.
Washington, 1889.
13 maps.
At head of title: Department of the Interior,
United States Geological Survey, J. W. Powell,
director.

15948   Beckwith, Frank.
A field of small fossils in western Utah. A spot
that "slept", by Frank Beckwith, Sr. Salt Lake
City, Utah State Historical Society, 1931. (In
Utah historical quarterly, v. 4, no. 1, January
1931, p. 25-29)

15949   Beckwith, Frank.
Fossils of the Ordovician time period, at Ibex,
Utah, as told by the fossils themselves to Frank
Beckwith, Sr. Salt Lake City, Utah State Historical

Society, 1931. (In Utah historical quarterly, v. 4, no. 2, April 1931, p. 55-62)

15950 Bedford, Hilory G
Texas Indian troubles. The most thrilling events in the history of Texas illustrated. By Hilory G. Bedford... Dallas, Tex., Hargreaves printing co., inc., 1905.
249 p. illus. 21½ cm.

15951 Beebe, Henry S
The history of Peru, by Henry S. Beebe. Peru, Ill., J. F. Linton, 1858.
2 p.l., 162 p. 15 cm.

15952 Beede, Aaron McGaffey.
The Dakota Indian victory dance, by Aaron Beede McGaffey. [Bismarck, State Historical Society of North Dakota, 1942]
166-178 p. 24 cm.
Reprinted from North Dakota historical quarterly, v. 9, no. 3, April 1942.

15953 Beeson, John, b. 1803.
Are we not men and brethren? An address to the people of the United States, in behalf of the Indians. By John Beeson. [New York, National Indian aid office, 1859]
4 p. incl. map. 24 cm. fold. to 18 cm.
[With his Plea for the Indians. 3d ed. New York, 1858]

15954 Belcourt, George Antoine, 1803-1874.
Department of Hudson Bay: addressed to His Excellency, Alex. Ramsey, president of the Minnesota Historical Society by Rev. G. A. Belcourt: translated from the French by Mrs. Letitia May. St. Paul, Minnesota Historical Society, 1853. (In Annals of the Minnesota Historical Society, no. IV, 1853, p. 17-32)

15955 Belden, George P
Belden, the white chief; or, Twelve years among the wild Indians of the plains. From the diaries and manuscripts of George P. Belden... Ed. by Gen. James S. Brisbin, U.S.A. Cincinnati and New York, C. F. Vent; [etc., etc.] 1870.
iv, [5]-513 p. incl. illus., plates. front. 20½ cm.

24

15956 Belden, George P
        Brisbin's stories of the plains; or, Twelve years
        among the wild Indians. Chiefly from the diaries
        and manuscripts of George P. Belden... Together with
        a biographical sketch of "Belden, the white chief..."
        By Gen. James S. Brisbin. St. Louis, Mo. [etc.]
        Anchor publishing company; San Francisco, Cal., A. L.
        Bancroft & co., 1881.
            iv, [5]-541 p. incl. illus., plates.   19½ cm.
        An earlier edition, Cincinnati, 1870, published
        under title: Belden, the white chief.

15957 Bell, Earl H
        Chapters in Nebraska archaeology. Lincoln, 1936-
            v. illus., map.   23 cm.

15958 Bell, Horace.
        Reminiscences of a ranger; or, Early times in
        Southern California. By Major Horace Bell. Los
        Angeles, Yarnell, Caystile & Mathes, 1881.
            457 p.   21 cm.

15959 Bell, John Calhoun, 1851-
        The pilgrim and the pioneer; the social and
        material developments in the Rocky Mountains, by
        John C. Bell... College View, Lincoln, Neb., The
        International publishing ass'n [c1906]
            xii, 13-531 p. incl. front., illus., plates.
        21 cm.

15960 Bell, John Thomas, 1842-
        History of Washington County, Nebraska; its
        early settlement and present status, resources,
        advantages and future prospects. [By] John T. Bell
        ... Omaha, Neb., Printed at the Herald printing
        house, 1876.
            64 p.   22 cm.

15961 Bell, William Abraham.
        New tracks in North America. A journal of travel
        and adventure whilst engaged in the survey for a
        southern railroad to the Pacific Ocean during 1867-8.
        By William A. Bell... With contributions by General
        W. J. Palmer, Major A. R. Calhoun, C. C. Parry...
        and Captain W. F. Colton... London, Chapman and
        Hall; New York, Scribner, Welford & co., 1869.
            2 v.   col. fronts., illus., plates (part col.)
        fold. map.   22½ cm.

15962   Benedict, Harry Yandell, 1869-
        The book of Texas, by H. Y. Benedict and John A.
        Lomax... Garden City, N. Y., Doubleday, Page &
        company, 1916.
        xxiii, 448 p., 1 l. incl. front., illus. (maps)
        plates, ports., diagrs.   25 cm.

15963   Benjamin, Marcus, 1857-1932.
        John Bidwell, pioneer; a sketch of his career, by
        Marcus Benjamin. Washington, 1907.
        2 p.l., 52 p.   front., illus., plates, ports.
        27½ cm.

15964   Bennett, James, 1812 or 3-1869.
        Overland journey to California, journal of James
        Bennett whose party left New Harmony in 1850 and
        crossed the plains and mountains until the golden
        West was reached. New Harmony, Ind., Times print,
        1906.
        cover-title, 45 p.   21½ cm.

15965   Bennett, John C
        The history of the saints; or, An exposé of Joe
        Smith and Mormonism. By John C. Bennett. Boston,
        Leland & Whiting; New York, Bradbury, Soden, & co.;
        [etc., etc.] 1842.
        ii, 344 p. incl. plates, plan.   2 port. (incl.
        front.)   19 cm.
        Cover-title: Mormonism exposed.

15966   Bennett, William P
        The first baby in camp. A full account of the
        scenes and adventures during the pioneer days of '49.
        George Francis Train. - Staging in early days. -
        A mad, wild ride. - The pony express. - Some of the
        old time drivers. By Wm. P. Bennett... (Picture
        22 x 28 accompanies this book)   Salt Lake City,
        Utah, The Rancher publishing co., 1893.
        68 p.   fold. pl.   18½ cm.

15967   Bennion, Israel.
        Indian reminiscence, by Israel Bennion. Salt Lake
        City, Utah State Historical Society, 1929. (In
        Utah historical quarterly, v. 2, no. 2, April 1929,
        p. 43-46)

15968   Benton, Jesse.
        An address to the people of the United States on

26

the presidential election. By Jesse Benton.
Nashville, Printed by J. Norvell for the author,
1824.
34 p.   18 cm.

15969   Benton, Joseph Augustine.
The California pilgrim: a series of lectures, by
J. A. Benton, pastor of the First church of Christ
in Sacramento... Sacramento, Cal., S. Alter; San
Francisco, Marvin & Hitchcock, 1853.
viii, [9]-261 p.   plates.   20 cm.
In allegorical language.

15970   Benton, Thomas Hart, 1782-1858.
Selection of editorial articles from the St. Louis
Enquirer on the subject of Oregon and Texas, as
originally published in that paper and written by
the Hon. Thomas H. Benton, to which is prefixed, his
speech in the Senate of the United States, in March,
1825, on the bill for the occupation of the Columbia
River. St. Louis, Missourian office, 1844.
45 p.   21 cm.

15971   Berghold, Alexander.
The Indians' revenge; or, Days of horror. Some
appalling events,in the history of the Sioux. By Rev.
Alexander Berghold... San Francisco, P. J. Thomas,
printer, 1891.
240 p.   front., illus., pl., ports.   17½ cm.

15972   The Bering sea arbitration. Letters to the Times by
its special correspondent; together with the award...
London, William Clowes & Sons [etc., etc., n.d.]
87 p.   17 cm.

15973   Bernard du Hautcilly, Auguste, 1790-1849.
Viaggio interno al globo principalmente alla
California ed alle isole Sandwich negli anni 1826,
1827, 1828 e 1829 di A. Duhaut-Cilly... Con
Paggiunta delle osservazioni sugli abitanti di quei
paesi di Paolo Emilio Botta. Tr. dal francese
nell' italiano di Carlo Botta... Torino, Stabili-
mento tipografico Fontana, 1841.
2 v. in 1.   fronts.   21 cm.
Translation of the author's "Voyage autour du monde..."
Paris, 1834-35.

15974 Berthoud, Edward L
         Jefferson county, Colorado: a statistical review
       of its agricultural, mining, manufacturing and
       pastoral resources, from official and other docu-
       mentary sources... Golden City, Colorado transcript,
       1868.
         7 p.   21 cm.

15975 Bidwell, John, 1819-1900.
         Addresses, reminiscences, etc. of General John
       Bidwell. Comp. by C. C. Royce. Chico, Cal., 1907.
         2 p.l., 221 p.   plates, ports., map, facsims.
       25½ cm. [With Royce, Charles C. John Bidwell, pioneer,
       statesman, philanthropist... Chico, Cal., 1906]

15976 Bidwell, John, 1819-1900.
         Echoes of the past: an account of the first
       emigrant train to California, Frémont in the conquest
       of California, the discovery of gold and early
       reminiscences, by the late General John Bidwell...
       Chico, Calif., Chico advertiser [19-?]
         cover-title, 1 l., 91 p.   1 illus., pl.   17½ cm.
       Half-title: Echoes of the past about California.
       Vignette (portrait) on half-title.

15977 Bigler, Henry William, 1815-
         Extracts from the journal of Henry W. Bigler.
       Salt Lake City, Utah State Historical Society, 1932.
       (In Utah historical quarterly, v. 5, no. 2,
       April 1932, p. 35-64; v. 5, no. 3, July 1932, p. 87-
       112; v. 5, no. 4, October 1952, p. 134-160)

15978 Bill, Fred A
         Early steamboating on the Red River, by Captain
       Fred A. Bill. [Bismarck, State Historical Society
       of North Dakota, 1942]
         69-85 p.   24 cm.
       Reprinted from North Dakota historical quarterly,
       v. 9, no. 2, January 1942.

15979 Bingham, Helen.
         In Tamal land, by Helen Bingham. San Francisco,
       The Calkins publishing house [c1906]
         6 p.l., 141 p. incl. illus., plates.   23½ cm.

15980 Biographical and historical memoirs of eastern
       Arkansas, comprising a condensed history of the
       state... biographies of distinguished citizens...

a brief... history of... the counties... Chicago
[etc.] St. Louis, The Goodspeed pub. co., 1890.
820 p. incl. port.   28½ cm.

15981 Biographical and historical memoirs of northeast
Arkansas, comprising a condensed history of the state...
biographies of distinguished citizens... a brief
history... of the counties... Chicago [etc.]
St. Louis, The Goodspeed publishing co., 1889.
981 p.   ports.   28½ cm.

15982 Biographical and historical memoirs of western
Arkansas, comprising a condensed history of the
state... biographies of distinguished citizens...
a brief... history... of the counties... Chicago
and Nashville, The Southern publ. co., 1891.
497 p.   pl., port.   28½ cm.

15983 Biographical record of Salt Lake City and vicinity,
containing biographies of well known citizens of
the past and present. Chicago, National historical
record co., 1902.
3 p.l., [11]-654, [4] p.   plates, ports.
29 x 23½ cm.

15984 Biography of Henry Augustus Peirce. San Francisco,
Bancroft, 1880.
24 p.   front. (port.)   18 cm.

15985 Biography of Joseph Lane... By Western... Washington,
Printed at the Congressional Globe Office, 1852.
40 p.   22 cm.

15986 Bird, Horace A
History of a line (Colorado midland railway)
In two parts: from plains to peaks, fishing and
hunting in Colorado. A hand-book for tourists and
sportsmen in the Rocky mountains. By Horace A. Bird.
Published by the Passenger department of the Colorado
midland r'y, Pike's Peak route... [New York, Press
of the American bank note co., 1889]
133, [1] p.   illus.   23 cm.

15987 Birge, Julius Charles, 1839-1923.
The awakening of the desert, by Julius C. Birge;
with illustrations. Boston, R. G. Badger [c1912]
429 p.   front., plates, ports.   19½ cm.
Map on front lining-paper.

29

15988   Birkbeck, Morris, 1764-1825.
        An address to the farmers of Great Britain; with
        an essay on the prairies of the western country: by
        Morris Birkbeck: to which is annexed, the consti-
        tution of the state of Illinois.   London, J. Ridgway,
        1822.
            iv, [5]-52 p.   22½ cm.   [Miscellaneous pamphlets,
        v. 113, no. 10]

15989   Birkbeck, Morris, 1764-1825.
        An appeal to the people of Illinois on the question
        of a convention, by Morris Birkbeck...   Shawneetown,
        Printed by C. Jones, July, 1823.   [Springfield, Ill.,
        Reprinted, 1905]
            33 p.   23½ cm.
        Also published in Illinois state historical library.
        Publication no. 10, 1905.
        "A contribution toward a bibliography of Morris
        Birkbeck and the English settlement in Edwards county,
        Illinois, founded by Morris Birkbeck and George
        Flower, 1817-18.   By Charles Wesley Smith":   p. [21]-33.

15990   Bivins, Viola (Cobb) 1863-
            Memoirs.   [n.p., n.d.]
            138 p.   illus.   23 cm.

15991   Black, Jeremiah Sullivan, 1810-1883.
            Federal jurisdiction in the territories.   Right of
        local self-government.   Judge Black's argument for
        Utah before the Judiciary committee of the House of
        Representatives, Feb. 1, 1883.   Salt Lake City,
        Deseret news co., 1883.
            28 p.   22 cm.

15992   Blackmar, Frank Wilson, 1854-1931.
            ...   Spanish colonization in the Southwest, by
        Frank W. Blackmar...   Baltimore, Johns Hopkins
        University, 1890.
            79 p.   24½ cm.   (Johns Hopkins University
        studies in historical and political science...
        8th series, IV)

15993   [Blackmore, William]   -1878, ed.
            Colorado: its resources, parks and prospects as
        a new field for emigration; with an account of the
        Trenchara and Costilla estates, in the San Luis Park.
        Privately printed.   [London, Rankin & co.] 1869.
            2 v. in 1.   fold. maps.   24 cm.

15994 Blair, George E   ed.
       The mountain empire Utah; a brief and reasonably
       authentic presentation of the material conditions of
       a state that lies in the heart of the mountains of
       the West... Ed. and pub. by Geo. E. Blair & R. W.
       Sloan, Salt Lake City, Utah. [Chicago, Press of
       W. P. Dunn co., c1904]
          142, [2] p.   illus. (incl. ports.)   24 cm.

15995 [Blair, James]
       Notices of the harbor at the mouth of the Columbia
       river. By the Commander and other officers of the
       exploring expedition. [n.p., n.d.]
          22 p.   17 cm.

15996 Blake, Mary E[lizabeth] 1840-1907.
       On the wing. Rambling notes of a trip to the
       Pacific. Ed. 3.   Boston, Lee and Shepard, 1883.
          4 p.l., 235 p., 1 l.   21 cm.

15997 Blakiston, Thomas Wright, 1832-1891.
       Report on the exploration of the Kootanie and
       boundary passes of the Rocky mountains in 1858.
       Woolwich, Printed at the Royal Artillery institution,
       1859.
          237-254 p.   maps.   22 cm.   (Occasional papers
       of the Royal Artillery institution, no. 12, May 1859)

15998 Blanchard, Rufus, 1821-1904.
       Hand-book of Iowa; describing its agricultural,
       commercial and manufacturing resources, and other
       capabilities of producing wealth, also, its physical
       geography and geology. 2d ed. By Rufus Blanchard.
       Chicago, R. Blanchard, 1869.
          1 p.l., [5]-92, [2] p.   illus. (plan) fold. map,
       diagrs.   15 cm.
       First published, 1867.

15999 Blanchet, Francis Norbert.
       Historical sketches of the Catholic Church in
       Oregon during the past forty years [1838-1878]
       Second ed.
          72 p.   17 cm.

16000 Bland, Thomas Augustus, 1830-
       Life of Alfred B. Meacham. By T. A. Bland.
       Together with his lecture. The tragedy of the lava

31

beds. Washington, T. A. & M. C. Bland, 1883.
30, 48 p. front., illus., port. 23½ cm.

16001 Blaschke, Eduardo.
Topographia media. Portus Novi - Archangelsensis,
sedis principalis coloniarum rossicarum in Septen-
trionali America. Petropoli, Typis K. Wienhoberi
et filii, 1842.
82 p. illus., maps, tables. 17 cm.

16002 Bledsoe, Anthony Jennings, 1858-
History of Del Norte county, California, with a
business directory and traveler's guide. By A. J.
Bledsoe. Eureka, Wyman & co., 1881.
175, [3] p. 22½ cm.

16003 Bliss, Charles R
The new West. New Mexico, by Charles R. Bliss...
Boston, F. Wood, printer, 1879.
1 p.l., [5]-16 p. front. (map) illus.
23½ cm.

16004 Bliss, Robert S , 1805-
The journal of Robert S. Bliss, with the Mormon
Battalion. Salt Lake City, Utah State Historical
Society, 1931. (In Utah historical quarterly, v. 4,
no. 3, July 1931, p. 66-96; v. 4, no. 4, October 1931,
p. 110-128)

16005 Block, Ben A
Colorado: its resources; its men... A lesson in
prosperity. [n.p., 1901]
unpaged. illus., port. 24 cm.

16006 Blood, Henry H
First settlement of Kaysville, Utah, by Henry H.
Blood. Salt Lake City, Utah State Historical Society,
1929. (In Utah historical quarterly, v. 2, no. 1,
January 1929, p. 14-18)

16007 Boardman, John, 1824-1883.
The journal of John Boardman; an overland journey
from Kansas to Oregon in 1843. Salt Lake City,
Utah State Historical Society, 1929. (In Utah
historical quarterly, v. 2, no. 4, October 1929,
p. 99-121)

16008   Boillot, Leon.
        Aux mines d'or du Klondike. Du Lac Bennett &
        Dawson. Paris, Hachette, 1899.
        [256] p.   illus., map.   17 cm.

16009   Boller, Henry A
        Among the Indians. Eight years in the far West:
        1858-1866. Embracing sketches of Montana and Salt
        Lake. By Henry A. Boller... Philadelphia, T. E.
        Zell, 1868.
        xvi, 17-428 p.   front. (fold. map)   19½ cm.

16010   Bolton, Herbert Eugene, 1870-   ed.
        Athanase de Mezières and the Louisiana-Texas frontier,
        1768-1780; documents pub. for the first time, from
        the original Spanish and French manuscripts, chiefly
        in the archives of Mexico and Spain; tr. into English;
        ed. and annotated, by Herbert Eugene Bolton...
        Cleveland, The Arthur H. Clark company, 1914-
        2 v.   fold. front. (map)   facsims.   24½ cm.
        (Half-title: Spain in the West... vol. I)
        "Sources of the manuscripts": v. 1, p. [123]-126.

16011   Bolton, Herbert Eugene, 1870-
        Texas in the middle eighteenth century, studies in
        Spanish colonial history and administration.
        Berkeley, 1915.
        x, 501 p.   front. (map), facsim. maps, plans.   23 cm.
        (California. University. Publications in history,
        v. 3)

16012   Bond, J   Harman.
        A journey to the forks of the Red River of the
        North in 1860. The journal of Ensign J. H. Bond,
        Royal Canadian Rifles. [Ed. by Arthur Henry
        Moehlman. Bismarck, State Historical Society of
        North Dakota, 1932]
        230-237 p.   24 cm.
        Reprinted from North Dakota historical quarterly,
        v. 6, no. 3, April 1932.

16013   Bond, John Wesley, 1825-1903.
        The meteorology of Minnesota, by John W. Bond.
        St. Paul, Minnesota Historical Society, 1853. (In
        Annals of the Minnesota Historical Society, no. IV,
        1853, p. 65-72)

16014 Bonney, Edward.
The banditti of the prairies, or, The murderer's
doom!! A tale of the Mississippi valley, by Edward
Bonney. Chicago, E. Bonney, 1850.
2 p.l., [9]-196 p.   plates, port.   22 cm.

16015 Bonsal, Stephen, 1863-
Edward Fitzgerald Beale; a pioneer in the path of
empire, 1822-1903, with 17 illustrations. New York,
G. P. Putnam's sons, 1912.
xii p., 1 l., 312 p.   plates, ports.   23 cm.

16016 Bookwalter, John Wesley.
Canyon and crater; or, Scenes in California and
the Sandwich Islands. Springfield, O., 1874.
372 p.   illus., maps, pl.   20 cm.

16017 Borrett, George Tuthill.
Letters from Canada and the United States. By
George Tuthill Borrett... London, Printed for
private circulation, by J. E. Adlard, 1865.
2 p.l., 294 p.   20 cm.

16018 Borthwick, J   D
Three years in California [1851-54] by J. D. Borthwick, with eight illustrations by the author. Edin-
burgh and London, W. Blackwood and sons, 1857.
vi p., 1 l., 384 p.   front., plates.   22 cm.
Not by John Douglas Borthwick of Montreal, Can.

16019 [Boss, Henry Rush] 1835-
Sketches of the history of Ogle County, Ill., and
the early settlement of the Northwest. Written for
the Polo advertiser. Polo, Ill., H. R. Boss, 1859.
2 p.l., 88 p.   20 cm.

16020 Boucard, Adolphe.
Travels of a naturalist. A record of adventures,
discoveries, history and customs of Americans and
Indians, habits and descriptions of animals, chiefly
made in North America, California, Mexico, Central
America, Columbia, Chili, etc., during the last
forty-two years. By A. Boucard... London [Pardy &
son, printers, Bournemouth] 1894.
viii, ii, 204 p.   front. (port.)   22 cm.

16021 Bouis, Amédée Théodore.
Le Whip-poor-will, ou, Les pionniers de Orégon...

Paris, Les imprimeurs-unis, 1847.
428 p.   19 cm.

16022   Bourke, John Gregory, 1843-1896.
An Apache campaign in the Sierra Madre. An account
of the expedition in pursuit of the hostile Chiricahua
Apaches in the spring of 1883. By John G. Bourke...
New York, C. Scribner's sons, 1886.
iv p., 1 l., 112 p.   front., pl.   19 cm.
Originally published in serial form in the Outing
magazine, of Boston.

16023   Bourke, John Gregory, 1843-1896.
... Mackenzie's last fight with the Cheyennes: a
winter campaign in Wyoming and Montana. By Captain
John G. Bourke... Governor's Island, N. Y. H., 1890.
cover-title, 44 p.   front. (port.)   25 cm.
Reprinted from Journal Military service institution.

16024   Bourke, John Gregory, 1843-1896.
On the border with Crook; by John G. Bourke...
New York, C. Scribner's sons, 1891.
xiii p., 1 l., 491 p.   front., pl., port.
23 cm.

16025   Bourke, John Gregory, 1843-1896.
The snake-dance of the Moquis of Arizona; being a
narrative of a journey from Santa Fe, New Mexico,
to the villages of the Moqui Indians of Arizona,
with a description of the manners and customs of this
peculiar people, and especially of the revolting
religious rite, the snake-dance; to which is added
a brief dissertation upon serpent-worship in general,
with an account of the tablet dance of the pueblo of
Santo Domingo, New Mexico, etc. By John G. Bourke...
New York, C. Scribner's sons, 1884.
xvi p., 1 l., 371 p.   illus., plates (part col.,
1 fold.) $22\frac{1}{2}$ cm.

16026   Boutwell, W   T
Exploring tour, by W. T. Boutwell. St. Paul,
Minnesota Historical Society, 1952. (In Annals of
the Minnesota Historical Society, 1852, p. 49-58)

16027   Bowen, Alfred D
Oregon and the orient, a work designed to show the
great natural and industrial advantages of Oregon
and its unequaled position relative to trade with

the Orient... Portland, Ore. [C. H. Crocker company]
1901.
159 p.   illus., port.

16028 Bowles, Samuel, 1826-1878.
          Our new West. Records of travel between the
       Mississippi River and the Pacific Ocean. Over the
       plains - over the mountains - through the great
       interior basin - over the Sierra Nevadas - to and up
       and down the Pacific coast. With details of the
       wonderful natural scenery, agriculture, mines,
       business, social life, progress, and prospects...
       including a full description of the Pacific railroad;
       and of the life of the Mormons, Indians, and Chinese.
       With map, portraits, and twelve full page illus-
       trations. By Samuel Bowles. Hartford, Ct., Hartford
       publishing co.; New York, J. D. Dennison; [etc., etc.]
       1869.
          xx, [21]-524 p. incl. plates, map.   front. (ports.)
       23 cm.

16029 Bowles, Samuel, 1826-1878.
          The Pacific railroad - open. How to go: what to
       see. Guide for travel to and through western America.
       By Samuel Bowles... Boston, Fields, Osgood & co.,
       1869.
          122 p.   17 cm.
          "The Sandwich Islands": p. [91]-99.

16030 Bowles, Samuel, 1826-1878.
          The Switzerland of America. A summer vacation in
       the parks and mountains of Colorado. By Samuel
       Bowles... Springfield, Mass., S. Bowles & co.;
       New York, The American news co.; [etc., etc.] 1869.
          iv, [6]-166 p.   17 cm.

16031 Boyce, William Dickson, 1848-1929.
          The Hawaiian Islands and Porto Rico, illustrated,
       by William D. Boyce... Chicago, New York, Rand,
       McNally & co. [c1914]
          1 p.l., vii-ix, 135 p.   front. (port.) illus.
       22½ cm.
          "A part of my complete work, United States colonies
       and dependencies... printed originally in the
       Saturday blade." - Introd.

16032 Brace, Charles Loring, 1826-1890.
          The new West: or, California in 1867-1868...

New York, G. P. Putnam & son, 1869.
373 p.   18 cm.

16033   Bradford, Ward, b. 1809.
Biographical sketches of the life of Major Ward
Bradford, as related by the author in his eighty-
second year. Containing a graphic description of
the manners and life of early times; vivid incidents
in Indian wars, and wilds of the mountains; life in
the gold regions of Nevada; perils by land and sea.
Together with reliable statements concerning the
products and resources of many lands and many climes.
[Fresno? Cal.] For the author [1891?]
92 p. incl. front. (port.)   17 cm.

16034   Brady, Cyrus Townsend, 1861-1920.
The conquest of the Southwest; the story of a great
spoliation, by Cyrus Townsend Brady... New York,
D. Appleton and company, 1905.
xiii, 293 p.   front., 8 pl., 3 port., 4 maps.
20 cm.   [Expansion of the republic series]

16035   Brady, Cyrus Townsend, 1861-1920.
Recollections of a missionary in the great West,
by the Rev. Cyrus Townsend Brady... New York,
C. Scribner's sons, 1900.
6 p.l., 200 p.   front. (port.)   19 cm.
Experiences in Missouri, Colorado and Kansas,
1890-1895.

16036   Brake, Hezekiah, b. 1814.
On two continents. A long life's experience.
By Hezekiah Brake. Pub. by the author. Topeka, Kan.,
Crane & company, printers, 1896.
240 p.   2 port. (incl. front.)   19½ cm.

16037   Braman, D   E   E
Braman's information about Texas, carefully
prepared by D. E. E. Braman... Philadelphia, J. B.
Lippincott & co., 1857.
viii, 9-192 p.   18 cm.

16038   Bravo Arosemena, Daniel.
La antigüedad clásica en el pensamiento historio-
gráfico español del siglo XIX. Panamá, Dirección
Nacional de Cultura, Ediciones del Ministerio de
Educación, 1970.
316 p.   23½ cm.

37

16039 Breck, Daniel, 1788-1871.
         Speech of Mr. Breck, of Kentucky, on the message of
         the President relating to California. Delivered in
         the House of Representatives of the United States,
         Monday, March 25, 1850. [Washington] Gideon & co.,
         printers [1850]
            16 p.   24½ cm.

16040 Breese, Sidney, 1800-1878.
         The early history of Illinois, from its discovery
         by the French, in 1673, until its cession to Great
         Britain in 1763, including the narrative of Marquette's
         discovery of the Mississippi. By Sidney Breese...
         With a biographical memoir by Melville W. Fuller.
         Edited by Thomas Hoyne, LL.D. Chicago, E. B. Myers
         & company, 1884.
            xiii, 422 p.   front. (port.) 3 fold. maps.
         23½ cm.

16041 A brief notice of the recent outrages committed by
         Isaac I. Stevens, governor of Washington Territory.
         The suspension of the writ of habeas corpus, the
         breaking up of courts, and the kidnapping of judges
         and clerks. Olympia, May 17, 1857.
            32 p.   21 cm.

16042 Briggs, Harold E
         The Black Hills gold rush. [Bismarck, State
         Historical Society of North Dakota, 1931]
            71-102 p.   24 cm.
         Reprinted from North Dakota historical quarterly,
         v. 5, no. 2, January 1931.

16043 Briggs, Harold E
         Early freight and stage lines in Dakota, by
         Harold E. Briggs. [Bismarck, State Historical
         Society of North Dakota, 1929]
            229-261 p.   24 cm.
         Reprinted from North Dakota historical quarterly,
         v. 3, no. 4, July 1929.

16044 Briggs, Harold E
         The great Dakota boom, 1879 to 1886, by Harold E.
         Briggs. [Bismarck, State Historical Society of
         North Dakota, 1930]
            78-108 p.   24 cm.
         Reprinted from North Dakota historical quarterly,
         v. 4, no. 2, January 1930.

16045   Briggs, Harold E
        Pioneer river transportation in Dakota, by
        Harold E. Briggs. [Bismarck, State Historical
        Society of North Dakota, 1928]
        159-181 p.   24 cm.
        Reprinted from North Dakota historical quarterly,
        v. 3, no. 3, April 1929.

16046   Briggs, Horace.
        Letters from Alaska and the Pacific Coast.
        Buffalo, 1889.
        87 p.   21 cm.

16047   Bristol, Sherlock, 1815-1906.
        The pioneer preacher; incidents of interest, and
        experiences in the author's life. Revival labors
        in the frontier settlements. A perilous trip across
        the plains in time of Indian wars, and before the
        railroads. Three years in the mining camps of
        California and Idaho, twenty-one years' residence in
        southern California, etc., by Rev. S. Bristol...
        Illustrated by Isabelle Blood. Chicago, New York,
        Fleming H. Revell [c1887]
        viii, 9-330 p.   front. (port.) plates.   19½ cm.

16048   Bristol, William M
        Californiana: and sketches of the southwest.
        Halftone illustrations from nature; drawings by
        Constance Farris, from suggestions by the author.
        Los Angeles [1901]
        131 p.   22 cm.

16049   The Broadmoor and Pike's Peak region. [Brooklyn,
        The Albertyoe company, n.d.]
        11 unnumb. p.   illus.   26½ x 33 cm.
        Eleven hand-colored views.

16050   Broke, Horatio George.
        With sack and stock in Alaska, by George Broke...
        London and New York, Longmans, Green, and co., 1891.
        xi, 158 p.   fold. maps.   20 cm.
        From Sitka to Mount St. Elias.

16051   Bromley, George Tisdale, 1817-
        The long ago and the later on; or, Recollections
        of eighty years, by George Tisdale Bromley. San
        Francisco, A. M. Robertson, 1904.
        xiii p., 1 l., 289 p.   front. (port.)   20½ cm.

16052   Bronaugh, Warren Carter, b. 1839.
        The Youngers' fight for freedom; a southern soldier's
        twenty years' campaign to open northern prison doors -
        with anecdotes of war days, by W. C. Bronaugh...
        who spent the period from 1882 to 1902 to secure the
        release of Cole, Jim, and Bob Younger from the
        Minnesota state penitentiary... Columbia, Mo.,
        Printed for the author by E. W. Stephens publishing
        company, 1906.
        308 p. incl. front., plates, ports.   21 cm.

16053   Bronson, Edgar Beecher, 1856-1917.
        The red-blooded, by Edgar Beecher Bronson...
        Chicago, A. C. McClurg & co., 1910.
        5 p.l.. 3-342 p.   front., plates.   21 cm.
        Partly reprinted from various periodicals.

16054   Bronson, Edgar Beecher, 1856-1917.
        Reminiscences of a ranchman, by Edgar Beecher
        Bronson. New York, The McClure company, 1908.
        4 p.l., 3-314 p.   20 cm.

16055   Brook, Harry E   , comp.
        Land of sunshine, Southern California. An authentic
        description of its natural features, resources and
        prospects... Compiled for the Southern California
        World's Fair Association and Southern California
        Bureau of Information. Los Angeles, 1893.
        112 p.   map., pl.   20 cm.

16056   Brooker, William H
        Texas. An epitome of Texas history from the
        filibustering and revolutionary eras to the inde-
        pendence of the republic. From most approved
        sources... by William H. Brooker... Columbus, O.,
        Press of Nitschke brothers, 1897.
        100 p.   front., plates, ports.   23 cm.

16057   Brooks, Elizabeth.
        Prominent women of Texas, by Elizabeth Brooks.
        Akron, O., Manufactured by The Werner company [1896]
        iii-ix, 11-206 p.   ports.   25 cm.

16058   Brooks, Helen.
        The Heath family, by Helen Brooks. [Bismarck,
        State Historical Society of North Dakota; 1930]
        109-115 p.   24 cm.

Reprinted from North Dakota historical quarterly, v. 4, no. 2, January 1930.

16059 Brooks, Juanita.
Indian relations on the Mormon frontier, by Juanita Brooks. Salt Lake City, Utah State Historical Society, 1944. (In Utah historical quarterly, v. 12, nos. 1, 2, January, April 1944, p. 1-48)

16060 Brosnan, Cornelius James, 1882-
History of the state of Idaho, by C. J. Brosnan... New York, Chicago [etc.] C. Scribner's sons [c1918] 2 p.l., vii-xiii, 237 p. front., illus., maps. 20 cm.

16061 Bross, William, 1813-1890.
History of Chicago. Historical and commercial statistics, sketches, facts and figures, republished from the "Daily Democratic press." What I remember of early Chicago; a lecture, delivered in McCormick's hall, January 23, 1876, (Tribune, January 24th) by William Bross... Chicago, Jansen, McClurg & co., 1876.
126 p. 23 cm.

16062 Brouillet, Jean Baptiste Abraham, 1813-1884.
Authentic account of the murder of Dr. Whitman and other missionaries, by the Cayuse Indians of Oregon, in 1847, and the causes which led to that horrible catastrophe. By the Very Rev. J. B. A. Brouillet... 2d ed. Portland, Or., S. J. McCormick, 1869.
108 p. 18½ cm.

16063 Brown, Charles E
Survey of the State Historical Museum of North Dakota, 1929, by Charles E. Brown. [Bismarck, State Historical Society of North Dakota, 1929] 292-304 p. 24 cm.
Reprinted from North Dakota historical quarterly, v. 3, no. 4, July 1929.

16064 Brown, James Henry.
Brown's political history of Oregon... By J. Henry Brown. Portland, Or., W. B. Allen, 1892.
v. front., illus., port., fold. map., fold. facsim. 22½ cm.
Contents. - v. 1. Provisional government. 1892.

41

16065 Brown, James Stephens, b. 1828.
       California gold; an authentic history of the
       first find, with the names of those interested in
       the discovery. Pub. by the author, James S. Brown...
       Oakland, Cal., Pacific press publishing company,
       1894.
       1 p.l., 5-20 p.   front. (port.)   18 cm.

16066 Brown, James Stephens, b. 1828.
       Life of a pioneer; being the autobiography of
       James S. Brown. Salt Lake City, Utah, G. Q. Cannon
       & sons co., 1900.
       xix, [9]-520 p.   front. (port.)   illus., pl.
       22 cm.

16067 Brown, John, 1843-
       Twenty-five years a parson in the wild West; being
       the experience of Parson Ralph Riley [pseud.] by
       Rev. John Brown... Fall River, Mass., The author,
       1896.
       215 p.   front. (port.)   19 cm.
       Experiences principally in Nevada and Texas.

16068 Brown, John Henry, 1810-1905.
       Reminiscences and incidents of "the early days"
       of San Francisco by John H. Brown; actual experience
       of an eyewitness, from 1845 to 1850. San Francisco,
       Calif., Mission journal publishing co. [c1886]
       [106] p.   front. (fold. plan)   23 cm.
       "A small number only was printed, and the work is
       rare." - Cowan, Bibl. of the hist. of Calif.

16069 Brown, William H   1796-1867.
       Memoir of the late Hon. Daniel P. Cook: read
       before the Chicago historical society, June 9, 1857,
       by William H. Brown... Pub. by vote of the Society.
       Chicago, Scripps, Bross & Spears, book and job
       printers, 1857.
       30 p.   22 cm.

16070 Browne, Mrs. Alice (Harriman) 1861-1925.
       ... Pacific history stories. Montana edition by
       Alice Harriman... Volume 1. San Francisco, The
       Whitaker & Ray company (incorporated) 1903.
       198 p.   col. front., illus.   17½ cm.
       (Western series of readers)
       No more published.
       "Books of reference on Montana history": p. 198.

16071   Browne, John Ross, 1821-1875.
        Crusoe's island: a ramble in the footsteps of
        Alexander Selkirk. With sketches of adventure in
        California and Washoe. By J. Ross Browne... New
        York, Harper & brothers, 1867.
        vii, [9]-436 p.   illus.   20 cm.

16072   Browne, John Ross, 1821-1875.
        ... Indian war in Oregon and Washington territories...
        [Washington, D.C.? 1858?]
        62 p.   17 cm.   (U.S. Congress. House. 35th
        Cong., 1st Sess., Ex. doc. no. 38)

16073   Browne, John Ross, 1821-1875.
        Resources of the Pacific slope. A statistical and
        descriptive summary of the mines and minerals,
        climate, topography, agriculture, commerce, manu-
        factures, and miscellaneous productions, of the
        states and territories west of the Rocky mountains.
        With a sketch of the settlement and exploration of
        Lower California. By J. Ross Browne, aided by a
        corps of assistants. New York, D. Appleton and
        company, 1869.
        678, 200 p.   24 cm.

16074   Brownlow, William Gannaway, 1805-1877.
        Helps to the study of Presbyterianism; or, An un-
        sophisticated exposition of Calvinism, with Hopkinsian
        modifications and policy, with a view to a more easy
        interpretation of the same. To which is added a
        brief account of the life and travels of the author;
        interspersed with anecdotes. By William G. Brownlow...
        Knoxville, T., F. S. Heiskell, printer, 1834.
        xiii, [15]-299 p.   20 cm.

16075   Brownson, Orestes Augustus, jr.
        Caroline: a comic dramina, in two acts. By O. A.
        Brownson, jr. ... Dubuque [Ia.] Palmer & bro., 1870.
        24 p.   illus.   18½ cm.
        "Coriolanus: an historical dramina": p. [21]-24.

16076   Bruce, Miner W
        Alaska: its history, and resources, gold fields,
        routes and scenery, by Miner W. Bruce. Illustrated.
        Seattle, Wash., Lowman & Hanford stationery and
        printing co., 1895.
        128 p., 1 l.   front., illus. (incl. ports.)
        plates, fold. map.   23½ cm.

16077 Brunson, Alfred, 1793-1882.
A western pioneer: or, Incidents of the life and
times of Rev. Alfred Brunson... embracing a period
of over seventy years. Written by himself...
Cincinnati, Hitchcock and Walden; New York, Carlton
and Lanahan, 1872-[79]
2 v.   20 cm.

16078 Bryan, Roger Bates, 1860-
An average American army officer; an autobiography,
by Roger G. Bryan, captain U. S. army, retired.
San Diego, Cal., Buck-Molina co., printers, 1914.
7 p.l., 17 -166 p., 1 l. incl. front. (port.)
illus.   18 cm.

16079 Buel, James William, 1849-1920.
The border outlaws. An authentic and thrilling
history of the most noted bandits of ancient or
modern times, the Younger brothers, Jesse and Frank
James, and their comrades in crime. Comp. from
reliable sources only... By J. W. Buel... Illustrated
with portraits and colored plates. St. Louis, Mo.,
Historical publishing company, 1881.
252, [2], 148 p. incl. front., illus.   col. plates,
2 port. on 1 pl.   19½ cm.

16080 Buel, James William, 1849-1920.
Life and marvelous adventures of Wild Bill, the
scout... By J. W. Buel... Chicago, Belford, Clarke
& co., 1880.
92, [1] p.   front. (port.) illus.   18 cm.
Sketch of the life of J. B. Hickok (Wild Bill)

16081 Buffum, Edward Gould.
Six months in the gold mines: from a journal of
three years residence in Upper and Lower California.
1847-8-9. By E. Gould Buffum... Philadelphia,
Lea & Blanchard, 1850.
172 p.   18 cm.

16082 Buffum, George Tower, 1846-
On two frontiers, by George T. Buffum... frontispiece by Maynard Dixon; pen-and-ink illustrations
by Frank T. Merrill. Boston, Lothrop, Lee & Shepard
co. [1918]
vii, 375 p.   front., illus.   20 cm.

16083 Buffum, George Tower, 1846-
       Smith of Bear City, and other frontier sketches,
       by George T. Buffum; illustrated with six photo-
       gravures from original drawings, by F. T. Wood.
       New York, The Grafton press, 1906.
       xii, [1], 248, 1 p.   6 pl.   21½ cm.

16084 Bugbee, Lester G
       Some difficulties of a Texas empresario. Harris-
       burg, 1899.
       113 p.   21 cm.
       Reprinted from Publications of the Southern historical
       association, 1899.

16085 Bulloch, James Dunwody, 1823-1901.
       The secret service of the Confederate States in
       Europe: or, How the Confederate cruisers were equipped.
       By James D. Bulloch... New York G. P. Putnam's sons,
       1884.
       2 v.   23 cm.

16086 Bunker Hill Trading and Mining Association. Consti-
       tution. [Boston? 1849?]
       Broadside.   34 x 21 cm.

16087 Bunnell, Lafayette H
       Discovery of the Yosemite, and the Indian war of
       1851, which led to that event. Chicago [1880]
       331 p.   illus.   map, pl.   19 cm.

16088 Burdette, Mary G   ed.
       The heroine of Saddle Mountain. Chicago, R. R.
       Donnelley, 1897.
       52 p.   illus., ports.   19 cm.   (Young women
       among blanket Indians, no. 2)
       "For the Women's Baptist Home Mission Society."

16089 Burdette, Robert Jones, 1844-1914, ed.
       American biography and genealogy. California ed.
       Robert J. Burdette, D.D., editor... Chicago,
       New York, The Lewis publishing company [191-]
       2 v.   front., illus., plates, ports.   27½ cm.

16090 Burdette, Robert Jones, 1844-1914, ed.
       Greater Los Angeles and southern California, their
       portraits and chronological record of their careers;
       Robert J. Burdette, ed. Chicago, Los Angeles [etc.]
       The Lewis publishing company, 1906.

1 p.l., ii, 240 p.   illus. (incl. ports.)
2 col. pl.   24½ cm.

16091 Burdette, Robert Jones, 1844-1914, ed.
Greater Los Angeles and southern California;
portraits and personal memoranda. Chicago, Lewis
publ. co., 1910.
336 p.   illus., ports.   25 cm.

16092 Burdick, Usher L
Ranches in the Great American Desert, by Usher L.
Burdick. [Bismarck, State Historical Society of
North Dakota, 1941]
295-300 p.   24 cm.
Reprinted from North Dakota historical quarterly,
v. 8, no. 4, July 1941.

16093 Burke, John M
"Buffalo Bill" from prairie to palace; an authentic
history of the wild West, with sketches, stories of
adventure, and anecdotes of "Buffalo Bill," the hero
of the plains; comp. by John M. Burke ("Arizona John")
with the authority of General W. F. Cody ("Buffalo
Bill") Chicago and New York, Rand, McNally & company,
1893.
275 p.   illus. (incl. ports., facsims.)   20½ cm.
(On cover: Rialto series. no. 13)

16094 Burke, William S
The history of Leavenworth, the metropolis of
Kansas, and the chief commercial center west of the
Missouri River. The superior mercantile and manufacturing facilities of the city. The agricultural
advantages of Leavenworth County impartially discussed.
By W. S. Burke and J. L. Rock, under the supervision
of the Leavenworth board of trade. Leavenworth, Kan.,
The Leavenworth times book and job printing establishment, 1880.
84, [1] p.   21½ cm.

16095 Burlingame, Merrill G
The buffalo in trade and commerce, by Merrill G.
Burlingame. [Bismarck, State Historical Society
of North Dakota, 1929]
262-291 p.   24 cm.
Reprinted from North Dakota historical quarterly,
v. 3, no. 4, July 1929.

16096 Burlington & Missouri River Railroad Company.
       Great opportunities for farmers, businessmen
       and investors in Nebraska, northwestern Kansas, and
       eastern Colorado... Chicago, 1893.
       32 p.   map.   18 cm.

16097 Burlington & Missouri River Railroad Company.
       Nebraska; B. & M. railroad lands...   St. Louis,
       A. Gast & co. [1879?]
       cover-title, 36 p.   illus. maps.   18 cm.

16098 Burlington & Missouri River Railroad Company.
       Views and descriptions of Burlington & Missouri
       river railroad lands, with important information
       concerning where and how to select and purchase farms
       in Iowa and Nebraska... Burlington [1874?]
       unpaged.   map, plates.   18 cm.
       Composed of plates with descriptive text.

16099 Burnett, Peter H[ardeman] 1807-1895.
       Recollections and opinions of an old pioneer...
       New York, D. Appleton & co., 1880.
       xiii, 448 p.   19½ cm.

16100 Burnham, John Howard, 1834-1917.
       [History of Bloomington and Normal, in McLean county,
       Illinois]
       (In The history of McLean county... Chicago, 1879.
       24½ cm.   p. 299-456)

16101 Burr, A   G
       Address at the dedication of the memorial on
       Butte St. Paul, by A. G. Burr. [Bismarck, State
       Historical Society of North Dakota, 1941]
       284-294 p.   24 cm.
       Reprinted from North Dakota historical quarterly,
       v. 8, no. 4, July 1941.

16102 Burr, A   G
       Judge John McDowell Cochrane, 1859-1904, by A. G.
       Burr. [Bismarck, State Historical Society of North
       Dakota, 1942]
       203-218 p.   front. (port.)   24 cm.
       Reprinted from North Dakota historical quarterly,
       v. 9, no. 4, July 1942.

16103 Burr, A   G
       The organization of Bottineau County, by A. G. Burr.

47

[Bismarck, State Historical Society of North Dakota, 1941]
   2-26 p.   24 cm.
Reprinted from North Dakota historical quarterly, v. 9, no. 1, October 1941.

16104 Burr, A   G
   The Sinclair family in Bottineau County, bv A. G. Burr. [Bismarck, State Historical Society of North Dakota, 1943]
   217-243 p.   ports.   24 cm.
Reprinted from North Dakota historical quarterly, v. 10, no. 4, October 1943.

16105 Burr, Aaron, 1756-1836.
   The private journal of Aaron Burr, reprinted in full from the original manuscript in the library of Mr. William K. Bixby of St. Louis, Mo., with an introduction, explanatory notes, and a glossary... Rochester, N. Y. [The Post express printing co.] 1903.
   2 v.   front. (ports.)   25 cm.
Compiled and edited by William H. Samson.

16106 Burrows, John McDowell, b. 1814.
   Fifty years in Iowa: being the personal reminiscences of J. M. D. Burrows, concerning the men and events, social life, industrial interests, physical development, and commercial progress of Davenport and Scott County, during the period from 1838 to 1888. Davenport, Ia., Glass & company, printers, 1888.
   xi, 182 p.   19 cm.

16107 Burtt-Davy, Joseph, 1870-
   ... Stock ranges of northwestern California: notes on the grasses and forage plants and range conditions. By Joseph Burtt Davy... Washington, Govt. print. off., 1902.
   81 p.   illus., VIII pl., III maps.   26 cm.
(U. S. Bureau of plant industry. Bulletin no. 12)

16108 Busby, Allie B
   Two summers among the Musquakies, relating to the early history of the Sac and Fox tribe, incidents of their noted chiefs, location of the Foxes, or Musquakies, in Iowa, with a full account of their traditions, rites and ceremonies, and the personal experience of the writer for two and a half years among them. By Allie B. Busby. Vinton, Ia., Herald

book and job rooms, 1886.
vii, [9]-238 p.   19½ cm.

16109   Busch, Moritz, 1821-1899.
Geschichte der Mormonen, nebst einer darstellung
ihres glaubens und ihrer gegenwärtigen socialen und
politischen verhältnisse, von dr. Moritz Busch.
Leipzig, A. Abel [1870]
viii, 444, [4] p.   19½ cm.

16110   Butcher, Solomon Devore, 1856-
S. D. Butcher's pioneer history of Custer county,
and short sketches of early days in Nebraska...
Broken Bow, Neb. [Denver, Colo., The Merchants
publishing co., c1901]
4 p.l., [7]-403 p.   illus. (incl. ports.)
24 x 18 cm.
Some of the sketches contributed by various authors.

16111   Butler, James D
Nebraska: its characteristics and prospects.
[n.p., 1873]
36, 2 p.   illus., plates.   19 cm.

16112   Butler, James D
A September scamper. Nebraska after a three years'
absence. [Burlington, Ia., 1877]
32 p.   plates.   19 cm.

16113   Butler, Sir William Francis, 1838-1910.
Sir William Butler, an autobiography, by Lieut.-
General the Rt. Hon. Sir W. F. Butler... London,
Constable and company, ltd., 1911.
xi, 476 p.   4 port. (incl. front.) 2 fold. maps.
24 cm.
Completed and prepared for publication by his
daughter, Eileen Butler.

16114   Butterfield, Consul Willshire, 1824-1899.
History of the discovery of the Northwest by
John Nicolet in 1634, with a sketch of his life, by
C. W. Butterfield... Cincinnati, R. Clarke & co.,
1881.
ix, 11-113 p.   20½ cm.

16115   Butterfield, Consul Willshire, 1824-1899.
History of the Girty's; being a concise account of
the Girty brothers - Thomas, Simon, James and

George, and of their half-brother John Turner -
also of the part taken by them in Lord Dunmore's war,
in the western border war of the revolution, and in
the Indian war of 1790-95; with a recital of the
principal events in the West during these wars...
By Consul Willshire Butterfield... Cincinnati,
R. Clarke & co., 1890.
xiii, 425, [1] p.   24 cm.

16116 Byers, Samuel Hawkins Marshall, 1838-1933.
With fire and sword, by Major S. H. M. Byers...
New York, The Neale publishing company, 1911.
203 p.   2 port. (incl. front.)   19 cm.

16117 Byers, William Newton, 1831-1903.
Encyclopedia of biography of Colorado; history of
Colorado, by William N. Byers... vol. 1. Illustrated
with steel plate and copper plate engravings.
Chicago, The Century publishing and engraving company,
1901.
xi, 477 p.   ports.   30 cm.

16118 Byrne, P   E
The Custer myth. [Bismarck, State Historical
Society of North Dakota, 1932]
187-200 p.   24 cm.
Reprinted from North Dakota historical quarterly,
v. 6, no. 3, April 1932.

                            C

16119 Cady, John Henry, 1846-
Arizona's yesterday, being the narrative of John H.
Cady, pioneer, rewritten and rev. by Basil Dillon Woon,
1915. [Los Angeles, Times-Minor printing and
binding house, c1916]
120 p.   front., plates, ports.   18 cm.

16120 Caldwell, Howard Walter, 1858-
... Education in Nebraska, by Howard W. Caldwell...
Washington, Govt. print. off., 1902.
268 p.   plates.   23½ cm.   (Contributions to
American educational history, ed. by Herbert B. Adams,
no. 32. U.S. Bureau of Education, Circulars of
information, 1902, no. 3)

16121 California; its past history, its present position,
its future prospects... account of the discovery
of the gold region and the subsequent important
proceedings. Including a history of the rise,
progress, and present condition of the Mormon settlements. With an appendix containing the official
reports made to the government of the United States.
London, For the proprietors, 1850.
viii, 270 p.   front., col. pl., map.   22 cm.

16122 California, the cornucopia of the world; room for
millions of immigrants... [Chicago] 1883.
76 p.   illus. pl.   22 cm.

16123 California. Alaska-Yukon-Pacific Exposition Commission.
California: its products, resources, industries
and attractions; what it offers the immigrant,
homeseeker, investor and tourist; pub. by the
California Alaska-Yukon Exposition Commission...
Ed. by T. G. Daniells. Sacramento, W. W. Shannon,
superintendent state printing, 1909.
174 p.   illus. $22\frac{1}{2}$ cm.
Similar publications, under same title, were issued
by the Louisiana Purchase Exposition Commission, 1904,
and by the Lewis and Clark Exposition Commission, 1905.

16124 California. Constitutional Convention, 1849.
Report of the debates in the Convention of California,
on the formation of the state constitution, in
September and October, 1849. By J. Ross Browne.
Washington, Printed by J. T. Towers, 1850.
479, xlvi p., 1 l. $22\frac{1}{2}$ cm.
"Constitution of the state of California":
p. [iii]-xiii.

16125 California. Historical Survey Commission.
The care and use of the county archives of California.
By Owen C. Coy... director and archivist. Publica-
tion of the California Historical Survey Commission.
Sacramento, California state printing office, 1919.
viii, 92 p. $22\frac{1}{2}$ cm.
John F. Davis, chairman.
This study is a reprint of pt. I of the Guide to
the county archives of California. cf. Pref., p. v.

16126 California. Historical Survey Commission.
The genesis of California counties, by Owen C. Coy,
Ph.D., director of the commission. Publication of

51

the California Historical Survey Commission,
Berkeley, 1923. [Sacramento, California state
printing office, F. J. Smith, superintendent, 1923]
vii p., 2 l., 92 p.   maps (2 fold.)   23½ cm.

16127 California Federation of Women's Clubs. History
and Landmarks Section.
Historic facts and fancies. History and Landmarks
Section of California Federated Women's Clubs...
[San Francisco, Printed by the Stanley-Taylor company,
1907?]
148, [1] p.   illus.   26 cm.

16128 California gold regions, with a full account of their
mineral resources... with sketches of California,
and account of the life, manners, and customs of the
inhabitants... New York [1849]
48 p.   17 cm.

16129 California Historical Society.
Papers of the California Historical Society...
San Francisco, California Historical Society etc.
1887-93.
4 v. in 3.   maps.   27 cm.

16130 California Immigrant Union.
All about California, and the inducements to settle
there. San Francisco, 1870.
64 p.   18 cm.

16131 California Northwestern Railway Vacation. 1905.
[n.p.] 1905.
196 p.   illus., map.   18 cm.

16132 The California register. v. 1, no. 1; April 1900.
San Francisco, California genealogical society, 1900.
cover-title, 32 p.   fold. tab.   25 cm.
[California genealogical society, Publications, no. 1]
No more published.

16133 Calkins, Franklin Welles, 1857-
Indian tales, by Frank W. Calkins. Chicago, M. A.
Donohue & co. [1893]
150 p.   illus.   22½ cm.

16134 Callison, John James, 1855-
Bill Jones of Paradise Valley, Oklahoma; his life
and adventures for over forty years in the great

Southwest. He was a pioneer in the days of the
buffalo, the wild Indian, the Oklahoma boomer, the
cowboy and the outlaw; copiously illustrated from
photos and drawings from real life, by John J.
Callison... [Chicago, Printed by M. A. Donohue & co.,
c1914]
328 p.   front., illus.   19 cm.

16135   Campbell, Robert.
A journey to Kentucky for sheep. From the journal
of Robert Campbell, 1832-1833. [Bismarck, N. D.,
State Historical Society of North Dakota, 1926]
35-45 p.   25 cm.
In North Dakota historical quarterly, v. 1, no. 1,
October. 1926.

16136   Campbell, William Carey.
A Colorado colonel, and other sketches, by William
Carey Campbell. Topeka, Kan., Crane & co., 1901.
402 p. incl. illus., pl.   front.   20 cm.

16137   Campion, J   S
On the frontier. Reminiscences of wild sports,
personal adventures, and strange scenes. By J. S.
Campion... With eight illustrations. [2d ed.]
London, Chapman & Hall, 1878.
xiv p., 1 l., 372 p. incl. front.   6 pl., port.
22 cm.

16138   Canadian Pacific Railway Company.
... Reports and documents in reference to the
location of the line and a western terminal harbour.
1878. Ottawa, Printed by Maclean, Roger & co., 1878.
104 p.   fold. maps.   25½ cm.
At head of title: Canadian Pacific railway.
Sandford Fleming, C.M.G., engineer-in-chief.

16139   Canfield, Chauncey de Leon, 1843-1909, ed.
The diary of a forty-niner, ed. by Chauncey L.
Canfield. New York, San Francisco, M. Shepard
company, 1906.
2 p.l., 231 p.   map.   22 x 17 cm.

16140   Cannon, Frank Jenne, 1859-
Brigham Young and his Mormon empire [by] Frank J.
Cannon and George L. Knapp... New York, Chicago [etc.]
Fleming H. Revell company [c1913]
398 p.   front., plates, ports.   21 cm.

16141 Cannon, Frank Jenne, 1859-
       Under the prophet in Utah; the national menace of a
       political priestcraft, by Frank J. Cannon... and
       Harvey J. O'Higgins... Boston, Mass., The C. M. Clark
       publishing co., 1911.
       402 p.   front. (port.)   19½ cm.
       First published in Everybody's magazine.

16142 Cannon, Miles.
       Waiilatpu, its rise and fall, 1836-1847; a story of
       pioneer days in the Pacific Northwest based entirely
       upon historical research, by Miles Cannon; featuring
       the journey of Narcissa Prentiss Whitman, the first
       American woman to cross the continent and look upon
       the Columbia river... Boise, Id., Capital news job
       rooms, 1915.
       ix, 171 p.   front., plates, ports.   23½ cm.

16143 Cantonwine, Alexander.
       Star forty-six, Oklahoma. [Oklahoma City, printed
       by Pythian Times publishing co.] 1911.
       334 p.   front. (port.), illus.   24 cm.

16144 Cape, Wilson.
       Population changes in the west North Central states,
       1900-1930. [Bismarck, State Historical Society of
       North Dakota, 1932]
       276-291 p.   tables, diagrs.   24 cm.
       Reprinted from North Dakota historical quarterly,
       v. 6, no. 4, July 1932.

16145 Capron, E[lisha] S
       History of California, from its discovery to the
       present time; comprising also a full description of
       its climate, surface, soil, rivers... agriculture,
       commerce, mines, mining, &c., with a journal of the
       voyage from New York, via Nicaragua, to San Francisco,
       and back, via Panama... By E. S. Capron, counsellor
       at law. Boston, J. P. Jewett & company; Cleveland, O.,
       Jewett, Proctor & Worthington, 1854.
       1 p.l., [v]-xi, 356 p.   front. (fold. map)
       18½ cm.

16146 Carey, Charles Henry.
       A general history of Oregon prior to 1861. Portland,
       Or., Metropolitan press, 1935-[36]
       2 v.   front., plates, ports., maps, facsim.
       23½ cm.

16147   Carlton, Ambrose B
         The wonderlands of the wild West, with sketches of
         the Mormons. By A. B. Carlton... [n.p.] 1891.
         1 p.l., [v]-vii, [9]-346, 2 p.   front., plates,
         ports.   23 cm.

16148   Carpenter, Lewis C
         Tourist's guide to Colorado and the carbonate fields.
         Leadville, and how to reach there. Denver, 1879.
         80 p.   18 cm.

16149   Carr, John.
         Pioneer days in California, by John Carr. Historical
         and personal sketches. Eureka, Cal., Times publishing
         company, 1891.
         2 p.l., [11]-452 p.   front. (port.)   22½ cm.
         Biographical sketches of pioneers of Humboldt and
         Trinity counties, California: p. 420-452.

16150   Carrigan, Mrs. Wilhelmina (Buce)
         Captured by the Indians: reminiscences of pioneer
         life in Minnesota, by Minnie Buce Carrigan. Forest
         City, S. D., Forest City press, 1907.
         2 p.l., [3]-40 p.   illus. (port.) pl.   22½ cm.
         From the Buffalo Lake news.

16151   Carrington, Frances (Courtney)
         My army life and the Fort Phil. Kearney massacre,
         with an account of the celebration of "Wyoming opened,"
         by Frances C. Carrington... Philadelphia & London,
         J. B. Lippincott company, 1910.
         317, [1] p.   plates, ports., maps (part fold.)
         plans.   20½ cm.

16152   Carrington, Henry Beebee, 1824-1912.
         The Indian question. An address, by General Henry
         B. Carrington, U.S.A., before the geographical and
         biological sections of the British association for
         the advancement of science, at their forty-fifth
         meeting, at Bristol, 1875. [American reprint]...
         Boston, De Wolfe & Fiske company, 1909.
         32 p.   2 pl., 2 fold. maps.   22½ cm.

16153   [Carrington, Mrs. Margaret Irvin Sullivant)] 1831-1870.
         Ab-sa-ra-ka, home of the Crows: being the
         experience of an officer's wife on the plains, and
         marking the vicisitudes of peril and pleasure during
         the occupation of the new route to Virginia City,

Montana, 1866-7, and the Indian hostilities thereto;
with outlines of the natural features and resources
of the land, tables of distances, maps and other aids
to the traveler; gathered from observation and other
reliable sources. Philadelphia, J. B. Lippincott &
co., 1869.
xii, 13-284 p.   front. (fold. map) illus.   19 cm.
The name Ab-sa-ra-ka is applied to the territory
occupied by the Crow Indians in northern Wyoming
and southern Montana.

16154   Carroll, George Ryerson, 1831-1895.
Pioneer life in and around Cedar Rapids, Iowa, from
1839 to 1849. By Rev. George R. Carroll. Cedar
Rapids, Ia., Times printing and binding house, 1895.
xii, 251 p. incl. front. (port.) illus., plates.
20½ cm.

16155   Carroll, Mary Pius.
The influence of the missions on present-day
California. Berkeley, Cal., Newman Club [1915]
16 p.   23 cm.   (Newman Hall prize essay, 1915)
Reprinted from the University of California
Chronicle, v. 18, no. 4.

16156   Carson, Andrew Carlisle.
Colorado, top of the world, by Andrew Carlisle
Carson... Denver, The Smith-Brooks co., 1912.
82, [16] p. incl. col. front., illus. (1 col.)
23½ cm.

16157   Carson, James H   d. 1853.
Early recollections of the mines, and a description
of the great Tulare valley. By J. H. Carson...
Stockton [Calif.] Pub. to accompany the steamer
edition of the "San Joaquin republican" 1852.
64 p.   front.   20½ cm.
At head of cover-title: Second edition.
Cover-title: ... Life in California, together with
a description of the great Tulare valley.
"The first edition did not appear in book form,
having been issued as a supplement to a number of
the 'San Joaquin republican'." - R.E. Cowan, Bibl.
of the hist. of Calif., p. 43.

16158   Carson, Thomas.
Ranching, sport and travel, by Thomas Carson...
New York, C. Scribner's sons; London, T. F. Unwin

[1912]
　　319, [1] p. incl. front., plates.　22½ cm.
"The main portion of the volume is devoted to
cattle ranching in Arizona, New Mexico and Texas."

16159　Carstarphon, James E
　　My trip to California in '49 [with biographical and
genealogical sketch, comp. by Clayton Keith]
[Louisiana, Mo., 1914]
　　[8] p.　port.　18 cm.

16160　Carter, Charles Franklin.
　　Missions of Nueva California; an historical sketch.
San Francisco, 1900.
　　15, 189 p.　illus., map, pl.　26 cm.

16161　Carter, Charles Franklin.
　　Some by-ways of California. New York [1902]
　　2 p.l., iii-vi, 189 p.　19½ cm.

16162　Carter, William Giles Harding, 1851-1925.
　　From Yorktown to Santiago with the sixth U. S.
cavalry, by Lieutenant-colonel W. H. Carter...
Baltimore, The Friedenwald co., 1900.
　　vi p., 1 l., 317 p.　front., illus., ports.
23½ cm.

16163　Carter, William Giles Harding, 1851-1925.
　　Old army sketches, by General W. H. Carter...
Baltimore, Md., The Lord Baltimore press, The Friedenwald company, 1906.
　　203 p.　front., illus., plates.　20½ cm.

16164　Cartwright, David W
　　Natural history of western wild animals and guide
for hunters, trappers, and sportsmen; embracing
observations on the art of hunting and trapping, a
description of the physical structure, homes, and
habits of fur-bearing animals and others of North
America, with general and specific rules for their
capture; also, narratives of personal adventure.
By David W. Cartwright. Written by Mary F. Bailey,
A.M. Toledo, O., Blade printing & paper company,
1875.
　　x p., 1 l., 280 p.　19 pl. (incl. front.)
20½ cm.

16165   Carver, Hartwell.
        Proposal for a charter to build a railroad from
        Lake Michigan to the Pacific Ocean, by Dr. Hartwell
        Carver. Washington, Printed by J. & G. S. Gideon,
        1847.
        38 p., 1 l.   23 cm.

16166   Catlin, George, 1796-1872.
        Last rambles amongst the Indians of the Rocky
        mountains and the Andes. By George Catlin... New
        York, D. Appleton and company, 1867.
        x p., 1 l., 361 p.   front., illus., plates.
        17 cm.

16167   Catlin, George, 1796-1872.
        Life among the Indians, by George Catlin. London
        [etc.] Gall & Inglis [187-?]
        xiv p., 1 l., 17-252 p.   illus., 8 pl. (incl.
        front.)   19½ cm.

16168   Catlin, George, 1796-1872.
        0-kee-pa: a religious ceremony; and other customs
        of the Mandans. By George Catlin. With thirteen
        coloured illustrations. Philadelphia, J. B. Lippin-
        cott & co. [London, printed] 1867.
        4 p.l., 52 p.   col. pl.   26 cm.

16169   Cattermole, E   G
        Famous frontiersmen, pioneers and scouts; the
        vanguards of American civilization... including
        Boone, Crawford, Girty, Molly Finney, the McCulloughs
        ... Captain Jack, Buffalo Bill, General Custer with
        his last campaign against Sitting Bull, and General
        Crook with his recent campaign against the Apaches.
        By E. G. Cattermole... Chicago, The Coburn & Newman
        publishing company, 1883.
        xvi, [17]-540 p.   front., illus. (incl. ports.)
        19½ cm.

16170   Central Texas Genealogical Society.
        McLennan County, Texas, marriage record, v. 1-
        1850/70-   [Waco? n.d.]
        v.   28 cm.

16171   Ceuleneer, Adolphe de.
        Le Colorado. Conférence faite à la Société royale
        de géographie d'Anvers. Extrait des Bulletins de la
        Société royale de géographie d'Anvers. Anvers, 1890.
        27 p.   21 cm.

16172 Chambers, John, 1780-1852.
    Autobiography of John Chambers, ed. by John Carl
Parish. Iowa City, Ia., The State historical society
of Iowa, 1908.
    ix p., 3 l., 49 p.   front., ports.   27 cm.
    Also published in the Iowa journal of history and
politics, v. 6, no. 2.

16173 Chambers, Julius, 1850-1920.
    The Mississippi River and its wonderful valley;
twenty-seven hundred and seventy-five miles from
source to sea, by Julius Chambers... with 80 illustrations and maps. New York and London, G. P.
Putnam's sons, 1910.
    xvi, 308 p.   front., plates, ports., maps (part
fold.) facsim. $24\frac{1}{2}$ cm.

16174 Chapin, Frederick Hastings.
    Mountaineering in Colorado; the peaks about Estes
park, by Frederick H. Chapin. Boston, Appalachian
Mountain Club, 1889.
    3 p.l., [iii]-xi, [13]-168 p.   front., illus.,
plates.   20 cm.

16175 Chaplin, William Edwards.
    Public lands of Wyoming, how title thereto may be
obtained. Laramie, Wyo., 1904.
    16 p.   22 cm.

16176 Chapman, Charles Edward, 1880-1941.
    The founding of Spanish California, the northwestward
expansion of New Spain, 1687-1783, by Charles Edward
Chapman... New York, The Macmillan company, 1916.
    xxxii, 485 p.   front. (port.) maps, double facsim.
$22\frac{1}{2}$ cm.
    Issued also as thesis (Ph.D.) University of
California, 1915.
    "Bibliographical notes": p. 437-453.

16177 Chapman, Samuel D
    History of Tama county, Iowa. Its cities, towns and
villages, with early reminiscences, personal incidents
and anecdotes, and a complete business directory of
the county. By Samuel D. Chapman. [Toledo] Printed
at the Toledo times office, 1879.
    4 p.l., [13]-296 p.   illus.   22 cm.

16178 Chard, Thomas S
California sketches. by Thomas S. Chard. Chicago,
1888.
2 p.l., 26 p.   20 cm.

16179 Charles E. Shafer, hunter, Indian trader, and rancher.
[Bismarck, State Historical Society of North Dakota,
1941]
167-178 p.   front. (port.)   24 cm.
Reprinted from North Dakota historical quarterly,
v. 8, no. 3, April 1941.

16180 Chase, Charles Monroe.
The editor's run in New Mexico and Colorado,
embracing twenty-eight letters on stock raising,
agriculture, territorial history... [Montpelier,
Vt., Printed at the "Argus and patriot" steam book
and job printing house, 1882]
233 p.   front., illus.

16181 Chase, Joseph Smeaton, 1864-
California coast trails; a horseback ride from
Mexico to Oregon, by J. Smeaton Chase, with illustrations from photographs by the author. Boston and
New York, Houghton Mifflin company, 1913.
xviii p., 1 l., 326 p., 1 l.   front., plates.
21 cm.

16182 Chase, Joseph Smeaton, 1864-
California desert trails, by J. Smeaton Chase, with
illustrations from photographs by the author, and an
appendix of plants, also hints on desert travelling.
Boston and New York, Houghton Mifflin company [1919]
xvi p., 1 l., 387, [1] p.   front., plates.
$22\frac{1}{2}$ cm.

16183 ... Cherokee almanac for the year of our Lord 18--
Park Hill, Mission press; E. Archer, printer [18]
v.   18 cm.
Cherokee and English on opposite pages; title also
in Cherokee. Edited by Samuel A. Worcester.
"... calculated by Benjamin Greenleaf".

16184 The Cherokee messenger... [Ed. by Evan Jones] v. 1
(no. 1-12) Aug. 1844-May 1846. [Cherokee, H. Upham,
Baptist mission press] 1844-46.
192 p.   illus. $23\frac{1}{2}$ cm.   monthly (irregular)
Text in Cherokee and English.

16185 Cherokee nation.
Memorial of a delegation from the Cherokee Indians.
Presented to Congress, January 18, 1831...
[Washington? 1831]
8 p.   22½ cm.

16186 Cherokee nation.
"Oklahoma" and the rights of the five tribes of the
Indian territory. Submitted to Congress by the
Cherokee delegation. Washington, 1888.
13 p.   23 cm.

16187 Cherokee nation. Laws, statutes, etc.
Laws of the Cherokee nation: adopted by the Council
at various periods [1808-1935] Printed for the
benefit of the nation. Tahlequah, C. N., Cherokee
advocate office, 1852.
179 p.   18 cm.

16188 Chetlain, Augustus Louis, 1824-1914.
Recollections of seventy years, by Augustus L.
Chetlain, brigadier, and brevet major general U.S.
vols., civil war, 1861-65. Galena, The Gazette
publishing company, 1899.
304 p.   front. (port.)   22 cm.

16189 Chicago. World's Columbian Exposition, 1893. Board
of Lady Managers, Utah.
World's fair ecclesiastical history of Utah.
Compiled by representatives of the religious deno-
minations. Salt Lake City, G. O. Cannon, 1893.
vii, [9]-318 p.   illus., ports.   23 cm.

16190 Chicago & Northwestern Railway Co.
California: a brief description of the chief
points of interest in the state and the most conve-
nient means of reaching them, together with information
concerning train service to the coast via the Chicago,
Union Pacific & North-western line. Chicago, 1905.
53 p.   illus., map, plates.

16191 Chicago & Northwestern Railway Co.
Colorado: a complete tourists' guide to the
splendors of Colorado... Chicago, 1906.
41 p.   map, illus., plates.

16192 Chidlaw, Benjamin Williams, 1811-1892.
Yr American, yr hwn sydd yn cynnwys Nodau ar daith

61

o ddyffryn Ohio i Gymru, Golwg ar dalaeth Ohio;
Hanes sefydliadau Cymreig yn America; cyfarwyddiadau
i ymofynwyr eyn y daith, ar y daith, ac yn y wlad.
Gan y parch. B. W. Chidlaw... Yr ail argraffiad.
Llanrwst [Wales] Argraffwyd, gan J. Jones, 1840.
    48 p.   18½ cm.

16193 Chipman, Norton P
       Northern California. The Sacramento valley: its
    resources and industries. [Repr. from Overland
    Monthly of April, 1901] [n.p., 1901]
       79 p.   illus., map, pl.
    Reprinted from the Overland Monthly, April, 1901.

16194 Chipman, Norton P
       Report upon the fruit industry of California:
    its growth and development, and present and future
    importance... Adopted by the State Board of Trade
    of California, Nov. 12, 1899... [San Francisco,
    1889]
       35 p.   22 cm.

16195 Chittenden, Hiram Martin, 1858-1917.
       The American fur trade of the far West; a history
    of the pioneer trading posts and early fur companies
    of the Missouri valley and the Rocky mountains and
    of the overland commerce with Santa Fe... By Hiram
    Martin Chittenden... New York, F. P. Harper, 1902.
       3 v.   front., plates, fold. map, plan, facsims.
    24½ cm.

16196 Chorpenning, George.
       The case of George Chorpenning vs. the United States.
    A brief history of the facts by the claimant.
    Washington, D. C., May 1, 1874. Washington, D. C.,
    M'Gill & Witherow, printers [1874]
       cover-title, 56 p.   23½ cm.

16197 Chouteau, Auguste.
       Fragment of Col. Auguste Chouteau's narrative of
    the settlement of St. Louis. A literal translation
    from the original French ms., in possession of the
    St. Louis mercantile library association. St. Louis,
    G. Knapp & co., 1858.
       10 p.   22 cm.

16198 Church of Jesus Christ of Latter-Day Saints. Bureau
    of Information.

Utah: its people, resources, attractions and
institutions. Compiled from authentic information
and the latest reports. Salt Lake City, Utah
[1915]
79 p.   illus.   18 cm.

16199 Churchill, Mrs. Carolina M   (Nichols) 1833-
"Little sheaves" gathered while gleaning after
reapers, being letters of travel, commencing in
1870, and ending in 1873. San Francisco, 1875.
2 p.l., [3]-99 p.   17 cm.

16200 Churchill, Mrs. Carolina M   (Nichols) 1833-
Over the purple hills; or, Sketches of travel in
California of important points usually visited by
tourists. By Caroline M. Churchill... Chicago,
Hazlitt & Reed, printers, 1877.
256 p.   15½ cm.

16201 Churchill, Franklin Hunter, 1823-
Sketch of Bvt. Brig. Gen. Sylvester Churchill...
with notes and appendices, by Franklin Hunter Churchill.
New York, W. McDonald & co., printers, 1888.
vi, 201 p.   23½ cm.

16202 The Cincinnati excursion to California: its origin,
progress, incidents, and results. History of a
railway journey of six thousand miles - complete
newspaper correspondence... Cincinnati, 1870.
vii, 156 p.   front. (fold. map)   20 cm.

16203 Clamorgan Land Association.
[Papers relating to the Clamorgan grant in Missouri
and Arkansas] [n.p., n.d.]
41 p.   25 cm.

16204 Clamorgan Land Association.
Title papers of the Clamorgan grant, of 536.904 arpens
of alluvial lands in Missouri and Arkansas. New York,
1837.
24 p.   map.   22 cm.

16205 Clampitt, John Wesley, 1839-
Echoes from the Rocky mountains; reminiscences and
thrilling incidents of the romantic and golden age
of the great West, with a graphic account of its
discovery, settlement, and grand development. By
John W. Clampitt... Chicago, New York [etc.]
Belford, Clarke & co., 1889.

63

xvi, 19-671 p. incl. illus., plates, ports.,
facsim.   front.   25 cm.

16206   Clappe, Mrs. Louise Amelia Knapp Smith.
The Shirley letters from California mines in
1851-52. Being a series of twenty-three letters
from Dame Shirley... to her sister in Massachusetts
and now reprinted from the Pioneer Magazine of 1854-55,
with synopses of the letters... and emendations by
Thomas C. Russell, together with "an appreciation by
Mrs. M. V. T. Lawrence." San Francisco, printed by
Thomas C. Russell at his private press, 1922.
350 p.   front., plates.   24 cm.

16207   Clark, Francis D
... The First regiment of New York volunteers,
commanded by Col. Jonathan D. Stevenson, in the
Mexican war. Names of the members of the regiment
during its term of service in Upper and Lower
California, 1847-1848, with a record of all known
survivors on the 15th day of April, 1882, and those
known to have deceased, with other matters of interest
pertaining to the organization and service of the
regiment. Comp. by their comrade, Francis D. Clark.
New York, G. S. Evans & co., printers, 1882.
94 p. incl. front., port.   24 cm.

16208   Clark, Susie Champney, 1856-
The round trip from the Hub to the Golden Gate,
by Susie C. Clark... Boston, Lee and Shepard;
New York, C. T. Dillingham, 1890.
193 p.   19 cm.

16209   Clarke, S   A   1827-
Pioneer days of Oregon history, by S. A. Clarke...
Portland, J. K. Gill company, 1905.
2 v.   front., plates, ports.   24 cm.

16210   Clavijero, Francisco Javier, 1731-1787.
Storia della California; opera postuma del nob.
sig. abate D. Francesco Saverio Clavigero...
Venezia, M. Fenzo, 1789.
2 v. in 1.   fold. map.   18½ cm.

16211   Clay, Henry, 1777-1852.
Annexation of Texas; opinions of Messrs. Clay, Polk,
Benton & Van Buren, on the immediate annexation of

64

Texas. [n.p., 1844]
16 p.   22 cm.

16212 Clay, John, 1851-
New world notes: being an account of journeyings and
sojournings in America and Canada. By John Clay,
jun.... Kelso [Scotland] J. & J. H. Rutherfurd, 1875.
4 p.l., 200 p. $17\frac{1}{2}$ cm.

16213 Cleland, Robert Glass.
The early sentiment for the annexation of California:
an account of the growth of American interests in
California, 1835-1846. (In Southwestern historical
quarterly, v. 18, 1914-15, p. 1-40, 121-162, 231-260)
Bibliography: p. 257-260.

16214 Clemens, Orion, 1825-1897.
City of Keokuk in 1856. A view of the city,
embracing its commerce and manufactures, and containing
the inaugural address of Mayor Curtis, and statistical
local information; also, a sketch of the Black Hawk
war, and history of the Half breed tract. Historical
and statistical matter written by Orion Clemens.
Keokuk [Ia.] Printed by O. Clemens, 1856.
44 p.   22 cm.

16215 Clements, James I
The Klondyke, by J. I. Clements... A complete guide
to the gold fields... Edited by G. Wharton James.
Los Angeles, Cal., B. R. Baumgardt & co., 1897.
98, [2] p.   plates, port., map.   20 cm.

16216 Climate of Nebraska, particularly in reference to the
temperature and rainfall and their influence upon the
agricultural interests of the state. Five appendices
and twelve charts. Washington, 1890.
60 p.   charts.   29 cm.   (U. S. 51st cong.,
1st sess. Sen. ex. doc. 115)

16217 Clinch, Bryan J
California and its missions; their history to the
treaty of Guadalupe Hidalgo, by Bryan J. Clinch...
San Francisco, The Whitaker & Ray company (incorporated) 1904.
2 v.   fronts.(ports.) illus. $23\frac{1}{2}$ cm.

16218 Coale, Charles B
The life and adventures of Wilburn Waters, the

famous hunter and trapper of White Top Mountain;
embracing early history of southwestern Virginia,
sufferings of the pioneers, etc., etc. By Charles B.
Coale. Richmond, G. W. Gary & co., printers, 1878.
2 p.l., [vii]-xiv, [17]-265 p. 20½ cm.

16219 Cochran, John Salisbury, 1841-
Bonnie Belmont; a historical romance of the days
of slavery and the civil war, by Judge John S. Cochran.
[Wheeling, W. Va., Press of Wheeling news lith. co.,
c1907]
291, [1] p. 2 pl. (1 fold.) ports. 24 cm.

16220 Cocke, William Alexander, 1874-
The Bailey controversy in Texas, with lessons from
the political life-story of a fallen idol... by
William A. Cocke... San Antonio, Tex., The Cocke
company, 1908.
2 v. fronts., plates, ports. 26½ cm.

16221 Codman, John, 1814-1900.
The Mormon country. A summer with the 'Latter-day
Saints.' New York, United States pub. co., 1874.
225 p. illus., map. 19 cm.

16222 Codman, John, 1814-1900.
The round trip by way of Panama through California,
Oregon, Nevada, Utah, Idaho, and Colorado with notes
on railroads, commerce, agriculture, mining, scenery,
and people... New York, G. P. Putman's sons, 1881.
331 p. 21 cm.

16223 Cody, William Frederick, 1846-1917.
An autobiography of Buffalo Bill (Colonel W. F.
Cody) illustrated by N. C. Wyeth. New York,
Cosmopolitan book corporation, 1920.
4 p.l., 328 p. front. (port.) plates. 20½ cm.
On cover: Buffalo Bill's life story.

16224 Cody, William Frederick, 1846-1917.
The life of Hon. William F. Cody, known as Buffalo
Bill, the famous hunter, scout and guide. An autobiography. Hartford, Conn., F. E. Bliss [c1879]
xvi, 17-365 p. incl. illus., plates. front. (port.)
21½ cm.

16225 Cody, William Frederick, 1846-1917.
True tales of the plains, by Buffalo Bill (William

F. Cody)... New York, Cupples & Leon company, 1908.
2 p.l., 259 p.   front., illus., plates, ports.
19½ cm.

16226 Coffeen, Henry Asa, 1841-1913.
... Vermilion County, historical, statistical,
and descriptive. A handbook containing the description,
resources, prospects, and history of Vermilion County,
Illinois. Sketches of Fairmount, Rossville, Georgetown,
and other towns of this county. Official directory
of the United States government, state of Illinois,
Vermilion County, city of Danville, and the fifteen
townships of the county. Statistics of Danville and
the townships of Vermilion County. A description and
directory of Danville, a lithograph map of Vermilion
County, useful tables, items of progress, etc., etc.
Danville, Ill., H. A. Coffeen [1871?]
    116 p.   front. (map) illus.   18 cm.

16227 Coffin, Charles Carleton, 1823-1896.
    The seat of empire. By Charles Carleton Coffin,
"Carleton"... Boston, Fields, Osgood, & co., 1870.
    viii, 232 p.   front., plates, fold. map.   18 cm.

16228 Coffin, George.
    A pioneer voyage to California and round the world,
1849-1852, ship Alhambra, Captain George Coffin.
Chicago, 1908.
    235 p.   pl., port.   20 cm.
    Foreword signed: Gorham B. Coffin.

16229 Colborn, Edward F
    A glimpse of Utah; its resources, attractions and
natural wonders... Denver, Colorado, 1908.
    56 p.   illus., plates.   21 cm.

16230 Cole, Cornelius, 1822-1924.
    Memoirs of Cornelius Cole, ex-senator of the
United States from California. New York, McLoughlin
brothers, 1908.
    x, 354 p.   front. (port.)   24½ x 18½ cm.

16231 Cole, George E
    Early Oregon; jottings of personal recollections
of a pioneer of 1850. [Spokane, Wash., 1905]
    95 p.   port.   20 cm.

16232 Cole, Gilbert L
         In the early days along the overland trail in
         Nebraska Territory, in 1852, by Gilbert L. Cole,
         compiled by Mrs. A. Hardy. Kansas City, Mo., 1905.
         xi, 125 p.   front. (port.)   20 cm.

16233 Collection of pamphlets descriptive of various local-
         ities of California. Issued for the Panama-Pacific
         international exposition. 1915.
         2 v.   illus., maps.   23 cm.

16234 Collins, Dennis.
         The Indians' last fight; or, The Dull Knife raid,
         by Dennis Collins. [Girard, Kan., Press of the Appeal
         to reason, c1915]
         1 p.l., [5]-326 p.   front., plates, ports.
         23½ cm.

16235 Collins, John Sloan, 1839-
         Across the plains in '64; incidents of early days
         west of the Missouri River - two thousand miles in
         an open boat from Fort Benton to Omaha - reminiscences
         of the pioneer period of Galena, General Grant's
         old home. By John S. Collins. Omaha, Neb., National
         printing company, 1904.
         151 p.   19½ cm.

16236 Colorado (Ter.) Adjutant-General's Office.
         Biennial report of the adjutant-general. Central
         City, 1867.
              v.   22 cm.
         Continued by the Biennial report of the adjutant-
         general of the state of Colorado.

16237 Colorado (Ter.) Board of Immigration.
         Official information. Colorado: a statement of
         facts, prepared and published by authority of the
         territorial board of immigration. Denver, 1872.
         35 p.   21½ cm.

16238 Colorado (Ter.) Board of Immigration.
         Report of the Board of Immigration of Colorado
         territory, for the two years ending Dec. 31, 1873.
         Transmitted to the legislative assembly, Jan. 5,
         1874. Denver, 1874.
         53 p.   21½ cm.

16239　Colorado (Ter.)　Board of Immigration.
　　　　　Resources and advantages of Colorado.　Prepared
　　　and published by authority of the Territorial board
　　　of immigration.　Denver, 1873.
　　　　　47 p.　　21½ cm.

16240　Colorado.　State Teachers' Association, 1861-1885.
　　　　　Education in Colorado:　a brief history of the
　　　early educational interests of Colorado, together
　　　with the history of the State teachers' association,
　　　and short sketches of private and denominational
　　　institutions.　Comp. by order of the State teachers'
　　　association [by Horace M. Hale, Aaron Gove, Jos. C.
　　　Shattuck, committee]　Denver, 1885.
　　　　　99 p.　　port.　　22½ cm.

16241　Colorado.　University.
　　　　　Trails through romantic Colorado; a series of radio
　　　talks about various phases of the history of Colorado;
　　　seventh series...　presented over Radio Station KOA,
　　　January 6, 1935 to March 31, 1935.　Boulder, 1935.
　　　　　50 p.　　21 cm.　　(Colorado. University. Bulletin,
　　　v. 35, no. 11)

16242　Colorado:　its climate.　Denver, 1904.
　　　　　24 p.　　map.　　23 cm.

16243　Colorado, New Mexico, Utah, Nevada, Wyoming and
　　　Arizona gazetteer and business directory, 1884-5.
　　　Chicago, 1884.
　　　　　891 p.　　23 cm.

16244　Colorado & Southern Railway.
　　　　　Out of doors in Colorado.　Denver [1912]
　　　　　36 p.　　illus., plates.　　21½ cm.

16245　Colorado & Southern Railway.
　　　　　The Pike's Peak region.　Denver [1912?]
　　　　　32 p.　　illus., plates.　　21½ cm.

16246　Colorado outdoor life.　Denver, 1904.
　　　　　31 p.　　illus., plates.　　23 cm.

16247　Colorado Promotion & Publicity Committee.
　　　　　Colorado:　its agriculture, its horticulture.
　　　Denver, 1904.
　　　　　52 p.　　illus., plates.　　20 cm.

16248   Colorado Promotion & Publicity Committee
        Colorado, its hotels and resorts. Denver, 1904.
        100 p.   illus., plates.   21½ cm.

16249   Colorado state business directory, with Colorado mining
        directory and Colorado live stock directory depart-
        ments. Denver, 1880-
            v.   19 cm.
        (J. A. Blake, pub.)

16250   Colorado State Federation of Labor. Committee to Inves-
        tigate the conduct of the Colorado National Guard
        during the coal strike of 1913-1914.
            Militarism in Colorado; report. [Denver] Colorado
        State Federation of Labor, 1914.
            16 p.   22½ cm.

16251   Colorado territory. [n.p., n.d.]
            13 p.   map.   23½ cm.

16252   Colton, Joseph Hutchins, 1800-1893, pub.
            The state of Indiana delineated: geographical,
        historical, statistical & commercial, and a brief
        view of the internal improvements, geology, education,
        travelling routes, &c., prepared to accompany
        Colton's [large] map. New York, J. H. Colton, 1838.
            92 p.   15 cm.

16253   Colton, Water, 1797-1851.
            Deck and port; or, Incidents of a cruise in the
        United States frigate Congress to California. With
        sketches of Rio Janeiro, Valparaiso, Lima, Honolulu,
        and San Francisco. By Rev. Walter Colton, U.S.N. ...
        New York, A. S. Barnes & co.; Cincinnati, H. W. Derby
        & co., 1852.
            408 p.   front. (port.) illus. (incl. map)
        col. plates.   19½ cm.

16254   Commercial Herald and Market Review.
            "Commercial herald" review of the trade of California
        and the entire Pacific coast for the year 1876.
        San Francisco, "Commercial herald and market review"
        publishing house, 1877.
            136 p.   fold. tab.   24½ cm.

16255   Comparative chronological statement of the events con-
        nected with the rights of Great Britain and the
        claims of the United States to the Oregon Territory.

[London, Printed by W. S. Johnson, 1845?]
15 p.   17 cm.

16256   Compendious history of Ellsworth county, Kansas, from
        its early settlement to the present time. Embracing
        the executive and educational departments, population,
        sketches of prominent men, general character of the
        land, and condition of the people. Ellsworth, Kansas,
        Printed at the Recorder office, 1879.
        60 p.   18 cm.

16257   Compendium of history, reminiscence and biography of
        western Nebraska, containing a history of the state
        of Nebraska... also a compendium of reminiscences of
        western Nebraska containing biographical sketches...
        Illustrated. Chicago, 1909.
        1135 p.   pl., ports.

16258   Condra, George Evert.
            Geography of Nebraska, by George Evert Condra...
        Lincoln, Neb., The University publishing co., 1906.
            viii, 192 p. incl. front., illus.   2 maps.   19 cm.

16259   Cone, Mary.
            Two years in California... Chicago, S. C. Griggs
        & co., 1876.
            xii p., 1 l., 238 p.   front., pl., map.

16260   Congregational churches in Illinois. General association.
            Constitution, articles of faith, standing rules,
        and general principles of church polity of the
        General Congregational association of Illinois.
        Galesburg, Ill., "Intelligencer" print, 1848.
            12 p.   17 cm.

16261   Conn, William.
            Cow-boys and colonels. Narrative of a journey
        across the prairie and over the Black Hills of Dakota.
        From "Dans les montagnes rocheuses" of Baron E. de
        Mandat-Grancey, with additional notes not contained
        in the original edition. London, Griffith, Farran,
        Okeden & Welsh, 1887.
            xi, 352 p.   front., plates.   22 cm.

16262   Connelley, William E[lsey] 1855-1930, ed.
            The provisional government of Nebraska territory
        and the journals of William Walker, provisional
        governor of Nebraska territory... Lincoln, Neb.,

State journal co., 1899.
ix, 423 p.   front., port., map.   24 cm.
(Nebraska state historical society. Proceedings and
collections, 2d ser. v. 3)
"A special publication of the society." Includes
a brief sketch of Abelard Guthrie, p. 101-52.

16263 Connelley, William Elsey, 1855-1930.
Quantrill and the border wars, by William Elsey
Connelley... Cedar Rapids, Ia., The Torch press,
1910.
542 p.   front., illus. (incl. ports., facsim.)
fold. map, fold. plan.   24½ cm.

16264 [Connolly, Alonzo P   ]
A thrilling narrative of the Minnesota massacre
and the Sioux war of 1862-63; graphic accounts of
the siege of Fort Ridgely, battles of Birch coolie,
Wood lake, Big mound, Stony lake, Dead Buffalo lake
and Missouri river... Chicago, A. P. Connolly [c1896]
273 p. incl. illus., plates, ports.   20 cm.

16265 Considerant, Victor Prosper, 1808-1893.
Au Texas... Paris, La Librairie phalanstérienne,
1854.
2 p.l., 194 p.   2 fold. maps.   22½ cm.

16266 [Constitutions and organic laws]   (In Thorpe, Francis
N. The federal and state constitutions. 1909.
v. 1, pp. 261-375)

16267 [Constitutions and organic laws]   (In Thorpe, Francis
N. The federal and state constitutions. 1909.
v. 1, pp. 463-518)

16268 Cook, Darius B
Six months among Indians, wolves and other wild
animals, in the forests of Allegan county, Mich.,
in the winter of 1839 and 1840. Interesting stories
of forest life. The exploits of Tecumseh and other
chiefs, their cruelty to captives. How Tecumseh was
killed and who killed him. True Indian stories of
the war of 1812-13. By Darius B. Cook. Niles,
Mich., The Author, 1889.
2 p.l., 101 p.   illus. (incl. ports.)   19 cm.

16269 Cook, David J   1840-1907.
Hands up; or, Twenty years of detective life in

72

the mountains and on the plains. Reminiscences by
General D. J. Cook, superintendent of the Rocky
mountain detective association. A condensed
criminal history of the far West. Denver, Republican
publishing company, 1882.
285 p. front. (port.) plates. 24 cm.

16270 Cook, David J 1840-1907.
Hands up; or, Thirty-five years of detective life
in the mountains and on the plains. Reminiscences
by General D. J. Cook, chief of the Rocky mountain
detective association. Comp. by John W. Cook. A
condensed criminal history of the far West. Denver,
The W. F. Robinson printing co., 1897.
2 p.l., [3]-442 p. incl. illus., plates. 2 port.
(incl. front.) 23½ cm.

16271 Cook, John R 1844-1917.
The border and the buffalo, an untold story of the
southwest plains; the bloody border of Missouri and
Kansas. The story of the slaughter of the buffalo.
Westward among the big game and wild tribes. A story
of mountain and plain, by John R. Cook. Topeka, Kan.,
Printed by Crane & company, 1907.
xii, 351, 1 p. incl. front., illus., ports.
23½ cm.

16272 Cooke, Philip St. George, 1809-1895.
The conquest of New Mexico and California; an
historical and personal narrative. By P. St. Geo.
Cooke... New York, G. P. Putnam's sons, 1878.
iv p., 1 l., 307 p. fold. map. 19 cm.

16273 Cooke, Philip St. George, 1809-1895.
Report of Lieut. Col. P. St. George Cooke of
his march from Santa Fé, New Mexico to San Diego,
Upper California.
(In U. S. Engineer dept. Notes of a military
reconnoissance... Washington, 1848. 23cm. [549]-
562, [1] p.)
U.S. 30th Cong., 1st sess. House. Ex. doc. 41.

16274 Coolidge, Louis Arthur, 1861-1925.
Klondike and the Yukon country, a description of
our Alaskan land of gold from the latest official
and scientific sources and personal observations,
by L. A. Coolidge; with a chapter by John F. Pratt...
New maps and photographic illustrations. Philadelphia,

H. Altemus, 1897.
213 p.   plates, 2 maps (incl. fold. front.)
18 cm.

16275 Corner, William, comp. and ed.
San Antonio de Bexar; a guide and history, comp.
and ed. by William Corner. Illustrated. San Antonio,
Tex., Bainbridge & Corner, 1890.
vi, [2], 166 p.   front., illus., plates, plans,
facsim.   26½ cm.

16276 Cornwall, Bruce.
Life sketch of Pierre Barlow Cornwall, by Bruce
Cornwall, his son... San Francisco, A. M. Robertson,
1906.
5 p.l., 87 p.   front., ports.   22½ cm.

16277 Correll, Hal.
Into the West, by Hall Correll, and Along the road
to Freedom, a story from the stirring days before
the Civil War, by Christine Gordon Wheeler. Columbus,
Ohio, The Book Concern [n.d.]
149 p.   19 cm.

16278 Cortés, Hernando, 1485-1547.
Historia de Nueva España, escrita por su esclarecido
conquistador Hernan Cortes, aumentada con otros
docvmentos, y notas, por el ilustrissimo Señor Don
Francisco Antonio Lorenzana, arzobispo de Mexico.
Con las licencias necesarias. Mexico, Impr. del
superior gobierno, J. A. de Hogal, 1770.
10 p.l., xvi, 400, [18] p.   pl., 2 fold. maps,
facsim. on 31 pl.   26½ cm.

16279 Coues, Elliott, 1842-1899.
... Birds of the Northwest: a handbook of the
ornithology of the region drained by the Missouri
River and its tributaries. By Elliott Coues...
Washington, Govt. print. off., 1874.
xi, 791 p.   23½ cm.   (U.S. Geological [and
geographical] survey of the territories. Miscellaneous
publications, 3)

16280 The courts of justice and injustice of Oklahoma
territory. An appeal to congress for their investi-
gation. [Oklahoma City, 1896]
52 p.   23 cm.

16281 Cowan, Robert Ernest, 1862-
A bibliography of the history of California and
the Pacific west 1510-1906, by Robert Ernest Cowan;
together with the text of John W. Dwinelle's address
on the acquisition of California by the United States
of America. San Francisco, The Book Club of California,
1914.
xxxi p., 1 l., 318, [2] p.   27 cm.

16282 Cowan, Robert Ernest, 1862-
The Spanish press of California, 1833-1844. [n.p.,
n.d.]
[11] p.   24½ cm.
Reprinted from the California historic-genealogical
society, publication 3.

16283 Cox, Isaac Joslin, 1873-
Educational efforts in San Fernando de Bexar...
[Austin? Tex., 1902?]
cover-title, [27]-63 p.   23 cm.
"Reprinted from the quarterly of the Texas historical
association, vol. VI, no. 1, July, 1902."

16284 Cox, John E
Soldiering in Dakota Territory in the seventies:
a communication. [Bismarck, State Historical Society
of North Dakota, 1931]
63-81 p.   24 cm.
Reprinted from North Dakota historical quarterly,
v. 6, no. 1, October 1931.

16285 Cox, Ross, 1793-1853.
Adventures on the Columbia River, including the
narrative of a residence of six years on the western
side of the Rocky mountains, among various tribes
of Indians hitherto unknown; together with a journey
across the American continent, by Ross Cox. New
York, J. & J. Harper, 1832.
xv, [25]-335 p.   20½ cm.

16286 Coyner, David H
The lost trappers; a collection of interesting
scenes and events in the Rocky mountains; together
with a short description of California; also, some
account of the fur trade, especially as carried on
about the sources of Missouri, Yellowstone, and on
the waters of the Columbia, in the Rocky mountains.
By David H. Coyner. Cincinnati, Anderson, Gates &

Wright, 1859.
xv, 17-255 p.   18 cm.

16287   Cozzens, Samuel Woodworth, 1834-1878.
        The marvellous country; or, Three years in Arizona
        and New Mexico, the Apaches' home... By Samuel
        Woodworth Cozzens. Illustrated by upwards of one
        hundred engravings. Boston, Shepard and Gill, 1873.
        532 p.   front., illus., plates, map.   22½ cm.

16288   Craig, John Roderick, 1837-
        Ranching with lords and commons; or, Twenty years
        on the range, being a record of actual facts and
        conditions relating to the cattle industry of the
        North-west territories of Canada; and comprising the
        extraordinary story of the formation and career of
        a great cattle company. By John R. Craig...
        Toronto, Printed for the author by W. Briggs [c1903]
        vi p., 1 l., 9-293 p.   front., plates, ports.
        19½ cm.

16289   Craig, Lulu Alice.
        Glimpses of sunshine and shade in the far North;
        or, My travels in the land of the midnight sun.
        By Lulu Alice Craig. Cincinnati, The Editor
        publishing co., 1900.
        ix, 123 p.   front., plates (part col.) port.
        22 cm.

16290   Craighead, James Geddes, 1823-1895.
        The story of Marcus Whitman; early Protestant
        missions in the Northwest, by the Rev. J. G. Craig-
        head, D. D. Philadelphia, Presbyterian board of
        publication and Sabbath school work, 1895.
        viii, 9-211 p.   17½ x 14 cm.

16291   Crakes, Sylvester, jr.
        Five years a captive among the Black-Feet Indians;
        or, A thrilling narrative of the adventures, perils
        and suffering endured by John Dixon and his
        companions... Never before published. By Sylvester
        Crakes, jun. Columbus, Osgood & Pearce, printers,
        1858.
        vi, [7]-224 p.   front., plates.   16 cm.

16292   Crane, Alice Rollins, comp.
        Smiles and tears from the Klondyke; a collection
        of stories and sketches... by Alice Rollins Crane...

New York, Doxey's At the Sign of the lark [1901]
203 p.   front., plates, ports.   19½ cm.

16293 Crane, James M
       The past, the present and the future of the Pacific.
       By James M. Crane. San Francisco, Cal., Printed by
       Sterett & co., 1856.
       79 p.   22½ cm.

16294 Cranfill, James Britton, 1858-
       Dr. J. B. Cranfill's chronicle; a story of life in
       Texas, written by himself about himself. New York,
       Chicago [etc.] Fleming H. Revell company [c1916]
       xi, [1], 496 p.   front., illus. (facsim.) plates,
       ports.   21 cm.

16295 Crawford, Charles Howard.
       Scenes of earlier days in crossing the plains to
       Oregon, and experiences of western life, by C. H.
       Crawford. Petaluma, Cal., J. T. Studdert, book and
       job printer, 1898.
       3 p.l., 186 p.   front. (port.) illus.   20½ cm.

16296 Crawford, Medorem, d. 1891.
       ... Journal of Medorem Crawford. An account of his
       trip across the plains with the Oregon pioneers of
       1842... Eugene [Or.] Star job office, 1897.
       26 p.   23 cm.   (Sources of the history of
       Oregon. v. 1, no. 1. Contributions of the Department
       of economics and history of the University of Oregon.
       F. G. Young, editor)
       From the original ms.

16297 Cremony, John Carey, 1815-1879.
       Life among the Apaches: by John C. Cremony...
       San Francisco, New York, A. Roman & company, 1868.
       322 p.   19½ cm.

16298 Critchell, Robert Siderfin, 1844-
       Recollections of a fire insurance man, including
       his experience in U. S. Navy (Mississippi squadron)
       during the Civil war, by Robert S. Critchell...
       [Chicago] The author, 1909.
       164 p.   front., pl., ports., facsim.   20 cm.

16299 Crocheron, Augusta (Joyce) 1844-
       Representative women of Deseret, a book of bio-
       graphical sketches, to accompany the picture bearing

the same title. Comp. and written by Augusta Joyce
Crocheron... Salt Lake City, Printed by J. C. Graham
& co., 1884.
4 p.l., 131 p.   18 cm.

16300 Crockett, David, 1786-1836.
Col. Crockett's exploits and adventures in Texas:
wherein is contained a full account of his journey
from Tennessee to the Red river and Natchitiches,
and thence across Texas to San Antonio... London,
Kennett, 1837.
vii, 152 p.   18 cm.

16301 Crofutt, Geo[rge] A
Crofutt's grip-sack guide of Colorado. A complete
encyclopedia of the state: resources and condensed
authentic descriptions of every city, town, village,
station, post office... v. I [i.e. 1st ed.] 1881.
Omaha, The Overland pub. co. [1881]
3 p.l., [23]-183 p.   front. (port.) illus., pl.,
fold. maps.   20 cm.

16302 Crofutt, George A
Crofutt's grip-sack guide of Colorado. A complete
encyclopedia of the state. Resources and condensed
authentic descriptions of every city, town, village,
station, post office and important mining camp in the
state... By Geo. A. Crofutt... vol. II [i.e. 2d ed]
1885. Omaha, Neb., The Overland publishing co., [1885]
3 p.l., [23]-174 p.   illus., fold. map.
26 x 20 cm.

16303 Cronise, Titus Fey.
The natural wealth of California; comprising early
history; geography, topography, and scenery; climate;
agriculture and commercial products; geology,
zoology, and botany; mineralogy, mines, and mining
processes; manufactures; steamship lines, railroads,
and commerce; immigration, population and society;
educational institutions and literature; together
with a detailed description of each county... By
Titus Fey Cronise. San Francisco, New York, H. H.
Bancroft & company, 1868.
xvi, 696 p.   26½ cm.

16304 Crook, John, 1831-
John Crook's journal. Salt Lake City, Utah State
Historical Society, 1933. (In Utah historical

quarterly, v. 6, no. 2, April 1933, p. 50-62, and
v. 6, no. 3, July 1933, p. 110-112)

16305 Cross, Osborne, 1803-1876.
... A report, in the form of a journal to the
Quartermaster General, of the march of the regiment
of mounted riflemen to Oregon, from May 10 to October 5,
1849. [Washington, 1851]
7-127 p.   pl.   22 cm.   (In U.S. Quartermaster General
Annual report, 1849-50 [App.] A)

16306 Crumpton, Hezekiah John.
The adventures of two Alabama boys... by H. J. and
W. B. Crumpton. Pt. 1. The adventures of Dr. H. J.
Crumpton... in his efforts to reach the gold fields
in 1849. Pt. 2. The adventures of Rev. W. B. Crumpton,
going to and returning from California, including his
lecture, "The original tramp, or how a boy got through
the lines to the Confederacy." Pt. 3. To California
and back after a lapse of forty years. Montgomery,
Ala., Paragon Press, 1912.
238 p.   illus., ports.   19 cm.

16307 Culbertson, Thaddeus Ainsworth, 1823-1850.
Journal of an expedition to the Mauvaises Terres
and the Upper Missouri in 1850, by Thaddeus A.
Culbertson. Ed. by John Francis McDermott. Washington,
Government Printing Office, 1952.
viii, 164 p.   2 fold. maps.   24 cm.   (U. S.
Bureau of American Enthnology. Bulletin 147)

16308 Cummins, Sarah J   (Lemmon) 1828-
Autobiography and reminiscences of Sarah J. Cummins...
La Grande, Or., La Grande printing co. [c1914]
63 p.   front. (port.)   20 cm.
Includes a narrative of an overland journey to
Oregon in 1845.

16309 Curley, Edwin A
Glittering gold. The true story of the Black Hills.
Illustrated with accurate colored maps and engravings.
By Edwin A. Curley... Chicago, The author, 1876.
iv p., 1 l., [7]-128 p.   front. (double map)
illus.   19½ cm.

16310 Curley, Edwin A
Nebraska, its advantages, resources and drawbacks...

New York, American News co. [etc.] 1876.
vi, [2], 433 p.   pl., maps.

16311   Curran, John Joseph.
Mr. Foley of Salmon, a story of life in a California
village, by J. J. Curran. Published by the author.
San Jose, Cal., Printed by Melvin, Hillis & Black,
1907.
1 p.l., 5-186 p.   19½ cm.

16312   Curtis, George Ticknor, 1812-1894.
Admission of Utah. Limitation of state sovereignty
by compact with the United States. An opinion given
by George Ticknor Curtis. New York, 1887.
22 p.   20½ cm.

16313   Curtis, George William, 1824-1892.
Lotus-eating; a summer book. By George William
Curtis... Illustrated by Kensett... New York,
Harper & brothers, 1852.
206 p.   illus.   19½ cm.

16314   Curtis, William Eleroy.
Oklahoma, Indian Territory, Texas; a series of
articles... pub. in the Record-Herald of Chicago,
Ill. [St. Louis, L. S. Taylor printing company, 1905?]
31 p.   port.   23 cm.
Reprinted by the Frisco system.

16315   Curtiss, Daniel S
Western portraiture, and emigrants' guide: a description of Wisconsin, Illinois, and Iowa; with remarks
on Minnesota, and other territories. By Daniel S.
Curtiss. New York, J. H. Colton, 1852.
xxx, 31 -351 p.   front. (fold. map)   18 cm.
"Mr. Thompson's letters": p. 306-342.

16316   Cushing, S   W   b. 1818.
Wild oats sowings; or, The autobiography of an
adventurer... By S. W. Cushing. New York, D. Fanshaw,
1857.
483 p.   20 cm.

16317   Custer, Elizabeth (Bacon) 1842-1933.
"Boots and saddles": or, Life in Dakota with
General Custer, by Elizabeth B. Custer. With portrait
and map. New York, Harper & brothers, 1885.
312 p.   front. (port.) map.   19 cm.

80

16318   Custer, George Armstrong, 1839-1876.
        My life on the plains. Or, Personal experiences
        with Indians. By Gen. G. A. Custer, U.S.A. New York,
        Sheldon and company, 1874.
            256 p. incl. front.   plates, ports. $22\frac{1}{2}$ cm.
        Originally published in the Galaxy, v. 13-18,
        1872-74.

                                    D

16319   Dacus, Joseph A
        Life and adventures of Frank and Jesse James, the
        noted western outlaws. By Hon. J. A. Dacus... St.
        Louis, W. S. Bryan; Chicago, J. S. Goodman; [etc.,
        etc.] 1880.
            383 p. incl. illus., ports.   19 cm.

16320   [Daggett, Thomas F   ]
        Billy Le Roy, the Colorado bandit; or, The king of
        American highwaymen. A complete and authentic history
        of this famous young desperado and adventurer.
        New York, Published by Richard K. Fox, Police Gazette
        [1881]
            2 p.l., 7-66, [10] p.   front., illus.   24 cm.
        (Police Gazette library of sensation, no. 5)

16321   Daggett, Thomas F
        The outlaw brothers, Frank and Jesse James. Lives
        and adventures of the two scourges of the plains...
        [New York] Published by Richard K. Fox, Police Gazette
        [1881]
            2 p.l., 7-67, [7] p.   front., illus., plan.
        24 cm.   (Police Gazette series of famous criminals)

16322   Daines, Franklin David.
            ... Separatism in Utah, 1847-1870. By Franklin D.
        Daines... (In American historical association.
        Annual report... for the year 1917. Washington, 1920.
        $24\frac{1}{2}$ cm. p. 331-343)

16323   Dalton, Kit, 1843-1920.
        Under the black flag, by Captain Kit Dalton, a
        Confederate soldier, a guerilla captain under the
        fearless leader Quantrell, and a border outlaw for
        seventeen years following the surrender of the
        Confederacy. Associated with the most noted band of

                                   81

free booters the world has ever known. [Memphis,
Tenn., Lockard publishing company, c1914]
  252 p.   front., illus. (ports.) pl.   19½ cm.

16324 Damon, Samuel Chenery, 1815-1885.
      A trip from the Sandwich Islands to lower Oregon,
      and upper California; or, Thirty leaves selected
      from "Our log-book". By Samuel C. Damon, seamen's
      chaplain. Honolulu, Oahu, H.I., Printed at the
      Polynesian office, 1849.
        1 p.l., [41]-96 p.   30 x 23½ cm.

16325 [Dana, C   W   ]
      The garden of the world, or, The great West; its
      history, its wealth, its natural advantages, and its
      future. Also comprising a complete guide to emigrants,
      with a full description of the different routes west-
      ward. By an old settler. With statistics and facts,
      from Hon. Thomas H. Benton, Hon. Sam Houston, Col.
      John C. Frémont, and other "old settlers." Boston,
      Wentworth and company, 1856.
        7, [13]-396 p.   illus.   18½ cm.
        Later editions, 1857-1862, pub. under title:
      "The great West; or, The garden of the world" have
      author's name on t.-p.

16326 [Dana, Richard Henry] 1815-1882.
      Two years before the mast. A personal narrative of
      life at sea... New York, Harper & brothers [c1840]
        483 p.   15½ cm.   (On cover: Harper's school
      district library, 127)

16327 Daniell, L   E   comp.
      Personnel of the Texas state government, with
      sketches of distinguished Texans... Austin, 1887.
        317 p.   pl., ports.   18 cm.

16328 Darby, John Fletcher, 1803-1882.
      Personal recollections of many prominent people whom
      I have known, and of events - especially of those
      relating to the history of St. Louis - during the
      first half of the present century. By John F. Darby.
      Pub. by subscription. St. Louis, G. I. Jones and
      company, 1880.
        2 p.l., 480 p.   front. (port.)   21½ cm.

16329 Darley, George Marshall, 1847-
      Pioneering in the San Juan; personal reminiscences

of work done in southwestern Colorado during the
"great San Juan excitement," by the Rev. George M.
Darley... Chicago, New York [etc.] Fleming H.
Revell company, 1899.
225, [1] p. incl. front. (port.) plates. 20 cm.

16330 Darlington, Mary Carson (O'Hara) 1824-1915, comp.
Fort Pitt and letters from the frontier. Pittsburgh,
J. R. Weldin, 1892.
312 p. ports., maps, plan. 26 cm.

16331 [Davies, Henry Eugene] 1836-1894.
Ten days on the plains, by *** New York, Printed
by Crocker & co. [1871]
68 p. front. (fold. map) 26 cm.

16332 Davies, John Johnson, 1831-
Historical sketch of my life. Salt Lake City,
Utah State Historical Society, 1941. (In Utah
historical quarterly, v. 9, nos. 3, 4, July,
October 1941, p. 155-167)

16333 Davis, Carlyle Channing.
Olden times in Colorado, by Carlyle Channing
Davis... Los Angeles, Calif., The Phillips publishing
company, 1916.
8 p. 448 p. front., illus., plates, ports.,
map. 24½ cm.

16334 Davis, Ellis Arthur, ed.
Davis' commercial encyclopedia of the Pacific
southwest. California, Nevada, Utah, Arizona.
Oakland, Calif., E. A. Davis [c1915]
[132], 101-841, [5] p. illus., maps (part col.
fold.) ports. 38 cm.
"Men of California": p. 372-840.

16335 Davis, George Turnbull Moore,1810-1888.
Autobiography of the late Col. Geo. T. M. Davis,
captain and aid-de-camp Scott's army of invasion
(Mexico), from post-humous papers. Pub. by his
legal representatives. New York [Press of Jenkins
and McCowan] 1891.
395 p. 19 cm.

16336 Davis, Henry T[urner]
Solitary places made glad: being observations and
experiences for thirty-two years in Nebraska; with

sketches and incidents touching the discovery,
early settlement, and development of the state.
By the Rev. Henry T. Davis... Cincinnati, Printed
for the author by Cranston & Stowe, 1890.
422 p.   front. (port.)   19 cm.

16337   Davis, Mrs. Mary Evelyn (Moore) 1852-1909.
Under six flags; the story of Texas.   Boston [1897]
ix, 187 p.   front., illus. pl., port., maps.   19 cm.

16338   Davis, Richard Harding, 1864-1916.
The West from a car window.   By Richard Harding
Davis... New York, Harper & brothers, 1892.
4 p.l., 242, [1] p. incl. illus., plates.
front.   19 cm.

16339   Davis, Samuel Post, 1850-1918, ed.
The history of Nevada, ed. by Sam P. Davis...
Reno, Nev., Los Angeles, Cal., The Elms publishing
co., inc., 1913.
2 v.   fronts., illus., plates, ports.   25 cm.

16340   Davis, William Heath.
Sixty years in California, a history of events and
life in California; personal, political and military,
under the Mexican regime; during the quasimilitary
government of the territory by the United States,
and after the admission of the state into the union,
being a compilation by a witness of the events
described. By William Heath Davis. San Francisco,
A. J. Leary, 1889.
xxii, 639 p.   22½ cm.

16341   Davis, William Watts Hart, 1820-1910.
The Spaniard in New Mexico. (American hist.
assoc. Papers, v. 3, p. 164-176) New York, 1888.
On the search for the seven cities of Cibola,
New Mexico.

16342   Davis, William Watts Hart, 1820-1910.
The Spanish conquest of New Mexico, by W. W. H.
Davis... Doylestown, Pa., 1869.
xv, [17]-438 p.   front. (port.) fold. map.
23½ cm.

16343   Davis, Winfield J
History of political conventions in California,
1849-1892. Sacramento, 1893.

711 p.   22 cm.   (California. State Library.
Publication, no. 1)

16344 *Omitted.*

16345 Dawson, Charles.
Pioneer tales of the Oregon trail and of Jefferson
county, by Charles Dawson. Topeka, Crane & company,
1912.
xv, 488 p.   front., illus., ports., maps (1 fold.)
23½ cm.

16346 Dawson, Moses.
A historical narrative of the civil and military
services of Major-General William H. Harrison, and
a vindication of his character and conduct as a
statesman, a citizen, and a soldier. With a detail
of his negotiations and wars with the Indians, until
the final overthrow of the celebrated chief Tecumseh,
and his brother the Prophet. The whole written and
compiled from original and authentic documents
furnished by many of the most respectable characters
in the United States. By Moses Dawson, editor of
the Cincinnati Advertiser. Cincinnati, Printed by
M. Dawson, 1824.
vii, 464, [8] p.   21½ cm.

16347 Day, Luella.
The tragedy of the Klondike; this book of travels
gives the true facts of what took place in the
gold-fields under British rule. By Luella Day.
New York, 1906.
3 p.l., 5-181 p.   plates, port.   20 cm.

16348 A day in the cañons of the Rockies. [Denver, n.d.]
30 p.   23 cm.

16349 Dearborn, Henry Alexander Scammell, 1783-1851.
Letters on the internal improvements and commerce
of the West, by Henry A. S. Dearborn. Boston,
Dutton and Wentworth, printers, 1839.
119, [1] p.   23 cm.

16350 Death of Captain May (communicated)   Salt Lake City,
Utah State Historical Society, 1932. (In Utah
historical quarterly, v. 5, no. 1, January 1932,
p. 28)

16351 [Debray, Xavier Blanchard]
       Sketch of the history of Debray's (26th) regiment
       of Texas cavalry. Austin, E. von Boeckmann, printer,
       1884.
       26 p.   21 cm.

16352 De Cordova, J[acob]
       Texas; her resources and her public men. A companion
       for J. De Cordova's new and correct map of the state
       of Texas... 1st ed. Philadelphia, E. Crozet, 1858.
       371, [1] p.   20 cm.

16353 De Cordova, Jacob.
       The Texas immigrant and traveller's guide book,
       by J. DeCordova. (1st ed.) Austin [Tex.] DeCordova
       and Frazier, 1856.
       103 p.   18½ cm.

16354 De Groot, Henry.
       British Columbia; its condition and prospects, soil,
       climate, and mineral resources, considered. By Henry
       De Groot. San Francisco, Printed at the Alta California
       job office, 1859.
       24 p.   24 cm.

16355 Delaney, Matilda J   (Sager) 1839-
       A survivor's recollections of the Whitman massacre,
       by Matilda J. Sager Delaney. Spokane, Wash.,
       Sponsored by Esther Reed chapter, Daughters of the
       American revolution [c1920]
       46 p.   illus., ports.   23½ cm.

16356 [Delano, Alonzo] 1806-1874.
       ... A live woman in the mines; or, Pike county
       ahead! A local play in two acts. By "Old Block".
       To which are added a description of the costume...
       and the whole of the stage business. New York,
       S. French [c1857]
       36 p.   18½ cm.   (The minor drama. The acting
       edition. No. 130)

16357 [Delano, Alonzo] 1806-1874.
       Old Block's sketch-book; or, Tales of California
       life. Illustrated with numerous elegant designs,
       by Nahl, the Cruikshank of California. Sacramento,
       J. Anthony & co., 1856.
       1 p.l., iii, [1], 66, 69-78 p., 1 l. incl. plates.
       pl.   22½ cm.

16358   [Delano, Alonzo] 1806-1874.
             Pen knife sketches; or, Chips of the old block.
         A series of original illustrated letters, written by
         one of California's pioneer miners, and dedicated to
         that class of her citizens by the author. Sacramento,
         Published at the Union office, 1853.
             112 p. incl. illus., plates.   23 cm.
             Introduction signed: Old Block. On cover: Second
         ed.... 1854.

16359   [Delavan, James]
             Notes on California and the placers: how to get
         there, and what to do afterwards. By one who has
         been there. New York, 1850.
             128 p.   18½ cm.

16360   Dellenbaugh, Frederick Samuel.
             Frémont and '49: the story of a remarkable career
         and its relation to the exploration and development
         of our western territory, especially of California.
         New York, 1914.
             xxiii, 547 p.   col. front., illus., fold. maps,
         pl., ports.   21 cm.
             Bibliography, p. 483-502.

16361   DeMilt, A   P
             Story of an old town [Decatur, Neb.] with reminis-
         cences of early Nebraska and biographies of pioneers...
         a narrative... describing the birth of Nebraska,
         and its progress, of its oldest towns, and its first
         settlers. Omaha, 1902.
             173 p.   pl., ports.   22 cm.

16362   Denis, Ferdinand, 1798-1890.
             Les Californies, l'Orégon et l'Amérique Russe.
         Par M. Ferdinand Denis. [n.p., 1849?]
             108 p.   18½ cm.

16363   Denny, Arthur Armstrong, 1822-1899.
             Pioneer days on Puget Sound, by Arthur A. Denny.
         Seattle, W. T., C. B. Bagley, printer, 1888.
             83 p.   17½ cm.

16364   Denver [Colo.] Board of Trade Resources of Colorado.
         [Denver, 1868]
             12 p.   18 cm.

16365 Denver [Colo.] Chamber of Commerce.
Colorado: some pictures and a few facts. Published
by the Denver Chamber of Commerce, and presented to
the General federation of woman's clubs, biennial
meeting, Denver, 1898. Gathered for the Denver
meeting of the American medical association, by the
committee of arrangements... Denver [1898]
111 p.   illus., map, pl.   19½ cm.

16366 Denver & Rio Grande Railroad.
Around the circle: one thousand miles: through
the Rocky Mountains, being descriptive of a trip
among peaks, over passes, and through cañons of
Colorado... [Chicago] 1893.
56 p.   maps, pl.   21 cm.

16367 Denver & Rio Grande Railroad.
Denver & Rio Grande official guide to cities,
villages and resorts on the line of the Denver and
Rio Grande R.R. Denver [n.d.]
286 p.   illus., map, port.   21 cm.

16368 Denver & Rio Grande Railroad.
The fertile lands of Colorado: a concise description
of the vast area of agricultural, horticultural and
grazing lands located on the line of the Denver &
Rio Grande railroad in the state of Colorado and the
territory of New Mexico... Ed. 3. Denver, 1901.
72 p.   illus., map.   21 cm.

16369 Denver & Rio Grande Railroad.
Rhymes of the Rockies; or, What the poets have
found to say of the beautiful scenery on the Denver
& Rio Grande, the scenic line of the world, and the
Rio Grande Western. Chicago, 1887-1902.
7 nos.   illus.   21 cm.

16370 Denver & Rio Grande Railroad.
Slopes of the Sangre de Cristo: a book of the
resources and industries of Colorado. Denver, 1896.
126, 2 p.   illus., pl.   21 cm.

16371 Denver & Rio Grande Railroad.
Tourists' handbook descriptive of Colorado, New
Mexico and Utah. Ed. 11.... [Denver, 1893]
56 p.   illus., map.   21 cm.

16372   Denver Villa Park Association.
        Articles of incorporation and by laws of the
        Denver Villa Park Association, Denver, Colorado.
        Denver, The Denver tribune association print, 1872.
        12 p.   14½ cm.

16373   Depew, Chauncey Mitchell, 1834-1928.
        Statehood bill. Speech in the Senate of the
        United States, Feb. 11, 12, 13, and 17, 1903.
        Washington, 1903.
        64 p.   22 cm.

16374   De Rupert, A   E   D
        Californians and Mormons; by A. E. D. De Rupert.
        New York, J. W. Lovell, 1881.
        166 p.   19½ cm.

16375   Description of the town of Lawrence, Van Buren county,
        in the Des Moines valley, Iowa: its hydraulic power
        and manufacturing facilities. Keokuk, J. B. Howell
        & co., 1856.
        11 p.

16376   Deseret. Constitution.
        Constitution of the state of Deseret, with the
        journal of the convention which formed it, and the
        proceedings of the legislature consequent thereon.
        Kanesville, O. Hyde, 1849.
        16 p.   22 cm.

16377   The Deseret alphabet. Salt Lake City, Utah State
        Historical Society, 1944. (In Utah historical
        quarterly, v. 12, nos. 1, 2, January, April 1944,
        p. 99-102)

16378   The Deseret News, Salt Lake City.
        Utah, the inland empire, illustrated. The story
        of the pioneers, resources and industries of the
        state, attractions of Salt Lake City, leading men
        of the community. Salt Lake City, The Deseret news,
        1902.
        110 p.   illus.

16379   De Shields, James T   1861-
        Border wars of Texas; being an authentic and
        popular account, in chronological order, of the long
        and bitter conflict waged between savage Indian tribes
        and pioneer settlers of Texas... by James T. De

Shields... Matt Bradley, revising editor and
publisher. Tioga, Tex., The Herald company, 1912.
400 p.   front., illus., plates, ports., maps.
23 cm.

16380 De Shields, James T   1861-
Cynthia Ann Parker. The story of her capture at the
massacre of the inmates of Parker's fort; of her
quarter of a century spent among the Comanches, as
the wife of the war chief, Peta Nocona; and of her
recapture at the battle of Pease river, by Captain
L. S. Ross, of the Texian [!] rangers. By James T.
De Shields... St. Louis, Printed for the author, 1886.
vii, [9]-80 p.   front., ports.   18½ x 14 cm.

16381 De Veny, William, 1852-
The establishment of law and order on western
plains, by William De Veny. Portland, Or. [The author];
the Dalles, Or., Optimist print, 1915.
120 p.   front., 1 illus., plates, port. group.
17½ cm.
A narrative of the author's experiences in Nebraska
and Kansas, 1871-1892.

16382 Devinny, V
The story of a pioneer... an historical sketch in
which is depicted some of the struggles and exciting
incidents pertaining to the early settlement of
Colorado. Denver, The Reed publishing company,
1904.
164 p.   front., pl., ports.   20 cm.

16383 Dewey, Orville.
Discourse on slavery and the annexation of Texas.
New York, 1844.
18 p.   22 cm.

16384 [Dewey, Squire Pierce] 1818-
The Bonanza mines and the Bonanza kings of California.
Their 5 years reign: 1875-1879... [San Francisco?
1879?]
3 p.l., [3]-87 p.   illus.   22½ cm.
A reissue, with some additional matter, of "The
Bonanza mines of Nevada. Gross frauds in the manage-
ment exposed. Reply of S. P. Dewey."

16385 De Wolff, J   H
Pawnee Bill (Major Gordon W. Lillie), his experience

and adventures on the western plains; or, From the
saddle of a "cowboy and ranger" to the chair of a
"bank president," by J. H. De Wolff. [n.p.] Pawnee
Bill's historic wild west company, 1902.
  108 p. incl. front., illus., plates, ports.   23½ cm.

16386 Dexter, A   Hersey.
  Early days in California; by A. Hersey Dexter...
[Denver, Col.,Tribune-Republican press] 1886.
  3 p.l., 9 -214 p.   20 cm.
  Includes his "Old sea stories and other poems (p. 165-
214)

16387 Dexter, W   W
  Texas, imperial state of America, with her diadem
of cities. The official and exclusive book of the
Texas world's fair commission. St. Louis [1903]
  unpaged.   map, pl., port.   21½ cm.

16388 Dickenson, Mrs. Luella.
  Reminiscences of a trip across the plains in 1846
and early days in California, by Luella Dickenson.
San Francisco, The Whitaker & Ray company (incorporated)
1904.
  117, [1] p. incl. plates, port.   front. (port.)
20 cm.

16389 Dickerson, Philip Jackson.
  History of the Osage nation: its people, resources
and prospects. The last reservation to open in the
new state... By Philip Dickerson, M.A. [Pawhuska,
Okla.? c1906]
  cover-title, 144 p.   illus., plates, ports.
28½ cm.

16390 Dietz, Arthur Arnold.
  Mad rush for gold in frozen North, by Arthur
Arnold Dietz; illustrations from photographs by W. A.
Sharp. Los Angeles, Times-Mirror printing and
binding house, 1914.
  281 p. incl. front. (group of ports.) plates,
port. group.   20½ cm.
  "A thrilling adventure of a party of eighteen gold
seekers who left New York city in the winter of 1897,
headed by Arthur A. Dietz." - Pref.

16391 Dill, R   G
  The political campaigns of Colorado, with complete

tabulated statements of the official vote. By R. G.
Dill. Denver, The Arapahoe publishing co., John Dove,
book and job printer, 1895.
   286 p.   20 cm.

16392 Dimsdale, Thomas Josiah, d. 1866.
     The vigilantes of Montana, or Popular justice in the
Rocky mountains. Being a correct and impartial
narrative of the chase, trial, capture and execution
of Henry Plummer's road agent band, together with
accounts of the lives and crimes of many of the
robbers and desperadoes, the whole being interspersed
with sketches of life in the mining camps of the
"Far West"... By Prof. Thos. J. Dimsdale. Virginia
City, M. T., D. W. Tilton & co., 1866.
     iv, [5]-228 p.   17½ cm.

16393 Diomedi, Alexander, 1843-
     Sketches of modern Indian life. By Father A. Diomedi.
Woodstock, Md., 1894?
     79 p.   23 cm.
     "The following pages, save some trifling additions
were written in 1879." - Pref.
     Reprinted from Woodstock letters, Woodstock, Md.,
v. 22-23, 1893-94.

16394 Dobbs, Arthur, 1689-1765.
     An account of the countries adjoining to Hudson's
bay, in the north-west part of America: containing
a description of their lakes and rivers, the nature
of the soil and climates, and their methods of
commerce, &c. shewing the benefit to be made by
settling colonies, and opening a trade in these parts;
whereby the French will be deprived in a great measure
of their traffick in furs, and the communication
between Canada and Mississippi be cut off. With an
abstract of Captain Middleton's journal, and observations upon his behaviour during his voyage, and since
his return. To which are added, I. A letter from
Bartholomew de Fonte... giving an account of his
voyage from Lima in Peru, to prevent, or seize upon
any ships that should attempt to find a northwest
passage to the South sea. II. An abstract of all
the discoveries which have been publish'd of the
islands and countries in and adjoining to the great
western ocean between America, India, and China, &c.
... III. The Hudson's bay company's charter. IV.
The standard of trade in those parts of America;

with an account of the exports and profits made
annually by the Hudson's bay company. V. Vocabularies
of the languages of several Indian nations adjoining
to Hudson's bay. The whole intended to shew the
great probability of a north-west passage... By
Arthur Dobbs, esq. London, Printed for J. Robinson,
1744.
1 p.l., ii, 211 p.   front. (fold. map)
26 x 21½ cm.

16395   Documents relating to the Kansas-Nebraska act, 1854.
New York, A. Lovell & company, 1894.
20 p.   18 cm.   (American history leaflets;
colonial and constitutional, no. 17)

16396   Dodd, Ephraim Shelby, d. 1864.
Diary of Ephraim Shelby Dodd, member of Company D,
Terry's Texas rangers, December 4, 1862-January 1,
1864. Austin, Press of E. L. Steck, 1914.
32 p.   24 cm.

16397   Dodge, Grenville Mellen, 1831-1916.
The battle of Atlanta and other campaigns,
addresses, etc., by Major-General Grenville M. Dodge.
Council Bluffs, Ia., The Monarch printing company,
1910.
183 p. incl. front., illus., plates, ports.   23 cm.

16398   Dodge, Grenville Mellen, 1831-1916.
How we built the Union Pacific railway, and other
railway papers and addresses, by Major General
Grenville M. Dodge... [New York? 1910?]
1 p.l., 5-171 p.   plates, ports.   23 cm.

16399   Dodge, Grenville Mellen, 1831-1916.
The Indian campaign of winter of 1864-65. Written
in 1877 by Major General Grenville M. Dodge and read
to the Colorado commandery of the Loyal legion of
the United States at Denver, April 21, 1907.
[Denver? 1907?]
20 p., 1 l.   22½ cm.

16400   Dodge, Richard Irving, 1827-1895.
The Black hills. A minute description of the
routes, scenery, soil, climate, timber, gold, geology,
zoology, etc. With an accurate map, four sectional
drawings, and ten plates from photographs, taken on
the spot. By Richard Irving Dodge... New York,

J. Miller, 1876.
151 p.   front., plates, fold. map, diagrs. (1 fold.)
19½ cm.

16401   Dodge, Richard Irving, 1827-1895.
The hunting grounds of the great West; a description
of the plains, game, and Indians of the great North
American desert, by Richard Irving Dodge... with an
introduction by William Blackmore. With numerous
illustrations by Ernest Griset. London, Chatto &
Windus, 1877.
lvii, 440 p.   front., illus., plates, ports.,
fold. map.   23 cm.

16402   Dollard, Robert.
Recollections of the civil war and going West to
grow up with the country, by Robert Dollard. Scotland,
S. D., The author, 1906.
5 p.l., [5]-296 p.   front., ports.   23 cm.

16403   Dolwig, Jacob.
From Hungary to North Dakota; an excerpt from the
diary of Jacob Dolwig, translated from the original
by Richard J. Dolwig. [Bismarck, State Historical
Society of North Dakota, 1929]
204-208 p.   24 cm.
Reprinted from North Dakota historical quarterly,
v. 3, no. 3, April 1929.

16404   Domenech, [Emmanuel Henri Dieudonné] 1825 or 6-1886.
Missionary adventures in Texas and Mexico. A
personal narrative of six years' sojourn in those
regions... Tr. from the French under the author's
superintendence.ʿ London, Longman, Brown, Green,
Longmans, & Roberts, 1858.
xv, 366 p.   front. (map)   20 cm.

16405   Domenech, Emmanuel Henri Dieudonné, 1825 or 6-1886.
Voyage dans les solitudes américaines. Voyage
au Minnesota, par l'abbé E. Domenech... Paris,
Pouget-Coulon [etc.] 1858.
224 p.   16 x 9½ cm.   (Half-title: Bibliothèque
catholique de voyages et de romans. Série des voyages)
The principal part of the book is devoted to a
general account of the Indians of North America,
following a brief description of Minnesota.

16406 Domenech, Emmanuel Henri Dieudonné, 1825 or 6-1886.
Voyage pittoresque dans les grands déserts du
Nouveau monde, par l'abbé Em. Domenech... Paris,
Morizot, 1862.
3 p.l., 608, [2] p.   40 col. pl. (incl. front.)
27½ cm.

16407 Donald, Jay.
Outlaws of the border. A complete and authentic
history of the lives of Frank and Jesse James, the
Younger brothers, and their robber companions,
including Quantrell [!] and his noted guerrillas,
the greatest bandits the world has ever known.
Chicago, Coburn and Newman publishing co., 1882.
ix, 11-520 p.   front., plates, ports.   20 cm.

16408 Donan, Patrick.
... The Columbia river empire, a land of promise
for the homeseeker and homemaker. Portland, Or.,
The Passenger department of the Oregon railroad and
navigation company, 1902.
72 p.   illus., map.   23 cm.

16409 Donan, Patrick.
The land of golden grain. North Dakota. The lake-
gemmed, breeze-swept empire of the new Northwest...
By P. Donan. Chicago, Ill., C. R. Brodix, 1883.
1 p.l., 5-70 p.   23 cm.
Issued by the St. Paul, Minneapolis & Manitoba
railway.

16410 Donan, Patrick.
Utah: a peep into a mountain walled treasury of
the gods. Rhymes by Cy Warman. [Buffalo, N. Y.,
Matthews, Northrup co., 1891]
96 p.   22½ cm.

16411 Donnel, William M
Pioneers of Marion County, consisting of a general
history of the county from its early settlement to
the present date. Also, the geography and history
of each township, including brief biographical sketches
of some of the more prominent early settlers in each,
together with numerous incidents illustrative of
pioneer life more than twenty-five years ago. By
Wm. M. Donnel. Des Moines, Ia., Republican steam
printing house, 1872.
346 p.   22 cm.

16412 Donoho, Milford Hill, 1844-
       Circle-Dot, a true story of cowboy life forty years
       ago, by M. H. Donoho. Topeka, Monotyped and printed
       by Crane & company, 1907.
       256 p.   front.   20 cm.

16413 Donovan, Joseph Wesley, 1847-
       Skill in trials: containing a variety of civil
       and criminal cases won by the art of advocates; with
       some of the skill of Webster, Choate, Beach, Butler,
       Curtis, Davis, Fountain, and others, given in sketches
       of their work and trial stories, with hints on
       speeches and new selections of western eloquence.
       2d enl. ed. By J. W. Donovan... Rochester, N. Y.,
       Williamson law book company, 1899.
       3 p.l., 173 p.   19½ cm.

16414 Dosch, Henry Ernest, 1841-
       ... Horticulture in Oregon... [Portland, Or.]
       Printed by direction of the Lewis and Clarke centennial
       exposition commission, 1904.
       cover-title, 32 p.   illus.   18½ cm.
       At head of title: Louisiana Purchase Exposition,
       St. Louis, 1904.

16415 Doubleday, Charles William, 1829-
       Reminiscences of the "filibuster" war in Nicaragua,
       by C. W. Doubleday. New York and London, G. P.
       Putnam's sons, 1886.
       ix, 225 p.   front. (map)   19½ cm.

16416 Douglas, David, 1799-1834.
       Journal kept by David Douglas during his travels in
       North America, 1823-1827, together with a particular
       description of thirty-three species of American oaks
       and eighteen species of Pinus, with appendices
       containing a list of the plants introduced by Douglas
       and an account of his death in 1834. Published
       under the direction of the Royal Horticultural
       Society. London, W. Wesley, 1914.
       364 p.   illus., port.   26 cm.
       Edited with "Memoir" and various notes by W. Wilks,
       assisted by H. R. Hutchinson.

16417 Downie, William, 1819-1894.
       Hunting for gold; reminisences [!] of personal
       experience and research in the early days of the
       Pacific coast from Alaska to Panama. By Major

William Downie... San Francisco, Cal., Press of the
California publishing co., 1893.
407 p.   front. (port.)   illus.   23 cm.
Edited by C. M. Waage. cf. Pref.
"Some of my early friends": p. 379-397.

16418 Downs, Solomon Weathersbee, 1801-1854.
Speech of Hon. S. U. [!] Downs, of Louisiana, on
the bill to establish a territorial government in
Oregon. Delivered in the Senate of the United States,
June 3, 1848. Washington, Printed at the Congressional
globe office, 1848.
8 p.   24 cm.

16419 Dowse, Thomas.
The new Northwest. Montana. Helena; its past,
present and future. By Thomas Dowse... Chicago,
Commercial advertiser co., 1880.
cover-title, 24 p.   illus. (incl. map)
$26\frac{1}{2}$ x 20 cm.

16420 Doy, John.
The narrative of John Doy, of Lawrence, Kansas...
New York, T. Holman, printer, 1860.
132 p.   illus. $18\frac{1}{2}$ cm.

16421 Doyle, John Thomas, 1819-1906.
Memorandum as to the discovery of the bay of San
Francisco by John T. Doyle. With introductory
remarks by John D. Washburn... Read before the
American antiquarian society, at their annual
meeting, October 21, 1873. Worcester, Mass.,
Printed by C. Hamilton, 1874.
14 p.   25 cm.

16422 Dragoon expedition. Fort Leavenworth, Oct. 3, 1839.
(In Army and Navy Chronicle, 1839, v. 9, p. 285-286)

16423 Drake, Eugene B   comp.
Jimeno's and Hartnell's indexes of land concessions,
from 1830 to 1846; also, toma de razon, or, registry
of titles, for 1844-45; approvals of land grants by
the territorial deputation and departmental assembly
of California, from 1835 to 1846, and a list of
unclaimed grants. Comp. from the Spanish archives
in the U. S. Surveyor-general's office. San Francisco,
Kenny & Alexander, 1861.
68 p., 1 l.   21 cm.

97

16424 Drannan, William F   1832-1913.
       Thirty-one years on the plains and in the
       mountains; or, The last voice from the plains.
       An authentic record of a life time of hunting,
       trapping, scouting and Indian fighting in the far
       West, by Capt. William F. Drannan... Copiously
       illustrated by H. S. DeLay... Thos. W. Jackson
       publishing company, 1900.
           1 p.l., [7]-654 p.   front., illus., plates, ports.
       20 cm.

16425 Drips, Joseph H   b. 1828?
       Three years among the Indians in Dakota. By J. H.
       Drips, sergeant in company L, Sixth Iowa cavalry.
       Kimball, S. D., Brule index, 1894.
           1 p.l., 139 p.   illus., ports.   19½ x 15½ cm.

16426 Droulers, Charles.
       Marquis de Morès in North Dakota. Translated from
       the French by George F. Will. [Bismarck, State
       Historical Society of North Dakota, 1940]
           3-23 p.   24 cm.
       Chapter II of his Le Marquis de Morès, 1858-1896,
       Paris, 1932.
       Reprinted from North Dakota historical quarterly,
       v. 8, no. 1, October 1940.

16427 Drown, Simeon De Witt.
       Drown's record, and historical view of Peoria,
       from the discovery by the French Jesuit missionaries,
       in the seventeenth century, to the present time.
       Also, an almanac for 1851. To which is added a
       business directory... with business cards... by
       S. De Witt Drown. Peoria, Ill, Printed by E. O.
       Woodcock, 1850.
           164 p.   illus. (incl. maps)   18 cm.

16428 Drown, Simeon De Witt, comp.
       The Peoria directory, for 1844: containing an
       account of the early discovery of the country, with
       a history of the town, down to the present time...
       and much other statistical information... by S.
       De Witt Drown... Peoria, Printed for the author,
       1844.
           124 p.   illus. (incl. maps)   fold. map.   19 cm.

16429 Drumm, Mark, comp.
       Drumm's manual of Utah, and souvenir of the first

state legislature, 1896. Containing the state
Constitution... [and] biographies of members of
the legislature. Salt Lake City [1896]
   95 p.   ports.   20 cm.

16430 Dudley, John H
     The climax in crime of the 19th century, being an
authentic history of the trial, conviction and
execution of Stephen Merris Ballew for the murder
of James P. Golden, in Collin county, Texas, on the
21st day of October, 1870, with a short sketch of the
early life of the murderer. Quincy, 1872.
   208 p.   front. (port.)   21 cm.

16431 Duffield, George Crawford.
     Memories of frontier Iowa, related by George C.
Duffield for the Annals of Iowa. Des Moines,
Bishard brothers, printers, 1906.
   2 p.l., 54 p.   5 pl., 5 port.   23 cm.
   Ms. prepared by E. R. Harlan from verbal narrative
of Mr. Duffield. cf. Pref. note.

16432 Duflot de Mofras, Eugène, 1810-1884.
     Exploration du territoire de l'Orégon, des
Californies et de la mer Vermeille, exécutée pendant
les années 1840, 1841 et 1842, par M. Duflot de
Mofras... Ouvrage pub. par ordre du roi... Paris,
A. Bertrand, 1844.
   2 v.   8 pl. (incl. fronts.)   tables.   24 cm.
and atlas: 3 p.l., 26 [i.e. 27]   illus. on 18 pl.
(part fold., incl. maps, plans)   53 x 35½ cm.
   An historical and descriptive account of the
Pacific coast of North America.
   "Bibliographie chronologique des ouvrages cités ou
consultés": v. 2, p. 485-500.

16433 Dufur, A. J., company.
     Statistics of the state of Oregon, containing a
description of its agricultural development, and
natural and industrial resources; together with the
physical, geographical, geological and mineral
statistics of the state. Salem, A. J. Dufur, 1869.
   128 p.   22 cm.

16434 Dumbell, Kate Ethel Mary, 1868-
     California and the far West; suggestions for the
west bound traveler, by K. E. M. Dumbell. New York,

J. Pott & company [c1914]
198 p.   fold. map.   16½ cm.

16435 Dunbar, Edward E
The romance of the age; or, The discovery of gold
in California. By Edward E. Dunbar. New York, D.
Appleton & co., 1867.
134 p.   front. (port.) pl.   17 cm.

16436 [Duncan, Lew Wallace] 1861-   comp.
History of Montgomery county, Kansas. By its own
people... Published by L. Wallace Duncan. Iola,
Kan., Press of Iola register, 1903.
852 p.   front., plates, ports.   27½ cm.

16437 Duniway, Mrs. Abigail Scott, 1834-1915.
From the West to the West: across the plains to
Oregon, by Abigail Scott Duniway, with frontispiece
in color. Chicago, A. C. McClurg & co., 1905.
xii p., 1 l., 15-311 p. incl. col. front.   21 cm.

16438 Dunlevy, Ursula, Sister.
The Canadian halfbreed rebellions of 1870 and 1885.
[Bismarck, State Historical Society of North Dakota,
1942]
86-113, 137-165 p.   24 cm.
Reprinted from North Dakota historical quarterly,
v. 9, no. 2, January 1942, and no. 3, April 1942.
M.A. thesis - University of North Dakota.

16439 Dunn, J   E
Indian Territory, a pre-commonwealth. Approved
and sanctioned by parties connected with the
Commission to the Five Civilized Tribes. Illustrations by courtesy of the Twin Territories
Magazine. Indianapolis, American print. co., 1904.
250 p.   illus., ports., fold. map.   20 cm.

16440 Dunn, Jacob Piatt, 1855-1924.
Massacres of the mountains; a history of the Indian
wars of the far West, by J. P. Dunn, jr. ...
New York, Harper & brothers, 1886.
iii -ix, 784 p. incl. front., illus., plates,
ports., maps (part fold.) plans. fold. map.
21½ cm.

16441 Dunn, William Edward, 1888-
... Spanish and French rivalry in the Gulf region

of the United States, 1678-1702; the beginnings of
Texas and Pensacola, by William Edward Dunn...
Austin, Tex., The University [1917]
    238 p.   maps (1 fold.)   23½ cm.   (University
of Texas bulletin. no. 1705, Jan. 20, 1917)
    Studies in history, no. 1. Published also as thesis
(Ph.D.) Columbia university, 1917.

16442 Duran, Narciso, 1776-1846.
    ... Expedition on the Sacramento and San Joaquin
rivers in 1817; diary of Fray Narciso Duran, ed. by
Charles Edward Chapman... University of California,
Berkeley, California, December, 1911. Berkeley,
The University press, 1911.
    21 p.   23½ cm.   (Publications of the Academy
of Pacific coast history, vol. 2, no. 5)
    Spanish and English.

16443 Durrie, Daniel S[teele] 1819-1892.
    The early outposts of Wisconsin. A paper read
before the State historical society of Wisconsin,
December 26, 1872. Annals of Prairie du Chien. By
Daniel S. Durrie... [Madison? Wis., 1872?]
    15 p.   24 cm.

16444 Duval, John C
    Early times in Texas. Austin, H. P. N. Gammel &
co., 1892.
    135 p.   22 cm.

16445 Dwinelle, John Whipple, 1816-1881.
    The colonial history of the city of San Francisco:
being a narrative argument in the Circuit court of
the United States for the state of California, for
four square leagues of land claimed by that city
and confirmed to it by that court. 3d ed. By John
W. Dwinelle... San Francisco, Printed by Towne &
Bacon, 1866.
    xlv, 106, 391 p.   2 pl. (incl. front.) 3 maps
(2 fold.)   24. cm.

16446 Dye, Mrs. Eva (Emery)
    McLoughlin and old Oregon: a chronicle. Ed. 2.
Chicago, 1900.
    381 p.   port.

16447 Dye, Mrs. Eva (Emery)
    Stories of Oregon. San Francisco, Whitaker and

101

Ray company, 1900.
  203 p.   front., illus.   19 cm.   (Western
series of readers, v. 7)

16448 Dyer, Mrs. D   B
  "Fort Reno"; or, Picturesque "Cheyenne and Arrapahoe
  [!] army life," being the opening of "Oklahoma."
  New York, 1896.
  216 p.   front., pl.   21 cm.

E

16449 [Eastman, Edwin]
  Seven and nine years among the Camanches and
  Apaches. An autobiography. Jersey City, N. J.,
  C. Johnson, 1874.
  309 p.   front., illus., plates, port.   18½ cm.

16450 Edmunds, A. C. of Lincoln, Neb.
  Pen sketches of Nebraskans, with photographs.
  By A. C. Edmunds. Lincoln, Neb., Omaha, R. & J.
  Wilbur, 1871.
  510, [1] p.   front., ports.   19½ cm.

16451 Edwards, John Newman, 1839-1889.
  Shelby and his men; or, The war in the West.
  By John N. Edwards. Cincinnati, Miami printing
  and publishing co., 1867.
  ix, 10-551 p.   front. (port.) fold. map.   23 cm.

16452 Edwards, John Newman, 1839-1889.
  Shelby's expedition to Mexico. An unwritten leaf
  of the war. By John N. Edwards... Kansas City,
  Mo., Kansas City times steam book and job printing
  house, 1872.
  139 p.   23 cm.

16453 Edwards, Mrs. Mary Virginia (Plattenburg) comp.
  John N. Edwards, biography, memoirs, reminiscences
  and recollections. His brilliant career as soldier,
  author, journalist. Choice collection of his most
  notable and interesting newspaper articles together
  with some unpublished poems and many private letters.
  Compiled by his wife... Kansas, Mo., Jennie Edwards,
  publisher, 1889.
  vi, 9-228 p.   front. (port.)   19 cm.

102

16454　Edwards, Philip Leget, 1812-1869.
　　　　　California in 1837. Diary of Col. Philip L. Edwards,
　　　　containing an account of a trip to the Pacific coast.
　　　　Published in "Themis" by authority of the Board of
　　　　state library trustees of the state of California.
　　　　Sacramento, A. J. Johnston & Co., 1890.
　　　　　47 p.　　23 cm.

16455　Eells, Myron, 1843-1907.
　　　　　History of the Congregational association of Oregon,
　　　　and Washington territory; the Home missionary society
　　　　of Oregon and adjoining territories; and the North-
　　　　western association of Congregational ministers.
　　　　By Rev. M. Eells. Portland, Or., Publishing house
　　　　of Himes the printer, 1881.
　　　　　124 p.　　22½ cm.

16456　Eells, Myron, 1843-1907.
　　　　　Hymns in the Chinook jargon language, comp. by
　　　　Rev. M. Eells... 2d ed. Rev. and enl. Portland,
　　　　Or., D. Steel, 1889.
　　　　　40 p.　　14½ cm.
　　　　Chinook hymns and English translation on opposite
　　　　pages. "The Lord's prayer," p. 38-39, and "A blessing
　　　　before meals," p. 40, have interlinear translation.

16457　[Egmont, John Perceval, 2d earl of] 1711-1770.
　　　　　An examination of the principles, and an enquiry
　　　　into the conduct, of the two b***rs: in regard to
　　　　the establishment of their power, and their prosecution
　　　　of the war, 'till the signing of the preliminaries.
　　　　In a letter to a member of Parliament. The 2d ed.,
　　　　reviewed and corrected... London, Printed for
　　　　A. Price, M.DCC.XLIX.
　　　　　1 p.l., 79 p.　　19½ cm.
　　　　"Two b***rs" i.e. Thomas Pelham-Holles, 1st duke of
　　　　Newcastle-under-Lyme, and Hon. Henry Pelham.

16458　Elderkin, James D　　　　1820-
　　　　　Biographical sketches and anecdotes of a soldier
　　　　of three wars, as written by himself. The Florida,
　　　　the Mexican war and the great rebellion, together
　　　　with sketches of travel, also of service in a
　　　　militia company and a member of the Detroit light
　　　　guard band for over thirty years. By James D.
　　　　Elderkin. Detroit, Mich. [Record printing company]
　　　　1899.
　　　　　2 p.l., 202 p.　　front., pl., port.　　17½ cm.

16459 Eldredge, Zoeth Skinner, 1846-
  History of California. New York [1915]
  5 v. maps, pl., port. 24 cm.
  Vol. 5. Special articles.
  "The first three volumes and half of the fourth
 volume are the work of Mr. Clinton A. Snowden."

16460 Eldredge, Zoeth Skinner, 1846-
  The Spanish archives of California; paper read
 before the California genealogical society, July 13,
 1901, by Zoeth S. Eldredge. San Francisco, The
 Murdock press, 1901.
  8 p. 25 cm. [California genealogical society.
 Publications, no. II]

16461 Elliott, A   B
  Travelers' hand-book across the continent,
 Pacific railroad and California sketches. Troy,
 N. Y., 1870.
  85 p. 20 cm.

16462 Elliott, Howard.
  The relation of the railway to community and state-
 wide advertising; address before the Oregon development league, in annual convention, Salem, Oregon,
 Nov. 29, 1910. [n.p.] 1910.
  14 p.

16463 Elliott, Richard Smith, b. 1817.
  Notes taken in sixty years... By Richard Smith
 Elliott... St. Louis, R. P. Studley & co., printers,
 1883.
  2 p.l., 336 p. $22\frac{1}{2}$ cm.

16464 [Ellis, Edward Sylvester] 1840-1916.
  ... In the Pecos country, by Lieut. R. H. Jayne
 pseud. New York, The Merrian company [c1894]
  303 p. incl. front. plates. $19\frac{1}{2}$ cm.
 (War whoop series, no. 3)
 Sequel: The cave in the mountain.

16465 Ellis, Edward Sylvester, 1840-1916.
  ... Off the reservation: or, Caught in an Apache
 raid, by Edward S. Ellis... illustrated by Edwin
 J. Prittie. Philadelphia, Chicago [etc.] The J. C.
 Winston company [c1908]
  331 p. front., 3 pl. $19\frac{1}{2}$ cm. (Half-title:
 The Arizona series [v. 1])

16466 [Ellis, Edward Sylvester] 1840-1916.
... On the trail of Geronimo; or, In the Apache
country. By Lieut. R. H. Jayne [pseud.] New York,
F. F. Lovell & company [c1889]
    333 p.   front., plates.   19 cm.   (Wild
adventure series, no. 1)

16467 Ellis, Edward Sylvester, 1840-1916.
... The round up; or, Geronimo's last raid, by
Edward S. Ellis... illustrated by Edwin J. Prittie.
Philadelphia, Chicago [etc.] The J. C. Winston
company [1908]
    347 p.   col. front., 3 pl.   19 cm.   (Half
title: The Arizona series [v. 3])

16468 Ellis, Edward Sylvester, 1840-1916.
... Wyoming, by Edward S. Ellis... Philadelphia,
Porter & Coates [c1888]
    321 p. incl. front.   plates.   17½ cm.
(Wyoming Valley series, no. 1)

16469 Ellis, Elmer E
Recollections of a Bad Lands' rancher. [Bismarck,
N.D., State Historical Society of North Dakota,
1926]
    24-34 p.   25 cm.
In North Dakota historical quarterly, v. 1, no. 1,
Oct. 1926.

16470 Ellsworth, Henry William, 1814-1864.
Valley of the upper Wabash, Indiana, with hints
on its agricultural advantages: plan of a dwelling,
estimates of cultivation, and notices of labor-saving
machines. By Henry William Ellsworth. New York,
Pratt, Robinson & co., 1838.
    xii, 175 p.   front. (fold. map)   2 fold. pl.,
fold. plan.   18½ cm.

16471 Empey, Jessie K
The last squaw fight, by Jessie K. Empey. Salt
Lake City, Utah State Historical Society, 1941.
(In Utah historical quarterly, v. 9, nos. 3, 4,
July, October 1941, p. 137-140)

16472 Engelhardt, Zephyrin, father, 1851-1934.
The Franciscans in California. With a map and
numerous illustrations... Harbor Springs, Mich., 1897.
    2 p.   front., illus.   map.   21½ cm.

16473 [English, Mrs. Mary Katharine (Jackson)]
Prairie sketches, or Fugitive recollections of an
army girl of 1899. [n.p., 1899?]
76 p. illus. 21½ cm.

16474 Ermatinger, Edward, 1797-1876.
... Edward Ermatinger's York Factory express
journal, being a record of journeys made between Fort
Vancouver and Hudson Bay in the years 1827-1828.
With introduction by Judge C. O. Ermatinger and notes
by Judge C. O. Ermatinger and James White, F.R.S.C.
Presented by G. H. Coyne... (Read May 14, 1912)
[Ottawa, 1912]
67-132 p. front. (port.) fold. map. 25½ cm.
From the Transactions of the Royal society of Canada,
vol. VI, 1912, section II.

16475 Erwin, Marie H
Wyoming historical blue book; a legal and political
history of Wyoming, 1868-1943. Denver, Bradford-
Robinson print. co. [1943?]
xxiii, 1471 p. illus. (part col.), ports., maps,
charts. 24 cm.
"In part a Works Progress Administration project."
- cf. p. viii.

16476 Escudero, José Agustín de, 1801-1862.
Noticias estadísticas del estado de Chihuahua,
por J. A. de Escudero... México, J. Ojeda, 1834.
160 (i.e. 260) p. 21 cm.

16477 [Espinosa y Tello, José] 1763-1815.
Relacion del viage hecho por las goletas Sutil
y Mexicana en el año de 1792, para reconocer el
estrecho de Fuca; con una introduccion en que se da
noticia de las expediciones executadas anteriormente
por los españoles en busca del paso del noroeste de
la América. De orden del rey. Madrid, Imprenta
real, 1802.
8 p.l., clxviii, 185 p. fold. tab. 22½ cm.
and atlas. 31 x 19½ cm.
By some bibliographers the author is wrongly
supposed to be Dionisio Alcalá Galiano, commander of
the expedition; Medina and Leclerc ascribe the
historical introduction to Alcalá Galiano, commander
of the Sutil, and Cayetano Valdés, commander of the
Mexicana. Navarrete (Bibl. mar. esp., t. 2, p. 65)

106

states that Espinosa wrote the "Relacion" and that
he himself wrote the introduction.

16478   Essays in American history dedicated to Frederick
Jackson Turner. New York, H. Holt and company, 1910.
vii, 293 p.   22 cm.
Edited by Guy Stanton Ford.

16479   Esshom, Frank Ellwood, 1865-
Pioneers and prominent men of Utah, comprising
photographs, genealogies, biographies... the early
history of the Church of Jesus Christ of Latter-day
saints... by Frank Esshom... [Ed. de luxe]
Salt Lake City, Utah, Utah pioneers book publishing
company, 1913.
1319 p.   illus. (ports.)   31 cm.

16480   Estes Rocky Mountain National Park, Colorado. [Denver,
The H. H. Tammen co., n.d.]
12 unnumb. p.   illus.   25½ x 33 cm.
Twelve hand-colored views.

16481   Ethell, Henry C
The rise and progress of civilization in the Hairy
nation. A comparative topical review of the stages
of progress in the brief history of Davis county,
Iowa. By Henry C. Ethell. Bloomfield, Ia., H. C.
Ethell, 1883.
viii, 9-144 p.   19½ cm.

16482   Evans, Albert S
A la California. Sketches of life in the golden
state... With an introduction by Col. W. H. L.
Barnes, and illustrations from original drawings by
Ernest Narjot. San Francisco, A. L. Bancroft &
co., 1874.
379 p.   front., pl.

16483   Evans, Clement A[nselm] ed.
Confederate military history; a library of
Confederate States history... written by distinguished
men of the South, and edited by Gen. Clement A. Evans
of Georgia... Atlanta, Confederate pub. co., 1899.
12 v.   front., 1 col. pl., port., maps (partly
fold.)   24½ cm.

16484   Evans, Ellwood, 1828-1898.
Washington Territory: her past, her present and

the elements of wealth which ensure her future. Address delivered at the Centennial exposition, Philadelphia, Sept. 2, 1876 and in joint convention of the legislature of Washington Territory, Oct. 13, 1877, by Elwood Evans. Pub. by order of the Legislative assembly... Olympia, C. B. Bagley, public printer, 1877.
51 p.   23 cm.

16485 Eventful narratives... Designed for the instruction and encouragement of young Latter-day saints. Salt Lake City, Utah, Juvenile instructor office, 1887.
vii, [9]-98 p.   19 cm.   (Faith-promoting series. 13th book)
Contents. - Leaving home, by Robert Aveson. - A boy's love: a man's devotion. - A trip to Carson valley, by O. B. Huntington.

F

16486 Fabian, Bentham.
The resources of Utah, with statistics of progress for the year 1872. Comprising a description of the geographical position and area of the territory, the population, climate, soil, agricultural products, value of property, mineral resources... &c. By Bentham Fabian. Salt Lake City, Salt Lake Tribune printing and publishing company, 1873.
46 p.   21½ cm.

16487 The facts about Texas. [n.p., 1912]
[4] p.   18 cm.

16488 Fages, Pedro.
... Expedition to San Francisco Bay in 1770, diary of Pedro Fages; ed. by Herbert Eugene Bolton... Berkeley, Cal., University of California, 1911.
19 p.   23½ cm.   (Publications of the Academy of Pacific Coast history. vol. 2, no. 3)
Spanish and English on opposite pages.

16489 Fairfield, Asa Merrill, 1854-
Fairfield's pioneer history of Lassen county, California; containing everything that can be learned about it from the beginning of the world to the year of Our Lord 1870... Also much of the pioneer history

of the state of Nevada... the biographies of Governor
Isaac N. Roop and Peter Lassen... and many stories
of Indian warfare never before published. By Asa
Merrill Fairfield. San Francisco, Pub. for the author
by H. S. Crocker company [c1916]
3 p.l., ix-xxii, 506 p., 1 l., front., pl., ports.,
fold. map.   22½ cm.

16490 A faithful picture of the political situation of New
Orleans, at the close of the last and the beginning
of the present year 1807. Boston, Re-printed from
the New-Orleans edition, 1808.
48 p.   21 cm.
An attack on General James Wilkinson in connection
with the measures taken by him in relation to the
Burr conspiracy.

16491 Falconer, Thomas, 1805-1882.
On the discovery of the Mississippi, and on the
southwestern, Oregon, and north-western boundary of
the United States. With a translation from the
original ms. of memoirs, etc., relating to the discovery of the Mississippi, by Robert Cavelier de La
Salle and the Chevalier Henry de Tonty. By Thomas
Falconer... London, S. Clarke, 1844.
2 p.l., [iii]-iv, 5-100, 99, [1] p.   front. (fold.
map)   19½ cm.

16492 Famous Southern California scenes; a collection of
views of southern California scenery. Los Angeles,
1902.
[47] pl.

16493 Farish, Thomas Edwin, d. 1919.
The gold hunters of California, by Thomas Edwin
Farish: illustrated by F. I. Wetherbee... Chicago,
M. A. Donohue & co., 1904.
246 p.   front., plates, ports.   20 cm.

16494 Farnham, Eliza Woodson (Burhans) "Mrs. T. J. Farnman,"
1815-1864.
California, in-doors and out; or, How we farm,
mine, and live generally in the Golden state. By
Eliza W. Farnham... New York, Dix, Edwards & co.,
1856.
xiv p., 1 l., 508 p.   18½ cm.

16495 Farnham, Thomas Jefferson, 1804-1848.
          The early days of California: embracing what I saw
       and heard there, with scenes in the Pacific. By
       J. T. Farnham, esq. ... Philadelphia, J. E. Potter,
       1859.
          vi, [5]-314 p.   front., plates, ports.   19 cm.
       First edition, New York, 1844, published under title:
       Travels in the Californias and scenes in the Pacific
       Ocean.

16496 Farnham, Thomas Jefferson, 1804-1848.
          The early days of California: embracing what I saw
       and heard there, with scenes in the Pacific, by J. T.
       Farnham, esq. ... Philadelphia, J. E. Potter, 1862.
          vi, [5]-314 p. incl. pl.   front., plates, ports.
       18½ cm.
          The present edition includes only chapters 1-15 as
       published in the edition of 1844. Sequel to "Travels
       in the great western prairies".

16497 Farnham, Thomas Jefferson, 1804-1848.
          History of Oregon territory, it being a demonstration
       of the title of these United States of North America
       to the same. 2d ed. ... By Thomas J. Farnham...
       New-York, W. Taylor; Boston, Saxton & Kelt; [etc.,
       etc., 1845]
          1 p.l., [7]-83 p.   front. (fold. map)   22½ cm.

16498 Farrar, Victor John, 1886-
          The annexation of Russian America to the United
       States, by Victor J. Farrar. Washington, D. C., W. F.
       Roberts company, inc., 1937.
          vii, [1], 142 p.   23½ cm.

16499 Farrell, Ned E
          Colorado, the Rocky Mountain gem, as it is in 1868.
       Gazetteer and handbook of Colorado, containing a
       description of every county... information for the
       farmer, mechanic, miner, laborer, capitalist or
       tourist. Chicago, 1868.
          72 p.   map.

16500 Farrow, E   A
          The Kiabab Indians, by E. A. Farrow. Salt Lake
       City, Utah State Historical Society, 1930. (In Utah
       historical quarterly, v. 3, no. 2, April 1930,
       p. 57-59)

16501   Ferguson, Charles D   1832 or 3-
        The experiences of a Forty-niner during the
        thirty-four years' residence in California and
        Australia, by Charles D. Ferguson, ed. by Frederick
        T. Wallace. Cleveland, O., The Williams publishing
        company, 1888.
            xviii, 9-507 p.   front., illus., plates, port.
        22½ cm.
            Cover-title: A third of a century in the gold
        fields.

16502   Ferguson, James Edward, 1871-1944, defendant.
        Record of proceedings of the High court of impeach-
        ment... convened in the city of Austin, August 1,
        1917. Pub. by authority of the legislature. Austin,
        A. C. Baldwin [1918]
            873 p.   tables.   24 cm.

16503   Fernández Duro, Cesáreo, 1830-1908.
        Don Diego de Peñalosa y su descubrimiento del
        reino de Quivira. Informe presentado á la Real
        academia de la historia... Madrid, Tello, 1882.
            160 p.   28 cm.
            On cover: Del tomo x de la Colección de memorias.

16504   Ferris, John Alexander.
        The financial economy of the United States illus-
        trated, and some of the causes which retard the
        progress of California demonstrated... By John
        Alexander Ferris... San Francisco, New York, A.
        Roman & co., 1867.
            427 p.

16505   Ferry, Hippolyte.
        Description de la nouvelle Californie; géographique,
        politique et morale... par Hypolite Ferry... Avec
        une grande carte de la nouvelle Californie. Des
        cartes particulières des baies de Monterey et de
        San-Francisco. De l'isthme de Panama. Du Cap Horn
        et du l'étroit de Magellan... Paris, L. Maison, 1850.
            2 p.l., 386 p.   illus., plates, maps (1 fold.)
        18 cm.
            The words "Deuxième édition" appear on upper margin
        of map of California.

16506   Fewkes, Jesse Walter, 1850-
        ... Antiquities of the Mesa Verde national park,
        Cliff palace, by Jesse Walter Fewkes. Washington,

Govt. print. off., 1911.
    82 p.   illus., plates (1 double) fold. plan.
23½ cm.   (Smithsonian institution. Bureau of
American ethnology. Bulletin 51)

16507 Fewkes, Jesse Walter, 1850-
       ... Prehistoric villages, castles, and towers of
       southwestern Colorado, by J. Walter Fewkes.
       Washington, Govt. print. off., 1919.
           79 p.   illus., 17 pl.   24 cm.   (Smithsonian
       institution. Bureau of American ethnology. Bulletin
       70)

16508 Field, Henry Martyn, 1822-1907.
       Our western archipelago, by Henry M. Field...
       New York, C. Scribner's sons, 1895.
           ix p., 1 l., 250 p.   front., plates, map.   21 cm.
       Account of a trip through Canada to Alaska, returning
       by way of the Northern Pacific railway.

16509 Field, Joseph E
       Three years in Texas, including a view of the Texan
       revolution, and an account of the principal battles;
       together with descriptions of the soil, commercial
       and agricultural advantages, &c. Greenfield, Mass.,
       1836.
           36 p.

16510 Field, Stephen Johnson, 1816-1899.
       Personal reminiscences of early days in California
       with other sketches. By Stephen J. Field. To which
       is added the story of his attempted assassination by
       a former associate on the Supreme bench of the state.
       By Hon. George C. Gorham. Printed for a few friends.
       Not published. [Washington, D. C., 1893]
           6, 472 p.   23 cm.

16511 Fielder, E   D
       Story of the Alamo. Nashville, Tenn. [1897]
           42 p.   pl., port.   20 cm.

16512 Fielding, Mrs. Harriet Chapin (Root) 1847-
       The ancestors and descendants of Isaac Alden and
       Irene Smith, his wife (1599-1903) by Harriet Chapin
       Fielding. [East Orange? N. J., c1903]
           144 p.   front., ports., facsims.   23½ cm.

16513   Filcher, Joseph Adams.
        Untold tales of California; short stories illus-
        trating phases of life peculiar to early days in the
        West... By J. A. Filcher. [San Francisco?] 1903.
        3 p.l., [9]-161 p.   plates.   17½ x 13½ cm.

16514   Filisola, Vicente.
        Evacuation of Texas. Translation of the Representa-
        tion addressed to the supreme government, by Gen.
        Vicente Filisola, in defence of his honor, and
        examination of his operations as commander-in-chief
        of the army against Texas. Columbia [Tex.] G. & T. H.
        Borden, public printers, 1837.
        1 p.l., iv, [3]-68 p.   19½ cm.

16515   Finerty, John Frederick, 1846-1908.
        War-path and bivouac, or The conquest of the Sioux,
        a narrative of stirring personal experiences and
        adventures in the Big Horn and Yellowstone expedition
        of 1876, and in the campaign on the British border,
        in 1879. By John F. Finerty... Chicago [J. F.
        Finerty? c1890]
        xxi, 25-460 p.   front., port., fold. map.   21 cm.

16516   [Fish, Reeder McCandless]
        The Grim chieftain of Kansas, and other free-state
        men in their struggles against slavery. Some political
        seances, incidents, inside political views and move-
        ments in their career. By one who knows. Cherryvale,
        Kan., Clarion book print, 1885.
        2 p.l., 145 p.   14 cm.
        A sketch of the life of James Henry Lane.

16517   Fisher, Ezra, 1800-1874.
        Correspondence of the Reverent Ezra Fisher,
        pioneer missionary of the American Baptist home
        mission society in Indiana, Illinois, Iowa and
        Oregon; ed. by Sarah Fisher Henderson, Nellie
        Edith Latourette, Kenneth Scott Latourette.
        [Portland, Or., 1919]
        492 p.   24 cm.
        Reprinted from Quarterly of the Oregon historical
        society, v. 17, 19-20, 1916, 1918-1919.

16518   Fisher, Walter M
        The Californians; by Walter M. Fisher...
        London, Macmillan & co., 1876.
        x, 236 p.

16519 Fitch, Abigail Hetzel.
          Junipero Serra; the man and his work, by A. H. Fitch,
       with fifteen illustrations from photographs and a
       map. Chicago, A. C. McClurg & co., 1914.
          xiii, 364 p.   front. (port.) plates, fold. map,
       plan.   21 cm.

16520 Fitch, Franklyn Y
          The life, travels and adventures of an American
       wanderer: a truthful narrative of events in the life
       of Alonzo P. De Milt. Containing his early adventures
       among the Indians of Florida; his life in the gold
       mines of California and Australia; his explorations
       of the Andes and the Amazon and its tributaries, etc.,
       etc., interspersed with sketches and narratives illus-
       trating life, manners, customs and scenery in Mexico,
       Central America, Peru, Brazil, Australia, the South
       Sea Islands, and the United States... By Franklyn Y.
       Fitch. New York, John W. Lovell company [c1883]
          4 p.l., [vii]-viii, [9]-228 p.   front. (port.)
       11 pl.   19½ cm.

16521 Fitzgerald, Oscar Penn, bp., 1829-1911.
          California sketches... Nashville, Tenn., Southern
       Methodist publishing house, 1892.
          208 p.   16½ cm.

16522 Flack,   Capt. [pseud.?]
          A hunter's experiences in the southern states of
       America: being an account of the natural history of
       the various quadrupeds and birds which are the objects
       of chase in those countries, by Captain Flack (The
       ranger") London, Longmans, Green, and co., 1866.
          4 p.l., 359 p.   19½ cm.

16523 Flack,   Capt. [pseud.?]
          The Texan ranger, or, Real life in the backwoods.
       London, Darton & co. [pref. 1866]
          319 p.   front., 5 pl.   17 cm.

16524 Fletcher, Charles H
          Jefferson County, Iowa; centennial history. 1776.
       1876. By authority of Board of Supervisors, under
       the direction of S. M. Boling [and others]
       Citizens Committee. Fairfield, Ia., Printed at the
       Ledger Office, 1876.
          35 p.   23 cm.

16525 Fletcher, Daniel Cooledge.
       Reminiscences of California and the civil war; by
       Daniel Cooledge Fletcher, sergt. Co. H, 40th regt.,
       N. Y. V. Ayer, Mass., Press of H. S. Turner, 1894.
       196 p.   front. (port.)   22½ cm.

16526 Flint, Timothy, 1780-1840.
       The history and geography of the Mississippi valley.
       To which is appended a condensed physical geography
       of the Atlantic United States, and the whole American
       continent. 3d ed. By Timothy Flint... Cincinnati,
       E. H. Flint and L. R. Lincoln, 1833.
       2 v. in 1.   23 cm.

16527 Flory, J   S
       Thrilling echoes from the wild frontier. Interesting
       personal reminiscences of the author. By J. S.
       Flory... Chicago, Rhodes & McClure publishing
       company, 1893.
       3 p.l., 17-248 p.   front., plates.   19½ cm.

16528 Flower, Richard, 1761?-1829.
       Letters from the Illinois, 1820. 1821. Containing
       an account of the English settlement at Albion and
       its vicinity, and a refutation of various misrepre-
       sentations, those more particularly of Mr. Cobbett.
       By Richard Flower. With a letter from M. Birkbeck;
       and a preface and notes by Benjamin Flower. London,
       Printed for J. Ridgway, 1822.
       xi, [9]-76 p.   21 cm.

16529 Floyd, Charles, d. 1804.
       The new found journal of Charles Floyd, a sergeant
       under Captains Lewis and Clark. By James Davie
       Butler... Worcester, Mass., Press of C. Hamilton,
       1894.
       30 p.   24½ cm.
       "From Proceedings of the American antiquarian
       society, at the semi-annual meeting, held in Boston,
       April 25, 1894."
       Published from a manuscript in the collection of
       the Wisconsin state historical society. The journal
       extends from May 14 to August 17, 1804.

16530 Fogarty, Kate Hammond.
       The story of Montana, by Kate Hammond Fogarty.
       New York and Chicago, The A. S. Barmes company [c1916]
       x, 302 p.   front., illus., maps.   19½ cm.

16531　Foght, Harold Waldstein.
　　　　The trail of the Loup; being a history of the
　　　　Loup river region, with some chapters on the state.
　　　　[Ord, Nebr.] 1906.
　　　　8 p.l., [17]-296 p.　　front. (port.), illus.,
　　　　plates (1 fold.), ports., maps, plans.　　26 cm.

16532　Foley, Thaddeus J
　　　　Memories of the old West.　[n.p., n.d.]
　　　　54 p.　　17½ cm.
　　　　Articles reprinted from various newspapers are
　　　　included.　The author's experiences in Nebraska
　　　　1870-1880s.

16533　Font, Pedro.
　　　　The Anza expedition of 1775-1776; diary of Pedro
　　　　Font, ed. by Frederick J. Teggart... Berkeley, Cal.,
　　　　University of California, 1913.
　　　　131 p.　　front. (facsim.)　　24½ cm.　　(Publica-
　　　　tions of the Academy of Pacific coast history. v. 3,
　　　　no. 1)
　　　　Spanish original, with English translation, on
　　　　opposite pages. From the ms. in the University of
　　　　California dated at the mission of Ures, June 23, 1776.

16534　Font, Pedro.
　　　　... San Francisco bay and California in 1776; three
　　　　maps, with outline sketches reproduced in facsimile
　　　　from the original manuscript, drawn by Pedro Font,
　　　　chaplain and cartographer to the expedition led by
　　　　Juan Bautista de Ansa, which made the overland journey
　　　　from northern Mexico to the California coast during
　　　　the winter of 1775-1776; with an explanation by
　　　　Irving Berdine Richman.　Providence, R. I. [Boston,
　　　　Merrymount press] 1911.
　　　　2 p.l., 7 p.　　3 maps (1 fold.) facsims.　　41½ cm.

16535　Forbes, Alexander, 1778-1862.
　　　　California: a history of Upper and Lower California
　　　　from their first discovery to the present time,
　　　　comprising an account of the climate, soil...
　　　　a full view of the missionary establishments and
　　　　condition of the free and domesticated Indians, with
　　　　an appendix relating to steam navigation in the
　　　　Pacific... London, Smith, Elder & co., 1839.
　　　　xvi, 352 p.　　front., plates, fold. map.

16536   Forbes, [Harrie Rebecca Piper (Smith)] "Mrs. A. S. C.
Forbes."
California missions and landmarks and how to get
there; a practical guide, together with a historical
sketch of the missions and landmarks, the Pious fund
and El camino real: with methods of transportation
and accommodations, fares, rates and distances from
San Francisco and Los Angeles to each point... Issued
by Mrs. Armitage S. C. Forbes... Los Angeles,
Official guide, 1903.
104 p.   illus. (incl. ports., maps)   17½ cm.

16537   Ford, John S
Origin and fall of the Alamo, March 6, 1836. By
John S. Ford, one of a committee of the Alamo
association. San Antonio, Tex., Johnson brothers
printing company, 1895.
39, [1] p.   front., plates.   23 cm.

16538   Fortier, Alcée, 1856-1914.
... Central America and Mexico, by Alcée Fortier...
and John Rose Ficklen... Philadelphia, Printed for
subscribers only by G. Barrie & sons [c1907]
xxviii, 536 p.   col. front., plates (part col.)
ports., maps (part double) plan, facsim. (part double)
23 cm.   (Half-title: The history of North America;
Francis Newton Thorpe... ed. [v. 9])

16539   Fossett, Frank.
Colorado: a historical, descriptive and statistical
work on the Rocky Mountain gold and silver mining
region... Denver, Daily tribune, 1876.
1 p.l., 470, ix p.   front., illus., pl.

16540   Foster, George G   , d. 1850, ed.
The gold regions of California: being a succinct
description of the geography, history, topography,
and general features of California; including a
carefully prepared account of the gold region of that
fortunate country, prepared from official documents
and other authentic sources. New York, 1848.
80 p.   map.   22 cm.

16541   Foster, James S   , 1828-1890.
Outlines of history of the Territory of Dakota,
and emigrant's guide to the free lands of the Northwest... Accompanied with a new sectional map. By
James S. Foster... Yankton, Dakota Territory, M'Intyre

& Foster, printers, "Union and Dakotian" office, 1870.
127 p.   front. (fold. map)   23 cm.

16542 Fowler, Smith W   1829-1894.
Autobiographical sketch of Captain S. W. Fowler...
Together with an appendix containing his speeches on
the state of the Union, "Reconstruction" etc., also
his report on the "Soldiers' voting bill" made in the
Michigan Senate, etc. Manistee, Mich., Times and
standard steam power print, 1877.
2 p.l., 37, 61 p.   19 cm.

16543 France, George W
The struggles for life and home in the North-west.
By a pioneer homebuilder. Life, 1865-1889. [By] Geo.
W. France. New York, I. Goldmann, printer, 1890.
607, [1] p.   front. (port.)   illus. (incl. facsims.)
25 cm.
"The practical workings of Masonry, etc.": p. 551-607.

16544 France, Lewis B   , 1833-1907.
Mr. Dide, his vacation in Colorado. Madison, Wis.
[1890]
137 p.   pl.   19 cm.

16545 [France, Lewis B   ] 1833-1907.
With rod and line in Colorado waters. Denver, 1884.
151 p.   illus., map.

16546 Franklin, John Benjamin.
A cheap trip to the great Salt Lake City. An
annotated lecture delivered before the President of
America and representatives; the mayors of Liverpool
and Manchester. Ipswich, J. Scoggins [1864]
31 p.   19½ cm.

16547 Fraser, Mary (Crawford) d. 1922.
Seven years on the Pacific slope, by Mrs. Hugh
Fraser and Hugh C. Fraser... New York, Dodd, Mead
and company, 1914.
xii p., 1 l., 391 p. incl. front.   plates.
23½ cm.
A narrative of life in the Methow valley, Washington.

16548 Freeman, George D
Midnight and noonday; or, The incidental history
of southern Kansas and the Indian territory, giving
twenty years experience on the frontier... and

118

incidents happening in and around Caldwell, Kansas,
from 1871 until 1890. By G. D. Freeman. Caldwell,
Kan., 1892.
406 p.   front., plates, ports.   20 cm.

16549 Freemasons. Denver, Colorado.
Resolutions adopted by the Ancient and accepted
Scottish rite of freemasonry at Denver, Colo., Monday,
May 18th, 1914 [relative to the disturbances in the
coal mining districts of the state] [Denver, 1914]
[4] p.

16550 Freitas de Acosta, Alecia.
Ricardo Archila. Caracas, Escuela de Biblioteconomía
y Archivos, Facultad de Humanidades y Educación,
Universidad Central de Venezuela, 1968.
51 p., illus.   front. (port.)   17 cm.   (Serie
bibliográfica, 7)

16551 Frejes, Francisco, d. 1845.
Historia breve de la conquista de los estados inde-
pendientes del Imperio mexicano, escrita por fr.
Francisco Frejes... Edición del "Estado de Jalisco."
Guadalajara, Tip. de S. Banada, 1878.
277, [2] p.   23½ cm.

16552 Frémont, Donatien.
Archbishop Taché and the beginnings of Manitoba.
[Bismarck, State Historical Society of North Dakota,
1932]
107-146 p.   24 cm.
Reprinted from North Dakota historical quarterly,
v. 6, no. 2, January 1932.
Translated from the French by sister Mary Aquinas
Norton.

16553 Frémont, Mrs. Jessie (Benton) 1824-1902.
A year of American travel, by Jessie Benton Frémont.
New York, Harper & brothers, 1878.
1 p.l., [7]-190 p.   13 cm.   (On cover: Harper's
half-hour series. [v. 67])

16554 Frémont, John Charles, 1813-1890.
Memoirs of my life, by John Charles Frémont. Including in the narrative five journeys of western exploration, during the years 1842, 1843-4, 1845-6-7,
1848-9, 1853-4. Together with a sketch of the life
of Senator Benton, in connection with western expansion.

By Jessie Benton Frémont. A retrospect of fifty
years covering the most eventful periods of modern
American history... With maps and colored plates.
vol. 1. Chicago and New York, Belford, Clarke &
company, 1887.
    viii, [iii]-iv, [xv]-xix, 655 p.   front., plates,
ports., maps (part fold.)   28 cm.
    No more published.

16555 French, D'Arcy A
    English grammar simplified: in which it is clearly
    proved that in the grammars most commonly used in
    our schools, the principles, in the most important
    constructions, are grossly erroneous and defective:
    and in which some plain and very useful rules are
    laid down, for the direction of persons who have not
    sufficient leisure to enter into a minute study of
    this subject. In two lectures. By D. A. French...
    Galena [Ill.] W. C. E. Thomas, printer, 1846.
        48 p.   19 cm.

16556 French, Leigh Hill, 1863-
    Seward's land of gold; five seasons experience
    with the gold seekers in northwestern Alaska, by
    L. H. French... New York, Montross, Clarke & Emmons
    [1905?]
        3 p.l., xii p., 1 l., 101 p.   front., plates,
    ports.   22 cm.

16557 French, Samuel Gibbs, 1818-1910.
    Report of Captain S. G. French, United States Army,
    descriptive of the route from San Antonio to El Paso.
    [San Antonio, Tex.] 1849.
        23 p.

16558 Frewen, Moreton, 1853-
    Melton Mowbray, and other memories, by Moreton
    Frewen. London, H. Jenkins limited, 1924.
        viii p., 2 l., 311 p.   front., plates, ports.
    21½ cm.

16559 Frignet, Ernest, b. 1823.
    La Californie. Historie des progrès de l'un des
    États-Unis d'Amérique, et des institutions qui font
    sa prospérité; par Ernest Frignet... 2. ed., rev.
    et enrichie d'une carte de la California. Paris,
    Schlesinger frères, 1867.
        2 p.l., xxvi, 479 p.   fold. map.   23 cm.

16560   Frizzell, Mrs. Lodisa.
        Across the plains to California in 1852; journal
        of Mrs. Lodisa Frizzell, ed. from the original manu-
        script in the New York public library by Victor Hugo
        Paltsits... [New York] The New York public library,
        1915.
           30 p.   3 pl., 3 maps on 1 pl.   25½ cm.
        Reprinted, May 1915, from the Bulletin of the New
        York public library of April 1915."

16561   Frost, John, 1800-1859.
        ... History of the state of California from the
        period of the conquest by Spain, to her occupation
        by the United States of America... also advice to
        emigrants on the best routes, and the preparations
        necessary to get there... Auburn, N. Y., 1850.
           508 p.   front., illus., pl.
        At head of title: Frost's pictorial history of
        California.

16562   Frost, John, 1800-1859.
        Thrilling adventures among the Indians: comprising
        the most remarkable personal narratives of events
        in the early Indian wars, as well as of incidents in
        the recent Indian hostilities in Mexico and Texas.
        By John Frost... Illustrated with numerous engravings,
        from designs by W. Croome and other distinguished
        artists. Philadelphia, J. W. Bradley, 1849.
           448 p. incl. illus., plates, ports.   col. front.
        (port.)   23½ cm.

16563   Fuller, Henry Clay.
        Adventures of Bill Longley. Captured by Sheriff
        Milton Mast and Deputy Bill Burrows, near Keatchie,
        Louisiana, in 1877, and was executed at Giddings,
        Texas, 1878. Nacogdoches, Texas [Baker printing
        co., n.d.]
           4 p.l., [68] p.   front. (port.)   22 cm.

16564   Fullerton, T   M
        St. Louis River, by Rev. T. M. Fullerton. St. Paul,
        Minnesota Historical Society, 1852. (In Annals of
        the Minnesota Historical Society, 1852, p. 27-28)

16565   Fulmore, Zachary Taylor, 1846-
        The history and geography of Texas as told in
        county names, by Z. T. Fulmore... [Austin, Press
        of E. L. Steck, c1915]

ix, 312 p.   illus. (incl. ports., maps)
facsims., tables.   24 cm.

16566 Fulton, Alexander R   1825-1891.
       The red men of Iowa: being a history of the
       various aboriginal tribes whose homes were in Iowa;
       sketches of chiefs, traditions, Indian hostilities,
       incidents and reminiscences; with a general account
       of the Indians and Indian wars of the Northwest; and
       also an appendix relating to the Pontiac war. By
       A. R. Fulton... Des Moines, Mills & company, 1882.
       559 p.   front., plates, ports.   23½ cm.

16567 Fulton, Ambrose Cowperthwaite.
       A life's voyage; a diary of a sailor on sea and
       land, jotted down during a seventy-years' voyage.
       By Ambrose Cowperthwaite Fulton. New York, The author,
       1898.
       vii, 555 p.   front., plates, ports.   20 cm.

16568 Fulton, Frances I   Sims
       To and through Nebraska. By a Pennsylvania girl.
       Lincoln, Journal co., 1884.
       273 p.   18 cm.

16569 Furlong, Thomas, 1844-
       Fifty years a detective, by Thomas Furlong...
       35 real detective stories... St. Louis, Mo., For sale
       by C. E. Barnett [c1912]
       2 p.l., [3]-352 p., 1 l.   illus. (incl. ports.)
       20 cm.

16570 Furnas, Robert Wilkinson, 1824-1905.
       Nebraska. Her resources, advantages, advancement
       and promises. Prepared and comp. by Robt. W. Furnas.
       New Orleans, F. A. Brandao & co., 1885.
       32 p.   23 cm.

                              G

16571 Gage, Emma Abbott.
       Western wanderings and summer saunterings through
       picturesque Colorado... Baltimore, The Friedenwald
       co., 1900.
       2 p.l., 262 p.   pl., port.

16572　Gannett, Henry.
　　　　　A gazetteer of Texas. Washington, 1902.
　　　　　162 p.　　maps.　　　　　(U. S. Geological
　　　　　survey. Bulletin no. 190)

16573　Gannon, Clell G
　　　　　A short account of a rowboat journey from Medora to
　　　　　Bismarck. [Bismarck, N. D., State Historical Society
　　　　　of North Dakota, 1926]
　　　　　16-23 p.　　illus.　　25 cm.
　　　　　In North Dakota historical quarterly, v. 1, no. 1,
　　　　　Oct. 1926.

16574　Garland, Hamlin, 1860-1940.
　　　　　Boy life on the prairies, by Hamlin Garland...
　　　　　illustrated by E. W. Deming. New York, The Macmillan
　　　　　company; London, Macmillan & co., ltd., 1900.
　　　　　x, 423 p.　　front., illus., plates.　　20 cm.

16575　Garland, Hamlin, 1860-1940.
　　　　　A son of the middle border, by Hamlin Garland; with
　　　　　illustrations by Alice Barber Stephens. New York,
　　　　　The Macmillan company, 1917.
　　　　　vii p., 1 l., 467 p.　　front., plates.　　20 cm.
　　　　　A story of the author's early life.

16576　Garrard, Lewis Hector, 1829-1887.
　　　　　Memoir of Charlotte Chambers. By her grandson,
　　　　　Lewis H. Garrard. Philadelphia, Printed for the
　　　　　author, 1856.
　　　　　vii p., 2 l., lx, 135 p.　　22 cm.
　　　　　Historical sketch: lx p.
　　　　　"Consists [principally] of letters written by Mrs.
　　　　　Chambers, while living near Cincinnati, from 1797 to
　　　　　1821. These relate mainly to the early settlement
　　　　　of Cincinnati, and the Northwest territory, and also
　　　　　give an account of the Ludlow family, including a
　　　　　narrative of Israel Ludlow's connection with Mathias
　　　　　Denman and Robert Patterson in the proprietorship of
　　　　　the law on which Cincinnati now stands." - P. G.
　　　　　Thompson, Bibl. of ... Ohio, 1880, p. 129-130.

16577　Garrido, Luis.
　　　　　Antonio Caso, una vida profunda. Prólogo de Luis
　　　　　Recasens-Siches. México, Biblioteca de Ensayos
　　　　　Sociológicos, Instituto de Investigaciones Sociales,
　　　　　Universidad Nacional Autónoma de México, 1961.
　　　　　162 p.　　illus.　　19 cm.　　(Cuadernos de sociología)

16578 Garrison, George P
      Texas: a contest of civilizations. Boston, 1903.
      320 p.   facsim., map.   13 cm.   (American
      commonwealths)

16579 Garza Mereado, Ario.
      Las bibliotecas de la Universidad de Nuevo León;
      estudio de recursos y necesidades, bases para un
      proyecto de reforma. Monterrey, Departamento de
      Bibliotecas UNL, 1966.
      1 v. (various pagings)   forms.   28 cm.

16580 Gasparin, Agénor Étienne, comte de, 1810-1871.
      The uprising of a great people. The United States
      in 1861. From the French of Count Agénor de Gasparin,
      by Mary L. Booth. 4th ed. New York, Charles
      Scribner, 1861.
      1 p.l., [v]-x p., 1 l., [9]-263 p.   17 cm.

16581 Gaston, Joseph, 1833-
      The centennial history of Oregon, 1811-1912, by
      Joseph Gaston. [With notice of antecedent explorations]
      ... Chicago, The S. J. Clarke publishing company,
      1912.
      4 v.   front., plates, ports., maps, facsims.
      27½ cm.

16582 Gay, Frederick A
      ... Sketches of California. An account of the life,
      manners and customs of the inhabitants. Its history,
      climate, soil, productions, &c. By Frederick A. Gay.
      Also interesting information in relation to cancha-
      lagua, a Californian plan of rare medicinal virtues .
      [New York, 1848] [Tarrytown, N. Y., Reprinted,
      W. Abbatt, 1925]
      (In Magazine of history, with notes and queries.
      Tarrytown, N. Y., 1925. 26½ cm. Extra number.
      no. 110 (v. 28, no. 2) 3 p.l., [9]-47 p.)

16583 Gazeteer [!] of Utah, and Salt Lake City directory...
      1869, 1874. Salt Lake City, Utah, "Salt Lake
      herald" publishing company, 1869-1874.
      1 v.   fold. map.   24 cm.
      Title varies: 1869 The Salt Lake City directory
      and business guide, 1874 Gazeteer [!] of Utah, and
      Salt Lake City directory. Compiler: 1869, 1874 E. L.
      Sloan. Publishers: 1869 E. L. Sloan & co., 1874
      "Salt Lake Herald" publishing company.

16584 Gebow, Joseph A
       A vocabulary of the Snake, or, Sho-sho-nay dialect,
       by Joseph A. Gebow, interpreter. 2d ed., rev. and
       improved, January 1st, 1864. Green River City, Wg.
       Ter., Freeman & bro., printers, 1868.
       24 p.   20 cm.

16585 Geer, Theodore T   1851-
       Fifty years in Oregon; experiences, observations,
       and commentaries upon men, measures, and customs in
       pioneer days and later times, by T. T. Geer...
       New York, The Neale publishing company, 1912.
       536 p.   front., plates, ports.   22½ cm.

16586 Gems from the Pike's Peak route. [n.p., n.d.]
       50 mounted photographs in cover.

16587 Gerstäcker, Friedrich Wilhelm Christian, 1816-1872.
       Scènes de la vie californienne, par F. Gerstäcker;
       tr. de l'allemand par Gustave Revilliod. Genève,
       Impr. de J. G. Fick, 1859.
       260 p., 1 l.   plates.   23 cm.
       German original, Leipzig, 1856, pub. under title:
       Californische skizzen.

16588 Gerstäcker, Friedrich Wilhelm Christian, 1816-1872.
       Wild sports in the far West, by Frederick Gerstäcker.
       Translated from the German. Illustrated by Harrison
       Weir. Philadelphia, J. B. Lippincott & co., 1878.
       xi, 396 p.   front., plates.

16589 Gibbons, James Joseph.
       In the San Juan, Colorado; sketches, by Rev. J. J.
       Gibbons. [Chicago, Calumet book and engraving co.,
       1898]
       194 p.   plates.   18½ cm.

16590 Gibbs, Josiah Francis, 1845-
       Black Hawk's last raid - 1866, by Josiah F. Gibbs.
       Salt Lake City, Utah State Historical Society, 1931.
       (In Utah historical quarterly, v. 4, no. 4, October
       1931, p. 110-128)

16591 Gibbs, Josiah Francis, 1845-
       Gunnison Massacre - 1853 - Millard County, Utah -
       Indian Mareer's version of the tragedy - 1894, by
       Josiah F. Gibbs. Salt Lake City, Utah State
       Historical Society, 1928. (In Utah historical

quarterly, v. 1, no. 3, July 1928, p. 67-75)

16592 Gibbs, Josiah Francis, 1845-
Moshoquop, the avenger, as loyal friend, by Josiah
F. Gibbs. Salt Lake City, Utah State Historical
Society, 1929. (In Utah historical quarterly, v. 2,
no. 1, January 1929, p. 3-8)

16593 Gibbs, Josiah Francis, 1845-
The Mountain Meadows massacre, by Joseph F. Gibbs...
Illustrated by nine full-page and five half-page
engravings from photographs taken on the ground.
[Salt Lake City] Salt Lake tribune publishing co.
[c1910]
59 p. incl. illus. (incl. port.) pl.   22½ cm.
Second edition.

16594 Gibson, J   Watt, b. 1829.
Recollections of a pioneer, by J. W. (Watt) Gibson.
[St. Joseph, Mo., Press of Nelson-Hanne printing
co., 1912]
216 p.   front. (port.)   20 cm.

16595 Gifford, Ruth   comp.
Early California, historical highlights, 1540-1848,
compiled and edited by Ruth Gifford; together with
a few suggestions to give added interest to your
vacation. Los Angeles, Calif., C. T. Henderson [1935]
52 p.   illus.   25½ cm.

16596 Gift, George Washington, b. 1833.
Something about California: being a description
of its climate, health, wealth and resources, com-
pressed into small compass. Marin county: its
industries, roads... and paragraphs describing the
sanatarium [!] of San Rafael... By George W. Gift.
San Rafael, The San Rafael herald, 1875.
cover-title, 32 p.   23 cm.

16597 Gilbert, James H
... Trade and currency in early Oregon; a study
in the commercial and monetary history of the Pacific
northwest... New York, 1907.
126 p.   22 cm.   (Columbia University Studies
in history, economics, and public law, v. 26)

16598 Gillette, J   M
The advent of the American Indian into North

Dakota. [Bismarck, State Historical Society of
North Dakota, 1932]
     210-220 p.   24 cm.
     Reprinted from North Dakota historical quarterly,
v. 6, no. 3, April 1932.

16599 Gillette, J   M
       Mounds and mound builders of the United States, by
       J. M. Gillette. [Bismarck, State Historical Society
       of North Dakota, 1944]
          139-208 p.   24 cm.
          Reprinted from North Dakota historical quarterly,
       v. 11, no. 3, July 1944.
          Bibliographical footnotes.

16600 Gillette, J   M
       Study of population trends in North Dakota, by
       J. M. Gillette. [Bismarck, State Historical Society
       of North Dakota, 1942]
          179-198 p.   maps, diagrs.   24 cm.
          Reprinted from North Dakota historical quarterly,
       v. 9, no. 3, April 1942.

16601 Gillmore, Parker.
       A hunter's adventures in the great West. By Parker
       Gillmore ("Ubique")... London, Hurst and Blackett,
       1871.
          1 p.l., [vii]-x, 3-336 p.   front.   22 cm.

16602 Gilpin, William, 1822-1894.
       Mission of the North American people, geographical,
       social, and political. Illustrated by six charts
       delineating the physical architecture and thermal
       laws of all the continents. By William Gilpin...
       Philadelphia, J. B. Lippincott & co., 1873.
          217 p.   fold. maps (incl. front.)   23½ cm.
          First published in 1860 under title: The central
       gold region. The grain, pastoral, and gold regions
       of North America.
          The appendix, p. 125-217, contains speeches by the
       author, 1847-1868, etc.

16603 Gilpin, William, 1822-1894.
       Notes on Colorado; and its inscription in the
       physical geography of the North American continent,
       by William Gilpin, governor of the territory of
       Colorado. [London, Printed by Witherby and co.,
       1870?]
          52 p.   18 cm.

16604 [Gilpin, William] 1822-1894.
       The parks of Colorado. [San Luis di Calebra?]
       Col., 1866
       6 p.   23½ cm.
       Also printed as "Description of the San Luis park:
       by the Hon. William Gilpin" p. 22-34 of "Colorado:
       its resources, parks, and prospects... By William
       Blackmore... London, 1869".

16605 Gittinger, Roy.
       The formation of the state of Oklahoma (1803-1906)...
       Berkeley, University of California Press, 1917.
       xii, 256 p.   front., maps (part fold.)   25 cm.
       (Half-title: University of California publications
       in history, v. VI)

16606 Glaspell, Mrs. Kate Eldridge.
       Incidents in the life of a pioneer, by Mrs. Kate
       Eldridge Glaspell. [Bismarck, State Historical
       Society of North Dakota, 1941]
       184-190 p.   24 cm.
       Reprinted from North Dakota historical quarterly,
       v. 8, no. 3, April 1941.

16607 Glazier, Willard, 1841-1905.
       Ocean to ocean on horseback; being the story of a
       tour in the saddle from the Atlantic to the Pacific;
       with especial reference to the early history and
       development of cities and towns along the route;
       and regions traversed beyond the Mississippi...
       Philadelphia, W. Ziegler company [1895]
       xvii, [1] p., 1 l., 21-544 p. incl. front., plates.
       19 cm.

16608 Glisan, Rodney, 1827-1890.
       Journal of army life. By R. Glisan. San Francisco,
       A. L. Bancroft and company, 1874.
       xi, 511 p.   21 pl. (incl. front.)   fold. tab.
       22½ cm.
       Garrison life on the border; Oregon and Washington
       Indian wars, 1855-1858.

16609 Goodlander, Charles W
       Memoirs and recollections of C. W. Goodlander of the
       early days of Fort Scott, from April 29, 1858, to
       January 1, 1870, covering the time prior to the
       advent of the railroad and during the days of the
       ox-team and stage transportation. And biographies

of Col. H. T. Wilson and Geo. A. Crawford, the fathers
of Fort Scott. Fort Scott, Kan., Monitor printing
co., 1900.
    145, [3] p.   front., illus., plates, ports.
16½ cm.

16610 Goodwin, Cardinal Leonidas, 1880-
    The establishment of state government in California
1846-1850, by Cardinal Goodwin, M. A. New York, The
Macmillan company, 1914.
    xiv p., 1 l., 359 p.   21 cm.

16611 Goodwin, Cardinal Leonidas, 1880-
    The question of the eastern boundary of California
in the convention of 1849. Austin, Texas [1913]
    [31] p.
    Reprinted from the Southwestern historical quarterly,
vol. XVI, no. 3, January, 1913, p. 227-58.

16612 Goodwin, Charles Carroll, 1832-1917.
    As I remember them, by C. C. Goodwin... Pub. by a
special committee of the Salt Lake commercial club...
Salt Lake City, Utah, 1913.
    360 p.   front. (port.)   22½ cm.
    Reminiscences mainly of California and Nevada
pioneers.

16613 Goodwin, Charles Carroll, 1832-1917.
    The Comstock club. By C. C. Goodwin... Salt Lake
City, Utah, Tribune printing company, 1891.
    4 p.l., 288 p.   23 cm.

16614 Goodwin, Charles Carroll, 1832-1917.
    The wedge of gold. By C. C. Goodwin... Salt
Lake City, Tribune Job Printing Office, 1893.
    283 p.   23 cm.

16615 Goodwin, Nathaniel Carl, 1857-1919.
    Nat Goodwin's book, Nat C. Goodwin... Boston,
R. G. Badger; [etc., etc., c1914]
    xv p., 1 l., 17-366 p.   front., plates, ports.
24½ cm.

16616 Gordon, S   Anna.
    Camping in Colorado, with suggestions to gold-
seekers, tourists and invalids... New York, The
Authors' publishing co. [1879]
    201 p.   20 cm.

16617   Gordon-Cumming, Constance Frederica, 1837-
        Granite crags of California. New ed. Edinburgh,
        1886.
        384 p.   fold. map, pl.   22½ cm.

16618   Gottfredson, Peter, ed.
        History of Indian depredations in Utah... Comp.
        and ed. by Peter Gottfredson. [Salt Lake City,
        Press of Skelton publishing co., c1919]
        352 p.   front., plates, ports.   19½ cm.

16619   Gouge, William M   1796-1863.
        The fiscal history of Texas, embracing an account
        of its revenues, debts, and currency, from the
        commencement of the revolution in 1834 to 1851-52,
        with remarks on American debts. Philadelphia, 1852.
        327 p.   20 cm.

16620   Goulder, William Armistead, 1821-
        Reminiscences; incidents in the life of a pioneer
        in Oregon and Idaho, by W. A. Goulder. Boise, Id.,
        T. Regan, 1909.
        376 p.   front. (port.)   20 cm.

16621   Graff, John Franklin.
        "Graybeard's" Colorado; or, Notes on the centennial
        state. Describing a trip from Philadelphia to Denver
        and back, in the autumn and winter of 1881-82...
        Philadelphia, J. B. Lippincott & co., 1882.
        90 p.   19½ cm.

16622   Grand Army of the Republic. Colorado, Department of.
        Colorado souvenir. [Dedicated by the department of
        Colorado, to the G.A.R., 22d National encampment,
        Columbus, Ohio, 1888] [Denver, 1888]
        48 p.   pl.   21½ cm.

16623   Granger, Lewis, 1819-1890.
        Letters: reports of the journey from Salt Lake
        to Los Angeles in 1849, and of conditions in
        southern California in the early fifties. Introd.
        and notes by Le Roy R. Hafen. Los Angeles, G.
        Dawson, 1959.
        50 p.   illus., port.   19 cm.   (Early California
        travels series, 47)

16624   Grant County, New Mexico, and her mineral prospects.
        1881. Denver, Col., The Tribune publishing company,

1881.
cover-title, 17 p.   fold. map.   22 cm.

16625 Graves, H   A
Andrew Jackson Potter, the fighting parson of the
Texan frontier. Six years of Indian warfare in New
Mexico and Arizona. Many wonderful events in his
ministerial life... By the Rev. H. A. Graves...
Nashville, Tenn., Southern Methodist publishing
house, 1881.
471 p.   front. (port.)   19 cm.

16626 Graves, Richard S
Oklahoma outlaws; a graphic history of the early
days in Oklahoma; the bandits who terrorized the
first settlers and the marshals who fought them to
extinction; covering a period of twenty-five years.
By Richard S. Graves... [Oklahoma City, State printing
& publishing co., 1915?]
3 p.l., [3]-131, [1] p.   illus. (ports.)
17½ cm.

16627 [Graves, S   H   ]
On the "White Pass" pay-roll, by the president of
the White Pass & Yukon route. Chicago [The Lakeside
press] 1908.
vii, 9-258 p.   front., 14 pl.   20½ cm.

16628 Gravier, Gabriel, 1827-1904.
Cavelier de La Salle de Rouen, par Gabriel Gravier...
Paris, Maisonneuve et c^e., 1871.
3 p.l., [5]-123 p.   facsim. (port.)   25½ cm.
"Bibliographie": p. [107]-123.

16629 Gray, William H
History of Oregon, 1792-1849, drawn from personal
observation and authentic information. Portland,
Oregon, 1870.
624 p.

16630 Gt. Brit. Foreign Office.
British diplomatic correspondence concerning
the republic of Texas, 1838-1846; ed. by Ephraim
Douglass Adams... Austin, Tex., The Texas state
historical association [1918?]
xii, 636 p.   23 cm.
"Reprinted from the Quarterly of the Texas state
historical association xv, nos. 3 and 4, and from

131

the Southwestern historical quarterly, XVI, no. I-XXI, no. 2, January, 1912-October, 1917."
The present publication consists mainly of letters and reports to the British government, hitherto unpublished, written by the two principal British officials stationed in Texas. They were Charles Elliot, chargé d'affaires, and William Kennedy, consul at Galveston" - Introd.

16631 Great trans-continental railroad guide, containing a full and authentic description of over five hundred cities, towns, villages, stations, government forts... summer resorts; where to look for and hunt the buffalo, antelope, deer, and other game; trout fishing, etc., etc. In fact, to tell you what is worth seeing - where to see it - where to go - how to go - and whom to stop with while passing... from the Atlantic to the Pacific Ocean... By Bill Dadd, the scribe [pseud.] Chicago, G. A. Crofutt & co., 1869.
    244 p.   front., illus., plates, port., fold. tab.
    17½ cm.
    "Bill Dadd", pseud. of H. Wallace Atwell.

16632 Greatorex, Eliza (Pratt) "Mrs. H. W. Greatorex," 1819-1897.
    Summer etchings in Colorado. By Eliza Greatorex. Introduction by Grace Greenwood [pseud.] New York, G. P. Putnam's sons [c1873]
    2 p.l., [3]-4 p., 1 l., [5]-96 p.   plates.   24 cm.

16633 Greely, A. W. & Glassford, W. A.
    Report on the climate of California and Nevada, with particular reference to questions of irrigation and water storage in the arid region. Washington, 1891.
    219 p.   maps.   23 cm.   (U. S. 51st Cong., 2d sess., 1891. House exec. doc. no. 287)

16634 Green, Charles Ransley, 1845-1915.
    ... Early days in Kansas. In Keokuks time on the Kansas reservation. Being various incidents pertaining to the Keokuks, the Sac & Fox Indians (Mississippi band) and tales of the early settlers, life on the Kansas reservation, located on the headwaters of the Osage River, 1846-1870... Charles R. Green, historian and publisher... Olathe, Kan., 1913.
    [101] p., front. (diagr.) pl., ports.   21 cm.
    (Green's historical series)

16635   Green, James Stephen, 1817-1870.
        Substance of an argument, made by J. S. Green,
        of Mo., before the Supreme court, U. S., in the case
        concerning the boundary line, between the state of
        Missouri and the state of Iowa. St. Louis, Printed
        at the Union job office, 1849.
        30 p.   22½ cm.

16636   Greene, Jeremiah Evarts, 1834-1902.
        The Santa Fé trade: its route and character. By
        J. Evarts Greene. Read as part of the report of the
        Council at the semi-annual meeting of the American
        antiquarian society, at Boston, April 26, 1893.
        Worcester, Mass., Press of C. Hamilton, 1893.
        20 p.   24½ cm.

16637   Greene, Mrs. Mary.
        Life, three sermons, and some of the miscellaneous
        writings of Rev. Jesse Greene... by his surviving
        companion, Mary Greene... Lexington, Mo., Patterson
        & Julian - Express machine press, 1852.
        280 p.   front. (port.)   19 cm.

16638   Greenhow, Robert, 1800-1854.
        The history of Oregon and California, and the other
        territories on the northwest coast of North America;
        accompanied by a geographical view and map of those
        countries, and a number of documents as proofs and
        illustration of the history. By Robert Greenhow...
        2d ed., rev., cor. and enl. Boston, C. C. Little and
        J. Brown; [etc., etc.] 1845.
        3 p.l., [iii]-xviii, 492 p.   fold. map.   23½ cm.

16639   Greenhow, Robert, 1800-1854.
        The history of Oregon and California, and the other
        territories of the north-west coast of North America;
        from their discovery to the present day. Accompanied
        by a geographical view of those countries, and a
        number of documents as proofs and illustrations of
        the history. By Robert Greenhow... 4th ed., rev.,
        cor., and enl. Boston, Printed for the author, by
        Freeman and Bolles, 1847.
        3 p.l., [iii]-xviii, 491 p.   illus.   22 cm.

16640   Greenhow, Robert, 1800-1854.
        Memoir, historical and political, on the northwest
        coast of North America, and the adjacent territories;
        illustrated by a map and a geographical view of those

countries. By Robert Greenhow, translator and
librarian to the Department of state... Washington,
Blair and Rives, printers, 1840.
  xi, [1]-228 p.   fold. map.   25 cm.   ([U.S.]
26th Cong., 1st sess. Senate. [Doc.] 474)
  Notes on the Louisiana purchase and the Southwest
are included, with brief accounts of overland journeys,
notably those of Alvar Nuñez Cabeza de Vaca (whose
wanderings for eight years, 1528-1536, brought him
to Cullacan, near the gulf of California) and the Lewis
and Clark expedition of 1804-1806.

16641 Gregg, Thomas, b. 1808.
         History of Hancock County, Illinois, together with
       an outline history of the State, and a digest of
       State laws. Chicago, C. C. Chapman, 1880.
         1036 p.   illus., ports., fold. col. map.   26 cm.

16642 Grenfell, Helen L
         The school lands of Colorado. Before the Denver
       Real Estate Exchange, June 6, 1902. Denver [1902]
         25 p.

16643 Grey, Frederick William.
         Seeking fortune in America, by F. W. Grey. With a
       frontispiece. London, Smith, Elder & co., 1912.
         xiv, 307 p.   front. (port.)   20 cm.

16644 Griffis, Joseph K   1852-
         Tahan, out of savagery into civilization; an auto-
       biography, by Joseph K. Griffis. New York, George H.
       Doran company [c1915]
         263 p.   front., ports.   20 cm.
         The author, son of "California Joe", a western
       hunter and trapper, and of Al-Zada, an Osage half-breed,
       was reared among the Kiowa Indians.

16645 Griffiths, D   jr.
         Two years' residence in the new settlements of
       Ohio, North America: with directions to emigrants.
       By D. Griffiths, jun. London, Westley and Davis;
       [etc., etc.] 1835.
         vii, [9]-197 p.   front.   17½ cm.
         Principally an account of the Western Reserve.

16646 Griffiths, David.
         Forage conditions on the northern border of the
       Great Basin, by David Griffiths... Washington,

Government Printing Office, 1902.
60 p.   illus., map.   22 cm.   (U. S.   Bureau of Plant Industry, Bulletin, 15)

16647 Grinnell, Joseph, 1877-
Gold hunting in Alaska as told by Joseph Grinnell.
Ed. by Elizabeth Grinnell... Elgin, Ill., Chicago,
David C. Cook publishing company [c1901]
96 p.   illus.   21½ cm.

16648 [Grinnell, Josiah Bushnell] 1821-1891.
The home of the Badgers, or, A sketch of the early
history of Wisconsin, with a series of familiar letters
and remarks on territorial character and characteristics, etc. By Oculus [pseud.]... Milwaukie,
Wilshire & co., 1845.
36 p.   18 cm.

16649 Grinnell, Josiah Bushnell, 1821-1891.
Men and events of forth years. Autobiographical
reminiscences of an active career from 1850 to 1890,
by the late Josiah Busnell [!] Grinnell. With introduction by Prof. Henry W. Parker, D.D. Boston, D.
Lothrop company [c1891]
1 p.l., [vii]-xvi, 426 p.   front., plates, ports.
22½ cm.

16650 Griswold, Norman W
Beauties of California. Copyright 1883, by N. W.
Griswold. Views and descriptions of Yosemite Valley,
big trees, geysers, Lake Tahoe, Donner lake, San
Francisco, '49 & '83. Los Angeles, and towns...
of southern California. San Francisco, H. S. Crocker
& co., 1884.
[58] p.   col. plates.   23½ cm.

16651 Grund, Francis Joseph, 1805-1863.
Handbuch und wegweiser für auswanderer nach den
Vereinigten Staaten von Nordamerika und Texas...
Von Francis J. Grund. 2. aufl. Stuttgart und
Tübingen, J. G. Cotta, 1846.
iv, 278 p.   fold. map.   20 cm.

16652 Guinn, James Miller, 1834-
Historical and biographical record of southern
California; containing a history of southern California
from its earliest settlement to the opening year of
the twentieth century, by J. M. Guinn... 25 p.

Also containing biographies of well-known citizens
of the past and present. Chicago, Chapman pub. co.,
1902.
1295 p. incl. port.   29 cm.

16653 Guinn, James Miller, 1834-
A history of California and an extended history of
its southern coast counties, also containing biographies of well-known citizens of the past and
present. By J. M. Guinn... Los Angeles, Cal.,
Historic record company, 1907.
2 v.   ports.   29½ cm.

16654 Guinn, James Miller, 1834-
History of the state of California and biographical
record of Oakland and environs, also containing biographies of well-known citizens of the past and
present. Los Angeles, Historic record co. [1907]
2 v.   illus.   30 cm.

16655 Guinn, James Miller, 1834-
History of the state of California and biographical
record of Santa Cruz, San Benito, Monterey and San
Luis Obispo counties. An historical story of the
state's marvelous growth from its earliest settlement
to the present time, by Prof. J. M. Guinn... Also
containing biographies of well-known citizens of
the past and present. Chicago, The Chapman publishing
co., 1903.
3 p.l., 19-742 p. incl. ports.   29 cm.
On cover: Central coast, California.

16656 Guinn, James Miller, 1834-
History of the state of California and biographical
record of the San Joaquin Valley, California. An
historical story of the state's marvelous growth
from its earliest settlement to the present time,
by Prof. J. M. Guinn... Also containing biographies
of well-known citizens of the past and present.
Chicago, The Chapman pub. co., 1905.
3 p.l., 19-27, vii, [33]-1613 p.   plates, ports.
30 cm.

16657 Gunn, Lewis Carstairs, 1813-1892.
Records of a California family; journals and
letters of Lewis C. Gunn and Elizabeth Le Breton Gunn,
edited by Anna Lee Marston. San Diego, Cal., 1928.

6 p.l., 3-279, [2] p., 1 1.   col. front., illus.
(incl. map) pl., ports., facsims.   23½ cm.

H

16658 Hadden, James, 1845-
       Washington's expeditions (1753-1754) and Braddock's
       expedition (1755) with history of Tom Fausett, the
       slayer of General Edward Braddock, by James Hadden...
       [Uniontown? Pa., c1910]
       139 p.   front., plates, ports.   19 cm.

16659 Hafen, LeRoy R   , 1893-
       Utah food supplies sold to the pioneer settlers
       of Colorado, by LeRoy R. Hafen, historian and custo-
       dian, State Historical Society of Museum, Denver.
       Salt Lake City, Utah State Historical Society, 1931.
       (In Utah historical quarterly, v. 4, no. 2, April
       1931, p. 62-64)

16660 Hagadorn, Henry J   , 1832-1903.
       On the march with Sibley in 1863. The diary of
       Private Henry J. Hagadorn. [Bismarck, State Histori-
       cal Society of North Dakota, 1931]
       103-129 p.   24 cm.
       Reprinted from North Dakota historical quarterly,
       v. 5, no. 2, January 1931.
       Edited by John Perry Pritchett.

16661 Hailey, John, 1835-1921.
       The history of Idaho, by John Hailey. Boise, Id.,
       Press of Syms-York company, inc., 1910.
       5 p.l., 395, [5] p.   front. (port.)   25 cm.

16662 Hale, Edward Everett, 1822-1909.
       Kansas and Nebraska; history, geographical and
       physical characteristics, and political position of
       those territories, and account of the emigrant aid
       companies, and directions to emigrants... Boston,
       Phillips, Sampson & co.; New York, J. C. Derby, 1854.
       256 p.   map.   23 cm.

16663 Hall, A   J
       ... Early and authentic history of Omaha, 1857-1870.
       [Omaha] A. J. Hall [1870]
       cover-title, 64 p.   21½ cm.

137

16664 Hall, Angelo, 1868-
Forty-one thieves; a tale of California [by]
Angelo Hall. Boston, The Cornhill company [c1919]
4 p.l., 133 p., 1 l.   19½ cm.

16665 Hall, Barnes M   1803-1886.
The life of Rev. John Clark. By Rev. B. M. Hall.
With an introduction, by Bishop Morris. New-York,
Carlton & Porter, 1857.
276 p.   front. (port.)   18½ cm.

16666 Hall, Frank, 1836-1918.
History of the state of Colorado, embracing accounts
of the pre historic races and their remains; the
earliest Spanish, French and American explorations...
the first American settlements founded; the original
discoveries of gold in the Rocky mountains; the
development of cities and towns, with the various
phases of industrial and political transition,
from 1858 to 1890... By Frank Hall, for the Rocky
mountain historical company. Chicago, The Blakely
printing company, 1889-95.
4 v.   front., plates, ports.   26½ cm.

16667 Hall, Frederic, 1825-1898.
The history of San José and surroundings, with
biographical sketches of early settlers, by Frederic
Hall... San Francisco, A. L. Bancroft and co.,
1871.
xv, 537 p.   front., fold. map.   23½ cm.

16668 Hall, Trowbridge.
California trails, intimate guide to the old
missions; the story of the California missions, by
Trowbridge Hall. New York, The Macmillan company,
1920.
8 p.l., 3-243 p.   front., plates.   22 cm.

16669 Halley, William.
The centennial year book of Alameda County,
California, containing a summary of the discovery
and settlement of California; a description of the
Contra Costa under Spanish, Mexican and American
rule; an account of the organization and settlement
of Alameda County, with a yearly synopsis of important
events, down to the centennial year of American
independence, together with the important events
of the year 1876. Also, a gazetteer of each township,

138

useful local and general statistical information,
appropriate for the present time. To which are
added biographical sketches of prominent pioneers
and public men, by William Halley... Oakland, Cal.,
W. Halley, 1876.
xv, [1], 586 p.   front., plates, ports.   23 cm.

16670 Halliburton, William Henry, b. 1816.
History of Arkansas County, Arkansas, 1541 to 1875.
[n.p., n.d.]
190 p.   21½ cm.

16671 Hallock, Leavitt Homan, 1842-
Why our flag floats over Oregon; or, The conquest
of our great Northwest by Leavitt H. Hallock...
Portland, Me., Smith & Sale, 1911.
vii, [1] p., 1 l., 3-76 p., 1 l.   front., plates,
ports.   19½ x 10½ cm.
An account of Marcus Whitman and his relation
to the acquisition of Oregon.

16672 Hallum, John.
Biographical and pictorial history of Arkansas.
Vol. 1. Albany, 1887.
14-581 p.   port.
Vol. 1 all published.

16673 Halsey, Francis Whiting, 1851-1919.
The pioneers of Unadilla village, 1784-1840, by
Francis Whiting Halsey... Reminiscences of village
life and of Panama and California from 1840-1850, by
Gaius Leonard Halsey... Unadilla, N. Y., Sold by
the vestry of St. Matthew's church, 1902.
xv, 323 p.   front., plates, ports., fold. plan.
19½ cm.

16674 Hambleton, Chalkley J   1829-
A gold hunter's experience, by Chalkley J. Hambleton.
Chicago [Printed by R. R. Donnelley and sons company]
1898.
1 p.l., 116 p., 1 l.   18½ cm.

16675 Hamblin, Jacob, 1819-
Early days in "Utah's Dixie". Salt Lake City,
Utah State Historical Society, 1932. (In Utah
historical quarterly, v. 5, no. 4, October 1932,
p. 130-134)

16676   Hamblin, Jacob, 1819-
        Jacob Hamblin, a narrative of his personal experience,
        as a frontiersman, missionary to the Indians and
        explorer, disclosing interpositions of providence,
        severe privations, perilous situations and remarkable
        escapes. Fifth book of the faith-promoting series,
        by James A. Little. Designed for the instruction
        and encouragement of young Latter-Day Saints. Salt
        Lake City, Juvenile Instructor Office, 1881.
        viii, [9]-144 p.   18 cm.

16677   Hamilton, B   B
        Historical sketch of Jersey county, Illinois.
        Delivered at Jerseyville, July 4, 1876, by B. B.
        Hamilton. Jacksonville, Ill., Courier steam
        printing house, 1876.
        36 p.   22 cm.

16678   Hamilton, H   W
        Rural sketches of Minnesota, the El Dorado of the
        Northwest; containing full descriptions of the
        country - its productions, villages, state of
        society, &c.; together with a series of letters upon
        northern Wisconsin, its appearance, improvements, &c.:
        with a table of distances. By H. W. Hamilton.
        Milan, O., G. Waggoner, 1850.
        40 p.   23 cm.

16679   Hamilton, Henry S   1836?-
        Reminiscences of a veteran, by Henry S. Hamilton.
        Concord, N. H., Republican press association, 1897.
        2 p.l., 180 p.   front., illus. (incl. ports.)
        18½ cm.

16680   Hamilton, William B
        ... A social survey of Austin, by William B.
        Hamilton. Austin, University of Texas, 1913.
        89, xix p.   illus. tables.   23 cm.   (Texas.
        University. Bulletin, no. 273. Humanities series,
        no. 15. 15 March 1913)

16681   Hamilton, William Thomas, 1822-1908.
        My sixty years on the plains trapping, trading,
        and Indian fighting, by W. T. Hamilton ("Bill
        Hamilton") ed. by E. T. Sieber; with eight full-
        page illustrations by Charles M. Russell. New York,
        Forest and stream publishing co., 1905.
        244 p. incl. front. (port.)   17 pl.   21½ cm.

16682 Hamilton, Wilson.
The new empire and her representative men; or,
The Pacific coast, its farms, mines, vines, wines,
orchards and interests... with interesting biographies and modes of travel. Oakland, Cal., 1886.
184 p.   pl.   22 cm.

16683 Hamlin, Hannibal, 1809-1891.
Speech... on the proposition to admit California
as a state into the Union delivered in the Senate of
the United States. March 5, 1850. Washington, 1850.
14 p.   24 cm.

16684 Hammond, Isaac B
Reminiscences of frontier life, compliments of
I. B. Hammond... [Portland? Or.] 1904.
134 p., 1 l. incl. illus., ports.   21 cm.

16685 Hanbury, David T
Sport and travel in the northland of Canada, by
David T. Hanbury. New York, The Macmillan company;
London, E. Arnold, 1904.
xxxii, 319 p.   col. front., illus., 36 pl. (4 col.)
2 fold. maps.   23 cm.
"Eskimo words and phrases": p. 294-312.

16686 Hand-book of Colorado... Denver, J. A. Blake &
F. C. Willett, 1872-
136 p.   illus., fold. maps.   15½ cm.
Advertising matter interspersed. Title varies;
edition of 1880: Tenth ed. Blake's hand-book of
Colorado... a guide for miners, settlers, tourists
and investors. 1872-73; 2d-3d year of publication.

16687 A handbook of reference to the history, chronology,
religion and country of the Latter-day Saints,
including the revelation on celestial marriage.
For the use of Saints and strangers. Salt Lake City,
Juvenile Instructor Office, 1884.
157 p.   19 cm.

16688 Handly, James.
The resources of Madison County, Montana. By
James Handly. [San Francisco, Francis & Valentine,
1872]
60 p.   23 cm.

16689   Handsaker, Samuel.
             Pioneer life. Eugene, Or., 1908.
             104 p.   pl., port., facsim.   23 cm.

16690   Hanna, Joseph A
             Dr. Whitman and his ride to save Oregon, by Rev.
        J. A. Hanna. [Los Angeles? 1903]
             8 p.   front. (port.)   23 cm.
             Read before the Association of Presbyterian ministers
        of Los Angeles, April 8, 1903.

16691   Hans, Frederic Malon, 1861-
             The great Sioux nation, by Fred M. Hans. A complete
        history of Indian life and warfare in America.
        The Indians as nature made them... Chicago, M. A.
        Donohue and company [c1907]
             575 p. incl. front. (port.)   illus.   22½ cm.

16692   Hanson, John Wesley, 1823-1901.
             The American Italy: the scenic wonderland of
        perfect climate, golden sunshine, ever-blooming
        flowers and always-ripening fruits. Southern California.
        By J. W. Hanson... Chicago, W. B. Conkey company
        [1896]
             xii, 13-296 p.   front., illus.   17½ x 23 cm.

16693   Hanson, Joseph Mills, 1876-
             ... With Sully into the Sioux land, by Joseph Mills
        Hanson... illustrated by John W. Norton. Chicago,
        A. C. McClurg & co., 1910.
             5 p.l., 9-407 p.   front., plates.   21 cm.
        ("Among the Sioux" series)

16694   Harby, Mrs. Lee (Cohen)
             The earliest Texas. Washington, 1892. American
        historical association, annual report for 1891.
        p. 199-205.

16695   Hardin, John J
             Speech on the annexation of Texas, delivered
        in the House of Representatives, Jan. 15, 1845.
        [Washington, 1845]
             13 p.   18 cm.

16696   Hardin, John Wesley, 1853-1895.
             The life of John Wesley Hardin, from the original
        manuscript, as written by himself. Seguin, Texas,

Smith & Moore, 1896.
1 p.l., 144 p.   illus. (incl. ports.)   19 cm.

16697   Hardy, Dermont H   ed.
        Historical review of south-east Texas and the
        founders, leaders and representative men of its
        commerce, industry and civic affairs; associate
        editors, Hon. Dermont H. Hardy... Major Ingham S.
        Roberts... Chicago, The Lewis publishing company,
        1910.
        2 v.   front., illus., ports. $27\frac{1}{2}$ x $21\frac{1}{2}$ cm.

16698   Hare, Mrs. Maud (Cuney)
        Norris Wright Cuney, a tribune of the black people...
        with an introduction by James S. Clarkson. New York,
        1913.
        xv, 230 p.   front., pl., port.   20 cm.

16699   Harlan, Jacob Wright.
        California '46 to '88; by Jacob Wright Harlan.
        Oakland, Pub. by the author, 1896.
        242 p.   front. (port.)   22 cm.
        Autobiography.

16700   Harman, S   W
        Hell on the border; he hanged eighty-eight men.
        A history of the great United States criminal court
        at Fort Smith, Arkansas, and of crime and criminals
        in the Indian Territory, and the trial and punishment
        thereof before... Judge Isaac C. Parker... and by the
        courts of said territory, embracing the leading
        sentences and charges to grand and petit juries
        delivered by the world famous jurist - his acknowl-
        edged masterpieces, besides much other legal lore.
        ... illustrated with over fifty fine half-tones.
        By S. W. Harman, compiled by C. P. Sterns. Fort
        Smith, Ark., The Phoenix publishing company [c1898]
        xiii, 720 p.   front., illus. (incl. ports.)
        22 cm.

16701   Harpending, Asbury.
        The great diamond hoax and other stirring incidents
        in the life of Asbury Harpending. Ed. by James H.
        Wilkins... San Francisco, The J. H. Barry co. [c1913]
        283 p.   ports. (incl. front.)   21 cm.

16702   [Harrington, Charles]
        Summering in Colorado. Denver, Richards & Co.,

1874.
158 p.   14 phot.   19½ cm.

16703 Harrington, Leonard E   , 1816-1883.
       Journal of Leonard E. Harrington. Salt Lake City,
       Utah State Historical Society, 1940. (In Utah
       historical quarterly, v. 8, no. 1, January 1940,
       pp. 3-64, i-vi)

16704 Harris, Branson Lewis, b. 1817.
       Some recollections of my boyhood [by] Branson L.
       Harris... [Indianapolis, The Hollenbeck press, 19-]
       1 p.l., 70 p.   1 illus.   20 cm.

16705 Harris, Frank, Judge, of Idaho.
       History of Washington county and Adams county;
       biography of Judge Frank Harris. [Weiser, Idaho,
       n.d.]
       3 p.l., 7-74 p.   front. (port.)   22 cm.

16706 Harris, J[ames] Morrison, 1818-1898.
       A paper upon California; read before the Maryland
       historical society... March 1849. Baltimore,
       For the Society, 1849.
       32 p.   20 cm.   [Maryland historical society.
       Publications]

16707 Harris, Sarah Hollister.
       An unwritten chapter of Salt Lake, 1851-1901, by
       Sarah Hollister Harris. New York, Printed privately,
       1901.
       88, [1] p.   18½ cm.

16708 Harris, William Richard, 1847-1923.
       The Catholic church in Utah, including an exposition
       of Catholic faith, by Bishop Scanlan. Salt Lake City,
       Intermountain Catholic Press [c1909]
       iii, iii, 350 p.   illus., ports., plates (1 double),
       double map.   25 cm.

16709 Hartford Union Mining and Trading Company.
       Around the Horn in '49. Journal of the Hartford
       Union Mining and Trading Company. Containing the
       name, residence and occupation of each member, with
       incidents of the voyage, &c. &c. Printed by L. J.
       Hall, on board the Henry Lee, 1849. [Wethersfield,
       Ct., Reprinted by Rev. L. J. Hall, 1898]

2 p.l., v, [1] p., 2 l., 252 p. incl. 21 pl.,
2 port.   front. (port.)   2 pl.   19 cm.

16710 Hartmann
Le Texas, ou Notice historique sur le Champ-d'asile
comprenant tout ce qui s'est passé depuis la formation
jusqu'à la dissolution de cette colonie, les causes
qui l'ont amenée, et la liste de tous les colons
français, avec renseignemens utiles à leurs familles...
Paris, Béguin [etc.] 1819.
5 p.l., ix, 11-135 p.   front.
"Par MM. Hartmann et Millard."

16711 Hartmann, Carl.
Geographisch-statistische beschreibung von Californien.
Aufschlüsse über die lage, den boden und das clima
des landes... mit besonderer berücksichtigung seines
mineralrichthums, namentlich der neuerlich so wichtigen
goldgewinnung und der vorzüglichsten dorthin gemachten
reisen. Nach den besten quellen bearbeitet...
Weimar, 1849.
2 v.   maps.   23 cm.

16712 Harvey, Fred.
California and the Grand canyon of Arizona. Los
Angeles, Cal., F. Harvey [c1914]
90 p.   21½ cm.

16713 Harwood, Thomas.
History of New Mexico Spanish and English missions
of the Methodist Episcopal church from 1850 to 1910.
In decades... By the Rev. Thomas Harwood... With
introductory notes. Albuquerque, N. M., El Abogado
press, 1908-10.
2 v.   front., illus., pl., ports.   19 cm.
On cover: v. 1, 1850-1884; v. 2, 1884-1910.

16714 Haskell, Thales H   , 1834-1909.
Journal of Thales H. Haskell (prepared for publication by Juanita Brooks) Salt Lake City, Utah State
Historical Society, 1944. (In Utah historical
quarterly, v. 12, nos. 1, 2, January, April, 1944,
p. 69-98)

16715 Haskins, C   W
Argonauts of California; being the reminiscences
of scenes and incidents that occurred in California
in early mining days, by a pioneer... New York,

145

1890.
501 p.   illus., pl.   22 cm.
Names of pioneers, pp. 360-501.

16716 Hastings, Frank Stewart.
A ranchman's recollections; an autobiography in
which unfamiliar facts bearing upon the origin of the
cattle industry in the Southwest and of the American
packing business are stated, and characteristic
incidents recorded, by Frank S. Hastings... Chicago,
Ill., The Breeder's gazette, 1921.
xiii, 235 p.   front., plates, ports.   20 cm.

16717 Hastings, Lansford Warren, 1819-ca. 1870.
A new history of Oregon and California: containing
complete descriptions of those countries, together
with the Oregon treaty and correspondence, and a vast
amount of information relating to the soil, climate,
productions, rivers and lakes, and the various routes
over the Rocky mountains, by Lansford W. Hastings...
Cincinnati, G. Conclin, 1847.
1 p.l., [5]-160 p.   22½ cm.
First published 1845 under title: The emigrants'
guide to Oregon and California.

16718 Hawkins, John Parker, 1830-
Memoranda concerning some branches of the Hawkins
family and connections, by Genl. John Parker Hawkins...
[Indianapolis, Ind., 1913]
137 p.   front., plates, ports.   23½ cm.

16719 Hawley, James Henry, 1847-1929, ed.
History of Idaho, the gem of the mountains. James
H. Hawley, editor... Chicago, The S. J. Clarke
publishing company, 1920.
4 v.   front., plates, ports., map.   18½ cm.
Vols. 2-4: Biographical.

16720 Hawthorne, Julian, 1846-1934.
The story of Oregon. A history with portraits
and biographies. New York, 1892.
2 v.   illus., port.

16721 Hayden, E   V
... Atlas of Colorado and portions of adjacent
territory... [Washington, D.C.?] 1877.
unpaged.   illus., diagr., maps.   27 cm.

At head of title: Department of the interior.
U. S. Geological and geographical surveys of the
territories.

16722 Hayden, Ferdinand Vandeveer, 1829-1887.
        The great West: its attractions and resources.
Containing a popular description of the marvellous
scenery, physical geography, fossils, and glaciers
of this wonderful region; and the recent explorations
in the Yellowstone park, "The wonderland of America,"
by Prof. F. V. Hayden... being an article written for
a work entitled "The great West." Philadelphia,
Pa., Franklin publishing co.; Bloomington, Ill.,
C. R. Brodix, 1880.
        cover-title, 17-87 p.   plates.   24 cm.

16723 Hayden, Ferdinand Vandeveer, 1829-1887.
        Sun pictures of Rocky Mountain scenery, with a
description of the geographical and geological
features, and some account of the resources of the
great West; containing thirty photographic views
along the line of the Pacific rail road, from Omaha
to Sacramento, by F. V. Hayden... New York, J. Bien,
1870.
        viii, 150 p., 1 l.   xxx mounted phot. (incl. front.)
32 x 24½ cm.

16724 Hayes, Augustus Allen, 1837-1892.
        Lincoln and Texas. [Chicago, 1885]
        3 p.   23 cm.
        From the Chicago Times, 13 Dec. 1885.

16725 Hayes, Augustus Allen, 1837-1892.
        New Colorado and the Santa Fe trail... New York,
Harper & brothers, 1880.
        200 p. incl. front. (map) illus.   23 cm.
        Articles reprinted from Harper's magazine and the
International review.

16726 Hayes, Jeff W   1853-1917.
        Paradise on earth, by Jeff. W. Hayes... Portland,
Or., F. W. Baltes and company, 1913.
        5 p.l., 112 p.   front. (port.)   21 cm.

16727 Hayne, M   H   E
        The pioneers of the Klondyke; being an account of
two years police service on the Yukon; narrated by
M. H. E. Hayne... and recorded by H. West Taylor.

Illustrated by photographs taken on the spot by the narrator. London, S. Low, Marston and company (limited) 1897.
xii p., 1 l., [2], 184 p. incl. front. (port.) map. plates. 19 cm.

16728 Hayter, Earl W
The Ponca removal. [Bismarck, State Historical Society of North Dakota, 1932]
262-275 p. 24 cm.
Reprinted from North Dakota historical quarterly, v. 6, no. 4, July 1932.

16729 Hazen, William Babcock, 1830-1887.
Our barren lands. The interior of the United States west of the 100th meridian, and east of the Sierra Nevadas. By Gen'l W. B. Hazen...
Cincinnati, R. Clarke & company, printers, 1875.
53 p. 23½ cm.

16730 Health, wealth and pleasure in Colorado and New Mexico: a reliable treatise on the famous pleasure and health resorts and the rich mining and agricultural regions of the Rocky Mountains. Chicago, 1881.
127 p. 21½ cm.

16731 Hearne, Samuel, 1745-1792.
A journey from the Prince of Wales's fort in Hudson's bay, to the Northern ocean. Undertaken by order of the Hudson's bay company, for the discovery of copper mines, a northwest passage, &c., in the years 1769, 1770, 1771, & 1772. By Samuel Hearne. London, A. Strahan and T. Cadell, 1795.
xliv, 458, [2] p. front., plates (part fold.) fold. maps. 30½ x 24 cm.

16732 Hebard, Grace Raymond, 1861-1936.
The government of Wyoming: the history, constitution and administration of affairs... by Grace Raymond Hebard... San Francisco, The Whitaker & Ray company (incorporated) 1904.
250 p. incl. plates, maps. front. 20½ cm.

16733 Hebard, Grace Raymond, 1861-1936.
The pathbreakers from river to ocean; the story of the great West from the time of Coronado to the present [by] Grace Raymond Hebard... four maps and numerous illustrations. Chicago, The Lakeside press,

1911.
x p., 1 l., 263 p. incl. front., illus., ports.,
4 maps.   19½ cm.

16734   Heermans, Forbes, 1856-
Thirteen; stories of the far West, by Forbes Heermans.
Syracuse, N. Y., C. W. Bardeen, 1887.
263 p.   18½ cm.
Contents. - Shingles. - The widow of the late Smith. -
Alanascar and his uncle. - The ascent of Uncompahgre. -
The descent of Uncompahgre. - Buried under an avalanche.
The wedding at Puerta da Luna. - On watch with the
night herd. - Don Quixote de Santa Rosa. - The assayer's
story. - The log of a landsman. - Molokai. - Death's
valley. - The home of everlasting fire.

16735   Helms, Ludvig V
Pioneering in the far East, and journeys to
California in 1849 and to the White sea in 1878.
London, 1882.
[6],408 p.   illus.   19 cm.

16736   Helper, Hinton Rowan, 1829-1909.
The land of gold. Reality versus fiction. By
Hinton R. Helper. Baltimore, Pub. for the author,
by H. Taylor, 1855.
xii, [13]-300 p.   19 cm.

16737   Hempstead, Fay.
A history of the state of Arkansas. For the use
of schools... New Orleans, F. F. Hansell & bro.
[1889]
2 p.l., 236 p.   illus., port., maps.   19 cm.

16738   Henderson, John.
Speech on the resolution for the annexation of
Texas, in Senate, February 20, 1845. [Washington,
1845]
16 p.   19 cm.

16739   Henry, James P
Resources of the state of Arkansas, with description of counties, railroads, mines, and the city
of Little Rock, the commercial, manufacturing,
political and railroad center of the state. Ed. 2.
Little Rock, 1872.
166 p.   map.   21 cm.

16740   Henshaw, David, 1791-1852.
        Letters on the internal improvements and commerce
        of the West, by Hon. David Henshaw. Boston, Dutton
        and Wentworth, 1839.
        29 p.   24 cm.
        Published original in the Morning post, Boston.

16741   Henshaw, Henry Wetherbee, 1850-
        ... Perforated stones from California, by Henry W.
        Henshaw. Washington, Govt. print. off., 1887.
        34 p.   illus.   24½ cm.   (U. S. Bureau of
        American ethnology. [Bulletin, no. 2])
        At head of title: Smithsonian institution.
        Bureau of ethnology.

16742   Hermann, Binger.
        The Louisiana Purchase and our title west of the
        Rocky Mountains, with a review of annexation by the
        United States, by Binger Hermann... Republished by
        joint resolution of Congress. Washington, Govt.
        print. off., 1900.
        87 p.   fold. maps.   27 cm.

16743   Herndon, Dallas T
        Arkansas history commission and its work; address
        prepared for the forty-fourth annual session of the
        Arkansas state teachers' association. Dec. 27-29,
        1911, Little Rock, Ark. Little Rock, 1911.
        16 p.   19 cm.

16744   Herndon, Sarah (Raymond)
        Days on the road; crossing the plains in 1865, by
        Sarah Raymond Herndon. New York, Burr printing
        house, 1902.
        xvi, 270 p.   front. (port.)   18½ cm.

16745   Herndon, William Henry, 1818-1891.
        Herndon's Lincoln; the true story of a great life...
        The history and personal recollections of Abraham
        Lincoln, by William H. Herndon... and Jesse
        William Weik... Chicago, New York [etc.] Belford,
        Clarke & company; [etc., etc., c1889]
        3 v.   front., plates, ports., facsims. (1 fold.)
        20 cm.

16746   Hervey, George W[ashington] 1846-   comp.
        A condensed history of Nebraska for fifty years
        to date... comp. by Geo. W. Hervey... Omaha, Neb.,

Nebraska farmer co., 1903.
140 p. incl. front., illus.   21½ cm.
Cover-title: Nebraska's resources.

16747 Hess, John W   , 1824-
John W. Hess, with the Mormon Battalion. Salt Lake
City, Utah State Historical Society, 1931. (In
Utah historical quarterly, v. 4, no. 2, April 1931,
p. 47-55)

16748 [Hewitt, Girart]
Minnesota: its advantages to settlers. Being a
brief synopsis of its history and progress, climate,
soil, agricultural and manufacturing facilities,
commercial capacities, and social status; its lakes,
rivers and railroads; homestead and exemption laws;
embracing a concise treatise on its climatology, in
a hygienic and sanitary point of view... [St. Paul,
Press printing company] 1867.
36 p.   22 cm.

16749 Heye, George Gustav, 1874-
Certain aboriginal pottery from southern California,
by George G. Heye. [New York, Museum of the American
Indian, Heye foundation, 1919]
46 p.   illus., xxi pl. (incl. double map)   17 cm.
(Added t.-p.: Indian notes and monographs... vol. VII,
no. 1)

16750 Hichborn, Franklin.
Story of the session of the California legislature
of 1909, by Franklin Hichborn... San Francisco,
Press of the James H. Barry company, 1909.
296, ii-xxxiii p. incl. tables.   20 cm.

16751 Hickman, William A   1815-1877 or 8.
Brigham's destroying angel: being the life,
confession, and startling disclosures of the notorious
Bill Hickman, the Danite chief of Utah. Written by
himself, with explanatory notes by J. H. Beadle...
Introduction by Richard B. Shepard... Salt Lake
City, Utah, Shepard book company, 1904.
vii, [2], 10-221 p. incl. front. (port.)   illus.
17½ x 13½ cm.

16752 Hicks, Edmund Warne, 1841-
History of Kendall county, Illinois, from the
earliest discoveries to the present time, by Rev.

151

E. W. Hicks... Aurora, Ill., Knickerbocker & Hodder, 1877.
viii, [9]-438 p. incl. front. 19½ cm.

16753 Higgins, Charles A
To California and back; by C. A. Higgins, illustrations by J. T. McCutcheon. Chicago, Passenger dept. Santa Fe route, 1893.
1 p.l., 151, [1] p. incl. illus., map. 20½ cm.

16754 Hilgard, Theodor Erasmus, 1790-1873.
Meine erinnerungen. Von Theodor Hilgard, d. ält. (Nicht zur veröffentlichung bestimmt.) [Heidelberg, Druck von G. Mohr, 1860?]
1 p.l., 379, [1] p. front. (port.) plates. 20½ cm.
Dated at end: Heidelberg, geschrieben 1856-58.
The author came to the United States in 1835, and settled near Belleville, Illinois; he returned to Germany about twenty years later.

16755 Hill, Mrs. Alice (Polk) 1854-
Colorado pioneers in picture and story, by Alice Polk Hill. [Denver, Brock-Haffner press, c1915]
xv, 544 p. front., illus. (incl. ports.) 19½ cm.
Called by the author a "revised edition" of her "Tales of the Colorado pioneers," Denver, 1884.

16756 Hill, Mrs. Alice (Polk) 1854-
Tales of the Colorado pioneers. Denver, Pierson & Gardner, 1884.
319 p. illus. 19½ cm.

16757 Hill, John Alexander, 1858-1916.
Stories of the railroad, by John A. Hill. New York, Doubleday & McClure co., 1899.
5 p.l., 7-297 p. front., 7 pl. 19 cm.

16758 Hill, Joseph J
Spanish and Mexican exploration and trade northwest from New Mexico into the Great Basin, 1765-1853, by Joseph J. Hill. Salt Lake City, Utah State Historical Society, 1939. (In Utah historical quarterly, v. 3, no. 1, January 1930, p. 2-23)

16759 Hill, Luther B
A history of the state of Oklahoma, by Luther B.

Hill, A.B., with the assistance of local authorities...
Chicago, New York, The Lewis publishing company, 1908.
2 v.   ports., maps.   28 cm.

16760   [Himmelwright, Abraham Lincoln Artman] 1865-
In the heart of the Bitter-Root mountains; the
story of "the Carlin hunting party," September-
December, 1893. By Heclawa [pseud.]... New York
[etc.] G. P. Putnam's sons, 1895.
xx p., 1 l., 259 p.   front., illus., plates,
fold. map.   19½ cm.

16761   Hines, Gustavus.
Life on the plains of the Pacific. Oregon: its
history, conditions and prospects; containing a
description of the geography, climate and productions,
with personal adventures among the Indians during a
residence of the author on the plains bordering the
Pacific, while connected with the Oregon mission;
embracing extended notes of a voyage around the
world. Buffalo, 1851.
437 p.   port.   20 cm.

16762   Hines, Gustavus.
Oregon and its institutions; comprising a full
history of the Willamette university, the first
established on the Pacific coast. New York [1868]
326 p.   pl., ports.   20 cm.

16763   Hines, Gustavus.
A voyage round the world, with a history of the
Oregon mission, and notes of several years residence
on the plains bordering the Pacific ocean: comprising
an account of interesting adventures among the Indians
west of the Rocky mountains; to which is appended a
full description of Oregon territory, its geography,
history and religion; designed for the benefit of
emigrants to that rising country. Buffalo, 1850.
437 p.   20 cm.

16764   Hines, Gustavus.
Wild life in Oregon; being a stirring recital of
actual scenes of daring and peril among the gigantic
forests and terrific rapids of the Columbia river...
and giving life-like pictures of terrific encounters
with savages... including a full, fair and reliable
history of the state of Oregon... New York [1881]
437 p.   20 cm.

153

16765 Hines, Harvey K   1828-1902, comp.
       At sea and in port; or, Life and experience of
       William S. Fletcher, for thirty years seaman's
       missionary in Portland, Oregon. Comp. from his
       journal and other authentic sources by H. K. Hines,
       D.D., with an introduction by Bishop Earl Cranston...
       Portland, Or., The J. K. Gill company, 1898.
           251 p.   front. (port.)   19½ cm.

16766 Hines, Harvey K   1828-1902.
       Missionary history of the Pacific Northwest,
       containing the wonderful story of Jason Lee, with
       sketches of many of his co-laborers, all illustrating
       life on the plains and in the mountains in pioneer
       days. Portland [1899]
           510 p.   front., pl., port.   21 cm.

16767 A historical, descriptive and commercial directory of
       Owyhee County, Idaho. January 1898. Silver City,
       Id., Press of the Owyhee avalanche, 1898.
           140, [16], iv p.   front., illus., plates, ports.
       23½ cm.

16768 Historical outline of Lower California: extracts taken
       from the posthumous work of Father Francisco Javier
       Clavijero of the Company of Jesus, published in
       Venice in 1789; and from the memorial published by
       the citizen Ulises Urbano Lassepas in 1859, on the
       colonization of Lower California; and from the decree
       of the supreme government, of the 10th of March, A.D.
       1857. San Francisco, H. Payot [1862?]
           79 p.   22½ cm.
       Compiled and translated by M. E. R.

16769 Historical records survey. Oregon.
       A guide to the Angelus studio collection of
       historic photographs. Prepared by the Oregon Historical
       records survey project, Division of professional and
       service projects, Work projects administration.
       Sponsored by the University of Oregon. Portland, Or.,
       The Oregon Historical records survey project, Official
       project no. 65-1-94-25, 1940.
           v, 77 p.   27½ cm.
       Reproduced from typewritten copy.

16770 History of Alameda County, California, including its
       geology, topography, soil, and productions: together
       with a full and particular record of the Spanish

grants... Oakland, M. W. Wood, 1883.
2 p.l., vii, [9]-1001 p.   front., ports.   27 cm.
Preface signed by M. W. Wood and J. P. Munro-Fraser,
historian.
"Biographical sketches": p. 836-999.

16771 History of Arizona Territory, showing its resources
and advantages: with illustrations... from original
drawings. San Francisco, Cal., W. W. Elliott & co.,
1884.
[25]-322, [2] p.   front., illus., plates, ports.,
facsims., diagrs.   35 cm.

16772 History of Contra Costa County, California, including
its geography, geology, topography, climatography
and description; together with a record of the Mexican
grants... also, incidents of pioneer life; and biographical sketches of early and prominent settlers and
representative men... San Francisco. W. A. Slocum
& co., 1882.
xii p., 1 l., [17]-710 p. incl. front.   ports.
25 cm.
Preface signed: J. P. Munro-Fraser, historian.

16773 History of Idaho Territory, showing its resources and
advantages; with illustrations... from original
drawings. San Francisco, Cal., W. W. Elliott & co.,
1884.
3 p.l., [19]-302 p.   front., illus., plates
(part fold.) ports., maps.   36 cm.

16774 History of Placer county, California, with illustrations
and biographical sketches of its prominent men and
pioneers. Oakland, Cal., Thompson & West, 1882.
viii, [9]-416 p.   front., plates (part fold.)
ports.   31 cm.
Literary work under charge of Myron Angel, assisted
by M. D. Fairchild.

16775 History of San Luis Obispo County, California, with
illustrations and biographical sketches of its
prominent men and pioneers. Oakland, Cal., 1883.
391 p.   pl., port.   25 cm.

16776 History of Sanpete and Emery counties, Utah, with
sketches of cities, towns and villages, chronology of
important events, records of Indian wars, portraits
of prominent persons, and biographies of representative

155

citizens... Ogden, Utah, W. H. Lever, 1898.
681, [2] p. incl. front., plates, ports.   24½ cm.

16777 History of Santa Clara county, California, including
its geography, geology, topography, climatology and
description... also incidents of public life...
and biographical sketches of early and prominent
settlers and representative men... San Francisco,
Alley, Bowen & co., 1881.
xvi, [17]-798 p.   ports. (incl. front.)   plans.
24½ cm.
Preface signed: J. P. Munro Fraser, historian.

16778 History of Solano County... and histories of its
cities, towns... etc. ... also a full and particular
biography of its early settlers and principal
inhabitants... San Francisco, Cal., East Oakland,
Wood, Alley & co., 1879.
1 p.l., [v]-xv, [17]-503 p.   ports.   25½ cm.
Preface signed: Wood, Alley & co., J. P. Munro-
Fraser, historian.

16779 History of southeastern Dakota, its settlement and
growth, geological and physical features - counties,
cities, towns and villages - incidents of pioneer
life - biographical sketches of the pioneers and
business men, with a brief outline history of the
territory in general... Sioux City, Ia., Western
publishing company, 1881.
256, [35], 306-392 p.   23½ cm.

16780 History of Texas together with a biographical history
of Milam, Williamson, Bastrop, Travis, Lee and
Burleson counties... Chicago, 1893.
826 p.   ports.   22 cm.

16781 History of Texas, together with a biographical history
of Tarrant and Parker counties; containing a concise
history of the state, with portraits and biographies
of prominent citizens of the above named counties,
and personal histories of many of the early settlers
and leading families... Chicago, The Lewis publishing
co., 1895.
v p., 1 l., [9]-658 p.   pl., port.   27½ cm.

16782 History of the city of Denver, Arapahoe county, and
Colorado. Containing a history of the state of
Colorado from its earliest settlement to the present

156

time... a condensed sketch of Arapahoe county: a
history of the city of Denver... biographical sketches
... &c., &c. ... Chicago, O. L. Baskin & co.,
1880.
 vi, [11]-652 p. incl. plates, ports., double front.,
plates, ports. 25 x 21 cm.
 The historical portion of the work is by W. B.
Vickers.

16783 The history of the McGarrahan claim as written by
  himself. [n.p., n.d.]
   xxviii, 411 p. maps. 25 cm.

16784 History of the Pacific Northwest: Oregon and Washington;
  embracing an account of the original discoveries on
  the Pacific coast of North America, and a description
  of the conquest, settlement and subjugation of the...
  original territory of Oregon; also interesting biographies of the earliest settlers and more prominent
  men and women of the Pacific Northwest, including a...
  description of the climate, soil, productions...
  of Oregon and Washington... Portland, Or., North
  Pacific history company [1889]
   2 v. plates (part fold.) ports. 30½ cm.
  By Elwood Evans and other writers.

16785 History of the state of Nebraska; containing a full
  account of its growth from an uninhabited territory
  to a wealthy and important state; of its early
  settlements; its rapid increase in population, and
  the marvellous development of its great natural
  resources. Also an extended description of its
  counties, cities, towns and villages... biographical
  sketches... Chicago, Western historical co., 1882.
   4 p.l., 33-1506 p. incl. port., front. (map) illus.
  25 cm.

16786 Hitchcock, Ethan Allen, 1798-1870.
   Fifty years in camp and field, diary of Major-
  General Ethan Allen Hitchcock, U.S.A.; ed. by W. A.
  Croffut, Ph.D. .New York and London, G. P. Putnam's
  sons, 1909.
   xv, 514 p. front. (port.) 25 cm.

16787 Hitchcock, Mary E "Mrs. R. D. Hitchcock."
   Two women in the Klondike; the story of a journey
  to the gold-fields of Alaska, by Mary E. Hitchcock.
  With 105 illustrations and map. New York and London,
  G. P. Putnam's sons, 1899.

xiv p., 1 l., 485 p.   front., illus., fold. map
(in pocket)   22½ cm.

16788   Hite, Cass.
        Colorado River gold, by Cass Hite [in Beaver Utonian,
        January 13, 1893] Salt Lake City, Utah State Historical
        Society, 1939. (In Utah historical quarterly, v. 7,
        nos. 1-3, p. 139-140)

16789   Hittell, John Shertzer, 1825-1901.
        A history of the city of San Francisco and inci-
        dentally of the state of California. By John S.
        Hittell... San Francisco, A. L. Bancroft & company,
        1878.
        498 p.   22½ cm.

16790   Hittell, John Shertzer, 1825-1901.
        Marshall's gold discovery: a lecture (the fourth
        of the sixth annual course of Lick lectures) by John S.
        Hittell, delivered before the Society of California
        pioneers... San Francisco, on the 24th of January,
        1893, the 45th anniversary of the discovery. San
        Francisco, B. F. Sterett, printers, 1893.
        20 p.   illus. (facsims.)   24 cm.

16791   Hittell, John Shertzer, 1825-1901.
        The resources of California, comprising the society,
        climate, salubrity, scenery, commerce and industry
        of the state. 6th ed., rewritten. San Francisco,
        A. Roman, 1877.
        xxix, 443 p.   21 cm.

16792   Hittell, Theodore Henry, 1830-
        History of California. San Francisco, 1885-97.
        4 v.   23½ cm.

16793   Hobart, Charles F
        Pioneering in North Dakota, by Charles F. Hobart.
        [Bismarck, State Historical Society of North Dakota,
        1940-1941]
        50-62, 114-131 p.   24 cm.
        Reprinted from North Dakota historical quarterly,
        v. 8, no. 1, October 1940, and no. 2, January 1941.

16794   Hobart, Chauncey, b. 1811.
        Recollections of my life. Fifty years of itinerancy
        in the Northwest, by Chauncey Hobart, D.D. Red Wing

[Minn.] Red Wing printing co., 1885.
409 p.   front. (port.)   20 cm.

16795 Hobbs, James, b. 1819.
Wild life in the far West; personal adventures of
a border mountain man. Comprising hunting and
trapping adventures with Kit Carson and others;
captivity and life among the Comanches; services
under Doniphan in the war with Mexico, and in the
Mexican war against the French; desperate combats
with Apaches, grizzly bears, etc., etc. By Captain
James Hobbs... Hartford, Wiley, Waterman & Eaton,
1872.
488 p.   col. front., illus., plates, port.
21½ cm.

16796 Hodgkin, Frank E   1846-
Pen pictures of representative men of Oregon.
By Frank E. Hodgkin, J. J. Galvin... Portland, Or.,
Farmer and dairyman publishing house, 1882.
4 p.l., xxv p., 1 l., 199 p.   2 phot.   22½ cm.

16797 Hoffmann, Hermann.
Californien, Nevada und Mexico. Wanderungen eines
Polytechnikers. Basel, Schweighauser, 1871.
iv, 426 p.   22 cm.
Autobiographical.

16798 Hogan, John Joseph, bp., 1829-1913.
On the mission in Missouri. 1857-1868. By Rt.
Rev. John Joseph Hogan, bishop of Kansas City.
Kansas City, Mo., J. A. Heilmann, 1892.
2 p.l., 205, [1], ccvii-ccxxxi p.   18½ cm.

16799 Hogg, James Stephen, 1851-1906.
Speeches and state papers of James Stephen Hogg,
ex-governor of Texas, with a sketch of his life;
ed. by C. W. Raines... Austin, Tex., The State
printing company, 1905.
453 p.   front. (port.)   23 cm.

16800 Holcombe, Theodore Isaac, 1832-
An apostle of the wilderness, James Lloyd Breck,
D.D., his missions and his schools, by Theodore I.
Holcombe, B.D. New York, T. Whittaker, 1903.
xii, 195 p.   3 pl., 5 port. (incl. front.)
19½ cm.

16801   De Hollanders in Iowa. Brieven uit Pella, van een
         Gelderschman. Arnhem, D. A. Thieme, 1858.
         xxiii, 189 p.   plates.   19 cm.

16802   Holley, Frances (Chamberlain)
         Once their home; or, Our legacy from the Dahkotahs;
         historical, biographical, and incidental, from far-off
         days, down to the present. By Frances Chamberlain
         Holley... Chicago, Donohue & Henneberry, 1890.
         xvi, [7]-405, [1] p.   front., plates, ports.
         22½ cm.

16803   Hollister, Ovando James, 1834-1892.
         The resources and attractions of Utah. By O. J.
         Hollister. Pub. by A. Zeehandelaar, secretary and
         special agent for Utah at Denver exposition. Salt
         Lake City, Tribune printing and publishing co., 1882.
         1 p.l., [7]-93 p., 1 l.   fold. map.   23½ cm.

16804   Hollister, Uriah S   1838-
         The Navajo and his blanket, by U. S. Hollister.
         Denver, Col., 1903.
         144 p. incl. front., illus., plates.   8 col. pl.
         25 cm.

16805   Holman, Frederick V
         Dr. John McLoughlin the father of Oregon. Cleveland,
         O., 1907.
         301 p.   port.   20½ cm.

16806   Holton, Edward Dwight, 1815-1892.
         Travels with jottings. From midland to the Pacific.
         Letters by E. D. Holton. Written for, and published,
         chiefly, as souvenirs to personal acquaintances and
         friends. Milwaukee, Trayser brothers, printers, 1880.
         94 p.   front. (port.)   22½ cm.

16807   Holtz, Mathilde Edith.
         Glacier national park; its trails and treasures,
         by Mathilde Edith Holtz and Katharine Isabel Bemis...
         illustrated from photographs. New York, George H.
         Doran company [c1917]
         xv p., 1 l., 19-263 p.   front., plates.   20½ cm.

16808   Homes in Arkansas. 1,000,000 acres of choice river
         bottom and upland for sale... Little Rock, 1871.
         32 p.   maps.   22 cm.

16809 Hook, W   E
       O'er cañon and crag to the land of gold. [Denver,
       Col, 1904]
       [24] pl.   28 cm.
       Book of views.

16810 Hooker, William Francis, 1856-
       The prairie schooner, by William Francis Hooker.
       Chicago, Saul brothers, 1918.
       156 p. incl. col. front., illus., pl.   18 cm.

16811 Hooper, William Henry, b. 1813.
       Extension of boundaries. Speech of Hon. William
       H. Hooper, of Utah, delivered in the House of
       Representatives, February 25, 1869. Washington,
       F. & J. Rives & G. A. Bailey, printers, 1869.
       14 p.   23 cm.

16812 Hopewell, Menra.
       Legends of the Missouri and Mississippi. By M.
       Hopewell... London, Ward, Lock and Tyler [1874]
       vi, [7]-506 p. incl. front.   2 pl. $16\frac{1}{2}$ cm.

16813 Hopkins, Albert Allis, 1869-
       Our country and its resources; what we ought to
       know about agriculture - fisheries - forests - Panama
       canal - railroads - manufactures - automobiles -
       industrial preparedness - the new navy - the army -
       our money - aeronautics - motion pictures - the
       weather - astronomy - the nation's capital - the
       President - Congress - all about the government;
       by Albert A. Hopkins... with 800 illustrations...
       New York, Munn & co., inc., 1917.
       4 p.l., 598 p.   illus. (incl. ports., maps)
       diagrs.   20 cm.   (Scientific American series)
       Published 1916.

16814 Hopkins, Sarah Winnemucca, 1844?-1891.
       Life among the Piutes, their wrongs and claims.
       Edited by Mrs. Horace Mann. Boston, For sale by
       Cupples, Upham, 1883.
       268 p.   19 cm.

16815 Hoppe, Janus.
       Californiens gegenwart und zukunft, von J. Hoppe.
       Nebst beiträgen von A. Erman ueber die klimatologie
       von Californien und ueber die geographische verbeitung
       des goldes. Hierzu zwei karten... Berlin, G. Reimer,

161

1849.
viii, 151, [1] p.   2 fold. maps.   22½ cm.

16816   Horn, Tom, 1860-1903.
Life of Tom Horn, government scout and interpreter,
written by himself, together with his letters and
statements by his friends, a vindication; thirteen
full page illustrations. Denver, For J. C. Coble
by the Louthan book company [1904]
317 p. incl. front.   plates, ports., facsim.
19 cm.

16817   Hough, Emerson, 1857-1923.
The covered wagon, by Emerson Hough... New York,
London, D. Appleton and company, 1922.
4 p.l., 378, [1] p.   front.   19½ cm.

16818   Hough, Emerson, 1857-1923.
The story of the cowboy, by E. Hough... illustrated
by William L. Wells and C. M. Russell. New York,
D. Appleton and company, 1897.
xii, 349 p.   10 pl. (incl. front.)   19½ cm.
(Half-title: The Story of the West series, ed. by
R. Hitchcock)

16819   Hough, Emerson, 1857-1923.
The story of the outlaw; a study of the western
desperado, with historical narratives of famous
outlaws; the stories of noted border wars; vigilante
movements and armed conflicts on the frontier. By
Emerson Hough. New York, The Outing publishing
company, 1907.
xiv, 401 p.   front., 16 pl. (incl. ports.)
19 cm.

16820   Houghton, Eliza Poor (Donner) 1843-
The expedition of the Donner party and its tragic
fate, by Eliza P. Donner Houghton... Chicago,
A. C. McClurg & co., 1911.
xxi p., 1 l., 374, [1] p.   front., plates, ports.
21½ cm.

16821   How to conquer Texas before Texas conquers us. Boston,
1845.
16 p.   20 cm.
At head of title: A tract for the day.

162

16822 Howard, Oliver Otis, 1830-1909.
       Nez Perce Joseph, an account of his ancestors,
       his lands, his confederates, his enemies, his murders,
       his war, his pursuit and capture; by O. O. Howard,
       brig. gen. U.S.A. Boston, Lee and Shepard, 1881.
         xii, 274 p.   front., port., maps (part fold.)
       20½ cm.

16823 Howbert, Irving, 1846-
       The Indians of the Pike's peak region, including
       an account of the battle of Sand creek, and of
       occurrences in El Paso county, Colorado, during the
       war with the Cheyennes and Arapahoes, in 1864 and
       1868, by Irving Howbert... New York, The Knicker-
       bocker press, 1914.
         x, 230 p.   front., ports.   21 cm.

16824 Howison, Neil M
       Report to the commander of the Pacific squadron;
       being the result of an examination in the year 1846
       of the coast, harbors, rivers, soil, production,
       climate and population of the territory of Oregon.
       Washington, 1848.
         36 p.

16825 Howlett, William Joseph, 1848-1936.
       Life of the Right Reverend Joseph P. Machebeuf,
       D.D., pioneer priest of Ohio, pioneer priest of New
       Mexico, pioneer priest of Colorado, vicar apostolic
       of Colorado and Utah, and first bishop of Denver. By
       the Rev. W. J. Howlett... Pueblo, Col. [The Franklin
       press company] 1908.
         419 p.   front., plates, ports.   23½ cm.

16826 Hoyt, John W
       Concerning the foundations of the future state of
       Wyoming. Paper read before the Wyoming academy of
       sciences, at its semi-annual meeting for 1889.
       [n.p.] 1889.
         4 p.   22 cm.

16827 Hubbard, Gurdon Saltonstall, 1802-1886.
       Incidents and events in the life of Gurdon
       Saltonstall Hubbard. Collected from personal narra-
       tions and other sources, and arranged by his nephew,
       Henry E. Hamilton. [Chicago, Rand, McNally & co.,
       printers] 1888.
         3 p.l., 5-189 p.   front. (port.)   22½ cm.

163

Includes an account of the author's service with the American fur company in Michigan and Illinois, 1818-1828.

16828   Hubbard, Mrs. Mary Ann (Hubbard) 1820-1909.
Family memories, by Mary Ann Hubbard, November 2, 1820-July 19, 1909. [Chicago?] Printed for private circulation, 1912.
4 p.l., 146 p.   3 port. (incl. front.)   18 cm.
Sketches of the Tucker and Hubbard family history, pioneer life in Illinois and Iowa, the Chicago fire of 1871, etc.

16829   Hughes, Mrs. Elizabeth.
The California of the padres; or, Footprints of ancient communism. By Mrs. Elizabeth Hughes. San Francisco, I. N. Choynski, 1875.
2 p.l., 41 p.   22 cm.

16830   [Hughes, William Edgar] 1840-
The journal of a grandfather. [St. Louis, Priv. print., Nixon-Jones ptg. co., c1912]
239 p.   front., plates, ports.   22½ cm.
Served in the civil war in the 1st Texas artillery and as colonel of the 16th Confederate States cavalry.

16831   Humfreville, James Lee.
Twenty years among our hostile Indians. Describing the characteristics, customs, habits, religion, marriages, dances and battles of the wild Indians in their natural state, together with the entrance of civilization through their hunting grounds... By J. Lee Humfreville... Fully illustrated from original photographs. New York, Hunter & co. [18-?]
1 p.l., [xi]-xxxvi, [45]-479 p.   front., port., illus.   24½ x 19½ cm.

16832   Hunt, George W   1831-
A history of the Hunt family, from the Norman conquest, 1066, A.D., to the year 1890. Early settlement in America... settlement in Oregon; mining experience in California in 1849; incidents of pioneer life and adventures among the Indian tribes of the Northwest. By G. W. Hunt. Boston, Press of McDonald, Gill & co., 1890.
79 p.   17½ cm.

16833   Hunt, Rockwell Dennis, 1868-
        ... The genesis of California's first constitution
        (1846-49). By Rockwell Dennis Hunt... Baltimore,
        The Johns Hopkins press, 1895.
        59 p.   24½ cm.   (Johns Hopkins university
        studies in historical and political science...
        13th ser., VIII)

16834   Hunter, George, 1835-
        Reminiscences of an old timer. A recital of the
        actual events, incidents, trials... of a pioneer,
        hunter, miner and scout of the Pacific Northwest,
        together with his later experiences... the several
        Indian wars, anecdotes, etc., by Colonel George
        Hunter. 3d ed. Battle Creek, Mich., Review and
        herald, 1888.
        xxv, 508 p.   front. (port.) plates.   20½ cm.
        Reprint of the 1887 edition, with an appendix.

16835   Hunter, John Marvin, 1880-   comp. and ed.
        The trail drivers of Texas, interesting sketches
        of early cowboys and their experiences on the range
        and on the trail during the days that tried men's
        souls; true narratives related by real cowpunchers
        and men who fathered the cattle industry in Texas.
        Pub. under the direction of George W. Saunders,
        president of the Old trail drivers association.
        Comp. and ed. by J. Marvin Hunter. [San Antonio,
        Jackson printing co., c1920]
        498 p., 1 l.   illus., ports.   23½ cm.

16836   [Huntley, Sir Henry Veel] 1795-1864.
        California: its gold and its inhabitants. By the
        author of "Seven years on the Slave Coast of Africa"
        ... London, T. C. Newby, 1856.
        2 v. in 1.   19½ cm.

16837   Hutchings, James Mason.
        Scenes of wonder and curiosity in California...
        San Francisco, Hutchings & Rosenfield [1860]
        236 p.   illus.   20½ cm.

16838   Hutchison, John Russell, 1807-1878.
        Reminiscences, sketches and addresses selected
        from my papers during a ministry of forty-five years
        in Mississippi, Louisiana and Texas. By Rev. J. R.
        Hutchison, D. D. Houston, Tex., E. H. Cushing, 1874.
        1 p.l., [v]-vi, [7]-262 p.   19½ cm.

16839 Hyatt, H   S
        Manufacturing, agricultural and industrial resources
        of Iowa, with reliable information to capitalists
        seeking the best fields for investments, also,
        valuable information for emigrants seeking new and
        desirable homes: under the direction of the State
        board of immigration. By H. S. Hyatt... Des Moines,
        Ia., Republicam steam printing house, 1872.
        155 p.   maps (incl. fold. front.)   22 cm.

16840 Hyde, S   C
        Historical sketch of Lyon county, Iowa, and a
        description of the country and its resources, giving
        information with regard to the inducements which
        it offers to immigrants and others desiring to
        settle in the Northwest. "Homes, fortunes, health
        and happiness for all." Published by authority of
        County board of supervisors. By S. C. Hyde.
        Lemars, Ia., Sentinel print, 1872.
        40 p.   front. (fold. map) $18\frac{1}{2}$ cm.

16841 Hyenne, Robert.
        El bandido chileno Joaquín Murieta en California,
        por Roberto Hyenne; traducido del francés por C. M. ...
        Santiago [de Chile] Centro editorial "La Prensa",
        1906.
        123, [1] p.   plates.   19 cm.

16842 [Hyer, Joseph Keyes] d. 1882, comp.
        Dictionary of the Sioux language. [New York?
        Priv. print. for F. D. Potter, 1931?]
        [34] p.   20 cm.
        Caption title: half-title: Lahcotah.
        "Compiled with the aid of Charles Guerreu, Indian
        interpreter, by Lieuts. J. K. Hyer and W. S. Starring,
        U.S.A., and is as complete as a perfect knowledge of
        the Lahcotah language can make it." - Note at end,
        signed: Fort Laramie, Dakota, December, 1866.
        English and Teton vocabulary.

                            I

16843 Idaho. Constitution.
        Constitution of the state of Idaho. Adopted in
        convention at Boise City, August 6, 1889. Boise City,

                            166

Id., The Statesman printing co., 1889.
cover-title, 42 p.   23½ cm.

16844   [Ide, Simeon] 1794-1889.
A biographical sketch of the life of William B. Ide:
with a minute and interesting account of one of the
largest emigrating companies... from the East to
the Pacific coast. And... account of "the virtual
conquest of California, in June, 1846, by the Bear
flag party," as given by its leader, the late Hon.
William Brown Ide... [Claremont, N. H., S. Ide, 1880]
2 p.l., [3]-239, 1 p.   16½ cm.
Cover-title and half-title: "Scraps of California
history...
The letter of W. B. Ide to Senator Wambough (p. 100-
205) was reprinted in 1882 under title: Who conquered
California? ...

16845   Ide, William B
Who conquered California? ... The most particular,
the most authentic, and the most reliable history
of the conquest of California, in June, 1846, by the
"Bear flag party", ever before published. Written
by its organizer and leader, the late Hon. William
Brown Ide. Claremont, N. H., Printed and pub. by
Simeon Ide [1880]
8, 21, 137 p.   20 cm.

16846   Illinois Central Railroad Company.
... Documents relating to the organization of the
Illinois central rail-road company. (3d ed.)
New-York, G. S. Roe, printer, 1855.
73 p.   23 cm.

16847   Illinois College, Jacksonville.
Description of Jacksonville and of the plot of
lands hereto annexed, and now offered for sale in
behalf of Illinois college. [New York? 1836?]
12 p.   front. (fold. plan.)   21½ cm.

16848   The Illinois monthly magazine... Conducted by James
Hall. v. 1-2; Oct. 1830-Sept. 1832. Vandalia,
Printed by R. Blackwell, 1831; Cincinnati, Corey
and Fairbank, 1832.
2 v.   22-24½ cm.
Continued as the Western monthly magazine (1833-37)

16849   An illustrated history of New Mexico... from the
        earliest period of its discovery to the present time,
        together with... biographical mention of many of its
        pioneers and prominent citizens of today... Chicago,
        The Lewis publishing company, 1895.
        671, [1] p.   plates, ports.   30 x 23½ cm.

16850   Illustrated history of Southern California; embracing
        the counties of San Diego, San Bernardino. Los
        Angeles and Orange, and the peninsula of Lower
        California... Chicago, 1890.
        898 p.   pl., port.   22 cm.

16851   [Immigration Association of Northern California]
        Northern California: a description of its soil,
        climate, productions, markets, occupied and unoccupied
        lands... Sacramento, 1885.
        72 p.   map, plates.   22 cm.

16852   Ingersoll, Ernest, 1852-1946.
        Knocking round the Rockies, by Ernest Ingersoll.
        New York, Harper & Brothers, Pub., 1883.
        viii, 220 p.   illus.   22 cm.
        Narratives of the author's experiences in the field
        work of the Geological and geographical survey of
        the territories in Colorado, 1874 and Wyoming, 1877.

16853   Ingham, George Thomas, 1851-
        Digging gold among the Rockies; or, Exciting
        adventures of wild camp life in Leadville, Black
        Hills and the Gunnison country. Giving a graphic
        history of the various discoveries of gold and silver
        in the United States, the development and extent of
        our mining industries... By G. Thomas Ingham...
        Philadelphia, Hubbard bros.; [etc., etc., 1880]
        xiii p., 1 l., 17-508 p. incl. plates.   front.,
        plates.   20 cm.

16854   Inman, Henry, 1837-1899.
        The Great Salt lake trail, by Colonel Henry Inman...
        and Colonel William F. Cody... New York, The
        Macmillan company; London, Macmillan & co., ltd.,
        1898.
        xiii, 529 p.   front. (2 port.)   illus., plates,
        fold. map.   23 cm.

16855   Inman, Henry, 1837-1899.
        Stories of the old Santa Fe trail. By Col. Henry

Inman... Kansas City, Mo., Ramsey, Millett & Hudson, 1881.
4 p.l., 287 p.   illus.   18 cm.

16856   Inman, Henry, 1837-1899.
Tales of the trail; short stories of western life, by Colonel Henry Inman... Topeka, Kan., Crane & company, 1898.
1 p.l., v-viii, 280 p.   illus.   19½ cm.

16857   Introductory letter, additional explanation, bill for a law, and suggested amendments to the constitution of Oregon designed to provide a system by which the conduct of state and county government may be made as efficient and economical as the management by the citizens of their private business. [Portland, 1909]
40 p.   20 cm.

16858   Iowa. Board of Immigration.
Iowa: the home for immigrants, being a treatise on the resources of Iowa, and giving useful information with regard to the state, for the benefit of immigrants and others. Pub. by order of the Iowa Board of Immigration. Des Moines, Mills & co., 1870.
96 p.   front. (fold. map) illus.   23½ cm.

16859   Iowa. Constitutional convention, 1857.
Journal of the Constitutional convention of the state of Iowa, in session at Iowa City, from the nineteenth day of January, A.D., one thousand eight hundred and fifty-seven, to the fifth day of March of the same year inclusive. Muscatine, Printed by J. Mahin, 1857.
406, 26 p.   21½ cm.
"Constitution of the state of Iowa": 26 p. at end of volume.

16860   Iowa. State Historical Society.
Constitution of the State historical society of Iowa adopted at Iowa City, February 7, 1857.
[Iowa City] Printed by Jerome & Duncan, 1861.
14 p.   14 cm.
"Address to the public": p. 7-14.

16861   Iowa (Ter.) Supreme Court.
Reports of the decisions of the Supreme court of Iowa, from the organization of the territory in July,

1838, to December, 1839, inclusive. Published by
order of the legislature. By Wm. J. A. Bradford,
reporter to the Supreme court. Galena, Printed by
W. C. Taylor, 1840.
20 p., 1 l., [2] p.   24½ cm.

16862 Irving, Leigh Hadley.
A history of the new California, its resources
and people; ed. by Leigh H. Irvine and associated
editors... New York, Chicago, The Lewis publishing
company, 1905.
2 v.   front., plates, ports.   27½ cm.

16863 Irwin, Mrs. Inez (Haynes)
The Californiacs, by Inez Haynes Irwin... San
Francisco, A. M. Robertson, 1916.
4 p.l., 63 p.   col. mounted front.   17½ cm.
"Published in Sunset, the Pacific monthly, for
February, 1916."

16864 Isom, Alice Parker, 1848-1924.
Memoirs of Alice Parker Isom. Salt Lake City,
Utah State Historical Society, 1942. (In Utah
historical quarterly, v. 10, nos. 1-4, 1942, p. 55-83)

16865 Ives, Butler.
Report of Butler Ives, commissioner of the boundary
survey between Nevada territory and California, 1863.
Carson City, 1864.
8 p.   20½ cm.

16866 Ivins, Virginia (Wilcox)
Pen pictures of early western days [by] Virginia
Wilcox Ivins; illustrations by Wm. S. Ivins.
[Keokuk? Ia., c1905]
157 p. incl. front.   plates.   22½ cm.

J

16867 Jack, O   G   comp.
A brief history of Muscatine; giving its location,
early settlement, trade, manufactures, fine resi-
dences, business houses, etc., together with many
accidents and incidents. Compiled by O. G. Jack.
Muscatine, Ia., Journal book and job printing house,

1870.
80 p.   21 cm.

16868   Jackson, A   P
Oklahoma! politically and topographically described. History and guide to the Indian territory.
Biographical sketches of Capt. D. L. Payne, W. L.
Couch, W. H. Osborn, and others, by A. P. Jackson
and E. C. Cole. Kansas City, Mo., Ramsey, Millett
& Hudson [1885]
150 p.   front. (fold. map) illus., plates, port.
20 cm.

16869   Jackson, George, 1838-
Sixty years in Texas. 2d ed. By George Jackson.
[Dallas, Tex., Wilkinson printing co., c1908]
5 p.l., 384 p. incl. illus., plates, ports.
front. (port.)   22½ cm.

16870   Jackson, Mrs. Helen Maria (Fiske) Hunt, 1831-1885.
Glimpses of California and the missions. With
illustrations by Henry Sandhum. Boston, 1902.
12, 292 p.   illus., pl.   20 cm.

16871   Jackson, Mrs. Helen Maria (Fiske) Hunt, 1831-1885.
Glimpses of three coasts. By Helen Jackson (H. H.)
... Boston, Roberts brothers, 1886.
2 p.l., 418 p.   19 cm.

16872   [Jackson, Mrs. Helen Maria (Fiske) Hunt] 1831-1885.
Nelly's silver mine. A story of Colorado life.
By H. H. [pseud.]... Boston, Roberts brothers,
1878.
379 p.   front., 3 pl.   17½ cm.

16873   Jackson, Mary E
The life of Nellie C. Bailey; or, A romance of
the West. Written by Mary E. Jackson... Topeka,
Kan., R. E. Martin & co., 1885.
5 p.l., [7]-399 p. incl. front., plates, ports.
19 cm.

16874   Jackson, Orick.
The white conquest of Arizona; history of the
pioneers, by Orick Jackson... Los Angeles, Cal.,
The West coast magazine, The Grafton co. [1908]
2 p.l., [9]-52 p.   plates, ports.   20½ cm.

171

16875   Jackson, Mrs. Pearl (Cashell) 1869-
        Texas governors' wives, by Pearl Cashell Jackson.
        Austin, Tex., E. L. Steck [c1915]
        155, [1] p.   illus. (incl. ports.)   pl.   21 cm.

16876   Jackson, William Turrentine.
        Dakota territorial papers in the Department of the
        Interior archives, by W. Turrentine Jackson.
        [Bismarck, State Historical Society of North Dakota,
        1944]
        209-220 p.   24 cm.
        Reprinted from North Dakota historical quarterly,
        v. 11, no. 3, July 1944.

16877   James, George Wharton, 1858-
        B. R. Baumgardt & co.'s tourists' guide book to
        south California... by G. Wharton James... Los
        Angeles, Cal., B. R. Baumgardt & co. [1895]
        457, [1] p.   illus., fold. map. $22\frac{1}{2}$ cm.

16878   James, George Wharton, 1858-
        California, romantic and beautiful; the history of
        its old missions and of its Indians; a survey of its
        climate, topography, deserts, mountains, rivers,
        valleys, islands and coast line; a description of
        its recreations and festivals; a review of its
        industries; an account of its influence upon prophets,
        poets, artists and architects; and some reference to
        what it offers of delight to the automobilist,
        traveller, sportsman, pleasure and health seeker,
        by George Wharton James... with a map and seventy-two
        plates, of which eight are in color. Boston, The
        Page company, 1914.
        xxv, 433 p.   col. front., plates (part col.)
        fold. map.   25 cm.   (On verso of half-title:
        See America first series)

16879   James, George Wharton, 1858-
        Heroes of California; the story of the founders
        of the golden state as narrated by themselves or
        gleaned from other sources. Boston, 1910.
        xxii, 515 p.   pl., ports. $20\frac{1}{2}$ cm.

16880   James, George Wharton, 1858-
        Travelers' handbook to southern California, by
        George Wharton James... Pub. annually. Pasadena,
        Cal., G. W. James, 19- .
            v.   illus. $15\frac{1}{2}$ x $12\frac{1}{2}$ cm.

16881 James, George Wharton, 1858-
       ... Utah, the land of blossoming valleys; the
       story of its desert wastes, of its huge and fantastic
       rock formations, and of its fertile gardens in the
       sheltered valleys; a survey of its rapidly developing
       industries; an account of the origin, development,
       and beliefs of the Mormon church; and chapters on the
       flora and fauna, and on the scenic wonders that are
       a heritage of all Americans. By George Wharton James...
       with a map and fifty-six plates of which eight are in
       color. Boston, The Page company, 1922.
          3 p.l., v-xix, 371 p.   col. front. (part col.)
       ports., fold. map.   24½ cm. (The "See America
       first" series)

16882 James, Jesse E   1875-
       Jesse James, my father. Written by Jesse James, jr.
       The first and only true story of his adventures ever
       written. Kansas City, Mo., J. James, jr.; Independence,
       Mo., The Sentinel printing co., 1899.
          194 p.   illus. (ports.)   19½ cm.

16883 James, John Towner, 1851-
       The Benders in Kansas, by John T. James, attorney
       for the defence in the trial of the "Bender women"
       at Oswego, Labette County, in 1889-1890; the complete
       story; facts, not fiction. Wichita, Kan., The Kan-Okla
       publishing co. [c1913]
          2 p.l., [7]-173 p.   illus. (incl. ports., plan)
       21 cm.

16884 Jamison, Matthew H   1840-
       Recollections of pioneer and army life, by Matthew
       H. Jamison, lieutenant E company, Tenth regiment,
       Illinois veteran volunteer infantry... Kansas City,
       Hudson press [1911]
          2 p.l., iv, 7-363 p.   front. (port.) illus.
       23 cm.

16885 Jefferson, H   E
       Oklahoma: the beautiful land; an exciting narrative
       of the scenes incident to the occupation of Oklahoma;
       a complete history of the country and its wondrous
       development. Chicago, 1889.
          202 p.   22 cm.

16886 Jenkins, F   H
       Journal of a voyage to San Francisco, 1849.

Northridge, Cal., California State University,
Northridge, Libraries, 1975.
2 p.l., [2] l., 91 p. of facsimile. 36 cm.
(American classics facsimile, series II)
Norman E. Tanis, series-editor.

16887   Jenney, Walter Proctor, 1849-1921.
        The mineral wealth, climate and rain-fall, and
        natural resources of the Black hills of Dakota. By
        Walter P. Jenney... Washington, Govt. print. off.,
        1876.
        1 p.l., 71 p.   fold. map, diagr.   23½ cm.
        ([U.S.] 44th Cong., 1st sess. Senate. Ex. doc.
        no. 51)

16888   Jennings, Alphonso J   1863-
        Beating back, by Al Jennings and Will Irwin;
        illustrated by Charles M. Russell. New York and
        London, D. Appleton and company, 1914.
        5 p.l., 354, [1] p.   front., 1 illus., plates,
        ports.   20 cm.
        Autobiography of Al Jennings, edited with an intro-
        ductory chapter by Will Irwin.

16889   Jennings, William.
        Material progress of Utah, dictated by William
        Jennings, ex-mayor of Salt Lake City, in 1884
        (Bancroft Library). Salt Lake City, Utah State
        Historical Society, 1930. (In Utah historical
        quarterly, v. 3, no. 3, July 1930, p. 89-90)

16890   Jerrett, Herman Daniel, 1877-
        California's El Dorado yesterday and today [by]
        Herman Daniel Jerrett. Sacramento, Press of J.
        Anderson, 1915.
        141 p.   illus. (incl. ports.)   19½ cm.

16891   Jocknick, Sidney, 1849-
        Early days on the western slope of Colorado and
        camp-fire chats with Otto Mears, the pathfinder,
        from 1870 to 1883, inclusive, by Sidney Jocknick.
        Denver, Colo., The Carson-Harper co., 1913.
        384 p.   front., plates, ports., map.   20½ cm.

16892   Johnson, Francis White, 1799-1884.
        A history of Texas and Texans, by Frank W. Johnson...
        ed. and brought to date by Eugene C. Barker... with
        the assistance of Ernest William Winkler... To which

are added historical, statistical and descriptive
matter pertaining to the important local divisions
of the state, and biographical accounts of the
leaders and representative men of the state...
Chicago and New York, The American historical society,
1914.
5 v.   front., illus., plates, ports., plan.
27½ cm.

16893 Johnson, Laura (Winthrop) 1825-1889.
Eight hundred miles in an ambulance. By Laura
Winthrop Johnson. Philadelphia, J. B. Lippincott
company, 1889.
131 p.   18½ cm.
First printed in Lippincott's magazine, June and
July 1875.

16894 Johnson, Sidney Smith, 1840-
Texans who wore the gray, by Sid S. Johnson, capt.
3rd Texas cavalry, Ross brigade, C.S.A., and brigadier
general Texas brigade, Forrest's cavalry, U.C.V. ...
v. 1-   [Tyler? Tex., c1907-   ]
    v.   illus. (ports.)   23 cm.

16895 Johnson, Sidona V   comp.
A short history of Oregon; early discoveries -
the Lewis and Clark exploration - settlement -
government - Indian wars - progress; comp. by Sidona
V. Johnson. Chicago, A. C. McClurg & co., 1904.
329 p.   front., plates, ports., fold. facsims.,
fold. map.   18 cm.

16896 Johnson, Theodore T
California and Oregon; or Sights in the gold region,
and scenes by the way, with a map and illustrations.
Ed. 4. With an appendix, containing full instructions
to emigrants by the overland route to Oregon, by
Samuel R. Thorston... Philadelphia, 1865.
12, 348 p.   pl.   19 cm.

16897 Johnson, Theodore T
Sights in the gold region, and scenes by the way.
New York, 1849.
12, 273 p.   21 cm.

16898 Johnston, Charles W
Along the Pacific by land and sea, through the
Golden Gate, by C. W. Johnston. Chicago, Rand,

McNally & co., 1916.
ix p., 1 1., 259 p.   19½ cm.

16899 Johnson, Arthur Tysilio.
California: an Englishman's impression of the
Golden state... with illustrations by E. Nora Meek.
London [1913]
346 p.   front., pl.   22 cm.

16900 Jones, Charles Jesse, 1844-
Buffalo Jones' forty years of adventure; a volume
of facts gathered from experience, by Hon. C. J. Jones,
whose eventful life has been devoted to the preservation
of the American bison and other wild animals... Comp.
by Colonel Henry Inman. Topeka, Kan., Crane & company,
1899.
xii, 469 p.   illus., plates, ports.   23½ cm.

16901 Jones, Daniel Webster.
Forty years among the Indians. A true yet thrilling
narrative of the author's experiences among the
natives. By Daniel W. Jones. Salt Lake City, Utah,
Juvenile instructor office, 1890.
[iii]-xv, [17]-400 p.   23 cm.

16902 Jones, Kumen.
First settlement of San Juan County, Utah, by
Kumen Jones. Salt Lake City, Utah State Historical
Society, 1929. (In Utah historical quarterly, v. 2,
no. 1, January 1929, p. 8-13)

16903 Jones, Lloyd.
Life and adventures of Harry Tracy, "the modern
Dick Turpin," by Lloyd Jones. Chicago, Jewett &
Lindrooth, 1902.
219, [5] p.   front. (ports.) illus.   20½ cm.

16904 Jones, Rebecca M   Burton.
Extracts from the life sketch of Nathaniel V. Jones,
by his wife, Rebecca M. Jones. Salt Lake City, Utah
State Historical Society, 1931. (In Utah historical
quarterly, v. 4, no. 1, January 1931, p. 2-24)
Includes extracts from Sergeant Jones' journal,
16 July 1846-24 August 1847.

16905 Jones, Thomas Lewis, 1841-
From the gold mine to the pulpit; the story of the
Rev. T. L. Jones, backwoods Methodist preacher in the

Pacific Northwest, during the closing years of the
nineteenth century. Cincinnati, Printed for the
author by Jennings and Pye [c1904]
169 p.   front., plates, ports.   19½ cm.

16906 Jones, William C
        ... Report on the subject of land titles in
        California, made in pursuance of instructions from the
        secretary of state and the secretary of the interior,
        together with a translation of the principal laws on
        that subject. Washington, 1860.
        60 p.   23 cm.

16907 Jordan, David S
        California and the Californians, and The alps of
        King-Kern Divide. New ed. San Francisco, 1903.
        63 p.   pl., port.   20½ cm.

16908 Judd, A   N
        Campaigning against the Sioux. By A. N. Judd.
        Being extracts from a diary kept during one of three
        expeditions participated in by the author against the
        Sioux, under General Alfred Sully in 1863-4-5.
        Illustrated by the author, some of the sketches being
        modifications from Catlin. [Watsonville, Calif.,
        Press of the Daily Pajaronian, July, 1906]
        45 p., 1 l.   illus., port.   25½ cm.

16909 Judson, Katharine Berry.
        Early days in old Oregon, by Katharine Berry Judson...
        with numerous illustrations and four maps. Chicago,
        A. C. McClurg & co., 1916.
        6 p.l., 263 p.   front., illus. (incl. maps)
        plates.   20 cm.
        Bibliography: p. 253-260.

16910 Judson, Katharine Berry.
        Montana, "the land of shining mountains", by
        Katharine Berry Judson; with 24 illustrations and a
        map. Chicago, A. C. McClurg & co., 1909.
        vii, [4] p., 1 l., 15-244 p.   front., plates,
        ports., fold. map.   19 cm.
        "Brief annotated bibliography of books touching
        upon Montana history": p. 179-188.

16911   Kane, Thomas L[eiper] 1822-1883.
          Coahuila. By Thomas L. Kane.   Read before the
        American philosophical society.   January 19, 1877.
        [Philadelphia, 1877]
          cover-title, 13 p.   23 cm.

16912   Kansas. Constitution.
          Conditions of the state of Kansas; adopted at
        Wyandot, July 29, '59.   [Wyandot, 1859]
          16 p.   23 cm.

16913   Kearns, Thomas.
          Conditions in Utah.   Speech in the Senate of the United
        States, Tuesday, Feb. 28, 1905.   Washington, 1905.
          14 p.   20 cm.

16914   Kearny, Stephen Watts, 1794-1848.
          The 1820 journal of Stephen Watts Kearny, comprising
        a narrative account of the Council Bluff-St. Peter's
        military exploration and a voyage down the Mississippi
        river to St. Louis.   Ed. by Valentine Mott Porter...
        St. Louis, Reprinted from Missouri historical society
        collections, vol. III, 1908.
          cover-title, 54 p.   2 pl., 3 port., map. $24\frac{1}{2}$ cm.

16915   Keeler, Charles Augustus.
          Southern California, illustrated with drawings
        from nature and from photographs by Louise M. Keeler.
        Los Angeles, 1899.
          141 p.   front., illus.   23 cm.

16916   Kelley, Hall Jackson, 1790-1874.
          A general circular to all persons of good character,
        who wish to emigrate to the Oregon territory, embracing
        some account of the character and advantages of the
        country; the right and the means and operations
        by which it is to be settled; - and all necessary
        directions for becoming an emigrant.   [By] Hall J.
        Kelley, general agent.   By order of the American
        society for encouraging the settlement of the Oregon
        territory.   Instituted in Boston, A.D. 1829.   Charles-
        town, Printed by W. W. Wheildon; Boston, R. P. & C.
        Williams, 1831.
          27 p. $24\frac{1}{2}$ cm.

16917   Kelley, Hall Jackson, 1790-1874.
        Geographical sketch of that part of North America
        called Oregon... Boston, 1830.
        80 p.   map.   20½ cm.

16918   Kelley, Hall J[ackson] 1790-1874.
        A history of the settlement of Oregon and the
        interior of upper California; and of persecutions
        and afflictions for forty years' continuance,
        endured by the author, Hall J. Kelley, A.M.
        Springfield, Mass., Union printing company, 1868.
        xv, [2], 7, 128 p.   22 cm.

16919   Kelley, Hall Jackson, 1790-1874.
        A narrative of events and difficulties in the
        colonization of Oregon, and the settlement of
        California; and, also, a history of the claim of
        American citizens to lands on Quadra's island;
        together with an account of the troubles and tribu-
        lations endured between the years 1824 and 1852, by
        the writer, Hall J. Kelley. Boston, Printed by
        Thurston, Torry & Emerson, 1852.
        92 p.   23½ cm.

16920   Kelley, Joseph.
        Thirteen years in the Oregon penitentiary, by
        Joseph (Bunko) Kelley. Portland, Or., 1908.
        142 p.   front. plates.   21 cm.

16921   Kelley, William Darrah, 1814-1890.
        ... The new Northwest: an address by Hon. Wm. D.
        Kelley [reported by D.Wolfe Brown, phonographer] on the
        Northern Pacific railway, in its relations to the
        development of the northwestern section of the
        United States, and to the industrial and commercial
        interests of the nation. [Philadelphia? 1871?]
        32 p.   24 cm.

16922   Kelly, Charles, 1889-
        Antoine Robidoux, by Charles Kelly. Salt Lake City,
        Utah State Historical Society, 1933. (In Utah
        historical quarterly, v. 6, no. 4, October 1933,
        p. 114-116)

16923   Kelly, Charles, 1889-
        The Hastings Cutoff, by Charles Kelly. Salt Lake
        City, Utah State Historical Society, 1930. (In Utah
        historical quarterly, v. 3, no. 3, July 1930, p. 66-82)

179

16924 Kelly, Charles, 1889-
Jedediah S. Smith on the Salt Desert Trail, by
Charles Kelly, continued in v. 3, no. 2, April 1930
under title, The Salt Desert Trail. Salt Lake City,
Utah State Historical Society, 1930. (In Utah histo-
rical quarterly, v. 3, no. 1, January 1930, p. 23-27)

16925 Kelly, Charles, 1889-
The mysterious "P. Julien". Salt Lake City, Utah
State Historical Society, 1933. (In Utah historical
quarterly, v. 6, no. 3, July 1933, p. 82-88)

16926 Kelly, Charles, 1889-
The Salt Desert Trail, by Charles Kelly. Salt Lake
City, Utah State Historical Society, 1930. (In Utah
historical quarterly, v. 3, no. 2, April 1930, p. 34-
56) Continuation of "Jedediah S. Smith on the Salt
Desert Trail," v. 3, no. 1, January 1930, p. 23-27.

16927 Kelly, Fanny (Wiggins) b. 1845.
Narrative of my captivity among the Sioux Indians.
By Fanny Kelly. With a brief account of General
Sully's Indian expedition in 1864, bearing upon events
occurring in my captivity. Cincinnati, Wilstach,
Baldwin & co., printers, 1871.
x, 11-285 p.   front. (port.)   plates.   20 cm.

16928 Kelly, J   Wells.
... Directory of Nevada Territory; embracing a
general directory of residents of all the principal
towns; business directory of advertisers... San
Francisco, Commercial Steam Press, Valentine & co.,
1862.
[14], 264 p.   15 cm.

16929 Kelly, William.
A stroll through the diggings of California. By
William Kelly, esq. London, Simms and M'Intyre,
1852.
xii, 18-240 p.   17½ cm.   (The Bookcase. v. 4)
Also printed as v. 2 of his Excursion to California
over the prairie... 1851.

16930 Kelsey, D   M
History of our wild West and stories of pioneer
life from experiences of Buffalo Bill, Wild Bill,
Kit Carson, David Crockett, Sam Houston, Generals
Crook, Miles and Custer, Geronimo, Sitting Bull,

great Indian chiefs, and other famous frontiersmen
and Indian fighters... By D. M. Kelsey... Chicago,
The Charles C. Thompson co. [c1901]
x p., 2 l., [15]-542 p.   illus.   21½ cm.

16931 Kelsey, Rayner W
The United States consulate in California. Berkeley,
1910.
107 p.   22½ cm.   (Academy of Pacific Coast
History, v. 1, no. 5)

16932 Kempker, John F   d. 1924.
History of the Catholic church in Iowa. Part I.
Comprising information of the early days, origin and
progress of the diocese of Dubuque, missions amongst
the Indian tribes, together with a chapter on Rt. Rev.
Dr. Smyth and Rt. Rev. Dr. Hennessy. By John F.
Kempker... Iowa City, Ia., Republican publishing
company, 1887.
64 p.   22 cm.

16933 Kendall, Reese P
Pacific trail camp-fires; containing the Missouri
column. The Applegate battalion. The "Pathfinder"
detachment. The Barneburg contingent. By Reese P.
Kendall, M.D. Chicago, Scroll pub. co., 1901.
6 p.l., [15]-437 p.   18½ cm.

16934 Kenderdine, Thaddeus S
California revisited, 1858-1897. Newtown, Pa.,
1898.
310 p.   illus., pl.

16935 Kenderdine, Thaddeus S
A California tramp and later footprints; or, Life
on the plains and in the Golden State thirty years
ago, with miscellaneous sketches in prose and verse.
Newtown, Pa., 1888.
415 p.   illus., pl., port.

16936 Kennedy, Elijah Robinson, 1844-
The contest for California in 1861; how Colonel
E. D. Baker saved the Pacific states to the Union,
by Elijah R. Kennedy... Boston and New York,
Houghton Mifflin company, 1912.
xiv p., 1 l., 361, [1] p.   front., ports.   22 cm.
"Authorities referred to": [343]-344.

16937 Kennedy, George W   1847-
The pioneer campfire, in four parts: With the
emigrants on the great plains. With the settlers in
the log cabin homes. With the hunters and miners.
With the preachers on the trails, at campmeetings and
in the log cabins. Anecdotes, adventures and reminiscences by G. W. Kennedy, pioneer of 1853. Portland,
Or., Printed for the author by the Clarke-Kundret
printing co., 1914.
240 p.   front. (port.) plates.   20 cm.

16938 Kennedy, William, 1799-1871.
Texas: its geography, natural history and topography. New York, Benjamin and Young, 1844.
118 p.   19 cm.

16939 Kenner, Scipio A
The practical politician; a digest of ready information
as to the fundamental differences between the great
national political parties, their rise and progress,
with past and present issues.... With a review of the
local political situation. Salt Lake City, Star print.
co., 1892.
181 p.   18 cm.

16940 Kerr, Lewis.
An exposition of the criminal laws of the territory
of Orleans; the practice of the courts of criminal
jurisdiction, the duties of their officers, with a
collection of forms for the use of magistrates and
others. Published in pursuance of an act of the
Legislature of the territory, entitled, "An act for
the punishment of crimes and misdemeanors" (section
48) passed May 4th, 1805. By order of government.
By Lewis Kerr... New-Orleans, Printed by John Mowry,
no. 36, Bienville street, 1806.
xii, 134, xxxiv p., 1 l.   18½ cm.

16941 Kershaw, W   L
History of Page County, Iowa, also biographical
sketches of some prominent citizens of the county,
by W. L. Kershaw, assisted by the following named
as an advisory board: Edwin C. Lane... W. P.
Ferguson... C. A. Lisle... G. B. Jennings...
Chicago, The S. J. Clarke publishing co., 1909.
2 v.   front., plates, ports.   27 cm.

16942 Keyes, Erasmus Darwin, 1810-1895.
Fifty years' observations of men and events, civil
and military. By E. D. Keyes... New York, C.
Scribner's sons, 1884.
vii, 515 p. 19½ cm.

16943 Kilbourne, David Wells, 1803-1876.
Strictures, on Dr. I. Galland's pamphlet, entitled,
"Villainy exposed", with some account of his transactions in lands of the Sac and Fox reservation, etc.,
in Lee County, Iowa. By D. W. Kilbourne. Fort
Madison, Printed at the Statesman office, 1850.
24 p. 19 cm.

16944 Kimball, Charles P
The San Francisco city directory, by Charles P.
Kimball. September 1, 1850. San Francisco, Journal
of commerce press, 1850.
139 p. 15 cm.

16945 Kimball, Heber Chase, 1801-1868.
Journal of Heber C. Kimball, an elder of the Church
of Jesus Christ of latter day saints. Giving an
account of his mission to Great Britain, and the
commencement of the work of the Lord in that land.
Also, the success which has attended the labors of
the elders to the present time. By R. B. Thompson...
Nauvoo, Ill., Printed by Robinson and Smith, 1840.
viii, [9]-60 p. 20 cm.

16946 Kimball, James P
Fort Buford, by James P. Kimball. [Bismarck,
State Historical Society of North Dakota, 1930]
73-77 p. 24 cm.
Reprinted from North Dakota historical quarterly,
v. 4, no. 2, January 1930.

16947 King, Charles, 1844-1933.
... Campaigning with Crook; by Capt. Charles King,
U.S.A. Milwaukee, Printed by the Sentinel company,
1880.
4 p.l., 133, [1] p. 24 cm.
At head of title: The Fifth cavalry in the Sioux
war of 1876.
First issued in the Milwaukee Sentinel.

16948 King, Charles, 1844-1933.
Trials of a staff-officer. By Capt. Charles King...

Philadelphia, L. R. Hamersly & co., 1891.
214 p.   19½ cm.

16949 King, Clarence, 1842-1901.
Mountaineering in the Sierra Nevada. By Clarence
King... Boston, J. R. Osgood and company, 1872.
3 p.l., 292 p.   21 cm.

16950 King, Thomas B
Report on California. Washington, 1850.
72 p.   21 cm.

16951 Kino, Eusebio Francisco, 1644-1711.
Kino's historical memoir of Pimeria Alta; a contem-
porary account of the beginnings of California,
Sonora, and Arizona, by Father Eusebio Francisco
Kino, S. J., pioneer missionary explorer, cartographer,
and ranchman, 1683-1711; pub. for the first time from
the original manuscript in the archives of Mexico;
tr. into English, ed. and annotated, by Herbert
Eugene Bolton... Cleveland, The Arthur H. Clark
company, 1919.
2 v.   fronts., maps (1 fold.) plan, facsim.
24½ cm.   (Half-title: Spain in the West; a series
of original documents from foreign archives, vol.
III-IV)
"Pimeria Alta included what is now northern Sonora
and southern Arizona." - v. 1, p. 50.
"Printed works": v. 2, p. [279]-286; "Manuscripts":
v. 2, p. [287]-296.

16952 [Kinzie, Juliette Augusta (Magill) "Mrs. John H. Kinzie"]
1806-1870.
Narrative of the massacre at Chicago, August 15,
1812, and of some preceding events. Chicago, Printed
by Ellis & Fergus, 1844.
34 p.   front. (map)   23 cm.
With some changes, this forms chapters XVIII and XIX
of the author's Wau-bun, the "early day" in the Northwest.

16953 Kip, Lawrence, 1836-1899.
Army life on the Pacific; a journal of the expedition
against the northern Indians, the tribes of the Coeur
d'Alenes, Spokans, and Pelouzes, in the summer of
1858. By Lawrence Kip, second lieutenant of the Third
regiment of artillery, U. S. Army. New York,

184

Redfield, 1859.
vi p., 1 l., [9]-144 p.   18½ cm.

16954 [Kip, Leonard] 1826-1906.
California sketches, with recollections of the
gold mines [anon.]   Albany, E. H. Pease & co., 1850.
57 p.   20½ cm.

16955 Kip, William Ingraham, bp., 1811-1893.
The early days of my episcopate. By the Right Rev.
Wm. Ingraham Kip... New York, T. Whittaker, 1892.
x, 263 p.   front. (port.)   19½ cm.

16956 Kip, William Ingraham, bp., 1811-1893.
The early Jesuit missions in North America; comp.
and tr. from the letters of the French Jesuits,
with notes. By the Rev. William Ingraham Kip...
New York, Wiley and Putnam, 1846.
2 v. in 1.   front. (fold. map)   18 cm.
(Half-title: Wiley and Putnam's library of American
books. [21-22])
A translation of parts relating to America in
"Letters édifiantes et curieuses, écrites des missions
étrangères."

16957 Kirchoff, Theodor.
Californische kulturbilder. Von Theodor Kirchoff...
Cassel, T. Fischer, 1886.
viii, 376 p.   24 cm.

16958 Kirk, Robert C
Twelve months in Klondike, by Robert C. Kirk; with
one hundred illustrations and a map. London, W.
Heinemann, 1899.
xii, 273 p.   front., illus., plates, map.   19½ cm.

16959 Klein, Julius.
The making of the treaty of Guadaloupe Hidalgo, on
February 2, 1848; the James Bryce historical prize
essay for 1905, by Julius Klein... Berkeley, The
University press, 1905.
1 p.l., 73 p. incl. map.   23½ cm.
Reprinted from the University chronicle, vol. VII,
no. 4.
"Sources cited and used": p. 71-73.

16960 Kneedler, H   S
Through storyland to sunset seas; what four people

185

saw on a journey through the Southwest to the Pacific coast. By H. S. Kneedler... Chicago, Knight, Leonard & co., printers, 1895.
2 p.l., [3]-205 p.   illus. $23\frac{1}{2}$ cm.

16961 Knower, Daniel.
The adventures of a forty-niner. An historic description of California, with events and ideas of San Francisco and its people in those early days... Albany, Weed-Parsons print co., 1894.
200 p.   pl., port.

16962 Koerner, Gustave Philipp, 1809-1896.
Memoirs of Gustave Koerner, 1809-1896, life-sketches written at the suggestion of his children; ed. by Thomas J. McCormack... Cedar Rapids, Ia., The Torch press, 1909.
2 v.   front., ports.   25 cm.

16963 Köhler, Karl.
Briefe aus Amerika. Ein lehrreicher wegweiser für deutsche auswanderer, und unterhaltendes lesebuch fur gebildete jeden standes... Bearbeitet von Carl Köhler... 2. verm. und verb. aufl. Darmstadt G. G. Lange, 1854.
viii, 288 p.   front., pl. $17\frac{1}{2}$ cm.

16964 Kopperl, Moritz.
Growth and material development of Texas. Address delivered at the annual convention of the American Bankers' Association, at Niagara Falls, August 12th, 1881. New York, Bankers' Pub. Association, 1881.
4 p.   24 cm.

L

16965 Ladue, Joseph.
Klondyke facts; being a complete guide book to the gold regions of the great Canadian northwest territories and Alaska, by Joseph Ladue... New York, American technical book co. [1897]
205 p.   plates, maps.   19 cm.   (On cover: Engineering and mining series, no. 1)

16966 Laird, Wilson M
The geology of the Turtle River State Park, by

Wilson M. Laird. [Bismarck, State Historical
Society of North Dakota, 1943]
244-261 p.   illus., fold. maps, diagrs.   24 cm.
Reprinted from North Dakota historical quarterly,
v. 10, no. 4, October 1943.

16967 Lambert, Will.
"One Texas." Report of the ceremonies of laying
the corner stone of the new state capitol, Austin,
March 2, 1885. [Austin, 1885]
43 p.   23 cm.

16968 Lambourne, Alfred.
Pictures of an inland sea, by Alfred Lambourne.
[Salt Lake City] The Deseret news [1902]
150 p.   front., pl.   21 cm.

16969 Lambourne, Alfred.
Scenic Utah: pen and pencil, by Alfred Lambourne.
New York, J. Dewing publishing co., 1891.
iv p., 45 l.   20 pl.   49 cm.

16970 [Lancaster, Columbia]
Citizens of Washington Territory. [Washington,
1854]
32 p.   24 p.
A report of debates in Congress relating to Washington
Territory by the territorial delegate in Congress.

16971 Lancaster, James A
Archeological excavations in Mesa Verde National
Park, Colorado, 1950, by James A. Lancaster [and
others] Washington, National Park Service, U.S.
Dept. of the Interior, 1954.
x, 118 p.   illus.   29 cm.   (U.S.   National
Park Service.   Archeological research series, no. 2)

16972 Lancaster, Samuel Christopher.
The Columbia, America's great highway through
the Cascade mountains to the sea, by Samuel Christopher
Lancaster; with thirty-one color plates and other
illustrations... Portland, Ore., S. C. Lancaster,
1915.
140 p. incl. illus., col. plates, ports.
col. front., col. fold. pl.   26½ cm.

16973 Lander, Frederick West, 1821-1862.
Remarks on the construction of a first class

double track railway to the Pacific, and the
difficulties attending its solution as a practical
and scientific problem. By Fred. W. Lander...
Washington, H. Polkinhorn, printer, 1854.
14 p.   23 cm.

16974   Lane, John J   b. 1833.
... History of education in Texas. By J. J.
Lane... Washington, Govt. print. off., 1903.
334 p.   front., plates. ports.   23½ cm.
(Contributions to American educational history.
Ed. by Herbert B. Adams. no. 35)
U.S. Bureau of education. Circulars of information.
1903. no. 2.

16975   Lane, Mrs. Lydia Spencer (Blaney)
I married a soldier; or, Old days in the old army.
By Lydia Spencer Lane. Philadelphia, J. B.
Lippincott company, 1893.
214 p.   18½ cm.
The wife of William B Lane, lieut. in the Mounted
rifle regiment, and captain and major in the 3d
U.S. cavalry.

16976   Lane, Samuel Alanson, b. 1815.
Fifty years and over of Akron and Summit county [O.]
by Samuel A. Lane... Akron, O., Beacon job department,
1892.
1 p.l., xl, 1167, [1] p.   front., illus. (incl.
ports.)   27 cm.

16977   Lang, H[erbert] O   ed.
History of the Willamette Valley, being a description
of the valley and resources, with an account of its
discovery and settlement by white men, and its
subsequent history; together with personal reminiscences
of its early pioneers. Ed. by H. O. Lang...
Published by Himes & Land. Portland, Ore., G. H.
Himes, book and job printer, 1885.
xv,[17]-902, xiii p.   front. (port.) plates.
25½ cm.

16978   Lang, William W
A paper on the resources and capabilities of Texas,
read before the Farmer's club of the American
institute, Cooper Union, New York, March 8th, 1881.
To which is appended a brief summary of the advantages
of the state as a field for immigration. Austin,

188

Texas [1881]
61 p.   tab., pl.   20½ cm.

16979 Langford, Nathaniel Pitt, 1832-1911.
Diary of the Washburn expedition to the Yellowstone
and Firehole rivers in the year 1870, by Nathaniel
Pitt Langford. [Salt. Paul? Minn., c1905]
xxxi, [1], 122 p.   front., illus., plates, ports.
21 cm.

16980 Langford, Nathaniel Pitt, 1832-1911.
Vigilante days and ways; the pioneers of the
Rockies; the makers and making of Montana, Idaho,
Oregon, Washington, and Wyoming. By Nathaniel Pitt
Langford... Boston, J. G. Cupples co., 1890.
2 v.   front., ports.   19½ cm.

16981 Langsdorff, Georg Heinrich, freiherr von, 1774-1852.
Voyages and travels in various parts of the world,
during the years 1803, 1804, 1805, 1806, and 1807.
By G. H. von Langsdorff... Illustrated by engravings
from original drawings. London, H. Colburn; [etc.,
etc.] 1813-14.
2 v.   21 pl. (incl. fronts., ports.) fold. map.
28 cm.
Translation of the author's Bemerkungen auf einer
reise um die welt, Frankfurt am Mayn, 1812.

16982 Langworthy, Lucius H[art]
Dubuque; its history, mines, Indian legends, etc.,
in two lectures, delivered before the Dubuque literary
institute, Dec. 18th, 1854, and Feb. 26th, 1855.
Dubuque, The Institute [1855]
82 p.   19 cm.

16983 Lanier, James Franklin Doughty, 1800-1881.
Sketch of the life of J. F. D. Lanier. (Printed for
the use of his family only) New York [Hosford & sons,
printers] 1871.
62 p.   front., port. (mounted phot.)   22 cm.
"The late Richard H. Winslow": p. 56-58.

16984 Lanning, C   M
A grammar and vocabulary of the Blackfoot language
... Comp. by C. M. Lanning from original translations,
by Joseph Kipp and W. S. Gladston, jr. Fort Benton
[Mont. Ter.] The author [1882]
iv, [5]-143 p.   15 cm.

16985 Lapham, Increase Allen, 1811-1875.
A geographical and topographical description of
Wisconsin; with brief sketches of its history,
geology, mineralogy, natural history, population...
by I. A. Lapham. Milwaukee, Wis., P. C. Hale, 1844.
iv, [5]-255, [1] p. front. (fold. map) 16 cm.

16986 Larimer, Mrs. Sarah Luse.
The capture and escape; or, Life among the Sioux.
By Mrs. Sarah L. Larimer... Philadelphia, Claxton,
Remsen & Haffelfinger, 1870.
xii, 13-252 p. front. (port.) pl. 19½ cm.

16987 Larimer, William Henry Harrison, 1840-1910.
Reminiscences of General William Larimer and of his
son William H. H. Larimer, two of the founders of
Denver City; comp. from letters: and from notes
written by the late William H. H. Larimer... by
Herman S. Davis, Ph.D. Printed for private circulation
under the auspices of William Larimer Mellon...
Lancaster, Pa., Press of the New era printing company,
1918.
1 p.l., [5]-256 (i.e. 266) p. incl. illus., ports.,
facsims. plates, ports., facsim., fold. geneal.
tab. 25 cm.

16988 La Roche, Frank.
En route to the Klondike; a series of photographic
views of the picturesque land of gold and glaciers...
Chicago, New York, W. B. Conkey [1898]
[144] p. front. (fold. map.) illus.

16989 Larocque, François Antoine.
... Journal of Larocque from the Assiniboine to
the Yellowstone, 1805. Ed. with notes by L. J.
Burpee... Pub. by authority of the minister of
agriculture under the direction of the archivist.
Ottawa, Government printing bureau, 1910.
1 p.l., 82 p. 25 cm. (Publications of the
Canadian archives, no. 3)
Laroque crossed the present states of North Dakota
and Montana.
"Bibliographical notes": p. 7-10.
"A few observations on the Rocky mountain Indians":
p. 55-78.

16990 Larpenteur, Charles, 1803?-1872.
Forty years a fur trader on the upper Missouri;

190

the personal narrative of Charles Larpenteur,
1833-1872; ed., with many critical notes, by Elliott
Coues... New York, F. P. Harper, 1898.
2 v.   fronts., plates, ports., maps (part fold.)
23½ cm.   (Half-title: American explorers series, II)

16991 Larrabee, Charles Hathaway, 1820-1883.
In the matter of the survey of the Ranchos San José,
Addition & Azusa before Hon. Sherman Day, U.S. Surveyor-
General, Charles H. Larrabee, and Henry Hancock,
counsel for settlers. San Francisco, Women's
Cooperative Union Print, 1869.
50 p.   23 cm.

16992 Larsen, Arthur J   , ed.
The Black Hills gold rush. Letters from men who
participated. [Bismarck, State Historical Society
of North Dakota, 1932]
302-318 p.   24 cm.
Reprinted from North Dakota historical quarterly,
v. 6, no. 4, July 1932.

16993 Larsen, Arthur J
The Northwestern Express and Transportation Company.
[Bismarck, State Historical Society of North Dakota,
1931]
42-62 p.   24 cm.
Reprinted from North Dakota historical quarterly,
v. 6, no. 1, October 1931.

16994 La Salle, Nicolas de.
Relation of the discovery of the Mississippi river,
written from the narrative of Nicolas de La Salle,
otherwise known as the little M. de La Salle; the
translation done by Melville B. Anderson. Chicago,
The Caxton club, 1898.
5 p.l., [3]-69 p., 1 l.   24 cm.
French and English on opposite pages.
The text is a reprint of "Récit de Nicolas de la
Salle - 1862" as published in "Découvertes et établissements des Français dans l'ouest et dans le sud
de l'Amérique Septentrionale 1614-1754; mémoires et
documents originaux recueillis et publiés par Pierre
Margry", 1. ptie., Paris, 1876, p. [545]-570.

16995 La Salle, Robert Cavelier, sieur de, 1643-1687?
Relation of the discoveries and voyages of Cavelier
de La Salle from 1679 to 1681, the official narrative;

the translation done by Melville B. Anderson.
Chicago, The Caxton club, 1901.
4 p.l., 299 p., 1 l.   24 cm.
French text and English translation on opposite
pages; the former from Margry's "Voyages des Français":
v. 1.
Authorship of the work uncertain; Parkman, Margry
and Winsor agree that it may have been compiled from
La Salle's letters rather than written by him.

16996   [Latham, Henry Jepson]
Among the Mormons. How an American and an Englishman went to Salt Lake City, and married seven wives
apiece. Their lively experience. A peep into the
mysteries of Mormonism. By Ring Jepson [pseud.]
San Francisco, The San Francisco news company, 1879.
115 p.   17 cm.

16997   Lathrop, George, b. 1830.
Some pioneer recollections, being the autobiography
of George Lathrop, one of the first to help in the
opening of the West, and a statement made by John
Sinclair relative to the rescue of the Donner party,
also an extract from a letter written by Geo. McKinstry
with reference to the rescue of the Donner party,
together with Personal recollections of pioneer life,
by Luke Voorhees. Philadelphia, G. W. Jacobs & co.,
1927.
32, 75 p. incl. port.   23½ cm.

16998   Latrobe, Benjamin Henry, 1764-1820.
The journal of Latrobe; being the notes and sketches
of an architect, naturalist and traveler in the
United States from 1797 to 1820, by Benjamin Henry
Latrobe, architect of the capitol at Washington;
with an introduction by J. H. B. Latrobe. New York,
D. Appleton and company, 1905.
xiii, 269 p.   front., illus., plates, ports.
23½ cm.

16999   Latta, Robert Ray, 1836-
Reminiscences of pioneer life, by Robert R. Latta.
Kansas City, Mo., Franklin Hudson publishing co.,
1912.
186 p.   front., illus. (incl. ports.)   20 cm.

17000   La Verendrye, Pierre Gautier de Varennes, sieur de,
1685-1749.

The journal of La Verendrye, 1738-39, tr. and
annotated by Henry E. Haxo. [Bismarck, State
Historical Society of North Dakota, 1941]
229-271 p., maps (part fold.)   24 cm.
Reprinted from North Dakota historical quarterly,
v. 8, no. 4, July 1941.

17001 Law, John, 1796-1873.
Address delivered before the Vincennes historical
and antiquarian society, February 22, 1839. By
Judge Law. Louisville, Ky., Prentice and Weissinger,
printers, 1839.
48 p.   front. (fold. map) $22\frac{1}{2}$ cm.

17002 Lazell, Frederick John.
Some autumn days in Iowa, by Frederick John Lazell.
Cedar Rapids, Ia., The Ioway club, 1906.
33 p. $24\frac{1}{2}$ cm.

17003 Lea, Albert M[iller]
A Pacific railway: by Albert M. Lea... [Knoxville,
Tenn., 1858?]
16 p.   23 cm.

17004 Leach, A   J
Early day stories; the overland trail; animals
and birds that lived here; hunting stories;
looking backward. 2d ed. By A. J. Leach. [Norfolk,
Neb., Huse publishing co., pref. 1916]
3 p.l., 9-244 p.   front. (port.)   plates.
$20\frac{1}{2}$ cm.

17005 Leach, A   J
A history of Antelope County, Nebraska, from its
first settlement in 1868 to the close of the year
1883. By A. J. Leach, secretary and historian of
the Antelope County pioneers. Cor. and rev. by
the advice of a committee of five elected for that
purpose... [Chicago, R. R. Donnelley & sons company]
1909.
3 p.l., 262 p. $20\frac{1}{2}$ cm.

17006 Leach, Frank Aleamon, 1846-
Recollections of a newspaperman: a record of life
and events in California, by Frank A. Leach. San
Francisco, S. Levinson, 1917.
7 p.l., 416 p.   front. (port.) plates, facsim.
$23\frac{1}{2}$ cm.

17007   Lecouvreur, Frank, 1829-1901.
From East Prussia to the Golden Gate, by Frank
Lecouvreur; letters and diary of the California
pioneer, edited in memory of her noble husband, by
Mrs. Josephine Rosana Lecouvreur; translated and
compiled by Julius C. Behnke... New York and Los
Angeles, Cal., Angelina book concern; [etc., etc.]
1906.
xiii, 15-355 p.   plates, ports. (incl. front.)
double maps.   23½ cm.

17008   Ledyard, Edgar M
American posts, by Edgar M. Ledyard.   Salt Lake City,
Utah State Historical Society, 1928-1933. (In Utah
historical quarterly, v. 1, no. 2, April 1928, p. 56-64;
v. 1, no. 3, July 1928, p. 86-96; v. 1, no. 4,
October 1928, p. 114-127; v. 2, no. 1, January 1929,
p. 25-30; v. 2, no. 2, April 1929, p. 54-64; v. 2,
no. 3, July 1929, p. 90-96; v. 2, no. 4, October 1929,
p. 127-128; v. 3, no. 1, January 1930, p. 27-32;
v. 3, no. 2, April 1930, p. 59-64; v. 3, no. 3,
July 1930, p. 90-96; v. 5, no. 2, April 1932, p. 65-80;
v. 5, no. 3, July 1932, p. 113-128; v. 5, no. 4,
October 1932, p. 161-176; v. 6, no. 1, January 1933,
p. 29-48; v. 6, no. 2, April 1933, p. 64-80)

17009   Lee, John Doyle, 1812-1877, defendant.
The Lee trial! An expose of the Mountain Meadows
massacre, being a condensed report of the prisoner's
statement, testimony of witnesses, charge of the judge,
arguments of counsel, and opinions of the press upon
the trial. By the Salt Lake daily tribune reporter.
Salt Lake City, Utah, Tribune printing company, 1875.
64 p.   21 cm.
Copyright by George F. Prescott.

17010   Lee, John Doyle, 1812-1877.
The life and confession of John D. Lee, the Mormon.
With a full account of the Mountain Meadows massacre
and execution of Lee... Philadelphia, Barclay & co.,
[1877]
1 p.l., 19-46 p. incl. pl.   pl.   24 cm.

17011   Lee, John Doyle, 1812-1877.
Mormonism unveiled; or, The life and confessions
of the late Mormon bishop, John D. Lee; (written
by himself) embracing a history of Mormonism from its
inception down to the present time, with an exposition

of the secret history, signs, symbols and crimes of
the Mormon church. Also the true history of the
horrible butchery known as the Mountain meadows
massacre... St. Louis, Mo., Bryan, Brand & co., 1877.
1 p.l., v-xiv, [15]-390 p.   front., plates, ports.
22 cm.
Edited by W. W. Bishop.

17012 Lee, L   P
History of the Spirit lake massacre: 8th March,
1857, and of Miss Abigail Gardiner's three month's
captivity among the Indians. According to her own
account, as given to L. P. Lee. New Britain, Conn.,
L. P. Lee, 1857.
47, [1] p.   illus. (incl. ports.)   23 cm.
Not the same as Mrs. Abigail Gardner-Sharp's
"History of the Spirit lake massacre" published 1885.

17013 Leeper, David Rohrer.
The argonauts of 'forty-nine; some recollections
of the plains and the diggings... illustrated by
O. Marion Elbel. South Bend, 1894.
146, xvi p.   illus.

17014 [Leeson, Michael A   ] ed.
History of Montana. 1739-1885. A history of its
discovery and settlement, social and commercial
progress, mines and miners, agriculture and stock-
growing, churches, schools and societies, Indians
and Indian wars, vigilantes, courts of justice,
newspaper press, navigation, railroads and statistics,
with histories of counties, cities, villages and
mining camps... Chicago, Warner, Beers & company, 1885.
1367 p. incl. plates, ports.   fold. map.   28 cm.

17015 Lefevre, Arthur.
Public education in Texas. [Austin, Tex., 1904]
12 p.   20 cm.

17016 Legard, Allayne Beaumont, 1847-
Colorado, by A. B. Legard. London, Chapman and
Hall, 1872.
2 p.l., 170 p.   19½ cm.

17017 The legion of liberty! And force of truth, containing
the thoughts, words and deeds, of some prominent
apostles, champions and martyrs. 2d ed. ... New York,
Sold at the office of the American a. s. society,

1843.
[308] p.   illus. (incl. ports.)   fold. map.
18½ cm.
"This Legion of liberty is a continuation of the
pamphlets, 'Liberty', published within the last five
years." Advertisement, p. [9]-[13] signed: J.R.A.
[i.e. Julius Rubens Ames?]
"The legion of liberty. Remonstrance of some free
men, states, and presses, to the Texas rebellion,
against the laws of nature and of nations..."
(p. [213-380]) has special t.-p.
An edition was published at Albany, 1845, under
title: The anti-Texass [!] legion. An edition under
the latter title, 1844, is ascribed to Benjamin Lundy.
cf. Cushing, Anonyms, 1889, p. 37.

17018 [Leisher, J   J   ]
The decline and fall of Samuel Sawbones, M.D., on
the Klondike, By his next best friend... Chicago,
New York [etc.] The Neely company [c1900]
2 p.l., [iii]-iv p., 1 l., [7]-197 p.   front.,
plates.   20 cm.

17019 Leland, Charles Godfrey, 1824-1903.
The Union Pacific railway, Eastern division; or,
Three thousand miles in a railway car, by Charles
Godfrey Leland... Philadelphia, Ringwalt & Brown,
1867.
95 p.   22 cm.

17020 Lenox, Edward Henry, 1827-
Overland to Oregon in the tracks of Lewis and
Clarke; history of the first emigration to Oregon
in 1843, by Edward Henry Lenox, ed. by Robert Whitaker;
illustrations and introduction by R. Morgenier.
Limited ed. Autograph copy. Oakland, Cal. [Dowdle
press] 1904.
2 p.l., vii-ix, 69 p. incl. plates, map.   ports.
23½ cm.

17021 Le Rossignol, James Edward, 1866-
... History of higher education in Colorado. By
James Edward Le Rossignol... Washington, Govt.
print. off., 1903.
67 p.   front., plates.   23½ cm.   (Contributions to American educational history. Ed. by
Herbert B. Adams. no. 34)

196

U.S. Bureau of education. Circulars of information.
1903, no. 1.

17022 Leslie, Miriam Florence (Folline) "Mrs. Frank Leslie,"
1851-1914.
California. A pleasure trip from Gotham to the
Golden Gate. (April, May, June, 1877) By Mrs. Frank
Leslie... New York, G. W. Carleton & co.; [etc.,
etc.] 1877.
6, [vii]-xiv, [17]-286 p.   front., illus., plates.
19 cm.

17023 Lester, Charles E
Life and achievements of Sam Houston, hero and
statesman. New York, 1883.
242 p.   port.   19 cm.
(Elzevir Library)

17024 Lester, Charles E
Sam Houston and his republic. New York, 1846.
208 p.   port.

17025 Lester, John Erastus.
The Atlantic to the Pacific. What to see, and
how to see it. By John Erastus Lester... Boston,
Shepard and Gill, 1873.
365 p.   front. (fold. map)   17 cm.

17026 Leuba, Edmond.
La Californie et les états du Pacifique;
souvenirs et impressions, par Edmond Leuba. Paris,
Sandoz et Thuillier; [etc., etc.] 1882.
318 p.   19 cm.

17027 Lévy, Daniel.
Les Français en Californie. San Francisco, 1884.
ix, 373 p.

17028 Lewis, Alfred Henry, 1857-1914.
The sunset trail, by Alfred Henry Lewis... New
York, A. S. Barnes & co., 1905.
x p., 3 l., 393 p.   front., illus., 7 pl.   19 cm.

17029 Lewis, Dio.
Gypsies; or, Why we went gypsying in the Sierras...
Boston, Eastern book co., 1881.
1 p.l., 416 p.   front. (port.) pl.   20½ cm.

17030 Lewis, Meriwether, 1774-1809.
Travels to the source of the Missouri river and across the American continent to the Pacific ocean. Performed by order of the government of the United States, in the years 1804, 1805, and 1806. By Captains Lewis and Clarke. Published from the official report, and illustrated by a map of the route, and other maps. London, Longman, Hurst, Rees, Orme and Brown, 1814.
1 p.l., [v]-xxiv, 663 p.   fold. front., maps. 28 cm.

17031 Lewis, Tracy Hammond.
Along the Rio Grande, by Tracy Hammond Lewis; illustrations by Oscar Frederick Howard. New York, Lewis publishing company, 1916.
5 p.l., 215 p.   front., plates.   19 cm.
Reprinted from the New York morning telegraph.

17032 Lewis, William Stanley, 1876-
The story of early days in the Big Bend country; breaking trails, rush of miners, coming of cattlemen, making homes, pioneer hardships in the Big Bend country, as told by William S. Lewis... Autograph ed. Spokane, Wash., W. D. Allen, 1926.
35 p.   front., pl.   24½ cm.

17033 [L'Héritier, Louis François] 1789-1852.
Le Champ-d'Asile, tableau topographique et historique du Texas, contenant des détails sur le sol, le climat et les productions de cette contrée; des documens authentiques sur l'organisation de la colonie des réfugiés français; des notices sur ses principaux fondateurs; des extraits de leurs pro- clamations et autres actes publics: suivi de lettres écrites par des colons à quelque-uns de leurs com- patriotes. Pub. au profit des réfugies) Par L.F.LH... Paris, Ladvocat, 1819.
viii, 247 p.   20½ cm.

17034 Lienhard, Heinrich.
Californien unmittelbar vor und nach der entdeckung des goldes. Bilder aus dem leben des Heinrich Lienhard von Bilton, kanton Glarus in Nauvoo, Nordamerika. Ein beitrag zur jubiläumsfeier der goldentdeckung und zur kulturgeschichte Californiens. Zürich, 1898.
318 p.   front. (port.)   22 cm.

17035 Linder, Usher F   1809-1876.
          Reminiscences of the early bench and bar of Illinois.
          By General Usher F. Linder. With an introduction and
          appendix, by the Hon. Joseph Gillespie. Chicago, The
          Chicago legal news company, 1879.
          406 p.   20 cm.

17036 Linderman, Frank Bird, 1868-1938.
          Indian why stories; sparks from War Eagle's lodge-
          fire, by Frank B. Linderman [Co-skee-see-co-cot]
          illustrated by Charles M. Russell [Cah-ne-ta-wah-see-
          na-e-ket]... New York, C. Scribner's sons, 1915.
          xvi, 236 p.   col. front., illus., col. plates.
          21 cm.
          "Tales told me by the older men of the Blackfeet,
          Chippewa and Cree tribes." - Pref.

17037 Lindley, Walter, 1852-
          California of the south; its physical geography,
          climate, mineral springs, resources, routes of travel
          and health-resorts, being a complete guide-book to
          southern California, by Walter Lindley, M.D., and
          J.P. Widney... With maps and numerous illustrations.
          3d ed., rewritten and printed from new plates. New
          York, D. Appleton and company, 1896.
          xii, 325 p.   front., illus., 2 maps (1 fold.)
          19½ cm.

17038 Lindsey, Benjamin Barr.
          The rule of plutocracy in Colorado: a retrospect
          and a warning. [Denver, Col., n.d.]
          68 p.   18 cm.

17039 Linn, William Alexander, 1846-1917.
          The story of the Mormons, from the date of their
          origin to the year 1901, by William Alexander Linn.
          New York, The Macmillan company; London, Macmillan &
          co., ltd., 1902.
          xxv, 637 p.   facsims., diagr.   23½ cm.

17040 Lĭsĭánskĭĭ, Ĭûrĭĭ Fedorovich, 1773-1837.
          A voyage round the world, in the years 1803, 4, 5,
          & 6; performed, by order of His Imperial Majesty
          Alexander the First, emperor of Russia, in the ship
          Neva, by Urey Lisiansky... London, Printed for
          J. Booth [etc.] 1814
          xxi, [2], 388 p. incl. tables.   front. (port.)
          5 pl. (2 col.) 8 maps (2 fold.)   27½ x 21½ cm.

199

Published originally in Russian, St. Petersburg,
1812; English translation by the author.

17041 Little, James Alexander, 1831-
What I saw on the old Sante Fe trail... A condensed
story of frontier life half a century ago. By James
A. Little... Plainfield, Ind., The Friends press
[1904]
1 p.l., 127 p. incl. ports.   front.   19½ cm.

17042 Little, James Amasa, 1822-1908.
From Kirtland to Salt Lake City.   Salt Lake City,
1890.
260 p.   illus.   23 cm.

17043 Little, James Amasa, 1822-1908.
Jacob Hamblin, a narrative of his personal
experience, as a frontiersman, missionary to the
Indians and explorer... Salt Lake City, Juvenile
instructor office, 1881.
144 p.   17 cm.

17044 Littlejohn, E   G
Texas history stories. Richmond, 1901.
various pagination.   pl., port.   21 cm.

17045 Lockley, Fred.
To Oregon by ox-team in '47; the story of the
coming of the Hunt family to the Oregon country and
the experiences of G. W. Hunt in the gold diggings
of California in 1849. Portland, Ore. [n.d.]
16 p.   20 cm.

17046 Lockwood, James D
Life and adventures of a drummer-boy; or, Seven
years a soldier. By James D. Lockwood... A true
story... Albany, N. Y., J. Skinner, 1893.
191 p.   front.   20 cm.

17047 Lockwood, Rufus A   1811-1857.
The Vigilance committee of San Francisco. Metcalf
vs. Argenti et al. Speeches of R. A. Lockwood, esq.
San Francisco, Cal., 1852.
47, [1] p.   22 cm.
Speeches before the Superior court of San Francisco
and the District court of Santa Clara in a suit against
members of the Vigilance committee.

17048   Long, John, Indian trader.
        Voyages and travels of an Indian interpreter and
        trader, describing the manners and customs of the
        North American Indians; with an account of the posts
        situated on the river Saint Laurence, lake Ontario,
        &c. To which is added a vocabulary of the Chippeway
        language... a list of words in the Iroquois, Mehegan,
        Shawanee, and Esquimeaux tongues, and a table,
        shewing the analogy between the Algonkin and Chippeway
        languages. By J. Long. London, Printed for the author,
        and sold by Robson [etc.] 1791.
        1 p.l., x p., 1 l., 295 p.   fold. map.
        28½ x 23 cm.

17049   Long, Stephen Harriman, 1784-1864.
        Voyage in a six-oared skiff to the Falls of Saint
        Anthony in 1817. By Major Stephen H. Long... With
        introductory note by Edward D. Neill... Philadelphia,
        H. B. Ashmead, printer, 1860.
        87, [1] p.   22 cm.   (Half-title: Collections
        of the Historical society of Minnesota. [pt. 1, 1860])
        Reprinted (2d edition) as the first part of
        "Collections of the Minnesota historical society.
        Volume II." 1889.

17050   Longley, William Preston, 1851-1878.
        Adventures of Bill Longley, captured by Sheriff
        Milton Mast and Deputy Bill Burrows, near Keatchie,
        Louisiana, in 1877, and was executed at Giddings,
        Texas, 1878. By Henry C. Fuller. Nacogdoches, Tex.,
        Baker Print. Co. [n.d.]
        1 v. (unpaged)   ports.   22 cm.
        A collection of the letters Longley wrote in jail,
        most of them to the Nacogdoches News.

17051   [Loomis, Augustus Ward] 1816-1891.
        Scenes in the Indian country. By the author of
        "Scenes in Chusan" [etc.] Philadelphia, Presbyterian
        board of publication [1859]
        283 p.   3 pl. (incl. front.)   15½ cm.
        "Some account... of about a year spent amongst the
        Creek Indians, who are located along the Arkansas
        River, west of the state of Arkansas."

17052   Loomis, Chester A   1789-1873.
        A journey on horseback through the great West,
        in 1825. By Chester A. Loomis. Visiting Allegany
        towns, Olean, Warren, Franklin, Pittsburg, New Lisbon,

Elyria, Norfalk, Columbus, Zanesville, Vermillion,
Kaskaskia, Vandalia, Sandusky, and many other
places. Bath, N. Y., Plaindealer press [182-?]
[29] p.   19½ x 15 cm.

17053 Lord, Mrs. Elizabeth (Laughlin)
       Reminiscences of eastern Oregon. [By] Mrs. Elizabeth
       Lord... Portland, Ore., The Irwin-Hodson co., 1903.
       255 p.   front., plates, ports.   21½ cm.

17054 Los Angeles. Chamber of Commerce.
       California's old mission scenic tour by motor or
       rail. Los Angeles [1916]
       folder.   illus., map.   22 cm.

17055 Los Angeles. Chamber of Commerce.
       Good roads in Southern California. Los Angeles [n.d.]
       unpaged.   illus.   22 cm.

17056 Los Angeles Times, Los Angeles, Cal.
       Los Angeles daily times, annual midwinter number,
       January 1, 1906. Los Angeles, 1906.
       184, 32 p.   illus.   28 cm.
       Published in 6 pt.
       Our Sister Republic - Mexican number supplementary
       part. 32 p.

17057 Loughborough, John.
       The Pacific telegraph and railway, an examination
       of all the projects for the construction of these
       works, with a proposition for harmonizing all sections
       and parties of the Union, and rendering these great
       works truly national in their character. By J. Lough-
       borough... Saint Louis, Printed by Charles & Hammond,
       1849.
       1 p.l., xx, [5]-80 p.   2 fold. maps (incl. front.)
       25½ cm.

17058 Lounsberry, Clement Augustus, 1843-1926.
       Early history of North Dakota; essential outlines
       of American history, by Colonel Clement A. Lounsberry...
       Washington, D. C., Liberty press, 1919.
       xv, 645 p.   front., plates (part.col.) ports.,
       maps.   27 cm.
       "Part one, Early history of North Dakota, was
       published in 1913, and three years later was merged
       into North Dakota history and people... in connection
       with two volumes of biographical sketches. The

historical features embraced in that work, with
added matter and illustrations, are now presented
in four parts, complete in one volume." -
Publisher's pref.

17059 Love, Nat, 1854-
Life and adventures of Nat Love, better known in
the cattle country as "Deadwood Dick," by himself;
a true history of slavery days, life on the great
cattle ranges... based on facts, and personal
experiences of the author. Los Angeles, Cal., 1907.
162 p.   illus., plates, ports.   23½ cm.

17060 Lowe, Percival Green, 1828-
Five years a dragoon ('49 to '54) and other
adventures on the great plains. By Percival G. Lowe.
Kansas City, Mo., The F. Hudson publishing co., 1906.
3 p.l., [5]-417, [1] p.   front., illus., ports.
20 cm.

17061 Lubbock, Francis Richard.
Six decades in Texas; or, Memoirs of Francis Richard
Lubbock... a personal experience in business, war,
and politics. Edited by C. W. Raines... Austin,
B. C. Jones & co., 1900.
xvi, 685 p.   illus., pl., port., facsim.   22½ cm.

17062 Lucas, C[orydon] L   1838-
The Milton Lott tragedy; a history of the first
white death in Boone County and the events which lead
up to the dark tragedy, and the placing of the
monument in memory of this historic event. Together
with two other short stories of pioneer happenings,
A sketch of the life of Col. Nathan Boone, the man
that explored the upper Des Moines Valley, and A sixty
mile race for one hundred and sixty acres of Iowa land.
Written by C. L. Lucas. Madrid, Ia., Pub. under the
auspices of the Madrid historical society [1906]
1 p.l., 24 p.   2 illus.   20½ cm.

17063 Ludlow, Fitz Hugh, 1836-1870.
The heart of the continent: a record of travel
across the plains and in Oregon, with an examination
of the Mormon principle. By Fitz Hugh Ludlow...
New York, Hurd and Houghton; Cambridge, Riverside
press, 1870.
vi, 568 p.   front., plates, ports.   22 cm.

17064   Lukens, Mrs. Matilda Barns.
         The inland passage. A journal of a trip to
         Alaska. By Matilda Barns Lukens. [n.p.] 1889.
         3 p.l., 84 p.   15 x 12 cm.

17065   [Lum, Dyer Daniel]
         Social problems of to-day; or, the Mormon question
         in its economic aspects. A study of cooperation and
         arbitration in Mormondom, from the standpoint of a
         wage-worker. By a Gentile. Port Jervis, N. Y.,
         D. D. Lum & Co., 1886.
         91 p.   23 cm.

17066   [Lundy, Benjamin] 1789-1839.
         The war in Texas; a review of facts and circumstances,
         showing that this contest is the result of a long
         premeditated crusade against the government, set on
         foot by slaveholders, land speculators, &c. with the
         view of re-establishing, extending, and perpetuating
         the system of slavery and the slave trade in the
         republic of Mexico. By a citizen of the United States.
         Philadelphia, Printed for the author, by Merrihew
         and Gunn, 1836.
         56, [1] p.   22 cm.

17067   Lydston, George Frank, 1858-1923.
         Panama and the Sierras; a doctor's wander days.
         Chicago, Riverton Press, 1900.
         283 p.   illus.   20 cm.
         "Illustrations from the author's original photo-
         graphs."

17068   Lyford, C   P
         Brigham Young's record of blood! or, The necessity
         for that famous "Bible and revolver"... A lecture
         delivered in the First M. E. church, Salt Lake City,
         Jan. 23d, 1876, by Rev. C. P. Lyford... [Salt Lake
         City, Tribune publishing company, 1876]
         15 p.   20½ cm.
         "Published in the Salt Lake daily tribune, Jan. 25th,
         1876, and Rocky Mountain Christian advocate, Feb. 1st,
         1876."

17069   Lyman, Albert.
         Journal of a voyage to California, and life in the
         gold diggings; and also of a voyage from California
         to the Sandwich Islands. Hartford, Conn., 1852.
         192 p.   illus.   20 cm.

17070 Lyman, Albert R
       Pahute biscuits, by Albert R. Lyman. Salt Lake
       City, Utah State Historical Society, 1930. (In Utah
       historical quarterly, v. 3, no. 4, October 1930,
       p. 118-120)

17071 Lyman, Horace S[umner] 1855-
       History of Oregon, the growth of an American state;
       by Horace S. Lyman, associate board of editors:
       Harvey W. Scott, Charles B. Bellinger and Frederic G.
       Young. New York, The North Pacific publishing
       society, 1903.
       4 v.   front., pl., port., maps, facsim.   24½ cm.

17072 Lyman, Horace S[umner] 1855-
       ... Mile posts in the development of Oregon and
       characteristics of Oregon as an American commonwealth,
       by Horace S. Lyman, with a supplement: A world move-
       ment and a national movement that had important
       relations to the making of Oregon, by the editor of
       the Historical series. Pub. with the approval of the
       Regents of the university. Eugene, Or., The University,
       1898.
       vi, 22, [3] p.   2 illus. (maps)   24½ cm.
       (Semi-centennial history of Oregon. [1])
       Supplement by Frederick George Young.
       At head of title: Bulletin of the University of
       Oregon. Historical series. vol. I, no. 1.

17073 [Lynch, James]
       With Stevenson to California, 1846. [n.p.,
       pref. 1896]
       65 p.   20½ cm.
       The author served in California, in a regiment
       commanded by Col. J. D. Stevenson, throughout the
       Mexican war.

17074 Lynch, James D
       The bench and bar of Texas... St. Louis, 1885.
       610 p.   port.   20 cm.

17075 Lynch, Jeremiah, 1849-
       A senator of the fifties: David C. Broderick,
       of California, by Jeremiah Lynch... San Francisco,
       A. M. Robertson, 1911.
       6 p.l., 246 p.   front., plates, ports., facsim.
       20 cm.

M

17076   McCain, Charles W
        History of the SS. "Beaver". Being a graphic and
        vivid sketch of this noted pioneer steamer and her
        romantic cruise for over half a century on the placid
        island-dotted waters of the north Pacific. Also
        containing a description of the Hudson's Bay company
        from its formation in 1670, down to the present time...
        Comp. by Charles W. McCain... [Vancouver, B.C., 1894]
        99 p. incl. plates, ports.   16½ cm.

17077   McCarty, W   C
        A few practical remarks about Texas, her resources,
        climate and soil, with many important facts and
        extracts from reliable sources. New York, 1871.
        27 p.   20 cm.

17078   McClellan, Rolander Guy.
        The golden state: a history of the region west of
        the Rocky mountains embracing California, Oregon,
        Nevada, Utah, Arizona, Idaho, Washington territory,
        British Columbia, and Alaska, from the earliest period
        to the present time... with a history of Mormonism
        and the Mormons. By R. Guy McClellan... Philadelphia
        [etc.] W. Flint & company; Chicago, Union publishing
        company [etc., etc., 1872]
        [4], 15-685 p.   front., plates, ports., maps.
        23 cm.

17079   McClernand, John Alexander, 1812-1900.
        Reprint of the separate report of Hon. John A.
        McClernand, as a member of the Utah Commission of
        the Mormon question. September 23, 1889. Washington,
        D.C., 1890.
        20 p.   23 cm.

17080   McClure, Alexander Kelly, 1828-1909.
        Three thousand miles through the Rocky Mountains.
        By A. K. McClure. Philadelphia, J. B. Lippincott & co.,
        1869.
        456 p.   front., pl., port.   19½ cm.

17081 McClurg, Virginia (Donaghe) 1858-1931.
      Picturesque Utah. Albertype illustrations from
      original photographs by Chas. R. Savage...
      Descriptive text by M. Virginia Donaghe. Denver,
      Col., F. S. Thayer, 1888.
      1 p.l., [7]-33 p. incl. 6 pl.   20½ x 28½ cm.

17082 McCoid, Moses Ayers, 1840-1904.
      John Williamson of Hardscrabble... by M. A. McCoid;
      drawings by H. Shriner. Chicago, M. A. Donohue &
      company [c1902]
      341 p.   front., pl., port.   20 cm.

17083 McConnell, William John, 1839-1925.
      Early history of Idaho, by W. J. McConnell, ex-U.S.
      senator and -governor, who was present and cognizant
      of the events narrated; published by authority of
      the Idaho state legislature. Caldwell, Id., The
      Caxton printers, 1913.
      2 p.l., [7]-420 p.   2 port. (incl. front.)
      23 cm.

17084 [McCoy, Isaac] 1784-1846.
      Address to the philanthropists in the United States,
      generally, and to Christians in particular, on the
      condition and prospects of the American Indians.
      [n.p., 1831?]
      8 p.   22 cm.

17085 McCoy, Isaac, 1784-1846.
      Remarks on the practicability of Indian reform,
      embracing their colonization. By Isaac M'Coy.
      Boston, Printed by Lincoln & Edmands, 1827.
      47 p.   22½ cm.

17086 McCoy, Joseph Geiting, 1837-1915.
      Historic sketches of the cattle trade of the West
      and Southwest. By Joseph G. McCoy... Kansas City,
      Mo., Ramsey, Millett & Hudson, 1874.
      3 p.l., 427 p.   front., illus. (incl. ports.)
      23 cm.

17087 McCulloch, Hugh, 1808-1895.
      Men and measures of half a century; sketches and
      comments, by Hugh McCulloch... New York, C. Scribner's
      sons, 1888.
      xxv, 542 p.   24 cm.

17088   Macdonald, Augustin S
          List of books - Californiana and the Pacific.
        Oakland, Cal., 1903.
          76 p.   20 cm.

17089   McDonald, Frank Virgil, 1852-1897.
          Notes preparatory to a biography of Richard Hayes
        McDonald of San Francisco, California. Comp. and ed.
        by his eldest child, Frank V. McDonald. v. 1...
        Cambridge, University press, 1881.
          xix, [1] p., 3 l., [29]-95, 119 p.   front., illus.,
        plates, ports.   34 x 25 cm.

17090   Macdonald, James, 1852-1913.
          Food from the far West; or, American agriculture,
        with special reference to beef production and import-
        ation of dead meat from America to Great Britain;
        by James Macdonald... London and Edinburgh, W. P.
        Nimmo, 1878.
          xvi, 331 p.   19 cm.

17091   McDougal, Henry Clay.
          Recollections 1844-1909, by Henry Clay McDougal.
        Kansas City, Mo., F. Hudson publishing co., 1910.
          1 p.l., 7-466 p.   front. (port.)   24 cm.

17092   McElrath, Thomson P
          The Yellowstone valley. What it is, where it is,
        and how to get to it. A hand-book for tourists and
        settlers... St. Paul, The pioneer press, 1880.
          138 p.   front. (fold. map)   19 cm.

17093   McElroy, Robert McNutt, 1872-
          The winning of the far West; a history of the
        regaining of Texas, of the Mexican war, and the
        Oregon question; and of the successive additions to
        the territory of the United States, within the
        continent of America: 1829-1867. By Robert McNutt
        McElroy... New York and London, G. P. Putnam's sons,
        1914.
          x p., 1 l., 384 p.   col. front., 3 pl., 10 fold.
        maps.   23½ cm.

17094   McGeeney, Patrick Sylvester, 1873-
          Down at Stein's Pass; a romance of New Mexico, by
        P. S. McGeeney... Boston, Mass., Angel guardian
        press, 1909.
          2 p.l., 114 p.   front. (port.)   19 cm.

17095 M'Gillivray, Duncan, d. 1808.
        The journal of Duncan M'Gillivray of the North west
        company at Fort George on the Saskatchewan, 1794-5,
        with introduction, notes and appendix by Arthur S.
        Morton... Toronto, The Macmillan company of Canada,
        limited, 1929.
        lxxviii, 79, 24, 6 p.   maps (1 double)   24 cm.

17096 McGlashan, Charles Fayette, 1847-1931.
        History of the Donner party. A tragedy of the
        Sierras. By C. G. McGlashan. Truckee, Cal., Crowley
        & McGlashan [1879]
        193 p.   23 cm.

17097 McGowan, Edward, 1813-1893.
        Narrative of Edward McGowan, including a full
        account of the author's adventures and perils while
        persecuted by the San Francisco vigilance committee
        of 1856... San Francisco, The author, 1857.
        viii, [9]-240 p.   illus.   19½ cm.

17098 MacGregor, John, 1825-1892.
        Our brothers and cousins; a summer tour in Canada
        and the States. By John MacGregor... London, Seeley,
        Jackson, and Halliday, 1859.
        xix, 156 p.   front., illus.   16½ cm.
        "Letters reprinted from the 'Record' newspaper." -
        Brit. mus. Catalogue.

17099 McGroarty, John Steven, 1862-
        California; its history and romance, by John S.
        McGroarty... Los Angeles, Grafton publishing company,
        1911.
        6 p.l., [3]-393 p.   front., 9 pl., map.   24½ cm.

17100 McIlhany, Edward Washington.
        Recollections of a '49er. A quaint and thrilling
        narrative of a trip across the plains, and life in
        the California gold fields during the stirring days
        following the discovery of gold in the far West.
        Kansas City, Mo., Hailman printing company, 1908.
        212 p.   illus.   20 cm.

17101 McIntire, James, 1846-
        Early days in Texas; a trip to hell and heaven.
        By Jim McIntire. Kansas City, Mo., McIntire
        publishing company [c1902]
        229 p.   front., plates, port.   20 cm.

209

17102   McKay, Robert Henderson, 1840-
          Little pills; an army story, by R. H. McKay...
          being some experiences of a United States army
          medical officer on the frontier nearly a half
          century ago. Pittsburg, Kan., Pittsburg headlight,
          1918.
          2 p.l., [7]-127 p.   2 pl., port.   22½ cm.

17103   McKee, James Cooper.
          Narrative of the surrender of a command of U.S.
          forces at Fort Fillmore, N. M. in July, A.D. 1861,
          at the breaking out of the civil war, between the
          North and the South. By James Cooper McKee...
          Prescott, A. T., 1878.
          cover-title, 15 p.   18½ cm.

17104   McKee, Lanier.
          The land of Nome; a narrative sketch of the rush to
          our Bering sea gold-fields, the country, its mines
          and its people, and the history of a great conspiracy
          1900-1901, by Lanier McKee. New York, The Grafton
          press [1902]
          ix p., 1 l., 260 p.   19½ cm.
          An attack on the operating of Alexander Mackenzie
          and the Alaska gold mining co.

17105   McKinley, William, pres. U.S., 1843-1901.
          ... Equitable distribution of the waters of the
          Rio Grande. Message from the president of the
          United States. [Washington, D. C., 1898]
          210 p.   maps, tables.   23 cm.   (U.S. Congress
          55th, 2d session, Senate document no. 229)

17106   McKitrick, Reuben.
          ... The public land system of Texas, 1823-1910.
          By Reuben McKitrick... Madison, Wis., 1918.
          172 p.   illus. (maps)   23½ cm.   (Bulletin
          of the University of Wisconsin, no. 905. Economics
          and political science series, v. 9, no. 1)
          Bibliography: p. 167-172.

17107   McLaughlin, James, 1842-1922.
          My friend the Indian, by James McLaughlin...
          Boston and New York, Houghton Mifflin company, 1910.
          viii p., 3 l., 416, [2] p.   front., plates,
          ports.   23 cm.

17108   McMaster, S   W   b. 1811.
        60 years on the upper Mississippi. My life and
        experiences, by S. W. McMaster. Rock Island, Ill.,
        1893 [i.e. 1895]
        2 p.l., 300 p.   18 cm.

17109   MacMechen, Edgar Carlisle, 1884-
        Life of Governor Evans, second territorial governor
        of Colorado, by Edgar Carlisle McMechen. [Denver,
        The Wahlgreen publishing co., c1924]
        x, 224 p.   front., plates, ports., facsims.
        20½ cm.

17110   McMurtrie, Douglas Crawford, 1888-1944.
        The beginnings of printing in Utah, with a biblio-
        graphy of the issues of the Utah press, 1849-1860.
        Chicago, Publ. by the John Calhoun Club, 1931.
        91 p.   facsim.   20 cm.

17111   McMurtrie, Douglas Crawford, 1888-1944.
        Early printing in Utah outside of Salt Lake City.
        Salt Lake City, Utah State Historical Society, 1932.
        (In Utah historical quarterly, v. 5, no. 3, July
        1932, p. 83-87)

17112   McMurtrie, Douglas Crawford, 1888-1944.
        Pioneer printing in North Dakota. [Bismarck,
        State Historical Society of North Dakota, 1932]
        221-230 p.   facsims.   24 cm.
        Reprinted from North Dakota historical quarterly,
        v. 6, no. 3, April 1932.

17113   McNaughton, Margaret.
        Overland to Cariboo; an eventful journey to Canadian
        pioneers to the gold-fields of British Columbia in
        1862. By Margaret McNaughton... Toronto, W. Briggs;
        [etc., etc.] 1896.
        vii, [xi]-xvi, [19]-176 p. incl. illus., plates,
        ports.   front., plates.   19 cm.

17114   McReynolds, Robert.
        Thirty years on the frontier, by Robert McReynolds...
        Colorado Springs, Co., El Paso publishing co., 1906.
        4 p.l., 256 p.   front., plates, ports.   19½ cm.

17115   McRoskey, Racine.
        The missions of California, with sketches of the
        lives of St. Francis and Junipero Serra, by Racine

McRoskey... illustrated from photographs... San Francisco, The Philopolis press, 1914.
7 p.l., [3]-174 p. incl. illus., plates. col. front., map. 25 cm.

17116 Magazine of travel.
Travels in the two hemispheres; or, Gleanings of a European tour, by George Duffield, D.D. "Land of pyramids," or, a winter in Egypt, together with a "Caravan journey" across the "long desert" by Warren Isham. "Sketches of border life," or Incidents of a railroad survey across the prairies of Iowa, by W. P. Isham. "Journal leaves of European rambles: ocean scenes, by D. Bethune Duffield. Travels in the Southwest - life in Arkansas and Texas by Gilbert Hathaway - 2d ed. Detroit, Doughty, Straw & co. [etc.] 1858.
2 p.l., vi, 576 p. front. 20½ cm.

17117 Maillard, N   Doran.
The history of the republic of Texas, from the discovery of the country to the present time: and the cause of her separation from the republic of Mexico... London, Smith, Elder and co., 1842.
xxiv, 512 p. fold. map. 23 cm.

17118 Majors, Alexander, 1814-
Seventy years on the frontier; Alexander Majors' memoirs of a lifetime on the border; with a preface by "Buffalo Bill" (General W. F. Cody) ed. by Colonel Prentiss Ingraham. Chicago and New York, Rand, McNally & company, 1893.
325 p. illus., plates, ports. (incl. front.) 20½ cm. (On cover: Rialto series, no. 10)

17119 *Omitted.*

17120 Mallet, Edmond.
The Canadians of Oregon. Tr. from La Minerve, of Montreal, Canada. Clippings from New York Freeman's Journal, April 30, 1881.
broadside (1 p., 3 cols.)

17121 [Maltby, William J   ] 1829-
Captain Jeff; or, Frontier life in Texas with the Texas rangers; some unwritten history and facts in the thrilling experiences of frontier life... By one of the nine, a member of Company "E" Texas rangers.

Colorado, Tex., Whipkey printing co., 1906.
161 p. incl. port.   2 pl.   23 cm.

17122   Mandat-Grancey, Edmond, baron de, 1842-1911.
Cow-boys and colonels; narrative of a journey across
the prairie and over the Black hills of Dakota. From
"Dans les Montagnes Rocheuses," of Baron E. de Mandat-
Grancey; with additional notes not contained in the
original editions, by William Conn. London, Griffith,
Farran, Dkeden, & Welsh, 1887.
xi, 352 p.   front., plates.   23 cm.

17123   Mandat-Grancey, Edmond, baron de, 1842-1911.
Dans les Montagnes Rocheuses, par le baron E. de
Mandat-Grancey, dessins de Crafty et carte spéciale;
couronné par l'Académie française, prix Montyon.
3. éd.   Paris, E. Plon, Nourrit et c^{ie}, 1894.
2 p.l., 314 p.   front., plates, fold. map.
18½ cm.

17124   Manly, William Lewis.
Death Valley in '49.   Important chapter of
California pioneer history: the autobiography of a
pioneer, detailing his life from a humble home in
the Green Mountains to the gold mines of California
and particularly reciting the sufferings of the band
of men, women and children who gave "Death Valley"
its name.   San Jose, 1894.
498 p.   port.   20 cm.

17125   Manning, William Ray.
Texas and the boundary issue, 1822-1829, by
William R. Manning... [Austin, Tex. 1914]
cover-title, p. 217 -261.   24½ cm.
"Reprint from the Southwestern historical quarterly,
volume XVII, number 3, January, 1914."

17126   Marcou, Jules, 1824-1898.
Une ascension dans les montagnes Rocheuses, par
J. Marcou...   Paris, Impr. de E. Martinet, 1867.
24 p.   22 cm.
Extrait du Bulletin de la Société de géographie
(mai 1867)

17127   Marcy, Randolph Barnes, 1812-1887.
Border reminiscences.   By Randolph B. Marcy...
New York, Harper & brothers, 1872.
ix, [11]-396 p. incl. front., illus., pl.   19½ cm.

213

17128 Marcy, Randolph Barnes, 1812-1887.
Thirty years of Army life on the border. Comprising
descriptions of the Indian nomads of the plains;
explorations of new territory; a trip across the
Rocky mountains in the winter; descriptions of the
habits of different animals found in the West, and
the methods of hunting them; with incidents in the
life of different frontier men, &c., &c. By
Colonel R. B. Marcy... With numerous illustrations.
New York, Harper & brothers, 1866.
1 p.l., [ix]-xvi, [17]-422 p. incl. illus., plates.
front.   22 cm.

17129 Margry, Pierre, 1818-1894, ed.
... Mémoires et documents pour servir à l'histoire
des origines françaises des pays d'outre-mer.
Découvertes et établissements des Français dans
l'ouest et dans le sud de l'Amérique Septentrionale
(1614-1754). Paris, Maisonneuve et cie., 1879-88.
6 v.   fronts. (port., v. 1, 4, 6)   fold. maps,
fold. facsim.   24½ cm.

17130 Markham, Edwin i.e. Charles Edwin, 1852-
California the wonderful; her romantic history, her
picturesque people, her wild shores, her desert
mystery, her valley loveliness, her mountain glory,
including her varied resources, her commercial
greatness, her intellectual achievements, her
expanding hopes; with glimpses of Oregon and
Washington, her northern neighbors. By Edwin Markham...
New York, Hearst's international library co. [c1914]
xiv p., 1 l., 400 p.   front. (map)   plates, ports.
21½ cm.

17131 Marks, Alfred, comp.
Mercantile guide to cities and suburbs of the
United States of America. California edition, 1891.
Issued annually. San Francisco, 1891.
654 p.   25 cm.

17132 Marmaduke, Meredith Miles, 1791-1864.
Journal of M. M. Marmaduke of a trip from
Franklin, Missouri, to Santa Fe, New Mexico, in 1824;
reprinted from the Missouri intelligencer, with notes
by F. A. Sampson... Columbia, Mo., 1911.
cover-title, 10 p.   23 cm.
Reprinted from Missouri historical review, v. 6,
no. 1, October, 1911.

17133   Marryat, Francis Samuel, 1826-1855.
        Mountains and molehills; or, Recollections of a
        burnt journal; by Frank Marryat... With illustrations
        by the author. New York, Harper & brothers, 1855.
        x p., 1 1., [13]-393 p. incl. illus., plates, front.
        20 cm.
        "Extracts from a work by Dr. J. B. Trask... on the
        geology of California": p. [383]-393.

17134   Marryat, Frederick, 1792-1848.
        The travels and romantic adventures of Monsieur
        Violet among the Snake Indians and wild tribes of the
        great western prairies, written by Capt. Marryat...
        London, Longman, Brown, Green, & Longmans, 1843.
        3 v.   front. (fold. map, v. 1)   20 cm.

17135   Marsh, Charles W   1834-
        Recollections 1837-1910, by Charles W. Marsh.
        Chicago, Farm implement news company, 1910.
        xv, 299 p. incl. front.   plates, ports.   21 cm.

17136   Marsh, James B
        Four years in the Rockies; or, The adventures of
        Isaac P. Rose, of Shenango township... Pennsylvania;
        giving his experience as a hunter and trapper in that
        remote region... By James B. Marsh. New Castle, Pa.,
        Printed by W. B. Thomas, 1884.
        262 p.   front. (port.)   19½ cm.

17137   Marshall, Mrs. A   J   , 1813-
        The autobiography of Mrs. A. J. Marshall, age,
        84 years. Pine Bluff, Ark., Adams-Wilson printing
        co., 1897.
        232 p.   20 cm.

17138   Marshall, Thomas Maitland.
        The southwestern boundary of Texas, 1821-1840.
        [n.p., n.d.]
        277-293 p.   22 cm.

17139   Marshall, William Isaac, 1840-1906.
        Acquisition of Oregon and the long suppressed
        evidence about Marcus Whitman... Seattle, Lowman &
        Hartford co., 1911.
        2 v.   front. (port.)   24 cm.

17140   Marshall, William Isaac, 1840-1906.
        History vs. the Whitman saved Oregon story; three

essays towards a true history of the acquisition of
the old Oregon territory... by William I. Marshall...
Chicago, The Blakely printing co., 1904.
82 p., 1 l., 221-236 p.   24 cm.

17141   Marshall, William Isaac, 1840-1906.
The Hudson's Bay company's archives furnish no
support to the Whitman saved Oregon story. Chicago,
1905.
36 p.   20 cm.

17142   Martin, Charles I
History of Door county, Wisconsin, together with
biographies of nearly seven hundred families, and
mention of 4,000 persons. By Chas. I. Martin.
Sturgeon Bay, Wis., Expositor job print, 1881.
viii p., 1 l., 136 (i.e. 138) p.   illus., port.
17 cm.

17143   Martin, George Washington, 1841-
The first two years of Kansas; or, Where, when and
how the Missouri bushwhacker, the Missouri train and
bank robber, and those who stole themselves rich in
the name of liberty, were sired and reared. An address
by George W. Martin... delivered at Pawnee Village,
Republic county, September 29, 1906, the one hundredth
anniversary of the flag in Kansas; also, before the
Fifty-sixers at Lawrence, September 14, 1907,
the fifty-first anniversary of the invasion of the
2700; also, at Old settlers' reunions at Highland
Station, Osage City, Emporia, Alma, and Lincoln Center.
Topeka, State printing office, 1907.
30 p.   23 cm.

17144   Martin, George Washington, 1841-
How the Oregon trail became a road, by George
Washington Martin... Salt Lake City, Utah, The
Deseret news, 1906.
52 p.   2 port. (incl. front.)   19½ cm.
"Published by resolution of the Presbyterian
teachers' association, Mount Pleasant, Utah, August,
1905."

17145   Mason, Charles, 1804-1882.
... The election in Iowa. By Hon. Charles Mason.
[New York, Office of the Society, 1863]
8 p.   22 cm.   (Society for the diffusion of
political knowledge, New York. Papers. no. 11)

17146   Massachusetts. Convention of Delegates on Annexation
        of Texas.
        Proceedings of a convention of delegates, chosen by
        the people of Massachusetts... assembled by Faneuil
        Hall, in the city of Boston... the 29th of January,
        1845, to take into consideration the proposed annexation
        of Texas to the United States. Boston, 1845.
        18 p.

17147   Massachusetts Emigrant Aid Company.
        Organization, objects, and plan of operations, of
        the Emigrant Aid Company: also, a description of Kansas
        for the information of emigrants. Boston, Printed
        by A. Mudge & son, 1854.
        24 p.   20 cm.
        "Notes of a trip up Kansas River, including
        observations on the soil, climate, scenery, &c. By
        Geo. S. Park": p. 9-19.

17148   Masson, Louis François Redrigue, 1833-1903.
        Les bourgeois de la Compagnie du Nord-Ouest; récits
        de voyages, lettres et rapports inédits relatifs au
        Nord-Ouest canadien. Pub. avec une esquisse historique
        et des annotations par L. R. Masson. Québec, Impr.
        générale A. Coté et Cie., 1889-90.
        2 v.   fold. map.   23 cm.

17149   Materials for the future history of Minnesota: being
        a report of the Minnesota Historical Society to the
        Historical Assembly. St. Paul, Minnesota Historical
        Society, 1956. (In Annals of the Minnesota Historical
        Society, 1856, p. 1-139)

17150   Mathews, Alfred E
        Gems of Rocky mountain scenery, containing views
        along and near the Union Pacific railroad... New York,
        The author, 1869.
        23 l.   pl. fol.   32 cm.

17151   Mathews, Alfred E
        Pencil sketches of Montana. By A. E. Mathews...
        New York, The author, 1868.
        3 p.l., 95 p. incl. front., xxxi pl.   33 x 27 cm.

17152   Mathews, Edward James, 1836-1901.
        Crossing the plains, adventures of Edward James
        Mathews in '59. Privately printed. [n.p., 1930]
        91 p.   18 cm.

17153   Mathews, Mrs. Mary McNair.
        Ten years in Nevada; or, Life on the Pacific coast.
        Buffalo, 1880.
        343 p.   front., port.   20 cm.

17154   Matson, Nehemiah, 1816-1883.
        Map of Bureau county, Illinois, with sketches of
        its early settlement. By N. Matson. Published by
        the author. Chicago, G. H. Fergus, book and job
        printer, 1867.
        88 p.   front., ports., maps.   20 x 20 cm.

17155   Matson, Nehemiah, 1816-1883.
        Memories of Shaubena. With incidents relating to
        the early settlement of the West. By N. Matson...
        Chicago, D. B. Cooke & co., 1878.
        4 p.l., 17-269 p.   front. (port.)   12 pl.   20½ cm.
        Includes several chapters on the Black Hawk war.

17156   Matson, Nehemiah, 1816-1883.
        Pioneers of Illinois, containing a series of
        sketches relating to events that occurred previous
        to 1813; also, narratives of many thrilling incidents
        connected with the early settlement of the West,
        drawn from history, tradition and personal reminiscences.
        By N. Matson... Chicago, Knight & Leonard, printers,
        1882.
        1 p.l., 11-306 p.   front. (port.)   20 cm.
        Many of the incidents given in the book entitled
        "French and Indians of Illinois river" have been
        revised and inserted in this volume. cf. Pref.
        Includes several chapters relating to the history
        of Peoria, Illinois.

17157   Matson, Nehemiah, 1816-1883.
        Reminiscences of Bureau county [Illinois] in two
        parts... By N. Matson. Princeton, Ill., Republican
        book and job office, 1872.
        6 p.l., [15]-209, [8], [231]-406 p. incl. front.,
        plates, mounted phot., ports.   20½ cm.

17158   Matthes, Benno.
        Reise-bilder, von Dr. Benno Matthes. Bilder aus
        Texas. Dresden, Buchhandlung von H. J. Zeh, 1861.
        4 p.l., 104 p.   17½ cm.

17159   Matthews, William Baynham, 1850-1914.
        Matthew's guide for settlers upon the public lands,

land attorneys, land agents, clerks of courts, notaries, bankers, brokers, and all persons interested in the public lands of the United State [!] and having business before the district land offices, the General land office and the Department of the interior... By William B. Matthews... Washington, D. C., W. H. Lowdermilk & co., 1889.
xiv, [2], 234 p.   fold. map.   23 cm.

17160 Matthews, William Baynham, 1850-1914.
The settler's map and guide book. Oklahoma. A brief review of the history, government, soil, and resources of the Indian Territory, Oklahoma proper, the public land strip, and Cherokee Outlet. The Springer bill. The Indian appropriation bill. President Harrison's proclamation. The homestead and townsite laws. Pub. by W. B. Matthews... Washington, D.C., W. H. Lepley, printer, 1889.
66 p.   fold. map.   24 cm.

17161 Mattson, Hans, 1832-1893.
Reminiscences: the story of an emigrant; by Hans Mattson... Saint Paul, D. D. Merrill company, 1891.
2 p.l., 314 p.   front. (port.)   illus. (incl. facsims.   22 cm.
First published in Swedish, 1890.

17162 Maverick, Mrs. Mary Ann (Adams) 1818-1918.
Memoirs of Mary A. Maverick, arranged by Mary A. Maverick and her son Geo. Madison Maverick; ed. by Rena Maverick Green... San Antonio, Tex., Alamo printing co., 1921.
136 p.   front., plates, ports., facsims.
22½ cm.

17163 Maxwell, William Audley, d. 1921.
Crossing the plains, days of '57; a narrative of early emigrant travel to California by the ox-team method, by Wm. Audley Maxwell. [San Francisco, Sunset publishing house, 1915]
4 p.l., 179 p.   front., illus., pl., ports.
18 cm.

17164 Mayer, Brantz, 1809-1879.
Tah-gah-jute; or, Logan and Captain Michael Cresap; a discourse by Brantz Mayer; delivered in Baltimore, before the Maryland historical society... 9 May,

219

1851. [Baltimore, Printed by J. Murphy & co.] 1851.
86 p., 1 l.   22 cm.

17165 Mayfield, Eugene O
The backbone of Nebraska, wherein is contained
many interesting matters pertaining to pioneer and
more modern days, by Eugene O. Mayfield. [Omaha,
Burkley printing co., c1916]
31 p.   illus. (incl. ports.)   23½ cm.

17166 Mayo, Robert, 1784-1864.
Political sketches of eight years in Washington;
in four parts, with annotations to each. Also a
general appendix; an alphabetical index; and a series
of charts, giving a comparative synopsis of the constitutions of the several states, and the United
States. By Robert Mayo... [Part 1] Baltimore,
F. Lucas, jr.; New York, G. & C. Carvill & co.;
[etc., etc.] 1839.
viii, [v]-x, [11]-216 p.   facsims., fold. tab.
22½ cm.

17167 [Mazzuchelli, Samuel Charles] 1806-1864.
Memoirs, historical and edifying, of a missionary
apostolic of the order of Saint Dominic among various
Indian tribes and among the Catholics and Protestants
in the United States of America... Chicago, Press
of W. F. Hall printing company, 1915.
xx, 2 l., xxiii-xxv, 375 p.   front. (port.)
pl., maps (part fold.)   23½ cm.
"Translator's preface" signed: Sister Mary
Benedicta Kennedy.

17168 Meares, John, 1756?-1809.
Voyages made in the years 1788 and 1789, from China
to the north west coast of America. To which are
prefixed, an introductory narrative of a voyage
performed in 1786, from Bengal, in the ship Nootka;
observations on the probable existence of a north
west passage; and some account of the trade between
the north west coast of America and China; and the
latter country and Great Britain. By John Meares,
esq. London, Printed at the Logographic press, 1790.
viii, [12], xcv, [1], 372, [108] p.   front.,
plates, ports. (part fold.) fold. maps.   30 x 25 cm.
Compiled by W. Combe from the papers of J. Meares.

17169 [Meears, George A   ]
        The geese of Ganderica; their history, the sense
        and nonsense. By a Utah goose. [Salt Lake City]
        Salt Lake herald print [c1882]
        35 p.   17 cm.

17170 [The Meears prize essay.   Salt Lake City, G. A. Meears,
        1881]
        20 p.   18 cm.

17171 Meeker, Ezra, 1830-
        ... The ox team; or, The old Oregon trail, 1852-
        1906; an account of the author's trip across the
        plains, from the Missouri River to Puget Sound, at
        the age of twenty-two, with an ox and cow team in
        1852, and of his return with an ox team in the year
        1906, at the age of seventy-six... by Ezra Meeker...
        New York, The author [1907]
        4 p.1., 5-6 p., 2 1., [13]-248, [6] p.   illus.
        19 cm.

17172 Meeker, Ezra, 1830-
        Washington Territory west of the Cascade Mountains,
        containing a description of Puget Sound, and rivers
        emptying into it, the lower Columbia, Shoalwater Bay,
        Gray's Harbor, timber, lands, climate, fisheries,
        ship building, coal mines, market reports, trade,
        labor, population, wealth and resources... By
        E. Meeker. Olympia, W. T., Printed at the Transcript
        office, 1870.
        52 p.   tables.   21 cm.

17173 Meeks, Priddy, 1795-1886.
        Journal of Priddy Meeks, Harrisburg, Washington
        County, Utah Territory, October 22, 1879 (and other
        dates in other years) Salt Lake City, Utah State
        Historical Society, 1942. (In Utah historical
        quarterly, v. 10, nos. 1-4, 1942, p. 145-223)

17174 Mekeel, Scudder.
        A short history of the Teton-Dakota, by Scudder
        Mekeel. [Bismarck, State Historical Society of
        North Dakota, 1943]
        136-205 p.   fold. map.   24 cm.
        Reprinted from North Dakota historical quarterly,
        v. 10, no. 3, July 1943.

17175 Meline, James Florant, 1811-1873.
       Two thousand miles on horseback. Santa Fé and back.
       A summer tour through Kansas, Nebraska, Colorado,
       and New Mexico, in the year 1866. By James F. Meline.
       New York, Hurd and Houghton, 1867.
       x, 317 p.   front. (fold. map)   19 cm.

17176 Memoirs of the principal transactions of the last war
       between the English and French in North America.
       From the commencement of it in 1744, to the conclusion
       of the treaty at Aix la Chapelle. Containing in
       particular an account of the importance of Nova Scotia
       or Acadie, and the island of Cape Breton to both
       nations. The third edition. London, printed.
       Boston, New England; Re-printed and sold by Green
       and Russell, at their printing-office in Queen street,
       1758.
       iv, [9]-80 p.   20½ cm.
       "Attributed sometimes to William Shirley" - Winsor.
       Harr. and crit. hist., v. 5, p. 568.

17177 A memorial and biographical history of northern California
       Illustrated. Containing a history of this important
       section of the Pacific coast from the earliest period...
       and biographical mention of many of its most eminent
       pioneers and also of prominent citizens of to-day...
       Chicago, The Lewis pub. co., 1891.
       834 p.   front., pl., port.   24 cm.

17178 Memorial to the senators and representatives of the
       Forty-first Congress. Memorial from the commissioners
       elected by the reconstruction convention of the
       state of Texas, to represent the condition of the
       state and the wants of the loyal people. [Washington,
       1859]
       9 p.   20 cm.

17179 Menefee, Eugene L
       History of Tulare and Kings counties, California,
       with biographical sketches of the leading men and
       women of the counties who have been identified with
       their growth and development from the early days to
       the present. History by Eugene L. Menefee and
       Fred A. Dodge... Los Angeles, Cal., Historic
       record company [1913]
       1 p.l., [v]-xiv, [5]-890 p. incl. illus., ports.,
       map.   plates.   28 cm.

17180   Mercer, Asa Shinn, 1839-1917.
         The banditti of the plains; or, The cattlemen's
         invasion of Wyoming in 1892. (The crowning infamy
         of the ages) [Cheyenne, Wyo., 1894]
         139 p.   illus., port.   21½ cm.

17181   Mercer, Asa Shinn, 1839-1917.
         The pioneer, by A. S. Mercer... Chicago, Printed
         by the Henneberry company [c1913]
         4 p.l., 11-47 p.   18½ cm.

17182   Mercer, Asa Shinn, 1839-1917.
         Washington territory. The great North-west, her
         material resources, and claims to emigration. A plain
         statement of things as they exist. By A. S. Mercer...
         Utica, N. Y., L. C. Childs, printer, 1865.
         38 p.   23 cm.

17183   Merkley, Christopher, 1808-
         Biography of Christopher Merkley. Written by
         himself. Salt Lake City, J. H. Parry & company, 1887.
         46 p.   18 cm.

17184   Merrick, George Byron, 1841-
         Old times on the upper Mississippi; the recollections
         of a steamboat pilot from 1854 to 1863, by George Byron
         Merrick. Cleveland, O., The A. H. Clark company, 1909
         [c1908]
         323 p., 1 l. incl. front., plates, 4 port. (on 1 pl.)
         maps, facsim.   25 cm.
         List of steamboats on the upper Mississippi river,
         1823-1868: p. 257-294.

17185   Messiter, Charles Alston.
         Sport and adventures among the North-American
         Indians. By Charles Alston Messiter, F. R. G. S.
         With original illustrations by Charles Whymper.
         London, R. H. Porter, 1890.
         xvi p., 1 l., 368 p. incl. plates.   front.
         21½ cm.

17186   Methvin, J   J
         Andele, or, The Mexican-Kiowa captive. A story of
         real life among the Indians, by Rev. J. J. Methvin...
         Louisville, Ky., Pentecostal herald press, 1899.
         184 p.   plates (1 col.) ports.   19½ cm.

17187 The Mexican war, 1845-1848.
In Great debates in American history, 1913.
v. 2, p. 333-377.
Contents: (Senate) John J. Crittenden and George
McDuffie on power of congress to make war or peace. -
Debate (House) on the annexation of Texas: in favor,
Charles J. Ingersoll, Stephen A. Douglas; opposed,
Robert C. Winthrop, John Quincy Adams. - Debate (Senate)
on the prosecution of the war with Mexico: in favor,
Samuel Houston, Lewis Cass; opposed, John C. Calhoun,
John M. Berrien, James D. Westcott, Crittenden. -
Debate (House) on admission of Texas into the Union:
in favor, Douglas; opposed, Julius Rockwell. -
Debate (House) on continuance of the war: in favor,
Douglas, J. H. Lumpkin; opposed, Joshua R. Giddings,
Columbus Delano, John W. Houston, John Quincy Adams,
Robert Toombs. - Speech of Thomas Corwin against the
war. - [(Senate)] Thomas H. Benton and Calhoun on
"Who is responsible for the war?" - [(House)] Arraign-
ment of Pres. Polk by Abraham Lincoln.

17188 Mexico. Legación. United States.
Correspondencia que ha mediado entre la Legacion
extraordinaria de Mexico y el Departamento de estado
de los Estados-Unidos, sobre el paso del Sabina por las
tropas que mandaba el general Gaines. Mexico,
Reimpreso por J. M. F. de Lara, 1837.
xxix, 122 p.   19½ cm.

17189 Meyer, Carl, of Basel.
Nach dem Sacramento. Reisebilder eines heimgekehrten,
von Carl Meyer. Aarau, H. R. Sauerländer, 1855.
2 p.l., 364 p., 1 l.   19 cm.

17190 Meyers, Augustus, 1841-
Ten years in the ranks, U. S. army, by Augustus
Meyers. New York, The Stirling press, 1914.
3 p.l., 356 p.   22 cm.

17191 Middleton, John W   1808-
History of the regulators and moderators and the
Shelby County war in 1841 and 1842, in the republic
of Texas, with facts and incidents in the early
history of the republic and state, from 1837 to
the annexation, together with incidents of frontier
life and Indian troubles and the war on the reserve
in Young County in 1857, by John W. Middleton...

Fort Worth, Tex., Loving publishing company, 1883.
40 p.   23 cm.

17192 Mighels, Ella Sterling (Clark) 1853-1934.
The story of the files; a review of California
writers and literature, by Ella Sterling Cummins...
[San Francisco, Cooperative printing co., c1893]
460 p.   front., illus. (incl. ports.) plates.
22½ cm.
"Issued under the auspices of the World's fair
commission of California, Columbia exposition, 1893."

17193 Miles, Nelson Appleton, 1839-1925.
Personal recollections and observations of General
Nelson A. Miles, embracing a brief view of the Civil
war; or, From New England to the Golden gate, and the
story of his Indian campaigns, with comments on the
exploration, development and progress of our great
western empire; copiously illustrated with graphic
pictures by Frederic Remington and other eminent
artists. Chicago, New York, The Werner company, 1896.
vii, 590 p. incl. front., illus., plates, ports.
25 x 21 cm.
A campaign against Apaches [1885-86] (Captain Maus'
narrative): p. 450-471.

17194 Milfort, Louis, 1750 (ca.)-1817.
Mémoire; ou, Coup-d'oeil rapide sur mes différens
voyages et mon séjour dans la nation Crëck. Par le
Gal. Milfort, Tastanégy ou grand chef de guerre de la
nation Crëck, et général de brigade au service de la
République Française. Paris, De l'Impr. de Giguet et
Michaud, an XI (1802)
2 p.l., 331, [1] p.   19½ cm.

17195 Miller, Joaquin, 1841-1913.
Songs of the Sierras. By Joaquin Miller. Boston,
Roberts brothers, 1880.
5 p.l., [3]-299 p.   18½ cm.

17196 Miller, William H
The history of Kansas City, together with a sketch
of the commercial resources of the country with which
it is surrounded. By W. H. Miller... Kansas City,
Birdsall & Miller, 1881.
vi, [5]-264 p.   illus., fold. map.   25 cm.

17197   Mills, Anson, 1834-1924.
        Big Horn expedition, August 15 to September 30, 1974.
        [n.p., n.d.]
        15 p.   fold. map.   23 cm.
        Two reports, dated Sept. 20 and 29, 1874, res-
        pectively, from Independence and Rawlins Station,
        W. T. to Gen. George D. Ruggles, Adjutant-General
        of the Department of the Platte.

17198   Mills, Anson, 1834-1924.
        My story, by Anson Mills... Ed. by C. H. Claudy.
        Washington, D. C., The author, 1918.
        412 p. incl. front., illus. (part col.) pl., port.
        21½ cm.

17199   Mills, Enos Abijah, 1870-
        The Rocky Mountain wonderland, by Enos A. Mills;
        with illustrations from photographs... Boston and
        New York, Houghton Mifflin company [1915]
        xiii, [1], 362, [2] p.   front., plates (1 double)
        map.   20½ cm.
        Reprinted in part from various periodicals.

17200   Mills, Enos Abijah, 1870-
        The spell of the Rockies, by Enos A. Mills; with
        illustrations from photographs by the author. Boston
        and New York, Houghton Mifflin company, 1911.
        xi, [1], 355, [1] p., 1 l.   front., plates.
        20½ cm.
        Partly reprinted from various periodicals.

17201   Mills, W[illiam] W
        Forty years at El Paso, 1858-1898; recollections
        of war, politics, adventure, events, narratives,
        sketches, etc., by W. W. Mills... [Chicago, Press
        of W. B. Conkey co., 1901]
        106 p. incl. front. (port.)   20 cm.

17202   Milton, William Fitzwilliam, viscount, 1839-1877.
        A history of the San Juan water boundary question,
        as affecting the division of territory between Great
        Britain and the United States. By Viscount Milton,
        M. P. Collected and comp. from official papers and
        documents printed under the authority of the
        governments respectively of Great Britain and
        Ireland and of the United States of America, and
        from other sources. With two maps. London and

New York, Cassell, Petter, and Galpin, 1869.
2 p.l., 442 p.   2 fold. maps (incl. front.)
23 cm.

17203 Milwaukee. Board of trustees.
Report of a committee appointed by the trustees of
the town of Milwaukee, relative to the commerce of
that town, and the navigation of Lake Michigan.
Published by order of the Board of trustees.
Milwaukee, W. T., Printed at the Courier office, 1842.
12 p. incl. tables.   23 cm.
Submitted by I. A. Lapham and F. Randall.

17204 The miners' own book, containing correct illustrations
and descriptions of the various modes of California
mining, including all the improvements introduced
from the earliest day to the present time. San
Francisco, Hutchings & Rosenfield, 1858.
32 p.   illus.   23 cm.

17205 Minnesota Historical Society.
Annals of the Minnesota Historical Society... [1850]
1850-51, 1852, 1853, 1856-57. Saint Paul, 1850-57.
6 v. in 3.   illus., plates, port.   24½ cm.

17206 Mission memories: the Franciscan missions of California.
Los Angeles, 1898.
unpaged.   illus.   21½ cm.

17207 A mission record of the California Indians, from a
manuscript in the Bancroft library, by A. L. Kroeber.
Berkeley, The University Press [1908]
cover-title, 27 p.   27½ cm.   (University of
California publications in American archaeology and
ethnology, vol. 8, no. 1... May 28, 1908)
Title of original: "Contestación al Interrogatorio
del año de 1811 por el presidente de las misiones
de esta Alta California, y los padres de las misiones
de San Miguel, San Antonio, Soledad [etc.]" It is
dated August 11, 1815, and comprises reports from the
Upper California missions to the vice regal government
of Mexico in the customs and condition of the Indians
connected with the missions... The present translation
consists of extracts only.

17208 Missouri. State Dept.
Document containing the correspondence, orders,
&c., in relation to the disturbances with the Mormons;

and the evidence given before the Hon. Austin A.
King, judge of the Fifth judicial circuit of the state
of Missouri, at the Court-house in Richmond, in a
criminal court of inquiry, begun November 12, 1838,
on the trial of Joseph Smith, jr., and others, for
high treason and other crimes against the state.
Pub. by order of the General assembly. Fayette, Mo.,
Printed at the office of the Boon's Lick democrat,
1841.
    2 p.l., 163 p.   23½ cm.

17209 Missouri Pacific Railway Co.
    Arkansas: statistics and information showing the
agricultural and mineral resources, the opportunities
for successful stock and fruit raising... Ed. 9.
[n.p., 1888]
    79 p.   illus., map.   20 cm.

17210 Missouri Pacific Railway Co.
    Statistics and information concerning the Indian
Territory, Oklahoma, and the Cherokee Strip, with its
millions of acres of unoccupied lands... Rev. ed.
[St. Louis, Woodward & Tiernan printing co., 1898]
    85 p.   illus., fold. map.   20 cm.

17211 Missouri Pacific Railway Co.
    Statistics and information concerning the state of
Texas, with its millions of acres of unoccupied lands,
for the farmer and stock raiser... Ed. 4. St. Louis,
1889.
    93 p.   illus., map.   20 cm.

17212 Missouri Pacific Railway Co.
    The Texarkana gateway to Texas and the Southwest.
Issued jointly by the Iron Mountain route, the Cotton
Belt route, the Texas & Pacific Railway, and the
International & Great Northern Railroad. St. Louis,
1896.
    224 p.   illus., map.

17213 Mitchell, John H
    Oregon presidential electoral vote. Shall the will
of the majority of the people of Oregon, as expressed
at the ballot box, be set aside by the edict of a
democratic governor? Speeches in the senate of the
United States, Friday, Dec. 15, 1876, and Tuesday,
Dec. 19, 1876. Washington, 1876.
    38 p.   18 cm.

17214 Mitchell, John L
Description of a trip to California, with the
board of managers of the National home for disabled
volunteer soldiers, delivered to the members of the
Northwestern branch, Milwaukee, Wis. Milwaukee, 1888.
20 p.   19½ cm.

17215 Mitchell, Samuel Augustus, 1792-1868.
Description of Oregon and California, embracing an
account of the gold regions; to which is added an
appendix, containing descriptions of various kinds
of gold, and methods of testing its genuineness;
with a large and accurate map of Oregon and California,
compiled from the latest authorities. Philadelphia,
Thomas Cowperthwait, 1849.
76 p.   illus. map.   19½ cm.

17216 Moffett, Cleveland, 1863-
True detective stories from the archives of the
Pinkertons, by Cleveland Moffett. New York, Doubleday
& McClure co., 1897.
4 p.l., 3-250 p.   17 cm.

17217 Möller, Joachim van.
Auf nach Alaska; ein führer für wagemutige, von
Joachim van Möller... Charlottenburg, F. Thiel,
1897.
198, [7] p.   illus., fold. map (in pocket)   23 cm.

17218 Möllhausen, Balduin, 1825-1905.
Diary of a journey from the Mississippi to the
coasts of the Pacific with a United States government
expedition. By Baldwin Möllhausen... With an
introduction by Alexander von Humboldt... Tr. by
Mrs. Percy Sinnett... London, Longman, Brown,
Green, Longmans, & Roberts, 1858.
2 v.   fronts., illus., plates (part col.)
fold. map.   22 cm.
The writer accompanied Lieut. Whipple's expedition.

17219 Monks, William.
A history of southern Missouri and northern
Arkansas; being an account of the early settlements,
the civil war, the Ku-klux, and times of peace. By
William Monks... West Plains, Mo., West Plains
journal co., 1907.
247 p. incl. front., illus., ports.   20 cm.

229

17220　Monnette, Orra Eugene.
　　　　California chronology, a period of three hundred
　　　　and fifty years, 1510-1860. Los Angeles, 1915.
　　　　52 p.　front., pl.　22 cm.

17221　Montana. Historical Society.
　　　　The Historical Society of Montana.　Helena, Mont.,
　　　　1874
　　　　7, [1] p.　23 cm.

17222　Montana (Ter.)　Laws, statutes, etc.
　　　　Organic act of Montana territory.　Virginia City,
　　　　D. W. Tilton & co., printers, 1867.
　　　　cover-title, 11 p.　21 cm.

17223　The Monthly recorder, a magazine... v. 1, no. 1;
　　　　Apr., 1813.　New-York, Pub. by D. Longworth, for the
　　　　editor [1813]
　　　　cover-title, [5]-68 p.　24 cm.

17224　Moody, Dan W　　　　1853-
　　　　The life of a rover, 1865-1926, by D. W. Moody,
　　　　author and publisher, known in early western life as
　　　　Dan Moody, the Indian scout... [Chicago, c1926]
　　　　2 p.l., 116 p.　illus., fold. map.　22½ cm.

17225　Moore, Edwin Ward, 1811-1865.
　　　　A brief synopsis of the doings of the Texas navy
　　　　under the command of Com. E. W. Moore; together
　　　　with his controversy with Gen. Sam Houston, president
　　　　of the republic of Texas... Washington, Printed by
　　　　T. Barnard, 1847.
　　　　32 p.　24 cm.

17226　[Moore, Edwin Ward] 1811-1865.
　　　　[Statements and documents on Texas and its
　　　　relations with Houston] [New Orleans? 1842]
　　　　204 p.

17227　Moore, Langdon W　　　　1830-
　　　　Langdon W. Moore.　His own story of his eventful
　　　　life.　Boston, L. W. Moore, 1893.
　　　　xi, 13-659 p. incl. illus., plates, ports.
　　　　front.　23 cm.

17228　Moore, William V
　　　　Indian wars of the United States, from the
　　　　discovery to the present time.　With accounts of

the origins, manners, superstitions, &c. of the
aborigines. From the best authorities. By
William V. Moore. Philadelphia, J. B. Smith & co.,
1858.
328 p. illus. 22 cm.

17229 Moreland, Sinclair, 1885-   ed.
The Texas women's hall of fame [by] Sinclair Moreland.
Austin, Tex., Biographical press, 1917.
3 p.l., [5]-272 p. illus. (ports.) 23½ cm.

17230 [Morgan, Dale L   ]
The State of Deseret. Salt Lake City, Utah State
Historical Society, 1940. (In Utah historical
quarterly, v. 8, nos. 2, 3, 4, April, July, October
1940, p. 65-251)

17231 Morgan, William Thomas.
A crisis in the history of the Hudson's Bay Company.
[Bismarck, State Historical Society of North Dakota,
1931]
197-218 p. 24 cm.
Reprinted from North Dakota historical quarterly,
v. 5, no. 4, July 1931.

17232 Morphis, J   M
History of Texas, from its discovery and settlement,
with a description of its principal cities and counties,
and the agricultural, mineral, and material resources
of the state... New York, United States publishing
co., 1874.
viii, [9]-591 p. front., pl., port., maps. 20 cm.

17233 Morrell, Z   N
Flowers and fruits from the wilderness; or, Thirty-
six years in Texas and two winters in Honduras.
Ed. 2, rev. Boston, 1872.
386 p. port.

17234 Morrill, A   Reed.
The site of Fort Robidoux, by A. Reed Morrill.
Salt Lake City, Utah State Historical Society, 1941.
(In Utah historical quarterly, v. 9, nos. 1, 2,
January, April 1941, p. 1-11)

17235 Morrill, Charles Henry, 1843-
The Morrills and reminiscences, by Charles Henry
Morrill. Chicago and Lincoln, University publishing

231

co. [c1918]
2 p.l., 160 p.   front., plates, ports., fold.
geneal. tab.   20 cm.
Autobiography.

17236 Morris, Earl H
Preliminary account of the antiquities of the
region between the Mancos and La Plata rivers in
southwestern Colorado, by Earl H. Morris.
(In U. S. Bureau of American Ethnology. Thirty-
third annual report, 1911-12. Washington, 1919.
30 cm. p. 155-206. illus., 45 pl. (incl. map))

17237 Morton, J[ulius] Sterling, 1832-1902.
Illustrated history of Nebraska; a history of
Nebraska from the earliest explorations of the trans-
Mississippi region, with steel engravings, photogravures, copper plates, maps, and tables; by J.
Sterling Morton succeeded by Albert Watkins... as
editor-in-chief, Dr. George L. Miller, associate
editor. v. 1-3. Lincoln, J. North & company, 1905-13.
3 v.   front., illus., ports.   28 cm.

17238 Moseley, Henry Nottidge, 1844-1891.
Oregon: its resources, climate, people, and
productions. By H. N. Moseley, F.R.S. London, E.
Stanford, 1878.
125 p.   front. (fold. map)   17 cm.

17239 Mowry, Sylvester, 1830-1871.
Arizona and Sonora: the geography, history, and
resources of the silver region of North America. By
Sylvester Mowry... 3d ed., rev. and enl. New York,
Harper & brother, 1864.
xiv, [15]-251 p. incl. front.   20 cm.
First edition published 1859 under title "The
geography and resources of Arizona & Sonora";
2d edition 1863.

17240 Mowry, Sylvester, 1830-1871.
The mines of the West. Shall the government
seize them? The mining states. How shall they be
taxed? By Sylvester Mowry... New York, G. E.
Currie, 1864.
16 p.   20½ cm.
"Letters, originally published in the New York
World and Herald." - Pref.

17241 Mowry, William A
Marcus Whitman and the early days of Oregon. New York [1901]
15, 341 p.   maps, pl., port.   21 cm.
Contains bibliography.

17242 [Mudge, Zechariah Atwell] 1813-1888.
Sketches of mission life among the Indians of Oregon.
New-York, Carlton & Phillips, 1854.
229 p. incl. front.   3 pl.   15 cm.

17243 Muir, John, 1838-1914.
Letters to a friend, written to Mrs. Ezra S. Carr, 1866-1879. Boston, 1915.
194 p.   19 cm.

17244 Muir, John, 1838-1914, ed.
Picturesque California and the region west of the Rocky Mountains, from Alaska to Mexico. Ed. by John Muir. Containing over six hundred... etchings, photogravures, wood engravings, etc., by eminent American artists... San Francisco and New York, The J. Dewing company, 1888.
2 v.   front., illus., plates.   42 cm.

17245 Muir, John, 1838-1914.
A thousand-mile walk to the Gulf, by John Muir.
Boston and New York, Houghton Mifflin company, 1916.
xxvi, [1], 219, [1] p.   front., plates, port., map, facsims.   24 cm.

17246 Munroe, Kirk.
The golden days of '49, a tale of the California diggings. New York [1889]
9, 351 p.   pl.   19 cm.

17247 Munsell, Marion Ebenezer, 1862-
Flying sparks, as told by a Pullman conductor, by M. E. Munsell. [2d ed.] Kansas City, Tiernan-Dart printing company, 1915.
2 p.l., xi-xvii, [1], 19-159 p.   illus., ports.
19½ cm.

17248 Murphy, John M
Oregon business directory and state gazetteer.
Portland, 1873.
382 p.   24 cm.

17249   Murphy, Thomas Dowler, 1866-
On sunset highways; a book of motor rambles in
California, by Thos. D. Murphy... with sixteen
illustrations in color from original paintings, mainly
by California artists, and forty duogravures from
photographs. Also Automobile club of southern
California road map of state. Boston, The Page
company, 1915.
6 p.l., 376 p.   col. front., plates (part col.)
fold. map.   21 cm.

17250   Murphy, Thomas Dowler, 1866-
Oregon, the picturesque; a book of rambles in the
Oregon country and in the wilds of northern
California; descriptive sketches and pictures of
Crater and Klamath lakes, the Deschutes River
Canyon, the New Columbia highway, the Willamette
and Rogue River valleys and the cities and towns of
Oregon; also of the little-known lakes, rivers,
mountains, and vast forests of northern California,
to which is added a trip to the Yosemite and to the
Roosevelt dam and the petrified forest of Arizona,
by motor car. By Thos. D. Murphy... with a map,
covering the country described and showing the author's
route, and with forty plates, of which sixteen are
in color. Boston, The Page company, 1917.
5 p.l., 317 p.   col. front., plates (part col.)
fold. map.   25 cm.

17251   Murray, Alexander Hunter, 1818-1874.
... Journal of the Yukon, 1847-48, by Alexander
Hunter Murray. Ed. with notes by L. J. Burpee...
Pub. by authority of the minister of agriculture
under the direction of the archivist. Ottawa,
Government printing bureau, 1910.
1 p.l., 125 p.   plates, fold. map, plan.   25 cm.
(Publications of the Canadian archives, no. 4)

17252   [Murray, Sir Charles Augustus] 1806-1895.
The trapper's bride; or, Spirit of adventure.
By the author of The prairie bird... Cincinnati, O.,
Stratton and Barnard, 1848.
154 p.   23½ cm.

17253   Murray, Mrs. Lois Lovina (Abbott) 1826-
Incidents of frontier life. In two parts.
Containing religious incidents and moral comment,
relating to various occurrences, evils of intemperance,

and historical and biographical sketches. By
Mrs. Louis L. Murray... Goshen, Ind., Ev. united
Mennonite publishing house, 1880.
x, 11-274 p.   2 port. (incl. front.)   20 cm.

17254 Musser, Amos Milton, 1830-1909.
The fruits of "Mormonism". By non-"Mormon"
witnesses. Being... extracts from letters,
addresses, lectures, etc., by statesmen, senators,
governors... all non-"Mormons" - about Utah and
the "Mormons". Salt Lake City, Deseret news steam
printing establishment, 1878.
35 p.   24 cm.

N

17255 Nash, Wallis.
The farm, ranch and range in Oregon. Lewis & Clark
centennial exposition... Portland, Oregon, 1905.
Salem, 1904.
32 p.   pl.   22 cm.

17256 Nash, Wallis.
Oregon: there and back in 1877. London,
Macmillan, 1878.
285 p.   map, pl.   20½ cm.

17257 Nash, Wallis.
Two years in Oregon. New York, Appleton, 1882.
311 p.   illus.   20½ cm.

17258 Nebecker, John, 1813-
Early justice in Utah, dictated by John Nebecker,
in 1884. Salt Lake City, Utah State Historical
Society, 1830. (In Utah historical quarterly,
v. 3, no. 3, July 1930, p. 87-89)

17259 Nebraska, the great wheat, corn, dairying, stock and
fruit country. [n.p.] 1904.
48 p.   illus., map.   18 cm.

17260 Nebraska state historical society.
Publications... v. 1-   Lincoln, Neb., 1885-19
v.   fronts., illus., plates, ports., maps,
fold. tab.   22-24½ cm.
Title varies: 1885-87 (1st ser., v. 1-2) Transactions

and reports... 1894/95-1902, 1907 (2d ser., v. 1-5,
10) Proceedings and collections... [1906-1913]
(2d ser., v. 6-8 [whole no.] v. 11-13)
Publications... 1911-13 (v. 16-17) Collections...
1917-   (v. 18-   ) Publications...

17261 Neill, Edward Duffield, 1823-1893.
       Addresses delivered at the opening of the
       State normal school, Winona, Minn., by Edward D.
       Neill... and John Ogden... With a report on the
       course of instruction, and other documents.
       Published by the prudential committee. Saint Paul,
       Pioneer printing co., 1860.
       55 p.   22 cm.

17262 Neill, Edward Duffield, 1823-1893.
       Address of Rev. Edward D. Neill, before the
       Minnesota Historical Society, at Saint Paul, Jan. 1,
       1850. St. Paul, Minnesota Historical Society,
       1850. (In Annals of the Minnesota Historical
       Society, 1850, ed ed., p. 9-28)

17263 Neill, Edward Duffield, 1823-1893.
       Dakota land and Dakota life, by Edward D. Neill.
       St. Paul, Minnesota Historical Society, 1853.
       (In Annals of the Minnesota Historical Society, no.
       IV, 1853, p. 45-64)

17264 Neill, Edward Duffield, 1823-1893.
       Indian trade. A sketch of the early trade and
       traders of Minnesota. By Edward D. Neill. St. Paul,
       Minnesota Historical Society, 1952. (In Annals of
       the Minnesota Historical Society, 1852, p. 29-48)

17265 Nelson, Nels Christian.
       ... Shellmounds of the San Francisco Bay region.
       By N. C. Nelson. Berkeley, The University press,
       1909.
       cover-title, p. [309]-356.   pl. 32-35, fold. map.
       27½ cm.   (University of California publications
       in American archaeology and ethnology. v. 7, no. 4)

17266 New Mexico (Ter.) Bureau of immigration.
       The resources of New Mexico. Prepared under the
       auspices of the Bureau of immigration for the
       Territorial fair, to be held at Albuquerque, N. M.,
       October 3d to 8th, 1861. Santa Fe, N. M., New
       Mexican book and job printing department, 1881.

64 (i.e. 68) p.   22½ cm.
An extra leaf, paged 12a-12b, and an unpaged leaf
are inserted between p. 12 and 13.
"Chronological annals of New Mexico, etc.": p. 13-45.

17267   New York (City)   Merchants' Association.
Natural resources and economic conditions of the
state of Texas. Report of an examination made by a
special committee of the Merchants' association of
New York, by invitation of the governor and legislature of Texas, December, 1901. New York, 1901.
146 p.   19½ cm.

17268   Newhall, John B
The British emigrants' "hand book," and guide to
the new states of America, particularly Illinois,
Iowa, and Wisconsin; comprising a general description
of the agricultural and commercial facilities, -
mineral production, - relative advantages that
different portions present for settlement, -
sketches of towns, - neighbourhoods, etc., with
practical advice to the emigrant, concerning the
different routes, time of sailing, &c. By J. B.
Newhall... London, Printed and pub. for the author,
by T. Stutter, 1844.
xi, [13]-99, [1] p.   17½ cm.

17269   Newhall, John B
A glimpse of Iowa in 1846; or, The emigrant's
guide, and state directory; with a description of
the New purchase: embracing much practical advice
and useful information to intending emigrants. Also,
the new state constitution. By J. B. Newhall...
2d ed. Burlington, Ia., W. D. Skillman, 1846.
2 p.l., [9]-106 p.   19 cm.

17270   Newhall, John B
Sketches of Iowa, or, The emigrant's guide;
containing a correct description of the agricultural
and mineral resources, geological features and
statistics of the territory of Iowa, a minute
description of each county...   a view of the rapid
increase and future prospects of the people, moral
and physical, traits of Indian character, with
sketches of Black Hawk, and others... by John B.
Newhall... New York, J. H. Colton, 1841.
252 p.   1 illus., fold. map.   15½ cm.

17271   Newmark, Harris, 1834-1916.
        Sixty years in Southern California, 1853-1913,
        containing the reminiscences of Harris Newmark, ed.
        by Maurice H. Newmark [and] Marco R. Newmark...
        with 150 illustrations. New York, The Knickerbocker
        press, 1916.
        xxviii p., 1 l., 688 p.   front., ports., facsims.
        23½ cm.

17272   Newson, Thomas McLean, 1827-1893.
        Thrilling scenes among the Indians. With a graphic
        description of Custer's last fight with Sitting Bull.
        By T. M. Newson... Chicago and New York, Belford,
        Clarke & co., 1884.
        241 p.   front., plates, ports.   18½ cm.

17273   Nicholson, Joh, 1839-1909.
        The martyrdom of Joseph Standing; or, the murder
        of a 'Mormon' missionary. A true story. Also an
        appendix, giving succint [!] description of the Utah
        penitentiary and some data regarding those who had,
        up to the date of this publication, suffered incar-
        ceration through the operations of the anti-'Mormon'
        crusade, begun in 1884. Written in prison. Salt
        Lake City, Deseret News, 1886.
        160 p.   19 cm.

17274   Nicolay, Charles G
        Oregon territory; geographical and physical
        account of that country and its inhabitants, with
        outlines of its history and discovery. London,
        Night & Co., 1846.
        226 p.   illus., map.   21 cm.

17275   Nimmo, Joseph, 1837-1909.
        The Mormon usurpation. An open letter addressed
        to the Committee on the Judiciary of the House of
        Representatives. Huntington, L. I., N. Y.,
        Long-Islander print. [1899]
        cover-title, 55 p.   23½ cm.

17276   Nixon, Oliver Woodson, 1825-
        How Marcus Whitman saved Oregon: a true romance
        of patriotic heroism, Christian devotion and final
        martyrdom; with sketches of life on the plains and
        mountains in pioneer days. Introduction by Rev. F. W.
        Gunsaulus, D.D., LL.D. Ed. 2. Chicago, 1895.
        339 p.   illus., map.

17277   Nixon, O[liver] W[oodson] 1825-
        Whitman's ride through savage lands with sketches
        of Indian life [by] O. W. Nixon... Introduction by
        James G. K. McClure... Chicago [The Winona]
        publishing company, 1905.
        3 p.l., 3-186 p.   front., plates, ports.   20 cm.

17278   Noall, Claire.
        Mormon midwives, by Claire Noall. Salt Lake City,
        Utah State Historical Society, 1942. (In Utah
        historical quarterly, v. 10, nos. 1-4, 1942,
        p. 84-144)

17279   Nordenskiöld, Gustaf Erik Adolf, 1868-1895.
        The Cliff dwellers of the Mesa Verde, southwestern
        Colorado; their pottery and implements; tr. by D. L.
        Morgan. Stockholm, Chicago [etc.] P. A. Norstedt
        & söner [1895?]
        4 p.l., 174 p., 34 l., iv, [1], xi p.   front.
        (port.) illus., pl., map, plans, fold. diagr.   fol.
        On verso of t.-p." "Stockholm, 1893. Royal
        printing office."
        Appendix by G. Retzius.

17280   Nordhoff, Charles, 1830-1901.
        California: for health, pleasure, and residence...
        New ed., thoroughly rev. New York, Harper & brothers,
        1882.
        206 p. incl. pl., maps.   20 cm.

17281   Nordhoff, Charles, 1830-1901.
        Northern California, Oregon, and the Sandwich
        Islands. By Charles Nordhoff... New York, Harper
        & brothers, 1874.
        256 p. incl. front. (map) illus., ports.   23 cm.

17282   Norman, Lucia.
        Popular history of California, from the earliest
        period of its discovery to the present time. Ed. 2,
        revised and enlarged by T. E. San Francisco, 1883.
        216 p.   pl.

17283   North Pacific History Company.
        History of the Pacific Northwest: Oregon and
        Washington; embracing an account of the original
        discoveries on the Pacific coast of North America,
        and a description of the conquest, settlement and
        subjugation of the vast country included in the

239

original territory of Oregon; also biographies
of the earliest settlers and more prominent men
and women of the Pacific Northwest. Portland, Ore.,
1889.
2 v.   pl., port.

17284   Norton, Harry J
Wonder-land illustrated; or, Horseback rides through
the Yellowstone national park. By Harry J. Norton.
Virginia City, Mont., H. J. Norton [c1874]
132 p.   front., plates, fold. map.   19½ cm.

17285   Norton, Henry Kittredge, 1884-
The story of California from the earliest days to
the present, by Henry K. Norton. Chicago, A. C.
McClurg & co., 1913.
6 p.l., 390 p.   front., plates, maps (1 fold.)
plan.   19½ cm.

17286   Norton, Lewis Adelbert, b. 1819.
Life and adventures of Col. L. A. Norton. Written
by himself. Oakland, Cal., Pacific press publishing
house, 1887.
viii, [9]-492 p.   front. (port.)   20 cm.

17287   Norton, Mary Aquinas, Sister.
Catholic missions and missionaries among the Indians
of Dakota. [Bismarck, State Historical Society of
North Dakota, 1931]
149-165 p.   24 cm.
Reprinted from North Dakota historical quarterly,
v. 5, no. 3, April 1931.

17288   Nourse, Charles Clinton, 1829-
Autobiography of Charles Clinton Nourse, prepared
for use of members of the family, containing the
incidents of more than fifty years' practice at the
bar in the state of Iowa. [Cedar Rapids, Ia.
Priv. print. [The Torch press] 1911.
235 p.   front., plates, ports.   24½ cm.

17289   Nourse, Charles Clinton, 1829-
Iowa and the Centennial. The state address,
delivered by Hon. C. C. Nourse, at Philadelphia,
Thursday, September 7, 1876. Des Moines, Iowa
state register print, 1876.
42 p.   21½ cm.

17290   Noyes, Alva Josiah, 1855-
        In the land of Chinook; or, The story of Blaine
        county, by Al. J. Noyes (Ajax)   Helena, Mont.,
        State publishing co. [c1917]
            152 p.   plates, ports., facsims.   24 cm.

17291   Noyes, Alva Josiah, 1855-
        The story of Ajax; life in the Big Hole Basin, by
        Alva J. Noyes.   Helena, Mont., State publishing
        company, 1914.
            4 p.l., 158 p.   front., plates, ports.   24 cm.

                                0

17292   Oakly, Obadiah.
        Expedition to Oregon [by] Obadiah Oakly.   New York,
        Reprinted from the Peoria register, 1914.
            19 p.   22½ cm.
        "The original from which this is reprinted is
        undated, however the Peoria register was published
        under this name only during the years 1842-1845."

17293   Objections of the Chickasaw, Choctaw, Seminole, Creek
        and Cherokee Indians to the bill for the organization
        of the Territory of Oklahoma pending in the House of
        Representatives of the United States.   [Washington,
        1885]
            22 p.   22 cm.

17294   O'Connor, Henry, 1820-1900.
        History of the First regiment of Iowa volunteers.
        By Henry O'Connor, a private in company "A".
        Originally prepared for the Iowa state historical
        society.   Muscatine, Printed at the Faust first
        premium printing house, 1862.
            24 p.   22 cm.

17295   O'Donovan, Jeremiah.
        A brief account of the author's interview with
        his countrymen, and of the parts of the Emerald isle,
        whence they emigrated.   Together with a direct
        reference to their present location in the land of
        their adoption, during his travels through various
        states of the Union in 1854 and 1855.   By Jeremiah
        O'Donovan.   Pittsburgh, Pa., The author, 1864.
            382 p.   20 cm.

                              241

17296 Official souvenir of California's golden jubilee
       held at San Francisco, California, beginning
       Jan. 24, 1898, and ending Jan. 29, 1898, containing
       the programme of each day's events, with much
       reading matter of interest pertaining to the
       discovery of gold, and many illustrations.
       Compiled and published under the supervision of the
       Jubilee committee. San Francisco [1898]
           88 p.   illus., pl., port.   23 cm.

17297 [O'Hanlon, John] 1821-1905.
       Life and scenery in Missouri. Reminiscences of a
       missionary priest. Dublin, J. Duffy & co., ltd., 1890.
       xii, 292 p.   15½ cm.
       "Under the heading 'Excursions through Missouri',
       many of [the sketches] first appeared in the columns
       of the American Celt... while others were written
       for later periodicals." - Pref.

17298 O'Hara, Edwin Vincent.
       Catholic history of Oregon. Ed. 2. Portland,
       Ore., 1916.
       xii, 165 p.   illus., map.   20 cm.
       Title of ed. 1: Pioneer Catholic history of Oregon.
       1911.

17299 Oklahoma in tabloid, 1911. [Oklahoma City, 1911]
           34 p.   illus., port.   22 cm.

17300 The Oklahoman almanac and industrial record...
       A year book and encyclopedia of information
       pertaining to the resources, industries and
       institutions of the great state of Oklahoma...
       v. 1-   1908-   Oklahoma City, Okla.,
       The Oklahoman [1908]
           v.   illus.   19½ cm.
       Edited and published by the Daily Oklahoman, 1908.

17301 Old, Robert Orchard.
       Colorado: United States, America. Its history,
       geography, and mining. Including a comprehensive
       catalogue of nearly six hundred samples of ores.
       By R. O. Old. London, Published under the auspices
       of the British and Colorado mining bureau [pref. 1869]
           64 p.   front. (fold. map)   21½ cm.

17302 The old Romish missions in California. In American
       quarterly church review, July, 1869. [n.p., 1869?]
           [15] p.   20 cm.

17303 Old settlers' association of Minnesota.
A sketch of the organization, objects and
membership of the Old settlers' association of
Minnesota; together with an account of its
excursion to the Red river of the North,
October 25 and 26, 1871. Prepared by order of the
Association... Saint Paul, Ramaley, Chaney & co.,
printers, 1872.
29 p.   21 cm.

17304 Olmsted, Frederick Law, 1822-1903.
A journey through Texas; or, A saddle-trip on the
southwestern frontier; with a statistical appendix.
By Frederick Law Olmsted... New York, Dix, Edwards
& co.; London, S. Low, son & co.; [etc., etc.] 1857.
4 p.l., [vii]-xxxiv, 516 p.   front., fold. map.
19 cm.

17305 Olmsted, John.
A trip to California in 1868. By John Olmsted.
New York, Trows printing and bookbinding company,
1880.
vi, [7]-131 p.   17½ cm.

17306 O'Meara, James.
Broderick and Gwin. The most extraordinary contest
for a seat in the senate of the United States ever
known; a brief history of early politics in
California. Sketches of prominent actors in the
scenes and an unbiased account of the fatal duel
between Broderick and Judge Terry, together with
death of Senator Broderick. San Francisco, 1881.
254 p.   20 cm.

17307 On horseback into Oregon. From Atlantic Monthly.
July, 1864.
75-86 p.   22 cm.

17308 Onderdonk, James Lawrence, 1854-1899.
Idaho; facts and statistics concerning its mining,
farming, stock-raising, lumbering and other
resources and industries. Together with notes on
the climate, scenery, game, and mineral springs.
Information for the homeseeker, capitalist, pros-
pector, and traveler. By James L. Onderdonk,
territorial controller. San Francisco, Cal., A. L.
Bancroft & company, 1885.
150 p.   22 cm.

17309   Oregon (Ter.)   Commissioner to collect the laws and
        archives of Oregon.
           The Oregon archives: including the journals,
        governors' messages and public papers of Oregon,
        from the earliest attempt on the part of the people
        to form a government, down to, and inclusive of the
        session of the territorial legislature, held in the
        year 1849, collected and published pursuant to an act
        of the Legislative assembly, passed Jan. 26, 1853.
        By La Fayette Grover, commissioner.   Salem, A. Bush,
        public printer, 1853.
           333, [1] p., 1 l.   22 cm.

17310   Oregon.   Governor, 1870-1877 (LaFayette Grover)
           Report of Governor Grover to General Schofield
        on the Modoc war, and reports of Maj. Gen. John F.
        Miller and General John E. Ross, to the governor.
        Also letter of the governor to the secretary of the
        interior on the Wallowa Valley Indian question.
        Salem, Or., M. V. Brown, state printer, 1874.
           68 p.   22 cm.

17311   Oregon.   Legislative assembly.
           Fortieth anniversary of the statehood of Oregon.
        Exercises before the Legislative assembly at Salem,
        Oregon, February 14, 1899.   Salem, Or., W. H. Leeds,
        state printer, 1899.
           60 p.   22 cm.

17312   Oregon.   People's Power League.
           Introductory letter: draft of suggested amendment
        to the constitution of Oregon for people's repre-
        sentative government; the short ballot; proportional
        representation in the legislature of all the voters...
        Portland, 1911.
           32 p.   18 cm.

17313   Oregon.   State Board of Immigration.
           Oregon.   Facts regarding its climate, soil,
        mineral and agricultural resources, means of
        communication, commerce and industry, laws, etc.,
        etc., for general information...   Boston, Oregon
        state board of immigration, 1877.
           48 p.   3 fold. maps.   23 cm.

17314   Oregon: its wealth and resources.   Ed. 2, revised.
        Chicago, 1889.
           67 p.   19 cm.

17315　Oregon Gulch Gold Mining Company, Butte County, Cal.
Oregon Gulch Gold Mining Company of Butte County,
California, 1852. Northridge, Cal., California
State University, Northridge, Libraries, 1976.
3 p.l., 102 p. of facsimile.　36 cm.
(American classics facsimile, series V)
Norman E. Tanis, series editor.

17316　Oregon Historical Society.
Proceedings of the fiftieth anniversary of the
admission of the state of Oregon to the Union, held
under the auspices of the 25th biennial session of
the legislative assembly and the Oregon historical
society, at the capitol, Salem, Monday, Feb. 15,
1909. Salem, 1909.
53 p.　21 cm.

17317　The Oregon native son, devoted to the history, industries
and development of the original Oregon, comprising
the states of Oregon, Washington, Idaho and part of
Montana. v. 1-2; May 1899-March 1901. Portland,
Or., Native son pub. co., 1899-1901.
2 v.　illus., port.　24-25 cm.

17318　Oregon Pioneer Association.
Transactions of the [1st]-56th annual reunion...
[1873]-1928. Salem, Ore., 1875-86; Portland, Ore.,
1887-1933.
7 v. in 7.　illus., ports., plan.　21-22 cm.

17319　Oregon Railroad & Navigation Company and Southern
Pacific Company. Passenger Department.
Outings in Oregon. [Portland, 1909]
62 p.　illus., map.　19 cm.

17320　The Oregon territory, consisting of a brief description
of the country and its productions; and of the
habits and manners of the native Indian tribes.
With a map of the territory. London, M. A. Nattali,
1846.
1 p.l., 78 p.　front. (map)　17½ cm.

17321　The Oregonian, and Indian's advocate. v. 1; Oct.
1838-Aug. 1839. [Boston, D. H. Ela, 1838-39]
352 p.　fold. map.　23½ cm.
Includes "Speech of Mr. Cushing... on the subject
of the Oregon Territory," his "Report on the Oregon
Territory in the House of representatives, Jan. 4, 1839,"
and "Supplemental report... Feb. 16, 1839."

17322 The Oregonian, Portland, Ore.
        The Oregonian's annual number. Portland,
        1899-1900.
        2 nos.   illus.   26 cm.
        Library has 1899 and 1900.

17323 The origin and true causes of the Texas insurrection,
        commenced in the year 1835. Philadelphia, 1836.
        32 p.   18 cm.
        Originally published in the Philadelphia "National
        Gazette" over the signature of "Columbus."

17324 Overland Traction Engine Company.
        ... Transportation by steam from Missouri river
        to the Rocky mountains. Reports of A. P. Robinson,
        esq. ... and Edw. Warner, esq. ... Boston, Wright &
        Potter, printers, 1865.
        61 p.   front., pl.   28½ cm.

17325 Owen, John, 1818-1889.
        The journals and letters of Major John Owen,
        pioneer of the Northwest, 1850-1871, embracing his
        purchase of St. Mary's mission; the building of Fort
        Owen; his travels; his relation with the Indians;
        his work for the government; and his activities as a
        western empire builder for twenty years. Transcribed
        and edited from the original manuscripts in the
        Montana historical society and the collection of
        W. R. Coe, esq., by Seymour Dunbar: and with notes
        to Owen's texts by Paul C. Phillips... with two
        maps and thirty plates... New York, E. Eberstadt,
        1927.
        2 v.   xxx pl. (incl. fronts., ports., plan,
        facsims.) II fold. maps.   24½ cm.

17326 Owen, Robert D
        Texas and her relations with Mexico. Speech
        delivered in the house of representatives of the
        United States, Jan. 8, 1845. [Washington, 1845]
        8 p.   18 cm.

                                P

17327 Pacific Coast Land Bureau.
        California guide book: the lands of the Central
        Pacific and Southern Pacific railroad companies...

in California, Nevada, and Utah... San Francisco
[1881?]
72, [2] p.   illus., map.   20 cm.

17328   Pacific Land Improvement Company.
Description of the towns on the great Santa Fé
route, on sale by the Pacific land improvement company.
Los Angeles, Press of Los Angeles printing co., 1888.
30 p.   20 cm.

17329   Paddock, Buckley B   1844-   ed.
A history of central and western Texas, comp. from
historical data supplied by commercial clubs,
individuals, and other authentic sources, under the
editorial supervision of Captain B. B. Paddock, of
Fort Worth...   Chicago, New York, The Lewis publishing
company, 1911.
2 v.   fronts., illus., plates, ports., facsim.
27½ x 21 cm.

17330   Paddock, Buckley B   1844-1922, ed.
A twentieth century history and biographical record
of north and west Texas. Capt. B. B. Paddock,
editor...   Chicago, New York, The Lewis publishing
co., 1906.
2 v.   front., ports.   28 cm.

17331   Painter, Charles C   C
The Oklahoma bill, and Oklahoma.   Philadelphia,
Indian Rights Association, 1889.
6 p.   18 cm.

17332   Painter, Orrin Chalfant, 1884-   comp.
William Painter and his father, Dr. Edward Painter;
sketches and reminiscences comp. by Orrin Chalfant
Painter...   Baltimore, The Arundel press, J. S.
Bridges & co., 1914.
152 p., 1 l.   front., illus. (incl. ports.,
facsims.)   31 cm.
"The Crown cork and seal company, by John Mifflin
Hood, jr.": p. 64-129.

17333   Palladino, Lawrence Benedict, 1837-1927.
Indian and white in the Northwest; or, A history
of Catholicity in Montana.   By L. B. Palladino, S.J.,
with an introduction by Right Reverend   John B.
Brondel...   Baltimore, J. Murphy & company, 1894.

3 p.l., v-xxv, 411 p.   front., plates, ports.,
fold. map, facsims.   24 cm.

17334 Palmer, Frederick, 1873-
In the Klondyke; including an account of a winter's
journey to Dawson, by Frederick Palmer... New York,
C. Scribner's sons, 1899.
x p., 1 l., 218 p. incl. front., plates.   19½ cm.

17335 Palmer, Joel, 1810-1881.
Journal of travels over the Rocky mountains,
to the mouth of the Columbia river, made during the
years 1845 and 1846, containing minute descriptions
of the valleys of the Willamette, Umpqua, and Calamet;
a general description of Oregon territory. Cincinnati,
1851.
189 p.   20 cm.

17336 Palmer, J[ohn] W[illiamson] 1825-1896.
The new and the old; or, California and India in
romantic aspects. By J. W. Palmer... With thirteen
illustrations, engraved by A. V. S. Anthony. From
original designs by John McLenan. New York, Rudd &
Carleton, 1859.
xiv p., 2 l., [19]-433 p. incl. front., illus., pl.
19½ cm.

17337 Palmer, William Jackson, 1836-1909.
Report of surveys across the continent, in 1867-'68,
on the thirty-fifth and thirty-second parallels, for
a route extending the Kansas Pacific railway to the
Pacific ocean at San Francisco and San Diego. By Gen.
Wm. J. Palmer. December 1st, 1868. Philadelphia,
W. B. Selheimer, printer, 1869.
6 p.l., 7-250 p.   front. (fold. plan) fold. map.
23 cm.
Report made to the Union Pacific railroad company,
Eastern division.

17338 Palmer, William R
Indian names in Utah geography, by Wm. R. Palmer.
Salt Lake City, Utah State Historical Society, 1934.
(In Utah historical quarterly, v. 1, no. 1, January,
1928, p. 5-32)

17339 Palmer, William R
The Pahute fire legend. Salt Lake City, Utah
State Historical Society, 1933. (In Utah historical
quarterly, v. 6, no. 2, April 1933, p. 62-64)

248

17340 Palmer, William R
       Pahute Indian government and laws, by William R.
       Palmer. Salt Lake City, Utah State Historical
       Society, 1929. (In Utah historical quarterly, v. 2,
       no. 2, April 1929, p. 35-42)

17341 Palmer, William R
       Pahute Indian homelands. Salt Lake City, Utah
       State Historical Society, 1933. (In Utah historical
       quarterly, v. 6, no. 3, July 1933, p. 88-102)

17342 Palmer, William R
       Pahute Indian medicine, by Wm. R. Palmer. Salt Lake
       City, Utah State Historical Society, 1942. (In Utah
       historical quarterly, v. 10, nos. 1-4, 1942, p. 1-13)

17343 Palmer, William R
       Utah Indians, past and present; an etymological
       and historical study of tribes and tribal names from
       original sources by Wm. R. Palmer, Cedar City, Utah.
       Salt Lake City, Utah State Historical Society, 1928.
       (In Utah historical quarterly, v. 1, no. 2, April,
       1928, p. 35-52)

17344 Palou, Francisco, 1723-1789.
       Francisco Palou's Life and apostolic labors of the
       Venerable Father Junipero Serra, founder of the
       Franciscan missions of California; with an intro-
       duction and notes by George Wharton James...
       English translation by C. Scott Williams. Pasadena,
       Cal., G. W. James, 1913.
       xxxiv, 338 p., 1 l. incl. illus., facsim.
       fold. map.   22½ cm.
       Translation of Palou's Relacion historica de la
       vida... del venerable padre fray Junipero Serra,
       Mexico, 1787, including reproduction of t.-p. of
       original.
       On cover: George Wharton James edition.

17345 Palou, Francisco, 1723-1789.
       Life of Ven. Padre Junipero Serra. Written by
       Very Rev. Francisco Palou... Tr. by Very Rev.
       J. Adam. San Francisco, P. E. Dougherty & co.,
       book and job printers, 1884.
       156 p.   front. (port.)   20 cm.
       A much abbreviated translation of the author's
       "Relacion historica de la vida... del venerable
       padre Fray Junipero Serra", Mexico, 1787.

17346 Pancoast, Charles Edward, 1818-1906.
  A Quaker forty-niner, the adventures of Charles
Edward Pancoast on the American frontier; edited by
Anna Paschall Hannum, with a foreword by John Bach
McMaster. Philadelphia, University of Pennsylvania
press; London, H. Milford, Oxford university press,
1930.
  xv, 402 p. front., illus. (map) plates, facsim.
(incl. port.) 23½ cm.

17347 Parisot, Pierre Fourier.
  The reminiscences of a Texas missionary. By Rev.
P. F. Parisot... San Antonio, Tex., Johnson bros.
printing co. [c1899]
  227, v p. incl. front. (port.) 19½ cm.

17348 Parker, Henry W
  How Oregon was saved to the United States. To appear
in the Homiletic review for July, 1901. [New York,
n.d.]
  10 p. 18 cm.

17349 Parker, James W b. 1797.
  Narrative of the perilous adventures, miraculous
escapes and sufferings of Rev. James W. Parker,
during a frontier residence in Texas, of fifteen
years; with an impartial geographical description
of the climate, soil, timber, water, &c., &c., &c.
of Texas; written by himself. To which is
appended a Narrative of the capture and subsequent
sufferings of Mrs. Rachel Plummer, (his daughter)
during a captivity of twenty-one months among the
Cumanche [!] Indians, with a sketch of their
manners, customs, laws, &c.; with a short description
of the country over which she travelled whilst with
the Indians; written by herself. Louisville, Ky.,
Morning courier office, 1844.
  95 p., 2 l., 35 (i.e. 36) p. 19½ cm.
  "Geographical description of the climate, soil,
timber, water, &c., of Texas": p. 43-81.
  This is the 2d edition of Rachel Plummer's
Narrative. It has separate paging and a separate
title-page, dated 1839.

17350 Parker, Nathan Howe.
  The Iowa handbook, for 1857... By Nathan H.
Parker... Boston, J. P. Jewett & co.; New York,

Sheldon, Lamport & Blakeman [etc.] 1857.
viii, 9-188 p.   front. (fold. map)   19 cm.

17351   Parker, N[athan] H[owe]
The Kansas & Nebraska hand-book. For 1857-8. With
a new and accurate map... Boston [etc.] J. P. Jewett
& co., 1857.
189 p.   fold. map.   18 cm.

17352   Parker, Nathan Howe.
The Minnesota handbook, for 1856-7... By Nathan H.
Parker... Boston, J. P. Jewett and company; New York,
Sheldon, Blakeman and company; [etc., etc.] 1857.
viii, 9-159, [1] p.   front. (fold. map)   19 cm.

17353   Parker, William Thornton, 1849-
Personal experiences among our North American
Indians from 1867 to 1885, by W. Thornton Parker...
Northampton, Mass., 1913.
232 p.   front., ports. $24\frac{1}{2}$ cm.
Articles reprinted from various periodicals.

17354   Parkinson, R   R
Pen portraits: autobiographies of state officers,
legislators, prominent business and professional men
of the capital of the state of California; also of
newspaper proprietors, editors, and members of the
corps reportorial. San Francisco, 1878.
142 p.   19 cm.

17355   The parks of Colorado. [San Luis de Calebra, 1866]
6 p.   19 cm.

17356   Parrish, Randall, 1858-1923.
The great plains; the romance of western American
exploration, warfare, and settlement, 1527-1870,
by Randall Parrish... Chicago, A. C. McClurg & co.,
1907.
xiv p., 1 l., 17-399 p.   front., plates, ports.
22 cm.

17357   Parsons, Eugene, 1855-
The making of Colorado; a historical sketch, by
Eugene Parsons... Chicago, A. Flanagan company
[c1908]
324 p. incl. front., illus. $17\frac{1}{2}$ cm.

251

17358   Parsons, George Frederic, 1840-1893.
        The life and adventures of James W. Marshall,
        the discoverer of gold in California. By George
        Frederic Parsons... Sacramento, J. W. Marshall and
        W. Burke, 1870.
        188 p.   front.   17 cm.

17359   Patterson, Lawson B
        Twelve years in the mines of California; embracing
        a general view of the gold region, with practical
        observations on hill, placer, and quartz diggings;
        and notes on the origin of gold deposits. Cambridge,
        1862.
        108 p.   18 cm.

17360   Paul Wilhelm, duke of Württemberg, 1797-1860.
        Erste reise nach dem nördlichen Amerika in den
        jahren 1822 bis 1824, von Paul Wilhelm, herzog von
        Württemberg. Stuttgart und Tübingen, J. G. Cotta,
        1835.
        vi, 394, [2] p.   fold. map.   23 cm.

17361   Paxson, Frederic Logan, 1877-1948.
        The constitution of Texas, 1845. (In The South-
        western historical quarterly, v. 18, April, 1915,
        p. 386-98)

17362   Paxson, Frederic Logan, 1877-1948.
        ... The county boundaries of Colorado, by Frederic
        L. Paxson. [Boulder, Col., 1906]
        197-215 p.   illus. (maps)   25 cm.
        Reprinted from the University of Colorado studies,
        vol. III, no. 4.

17363   Paxson, Frederic Logan, 1877-1948.
        The territory of Jefferson: a spontaneous
        commonwealth. [n.p., 1905]
        [16]-18 p.   22 cm.
        Reprinted from the University of Colorado studies,
        vol. 3, no. 1, Nov., 1905.

17364   Peabody, Alfred.
        On the early days and rapid growth of California.
        (In Essex Institute, Historical collections,
        v. 12, p. 104-23. 1874)

17365   Peareson, Philip E   d. 1895.
        Sketch of the life of Judge Edwin Waller, together

with some of the more important events of the early
Texas revolution, in which he participated, such as
the battle of Velasco... selecting the site and
founding the present capitol of Texas, &c., &c.
By P. E. Peareson. Galveston, Printed at the "News"
steam book and job establishment, 1874.
25 p.   22½ cm.

17366 Peck, George.
Wyoming; its history, stirring incidents, and
romantic adventures. By George Peck... New York,
Harper & brothers, 1858.
vi p., 1 l., 10-432 p.   illus.   20½ cm.

17367 Peck, John Mason, 1789-1858.
A new guide for emigrants to the West, containing
sketches of Ohio, Indiana, Illinois, Missouri,
Michigan, with the territories of Wisconsin and
Arkansas, and the adjacent parts. By J. M. Peck...
Boston, Gould, Kendall & Lincoln, 1836.
vii, [v]-x, [11]-374 p.   16 cm.

17368 Peck, Simon Lewis, 1844-
History of Ira, Vermont, by S. L. Peck, town clerk
for over forty years, to which is added The author's
early experiences upon the plains and the Rockies of
the great West during the years 1866-1867, from his
diary of the period. Rutland, Vt., The Tuttle
company, 1926.
83 p.   illus. (incl. ports.)   23½ cm.

17369 Peixotto, Ernest Clifford, 1869-
Romantic California, by Ernest Peixotto, illustrations by the author. New and enl. ed. New York,
C. Scribner's sons, 1914.
xvi, 272 p.   front., illus., plates.   23½ cm.

17370 Pendleton, Mark A   , 1868-
Dr. Calvin Crane Pendleton, by Mark A. Pendleton.
Salt Lake City, Utah State Historical Society,
1942. (In Utah historical quarterly, v. 10, nos.
1-4, 1942, p. 34-36)

17371 Pendleton, Mark A   , 1868-
Memories of Silver Reef, by Mark A. Pendleton.
Salt Lake City, Utah State Historical Society,
1930. (In Utah historical quarterly, v. 3, no. 4,
October 1930, p. 98-118)

17372 Pendleton, Mark A   , 1868-
       Naming Silver Reef, by Mark A. Pendleton. Salt
Lake City, Utah State Historical Society, 1932.
(In Utah historical quarterly, v. 5, no. 1, January
1932, p. 29-31)

17373 Pendleton, Mark A   , 1868-
       The Orderville United Order of Zion, by Mark A.
Pendleton. Salt Lake City, Utah State Historical
Society, 1939. (In Utah historical quarterly, v. 7,
no. 4, October 1939, p. 141-159)

17374 [Pengra, P   J   ]
       Oregon branch of the Pacific railroad. Washington,
D.C., McGill & Witherow, printers [1868]
       cover-title, 19 p.   23 cm.
       Memorial to the Senate and House of representatives.
Signed by P. J. Pengra and H. Cummins.

17375 Pennybacker, Mrs. Anna J   (Hardwicke)
       A new history of Texas for schools, also for
general reading and for teachers preparing themselves
for examination. Rev. ed. Palestine, Tex. [1895]
       xvi, 396 p.   illus., maps.   19 cm.

17376 Peters, Charles, b. 1825.
       The autobiography of Charles Peters, in 1915 the
oldest pioneer living in California, who mined in...
the days of '49... Also historical happenings,
interesting incidents and illustrations of the old
mining towns in the good luck era, the placer mining
days of the '50s. Sacramento, Cal., The La Grave
co. [1915?]
       3 p.l., 231 p.   illus.   17 cm.

17377 [Pettis, George Henry] 1834-
       ... The California column. Its campaigns and
services in New Mexico, Arizona and Texas, during
the civil war, with sketches of Brigadier General
James H. Carleton, its commander, and other officers
and soldiers. Santa Fe, New Mexican printing company,
1908.
       45 p.   illus. (ports.)   22 cm.   (Historical
society of New Mexico. [Publications] no. 11)

17378 Pettis, George Henry, 1834-
       Frontier service during the rebellion; or, A
history of Company K, First infantry, California

volunteers. By George H. Pettis... Providence,
The Society, 1885.
    54 p.   21 cm.   (Added t.-p.: Personal
narratives of events in the war of the rebellion,
being papers read before the Rhode Island soldiers
and sailors historical society. 3d ser., no. 14)

17379 Pettis, George Henry, 1834-
    Kit Carson's fight with the Comanche and Kiowa
Indians, at the Adobe Walls on the Canadian river,
November 25th, 1864. By George H. Pettis...
Providence, S. S. Rider, 1878.
    44 p.   21 cm.   (Added t.-p.: Personal narratives
of the battles of the rebellion, being papers read
before the Rhode Island soldiers and sailors historical
society. no. 5)

17380 Philbrook, Horace W
    The corrupt judges of the supreme court of the
state of California. Memorial to the legislature of
the state of California, to remove from office W. H.
Beatty, T. B. McFarland, W. C. Van Fleet, Ralph C.
Harrison, C. H. Garoutte, Jackson Temple, F. W.
Henshaw, justices of the Supreme Court, for corrupt
misconduct in office. San Francisco, 1897.
    207, 18 p.   19 cm.

17381 Phillips, A. & Co.
    New facts and figures concerning Southern California,
including the actual experience of individual
producers... from material furnished by the Los
Angeles Chamber of Commerce. Los Angeles, 1891.
    33 p.   19 cm.

17382 Phillips, A. & Co.
    ... Phillips' California guide, issued quarterly
by A. Phillips & Co., managers of Boston and
California excursion July, 1888. San Francisco,
1888.
    123 p.   illus.   19 cm.

17383 Phillips, D   L
    Letters from California: its mountains, valleys,
plains, lakes, rivers, climate, and productions,
also its railroads, cities, towns and people, as
seen in 1876. Springfield, Illinois, 1877.
    viii, 171 p.   19 cm.

255

17384 Phillips, Semira Ann (Hobbs) "Mrs. T. G. Phillips."
Proud Mahaska. 1843-1900... By Semira A.
Phillips. Oskaloosa, Ia., Herald print, 1900.
2 p.l., [13]-383 p.   2 port. (incl. front.)
22½ cm.

17385 Phillips, Stephen Clarendon, 1801-1857.
An address on the annexation of Texas, and the
aspect of slavery in the United States, in a
connection therewith. Delivered in Boston,
November 14 and 18, 1845. Boston, Wm. Crosby and
H. P. Nichols, 1845.
56 p.   20 cm.

17386 Phillips, William Allison.
The conquest of Kansas, by Missouri and her allies.
A history of the troubles in Kansas, from the
passage of the organic act until the close of July,
1856. By William Phillips... Boston, Phillips,
Sampson and company, 1856.
x, [11]-414 p.   19 cm.

17387 Piercy, Frederick.
Route from Liverpool to Great Salt Lake valley,
illustrated with steel engravings and wood cuts from
sketches made by Frederick Piercy... Together with
a geographical and historical description of Utah...
also an authentic history of the Later day saints'
emigration from Europe... 1855... Ed. by James
Linforth. Liverpool, F. D. Richards, 1855.
viii, 120 p.   front. (fold. map)   illus., plates,
ports.   32 cm.

17388 Pike, Albert, 1809-1891.
An address delivered by Albert Pike... to the
young ladies of the Tulip female seminary, and the
cadets of the Arkansas military institute: at Tulip,
on the 4th June, 1852. Little Rock, W. E. Woodruff,
printer, 1852.
31 p.   22½ cm.

17389 Pike, Warburton Mayer, 1861-1915.
The barren ground of northern Canada, by Warburton
Pike. London and New York, Macmillan and co.,
1892.
ix p., 1 l., 300 p.   2 fold. maps.   23 cm.

17390 Pike, Warburton Mayer, 1861-1915.
Through the subarctic forest; a record of a canoe
journey from Fort Wrangel to the Pelly lakes, and
down the Yukon River to the Behring Sea, by Warburton
Pike... London, New York, E. Arnold, 1896.
xiv p., 1 l., 295 p. incl. illus., plates,
front., 2 fold. maps.   23 cm.

17391 Pike, Zebulon Montgomery, 1779-1813.
Exploratory travels through the western territories
of North America: comprising a voyage from St. Louis,
on the Mississippi, to the source of that river, and
a journey through the interior of Louisiana, and the
north-eastern provinces of New Spain. Performed
in the years 1805, 1806, 1807, by order of the
government of the United States. By Zebulon Montgomery Pike... London, Printed for Longman, Hurst,
Rees, Orme, and Brown, 1811.
xx, 436 p.   front. (fold. map) map, tables.
$27\frac{1}{2}$ x $22\frac{1}{2}$ cm.
"This is the standard English edition, prepared under
the... editorship of Dr. Thomas Rees, from a manuscript
copy transmitted to England at the time that the
original manuscript went to press in America." -
Pike, Expeditions; ed. by Coues, 1895. The American
edition, Baltimore, 1810, was issued under title:
An account of expeditions to the sources of the
Mississippi, and through the western parts of
Louisiana...

17392 Pino, Pedro Bautista.
Noticias históricas y estadísticas de la antigua
provincia del Nuevo-Mexico, presentadas por su
diputado en Cortes d. Pedro Bautista Pino, en Cadiz
el año de 1812. Adicionadas por el lic. d. Antonio
Barreiro en 1839; y ultimamente anotadas por el
lic. don José Agustín de Escudero, para la Comisión
de estadística militar de la República Mexicana...
Mexico, Impr. de Lara, 1849.
1 p.l., iv, 96, [4] p.   fold. map.   22 cm.

17393 Player-Frowd, J   G
Six months in California. By J. G. Player-Frowd.
London, Longmans, Green, and co., 1872.
3 p.l., 164 p.   20 cm.

17394 Pleasants, W[illiam] J[ames] 1834-
Twice across the plains, 1849, 1856, by W. J.

257

Pleasants. San Francisco, Press of W. N. Brunt
co., 1906.
160 p. incl. front., plates, ports.   17½ cm.

17395 Plumbe, John.
Memorial against Mr. Asa Whitney's railroad
scheme. [Washington] Buell & Blanchard, printers
[1851]
48 p.   22 cm.

17396 Political essays; the annexation of Texas. The future
of the democracy. [n.p., 1844-1852]
38 p.

17397 Polk, R   L   , pub.
California state gazetteer and business directory,
1888. San Francisco, 1888.
1734 p.   24 cm.

17398 Polk, R   L   , pub.
Texas state gazetteer and business directory.
Detroit, 1892.
v.   24 cm.
Library has Vol. 4, 1892.

17399 Polley, Joseph Benjamin, 1840-
A soldier's letters to charming Nellie, by J. B.
Polley, of Hood's Texas brigade... New York and
Washington, The Neale publishing company, 1908.
vi p., 1 l., [9]-317 p.   front., ports.   21 cm.

17400 Pollock, J   M
The unvarnished West; ranching as I found it.
London, 1907.
252 p.   illus., plates, port.   20 cm.

17401 Pond, Samuel William, 1850-1916.
Two volunteer missionaries among the Dakotas;
or, The story of the labors of Samuel W. and Gideon
H. Pond, by S. W. Pond, jr.... Boston and Chicago,
Congregational Sunday-school and publishing society
[c1893]
xii, 278 p.   front., illus., 9 pl. (incl. 5 port.)
19 cm.

17402 Poole, De Witt Clinton, 1828-
Among the Sioux of Dakota; eighteen months
experience as an Indian agent... By Captain D. C.

Poole, 22d infantry, U.S.A. New York, D. Van
Nostrand, 1881.
235 p.   19 cm.

17403 Porter, Burton B   1832-
One of the people; his own story, by Burton B.
Porter. [Colton, Calif.] The author [c1907]
v p., 1 l., 382 p.   front. (port.)   19½ cm.

17404 Porter, Kenneth W
John Jacob Astor and Lord Selkirk. [Bismarck,
State Historical Society of North Dakota, 1930]
5-13 p.   24 cm.
Reprinted from North Dakota historical quarterly,
v. 5, no. 1, October 1930.

17405 Porter, Mrs. Lavinia Honeyman.
By ox team to California; a narrative of crossing
the plains in 1860, by Lavinia Honeyman Porter.
Oakland, Cal., Oakland enquirer pub. co., 1910.
xi, 139 p.   24½ cm.

17406 Portland, Or. Board of Statistics, Immigration and
Labor Exchange.
Oregon, its advantages as an agricultural and
commercial state. Statistics, climate, condition of
the people, markets, price of land, wages, cost and
routes of travel, etc., etc., etc. Issued by the
Board of Statistics, Immigration and Labor Exchange
of Portland, Oregon... Portland, Or., A. G. Walling,
book and job printer, 1870.
62 p.   22½ cm.

17407 Portland, Or. Chamber of Commerce.
Oregon, the land of opportunity. Portland [1911]
iv, 32, vii p.   map, plates.   21 cm.

17408 Portland, Or. Oregon Immigration Board.
The new empire: Oregon, Washington, Idaho;
its resources, climate, present development, and its
advantages as a place of residence and field for
investment. The city of Portland, its trade,
commerce, and position as metropolis... and center
of transportation lines. Portland [1889]
89 p.   21 cm.

17409 Portland, Or. Oregon Immigration Board.
The Pacific Northwest; its wealth and resources.

Oregon, Washington, Idaho the city of Portland.
[Portland, 1891]
158 p.   illus.   21 cm.

17410   Portland Press Club, Portland, Or.
Pictorial Oregon, the wonderland; an invitation to
visit Oregon extended by the Portland press club.
Portland, Or., Portland press club, 1915.
167, 1 p. incl. front., illus., ports., maps.
23½ x 31½ cm.
"Written by James V. Sayre and Lair H. Gregory
where not otherwise specified."

17411   Portrait and biographical album of Lancaster county,
Nebraska, containing full page portraits and biographical sketches of prominent and representative
citizens of the county... Chicago, Chapman brothers,
1888.
4 p.l., 19-796, [4] p. incl. plates, ports.
28 cm.

17412   Portrait and biographical album of Otoe and Cass
counties, Nebraska, containing full page portraits
and biographical sketches of prominent and representative citizens of the county, together with portraits
and biographies of all the governors of the state,
and of the presidents of the United States. Chicago,
Chapman brothers, 1889.
6 p.l., 23-1307, [5] p. incl. ports.   28 cm.

17413   Portrait and biographical record of Denver and vicinity,
Colorado, containing portraits and biographies of
many well known citizens of the past and present,
together with biographies and portraits of all the
presidents of the United States. Chicago, Chapman
publishing company, 1898.
4 p.l., [19]-112 p., 2 l., [115]-1306 p. incl.
pl., ports.   ports.   29 x 22½ cm.

17414   Portrait and biographical record of Oklahoma; commemorating the achievements of citizens who have contributed to the progress of Oklahoma and the development
of its resources. Chicago, Chapman publishing co.,
1901.
2 p.l., [7]-1298 p. incl. plates, ports.   ports.
29 cm.

17415 Portrait and biographical record of western Oregon,
containing original sketches of many well known
citizens of the past and present... Chicago,
Chapman publishing company, 1904.
5 p.l., [21]-1033 p. incl. ports. 29½ cm.

17416 Post, Truman Augustus.
Truman Marcellus Post, D.D., a biography, personal
and literary, by T. A. Post. Boston and Chicago,
Congregational Sunday-school and publishing society
[1891]
xv, 507 p. front., plates, port. 21½ cm.

17417 Potter, Albert W
The plain truth about California. Oakland, Cal.,
1886.
148 p.

17418 Potter, Theodore Edgar, 1832-1910.
The autobiography of Theodore Edgar Potter.
[Concord, N. H., The Rumford press, c1913]
ix, 228 p. front., ports. 21½ cm.

17419 Powell, John J
The golden state and its resources... San Francisco,
Bacon & co., 1874.
219 p. 21 cm.

17420 Powell, John J
Nevada: the land of silver... San Francisco,
Bacon & co., 1876.
vii, 306 p. 21 cm.

17421 Powell, John J
Wonders of the Sierra Nevada, and Coast range...
San Francisco, H. S. Crocker & co., 1881.
162 p. 4 maps. 24 cm.

17422 Powell, John Wesley, 1834-1902.
Canyons of the Colorado, by J. W. Powell...
Meadville, Pa., Flood & Vincent, 1895.
2 p.l., [iii]-xiv, [15]-400 p. incl. illus., plates.
front. (port.) 10 fold. pl. 30 x 22½ cm.
A republication (with six additional chapters) of
chapters 1-9 of part of Powell's original report,
published by the Smithsonian institution in 1875,
under title: Exploration of the Colorado river of
the West and its tributaries.

17423 Powers, Laura Bride.
Missions of California, their establishment,
progress and decay. San Francisco, W. Doxey, 1897.
vi, 106 p.   illus.   19 cm.
Earlier edition, 1893, had title: The story of the
old missions of California.

17424 Pratt, Orson, 1811-1881.
Mormonism. The state and prospects of Utah;
second epistle. [Washington, D. C., 1853]
Mounted clipping from an unidentified source
reprinting material first appearing in The Seer
(Washington, D. C., 1853-1854). Text signed and
dated Oct. 1, 1853.

17425 Pratt, Parley Parker, 1807-1857.
The autobiography of Parley Parker Pratt, one of
the twelve apostles of the Church of Jesus Christ of
latter-day saints, embracing his life, ministry and
travels, with extracts... from his miscellaneous
writings. Edited by his son, Parley P. Pratt...
New York, Published for the editor and proprietor by
Russell brothers, 1874.
502, x p.   front., illus., plates, ports.
22½ cm.

17426 Prentiss, A   , ed.
The history of the Utah volunteers in the Spanish-
American war and in the Philippine Islands. In two
parts. [Salt Lake City] W. F. Ford [1900]
xviii, 430 p.   illus., ports., maps.   23 cm.
Part II has special title-page: The story of the
Utah Battalion, United States light artillery.

17427 Press reference library (Southwest ed.)... being the
portraits and biographies of progressive men of the
Southwest... Los Angeles, Cal., The Los Angeles
examiner, 1912.
500 p.   illus. (ports.)   28½ cm.

17428 Price, George Frederic, d. 1888.
Across the continent with the fifth cavalry,
compiled by George F. Price... New York, D. Van
Nostrand, 1883.
705, [1] p.   front., ports.   24 cm.

17429 Price, Sir Rose Lambart, bart., 1837-1899.
A summer on the Rockies, by Major Sir Rose Lambart

Price, bart. ... London, S. Low, Marston & company, ltd., 1898.
x, 279, [1] p.   front. (port.) pl., fold. map.
20 cm.

17430 Prince, Le Baron Bradford, 1840-1922.
Historical sketches of New Mexico, from the earliest records to the American occupation, by L. Bradford Prince... New York, Leggat brothers; Kansas City, Ramsey, Millett & Hudson, 1883.
327 p.   illus.   20½ cm.

17431 Prosch, Thomas Wickham, 1850-1915.
David S. Maynard and Catherine T. Maynard; biographies of two of the Oregon immigrants of 1850... By Thomas W. Prosch... Seattle, Wash., Lowman & Hanford stationery & printing co. [1906]
83 p. incl. illus., 2 port.   23 cm.

17432 Public libraries of Wyoming. (In Wyoming historical society collections, 1897, v. 1, p. 123-127)

17433 Puckett, James Louis, 1863-
History of Oklahoma and Indian Territory and home-seekekers' [!] guide, by J. L. and Ellen Puckett. Vinita, Okla., Chieftain publishing company, 1906.
1 p.l., [7]-149, [1] p., 1 l. incl. plates, ports. front.   22 cm.

17434 [Puelles, José María de Jesús]
Informe que se dio al Excmo. Sr. Presidente de la República Mejicana, sobre limites de la Provincia de Tejas con la de la Luisiana. Zacatecas, 1828.
[39] p.   20 cm.

17435 Pumpelly, Raphael, 1837-1923.
My reminiscences, by Raphael Pumpelly... New York, H. Holt and company, 1918.
2 v.   fronts., plates (part col.) ports., maps (part fold.)   23 cm.

17436 Put's golden songster, containing the largest and most popular collection of California songs ever published. San Francisco [1858]
64 p.   25 cm.

17437 Putnam, George Palmer, 1887-1950.
In the Oregon country; out-doors in Oregon,

Washington, and California, together with some
legendary lore, and glimpses of the modern West
in the making, by George Palmer Putnam... with an
introduction by James Withycombe... with 52 illustrations. New York and London, G. P. Putnam's sons,
1915.
xxi, 169 p.   front., plates.   20 cm.
"Some of the material in this book has been printed
in substantially the same form in Recreation."

Q

17438 Qualey, Carlton C
Pioneer Norwegian settlement in North Dakota.
[Bismarck, State Historical Society of North Dakota,
1930]
14-37 p.   24 cm.
Reprinted from North Dakota historical quarterly,
v. 5, no. 1, October 1930.

R

17439 Rae, John, 1813-1893.
The Arctic regions and Hudson's Bay route. Report
of a lecture. [Winnipeg, 1882]
11 p.   21 cm.   (Manitoba historical and scientific
society transactions, no. 2)

17440 Rae, William Fraser.
Newfoundland to Manitoba through Canada's maritime
mining, and prairie provinces, by W. Fraser Rae.
With maps and illustrations. New York, G. P. Putnam's
sons, 1881.
x p., 1 l., 294 p.   fold. map.   19 cm.

17441 Raht, Carlysle Graham.
The romance of Davis mountains and Big Bend country;
a history of Carlysle Graham Raht, drawings by Waldo
Williams. El Paso, The Raht books company [1919]
3 p.l., 381 p.   front., plates, ports., double map.
20½ cm.

17442 Raines, Caldwell W
Bibliography of Texas; being a descriptive list of

books, pamphlets and documents relating to Texas
in print and manuscript since 1536, including a
complete collation of the laws: with an introductory
essay on the materials of early Texan history.
Austin, Texas, 1896.
16, 268 p.   pl.   22 cm.

17443 *Omitted.*

17444 Ranch life in California, extracted from the home
       correspondence of E. M. H.   London, W. H. Allen & co.,
       1886.
       iv, 171, [1] p.   front., pl.   16½ cm.

17445 Ranck, Glenn N
       Pictures from Northwest history.   [Vancouver, 1902]
       [37] p.   22 cm.

17446 Randall, P   K
       Traveller's companion and guide westward.   29th ed.
       Boston, Fred Rogers, printer, 1863.
       19 p.   fold. map.   11 cm.

17447 Rathmoll, William.
       Life of the Marlows; a true story of frontier life
       of early days as related by themselves. Revised by
       William Rathmoll. Ouray, Colo., Ouray Herald print
       [n.d.]
       100 p.   20 cm.

17448 Ratliff, Beulah Amidon.
       Charles Fremont Amidon, 1856-1937, by Beulah Amidon
       Ratliff. [Bismarck, State Historical Society of
       North Dakota, 1941]
       83-100 p.   front. (port.)   24 cm.
       Reprinted from North Dakota historical quarterly,
       v. 8, no. 2, January 1941.

17449 Ravoux, Augustin, bp., 1815-1906.
       Reminiscences, memoirs and lectures of Monsignor
       A. Ravoux, V. G.   St. Paul, Minn., Brown, Treacy & co.,
       1890.
       x, 223 p.   3 port. (incl. front.)   25½ cm.

17450 Rawlins, Joseph L
       Admission of Utah.   Speech in the House of
       representatives, Dec. 12, 1893. Washington, 1893.
       23 p.   22 cm.

17451 Read, Benjamin Maurice, 1853-
        Illustrated history of New Mexico, by Benjamin M.
        Read... tr. into English under the direction of the
        author, by Eleuterio Baca... [Santa Fe, New Mexican
        printing company, c1912]
        812 p. incl. illus., pl., ports., facsims.   26 cm.

17452 Reagan, Albert B
        Chipeta, queen of the Utes, and her equally illus-
        trious husband, noted Chief Ouray. Salt Lake City,
        Utah State Historical Society, 1933. (In Utah his-
        torical quarterly, v. 6, no. 3, July 1933, p. 103-110)

17453 Reagan, John Henninger, 1818-1905.
        Memoirs, with special reference to secession and the
        civil war, by John H. Reagan... ed. by Walter Flavius
        McCaleb... with introduction by George P. Garrison...
        New York and Washington, The Neale publishing company,
        1906.
        351 p.   front., pl., ports.   23 cm.

17454 Reavis, Logan Uriah, 1831-1889.
        The life and military services of Ben. William
        Selby Harney. By L. U. Reavis... Introduction by
        Gen. Cassius M. Clay. Saint Louis, Bryan, Brand & co.,
        1878.
        2 p.l., [iii]-xvii, 18-477 p. incl. illus., plates,
        ports.   front., ports.   22 cm.
        "The American Indian": p. 394-449.

17455 Reed, Henry E   , comp.
        Oregon: a story of progress and development,
        together with an account of the Lewis & Clark
        centennial exposition to be held in Portland, Oregon,
        from June 1 to October 15, 1905. Portland, 1904.
        96 p.   plates.   22 cm.

17456 Rees, William.
        Description of the city of Keokuk, Lee County,
        Iowa; exhibiting its geographical and local advantages,
        which render it the only point in sixteen hundred
        miles for bridging the Mississippi, and for the
        transit of the trade between the Atlantic & Pacific
        oceans: also, statement of the nature of the land
        titles. By William Rees. [Keokuk] Keokuk dispatch
        print, 1854.
        24 p.   illus.   24 cm.

17457   Reid, Russell.
         The De Morès Historical Site, by Superintendent
         Russell Reid. [Bismarck, State Historical Society of
         North Dakota, 1941]
            272-283 p.   illus., fold. map.   24 cm.
         Reprinted from North Dakota historical quarterly,
         v. 8, no. 4, July 1941.

17458   Reid, Russell.
         The earth lodge, by Russell Reid. [Bismarck,
         State Historical Society of North Dakota, 1930]
            174-185 p.   illus.   24 cm.
         Reprinted from North Dakota historical quarterly,
         v. 4, no. 3, April 1930.

17459   Reid, Russell.
         Fort Lincoln State Park, by Superintendent Russell
         Reid. [Bismarck, State Historical Society of North
         Dakota, 1941]
            101-113 p.   illus., fold. map.   24 cm.
         Reprinted from North Dakota historical quarterly,
         v. 8, no. 2, January 1941.

17460   Reid, Russell, ed.
         Journal of the Atkinson-O'Fallon Expedition, ed. by
         Russell Reid and Clell G. Gannon. [Bismarck, State
         Historical Society of North Dakota, 1929]
            5-56 p.   facsim.   24 cm.
         Reprinted from North Dakota historical quarterly,
         v. 4, no. 1, October 1929.

17461   Reid, Russell.
         Lake Metigoshe State Park, by Supt. Russell Reid.
         [Bismarck, State Historical Society of North Dakota,
         1942]
            114-124 p.   fold. map.   24 cm.
         Reprinted from North Dakota historical quarterly,
         v. 9, no. 2, January 1942.

17462   Reid, Russell.
         The North Dakota state park system, by Superintendent
         Russell Reid. [Bismarck, State Historical Society
         of North Dakota, 1940]
            63-78 p.   illus.   24 cm.
         Reprinted from North Dakota historical quarterly,
         v. 8, no. 1, October 1940.

17463 Reid, Russell.
Turtle River State Park, by Superintendent Russell
Reid. [Bismarck, State Historical Society of North
Dakota, 1941]
147-156 p.   illus., fold. map.   24 cm.
Reprinted from North Dakota historical quarterly,
v. 8, no. 3, April 1941.

17464 Reister, J   T
Sketches of Colorado: valuable information obtained
from personal observation of this new Eldorado.
Macon, Mo., 1876.
62 p.   19 cm.

17465 Remarks in the electoral commission on the Oregon case,
on the 23d of February, 1877. [n.p., 1877]
11 p.   18 cm.

17466 Renick, William, b. 1804.
Memoirs, correspondence and reminiscences of
William Renick. Circleville, O., Union-herald book
and job printing house, 1880.
3 p.l., 115 p.   front. (port.)   23½ cm.

17467 Remington, Frederic, 1861-1909.
Crooked trails. New York and London, Harper &
Brothers, 1898.
2 p.l., v, [1] p., 1 l., 150 p.   plates.   23 cm.

17468 Remington, Frederic, 1861-1909.
Drawings by Frederic Remington. New York, R. H.
Russell; London, Lawrence & Bullen, 1897.
3 p.l., 61 pl.   30 x 46½ cm.

17469 Remington, Frederic, 1861-1909.
Pony tracks, written and illustrated by Frederic
Remington. New York, Harper & brothers, 1895.
viii p., 1 l., 269 p. incl. illus., plates.   front.
23 cm.
Fifteen sketches of army and sporting life, chiefly
in the western part of the United States and in
northern Mexico.

17470 Reminiscences of the early days of Manti [from The
Home Sentinel, Manti, Utah, Aug. 15, 1889; Our price
articles, no. 1, written by A.B.C.'s] Salt Lake City,
Utah State Historical Society, 1933. (In Utah historical
quarterly, v. 6, no. 4, October 1933, p. 117-128)

17471   Remondino, Peter C
        The marine climate of the Southern California coast,
        and its relation to phthisis. Reprinted from Proceedings
        of Southern California medical society. [n.p., 1888?]
        58 p.   22 cm.

17472   Remondino, P[eter] C
        The Mediterranean shores of America. Southern
        California: its climatic, physical, and meteorological
        conditions: by P. C. Remondino, M.D. ... Philadelphia
        and London, The F. A. Davis co., 1892.
        xiv, 160 p.   illus., pl., map.   22 cm.

17473   Remsburg, George J
        An old Kansas Indian town on the Missouri, by George
        J. Remsburg. Plymouth, Ia., G. A. Chandler, printer
        [1919?]
        1 p.l., 11 p.   pl., port.   21½ cm.

17474   [Remsburg, John Eleazer] 1848-1919.
        Charley Reynolds. [Potter, Kan., 1915?]
        [40] p.   23½ cm.
        Reprinted from the Potter weekly Kansan, 1914-15.

17475   Renick, William, b. 1804.
        Memoirs, correspondence and reminiscences of William
        Renick. Circleville, O., Union-herald book and job
        printing house, 1880.
        3 p.l., 115 p.   front. (port.)   23½ cm.

17476   Resources and attractions of Colorado for the home
        seeker, capitalist and tourist: facts on climate,
        soil, farming stock raising... Ed. 2. St. Louis,
        1889.
        91 p.
        Issued by the passenger department of the Union
        Pacific railroad.

17477   Revere, Joseph Warren, 1812-1880.
        A tour of duty in California: including a description
        of the gold region; and an account of the voyage
        around Cape Horn; with notices of lower California,
        the Gulf and Pacific coasts, and the principal events
        attending the conquest of the Californias. By Joseph
        Warren Revere... Ed. by Joseph N. Balestier...
        With a map and plates from original designs. New York,
        C. S. Francis & co.; Boston, J. H. Francis, 1849.

3 p.l., [iii]-vi p., 1 l., 305 p.   front.,
plates, fold. map.   19½ cm.
Revere was at the time a lieutenant in the U.S.
Navy.

17478 Reynolds, John Hugh.
       ... Makers of Arkansas history, by John Hugh Reynolds
       ... New York, Boston [etc.] Silver, Burdett and
       company [c1905]
         294 p.   front. (fold. map)   illus.   19 cm.
       (Stories of the states)

17479 Reynolds, John Hugh.
       Public archives of Arkansas. American historical
       association. Annual report for 1906. v. 2, p. 23-51.
       Washington, 1908.

17480 Reynolds, John N
       The twin hells; a thrilling narrative of life in
       the Kansas and Missouri penitentiaries, by John N.
       Reynolds... Atchison, Kan., The Bee publishing co.
       [c1890]
         331 p. incl. front. (port.)   19 cm.

17481 Rice, Harvey, 1800-1891.
       Letters from the Pacific slope; or, First impressions.
       By Harvey Rice. New York, D. Appleton & company, 1870.
         iv, [5]-135 p.   19 cm.

17482 Rice, Martin, b. 1814.
       Rural rhymes, and talks and tales of olden times,
       being a collection of poems and old-time stories...
       by Martin Rice... 2d ed., enl. and improved. Kansas
       City, Ramsey, Millett & Hudson, 1882.
         v, [2], [9]-392 p.   front., ports., diagr.   20 cm.

17483 [Richards, Franklin Dewey] 1821-1899, comp.
       Latter-day Saints in Utah... Liverpool, F. D.
       Richards; London, T. C. Armstrong, 1852.
         iv, [5]-24 p.   21 cm.

17484 Richards, Jarrett Thomas.
       Romance on El camino real; reminiscences and romances
       where the footsteps of the padres fall, by Jarrett T.
       Richards, L.L.B.; illustrations by Alexander R. Harmer...
       St. Louis, Mo. [etc.] B. Herder, 1914.
         5 p.l., 538 p.   front., plates.   20½ cm.

17485   Richardson, Albert Deane, 1833-1869.
        Our new states and territories, being notes of a
        recent tour of observation through Colorado, Utah,
        Idaho, Nevada, Oregon, Montana, Washington Territory
        and California... By Albert D. Richardson. New York,
        Beadle and company [c1866]
        3 p.l. [9]-80 p.   illus.   22 cm.

17486   Richman, Irving Berdine.
        California under Spain and Mexico, 1535-1847.
        Boston, 1911.
        ix, 541 p.   charts, maps, plans.   21 cm.

17487   Riddle, George W   1839-
        History of early days in Oregon. By George W.
        Riddle. Riddle, Or., Reprinted from the Riddle enter-
        prise, 1920.
        1 p.l., 74 p.   pl., port.   19 cm.

17488   Rideing, William Henry, 1853-1918.
        ... A saddle in the wild West. A glimpse of travel
        among the mountains, lava beds, sand deserts, adobe
        towns, Indian reservations, and ancient pueblos of
        southern Colorado, New Mexico and Arizona. By William
        H. Rideing... New York, D. Appleton and company, 1879.
        165 p.   17 cm.   (Appleton's new handy-volume series,
        no. 36)

17489   Rideout, Mrs. J   B
        Camping out in California. San Francisco [1889]
        337 p.   plates.   20 cm.

17490   Ridge, John Rollin, 1827-1867.
        Poems. By John R. Ridge. San Francisco, H. Payot &
        company, 1868.
        137, [1] p.   front. (port.)   18½ cm.
        By a Cherokee Indian, with an account of the
        assassination of his father, John Ridge.

17491   Riggs, Stephen Return, 1812-1883.
        Tah-koo wah-kan; or, The gospel among the Dakotas.
        By Stephen R. Riggs... With an introduction, by S. B.
        Treat... Boston, Cong. Sabbath-school and publishing
        society [c1869]
        xxxvi, 491 p.   1 illus. (music) 4 port. (incl.
        front.)   17½ cm.
        "Written for the Congregational Sabbath-school and
        publishing society and approved by the Committee of
        publication."

17492 Riggs, Stephen Return, 1812-1883.
Mounds of Minnesota Valley, by Rev. S. R. Riggs,
Lac-qui-fable Mission. St. Paul, Minnesota Historical
Society, 1853. (In Annals of the Minnesota Historical
Society, no. IV, 1853, p. 34-39)

17493 Ripley, Henry, 1847-
Hand-clasp of the East and West; a story of pioneer
life on the western slope of Colorado, by Henry and
Martha Ripley. [Denver, Press of the Williamson-
Haffner engraving & printing co., 1914]
471 p. incl. front. (port. group) illus. 19½ cm.

17494 Ritch, William Gillet, 1830-1904.
Aztlan. The history, resources and attractions of
New Mexico, embellished with maps and seventy-five
characteristic illustrations. By Hon. Wm. G. Ritch,
who for twelve years served the territory either as
secretary or governor. 6th ed. 27th thousand. Rev.
and enl. Boston, D. Lothrop & co., 1885.
253 p. incl. front., illus., plates (part fold.)
fold. maps. 22½ cm.
Earlier editions have title: "Illustrated New
Mexico."

17495 Rittenhouse, Rufus, 1825-
Boyhood life in Iowa forty years ago, as found in
the memoirs of Rufus Rittenhouse... Dubuque, Ia.,
C. B. Dorr, book and job printer, 1880.
28 p. illus. 19½ cm.

17496 Roach, Philip A
Address on the opening of the fair for the erection
of the Roman Catholic cathedral, on Van Ness Avenue,
Nov. 15th, 1887, at the Mechanics' pavilion. San
Francisco, 1887.
24 p. pl. 21 cm.

17497 Roberts, Daniel Webster, 1841-
Rangers and sovereignty, by Dan W. Roberts, captain
Company "D" of the Texas rangers. San Antonio, Tex.,
Wood printing & engraving co., 1914.
3 p.l., [11]-190 p. 2 port. (incl. front. 20 cm.

17498 Roberts, Lou (Conway) "Mrs. D. W. Roberts."
A woman's reminiscences of six years in camp with
the Texas rangers, by Mrs. D. W. Roberts, "assistant
commander" Company D, Texas frontier battalion.

Austin, Tex., Press of Von Boeckmann-Jones co.
[1928?]
64 p.   front. (ports.) plates.   23 cm.

17499 Roberts, Morley, 1857-
The western Avernus; or, Toil and travel in further
North America, by Morley Roberts. London, Smith,
Elder & co., 1887.
4 p.l., 307 p.   front. (fold. map)   21 cm.

17500 Roberts, Oran Milo, 1815-1898.
Texas [in the Civil war] (In Evans, C. A., ed.
Confederate military history, 1899, v. 11, 713 p.)

17501 Roberts, Sidney.
Great distress and loss of the lives of American
citizens. An appeal to the citizens of the United
States, for and in behalf of suffering humanity, in
the western state of Iowa, and in the Indian Territory.
By Sidney Roberts... [n.p.] 1848.
iv, [5]-9, [3] p.   19 cm.
An appeal for contributions to relieve the sufferings
of the Mormons in Iowa.

17502 Robertson, Wyndham, 1803-1888.
Oregon, our right and title; containing an account
of the condition of the Oregon territory... together
with a statement of the claims of Russia, Spain,
Great Britain, and the United States; accompanied
with a map, prepared by the author... Washington,
J. & G. S. Gideon, 1846.
203, xxiv p.   fold. map.   20 cm.

17503 [Robinson, Alfred] 1806-1895.
Life in California: during a residence of several
years in that territory, comprising a description
of the country and the missionary establishments,
with incidents, observations, etc. ... By an American.
To which is annexed a historical account of the origin,
customs, and traditions, of the Indians of Alta-
California. Tr. from the original Spanish manuscript.
New York, Wiley & Putnam, 1846.
xii p., 1 l., 341 p.   front., plates, port.
19½ cm.
"Chinigchinich; a historical account of the ...
Indians at the missionary establishment of St. Juan
Capistrano, Alta California... By the reverend father

friar Geronimo Boscana... New York, Wiley & Putnam, 1846": p. [227]-341.

17504 Robinson, Edgar E
Frederick Jackson Turner. [Bismarck, State Historical Society of North Dakota, 1932]
259-261 p.   24 cm.
Reprinted from North Dakota historical quarterly, v. 6, no. 4, July 1932.

17505 Robinson, Fayette, d. 1859.
California and its gold regions; with a geographical and topographical view of the country, its mineral and agricultural resources. Prepared from official and other authentic documents; with a map of the U. S. and California, showing the routes of the U. S. mail steam packets to California, also the various overland routes. By Fayette Robinson... New York, Stringer & Townsend, 1849.
137 p.   front. (fold. map)   20½ cm.

17506 Robinson, Philip Stewart, 1847-1902.
Sinners and saints. A tour across the states and round them, with three months among the Mormons. Boston, Roberts, 1883.
x, 370 p.   19 cm.

17507 Robinson, W   W
Tarnished angels; paradisical turpitude in Los Angeles revealed. [Los Angeles, The Ward Ritchie press, 1964]
26 p.   [16] p. of facsim. illus.   17½ cm.
Facsimile pages reproduce "La Fiesta de Los Angeles, Souvenir Sporting Guide" (Los Angeles, 1897)

17508 Robinson, William Henry, 1867-
The story of Arizona, by Will H. Robinson... Phoenix, Ariz., The Berryhill company [c1919]
458 p.   front., plates, map.   20 cm.

17509 Rock, Marion Tuttle.
Illustrated history of Oklahoma, its occupation by Spain and France - its sale to the United States - its opening to settlement in 1889 - and the meeting of the first territorial legislature. By Marion Tuttle Rock. Topeka, Kan., C. B. Hamilton & sons, printers, 1890.
xii, 5-277, [1] p.   front., illus., plates, ports. 22 cm.

274

17510   Rock Island & Pacific R. R. Company.
        The golden state, California. Chicago, Rock
        Island lines, 1905.
        47 p.   illus.   18 cm.

17511   Rock Island - Frisco Lines.
        Under the turquoise sky in Colorado; in which is
        shown how pleasant, healthful and economical a sojourn
        in the ideal vacation-land may be. [Denver?] 1905.
        79 p.   illus., plates.   20 cm.

17512   Rock Island Railroad Company.
        Colorado and the Rocky Mountain national park.
        [Chicago] 1916.
        32 p.   illus., map.   20 cm.

17513   Rock Island Railway Company.
        Hotels and boarding houses in California. [San
        Francisco] 1915.
        74 p.   20 cm.

17514   Rocky Mountain directory and Colorado gazetteer for
        1871, comprising a brief history of Colorado and a
        condensed... account of her mining, agricultural,
        commercial and manufacturing interests... together
        with a directory of Denver, Golden City, Black Hawk,
        Central City, Nevada, Idaho, Georgetown, Boulder,
        Greeley... Denver [1871]
        442 p.   21 cm.

17515   Rocky Mountain News.
        Colorado condensed. Ed. 2. Industrial information
        for capitalists and immigrants, freshly compiled by
        the Rocky Mountain News. Denver, 1883.
        71 p.   illus., port.   19 cm.

17516   Roemer, Ferdinand.
        Texas, mit besonderer rücksicht auf deutsche
        auswanderung und die physischen verhältnisse des
        landes nach eigener beobachtung geschildert; mit einem
        naturwissenschaftlichen anhange und einer topographisch-
        geognistischen karte von Texas. Bonn, bei Adolph
        Marcus, 1849.
        xiv, 464 p.   fold. map.   20 cm.

17517   Rogers, Justus H
        Colusa County: its history... with a description

of its resources... Also biographical sketches of
pioneers and prominent residents. By Justus H. Rogers.
Orland, Cal., 1891.
    viii, 9-473, [1] p. incl. front.   plates, ports.,
fold. map.   24 cm.

17518 [Rollins, John R   ]
       Notes on Colorado territory. [n.p.] 1865.
       19 p.

17519 Romspert, George W
       The western echo: a description of the western
       states and territories of the United States. As
       gathered in a tour by wagon. By George W. Romspert.
       Dayton, O., United brethren publishing house, 1881.
       406 p. incl. front. (port.) illus.   18½ cm.

17520 Roosevelt, Theodore, pres. U.S., 1858-1919.
       Hunting trips of a ranchman; sketches of sport on
       the northern cattle plains, by Theodore Roosevelt...
       Illustrated by A. B. Frost, R. Swain Gifford, J. C.
       Beard, Fannie E. Gifford, Henry Sandham. New York &
       London, G. P. Putnam's sons, 1891.
       2 p.l., iii-xvi, 318 p.   front. (port.) plates.
       20 cm.

17521 Roosevelt, Theodore, pres. U.S., 1858-1919.
       The wilderness hunter; an account of the big game
       of the United States and its chase with horse, hound,
       and rifle; by Theodore Roosevelt... New York [etc.]
       G. P. Putnam's sons [c1893]
       xvi, 472 p.   front., pl.   24 cm.

17522 Root, Frank Albert, 1837-
       The overland stage to California. Personal remi-
       niscences and authentic history of the great overland
       stage line and pony express from the Missouri river
       to the Pacific ocean. By Frank A. Root... and William
       Elsey Connelley... Pub. by the authors. Topeka, Kan.,
       1901.
       1 p.l., xvii, [1], 680 p. incl. illus., port.
       front., map.   23½ cm.

17523 Root, Joseph Mosley, 1807-1879.
       California and New Mexico. Speech of Hon. Joseph M.
       Root, of Ohio, in the House of representatives,
       February 15, 1850. Washington, Printed at the

Congressional globe office, 1850?]
7 p.   22 cm.

17524 Rose, Blanche E
       Early Utah medical practice, by Blanche E. Rose.
       Salt Lake City, Utah State Historical Society, 1942.
       (In Utah historical quarterly, v. 10, nos. 1-4, 1942,
       p. 1-13)

17525 Rosen, Peter, 1850-
       Pa-ha-sa-pah; or, The Black hills of South Dakota.
       A complete history of the gold and wonder-land of the
       Dakotas, from the remotest date up to the present...
       By Rev. Peter Rosen... St. Louis, Nixon-Jones
       printing company, 1895.
          xiii, 645 p.   front., illus., plates, ports.
       24 cm.

17526 Ross, Alexander, 1783-1856.
       ... Letters of a pioneer, Alexander Ross; ed. by
       George Bryce... Winnipeg, Manitoba free press print,
       1903.
          cover-title, 15 p.   22 cm.   (Transaction no. 63...
       The historical and scientific society of Manitoba)

17527 Ross, Alexander, 1783-1856.
       The Red River Settlement: its rise, progress, and
       present state. With some account of the native races
       and its general history, to the present day. By
       Alexander Ross... London, Smith, Elder and co., 1856.
          xvi, 416 p.   front.   19½ cm.

17528 Rosser, Thomas L
       Rosser's journal, Northern Pacific Railroad survey,
       September 1871 [ed.] by William D. Hoyt, Jr.
       [Bismarck, State Historical Society of North Dakota,
       1943]
          47-51 p.   24 cm.
       Reprinted from North Dakota historical quarterly,
       v. 10, no. 1, January 1943.

17529 Rossi, L   abbé.
       Six ans en Amérique, Californie et Oregon...
       2. éd. Paris, E. Dentu [etc.] 1863.
          322, 2 p.   fold. maps.

17530 Routes of travel in Colorado; a handbook of information
       for the tourist, invalid, capitalist and immigrant...

Denver, Col., 1874.
66 p.   20 cm.

17531 Rowbotham, Francis Jameson.
A trip to prairie-land: being a glance at the
shady side of emigration, by Francis Jameson Rowbotham.
In two parts: Part I. - The life on the prairie.
Part 2. - The farming prospects of northern Dakota.
London, S. Low, Marston, Searle, & Rivington, 1885.
xii, 243, [1] p.   19½ cm.

17532 Rowell Art Publishing Company.
Representative men of Colorado in the nineteenth
century. A portrait gallery of many of the men who
have been instrumental in the upbuilding of Colorado,
including not only the pioneers, but others who,
coming later, have added their quota, until the once
territory is now the splendid state. New York, 1902.
xii, 272 p.   ports.   26 cm.

17533 Royce, Charles C   1845-
John Bidwell, pioneer, statesman, philanthropist;
a biographical sketch, by C. C. Royce. Chico, Cal.,
1906.
66 p. incl. front., illus., port.   facsims.
25½ cm.
"The first emigrant train to California" by John
Bidwell: p. 8-37.

17534 Royce, Josiah, 1855-1916.
... California, from the conquest in 1846 to the
second vigilance committee in San Francisco [1856]
A study of American character, by Josiah Royce...
Boston and New York, Houghton, Mifflin and company,
1886.
xv, 513 p.   front. (fold. map)   18 cm.   (Half-
title: American commonwealths. Ed. by H. E.
Scudder. [v. 7])

17535 Rozier, Firmin A
150th celebration of the bounding of Ste. Genevieve.
Address of Hon. Firmin A. Rozier, historian and
orator selected for the occasion, giving a full
history of Ste. Genevieve, the first permanent
settlement in the United States west of the Mississippi
River. Delivered at the city of Ste. Genevieve, Mo.,
July 21, 1885.   St. Louis, G. A. Pierrot & son,

printers, 1885]
1 p.l., 19 p.   25½ cm.

17536　Ruffner, Ernest Howard.
Report of a reconnaissance in the Ute country
[Colorado] made in the year 1873, by Lieut. E. H.
Ruffner, corps of engineers. Washington, U. S. War
Department, 1874.
101 p.   map.   24 cm.

17537　Rühl, Karl.
Californien. Ueber dessen bevölkerung und
gesellschaftliche zustände, politische, religiöse
und schul-verhältnisse, handel, industrie, minen,
ackerbau, u.s.w. Mit berücksichtigung der minen-
regionen der benachbarten staaten und territorien.
Von Karl Rühl... New York, E. Steiger, 1867.
viii, 283 p.   fold. map, fold. plan.   23½ cm.

17538　Russell, Ike.
The West vs. Harriman.
335-355 p.   illus., ports.   25 cm.
Tear sheets from Pearson's Magazine, Sept. 1909.

17539　Russell, Israel Cook.
Present and extinct lakes of Nevada. (In National
Geographic Society. The physiography of the United
States. [1895] p. 101-132)

17540　Russell, Morris Craw, 1840-
Uncle Dudley's odd hours; western sketches, Indian
trail echoes, straws of humor, by M. C. Russell
("Uncle Dudley") Lake City, Minn., "The Home printery",
1904.
256 p. incl. port.   25 cm.

17541　Russell, Osborne, b. 1814.
Journal of a trapper; or, Nine years in the Rocky
Mountains: 1834-1843; being a general description
of the country, climate, rivers, lakes, mountains,
etc., and a view of the life led by a hunter in those
regions, by Osborne Russell... [Boise, Id., Syms-
York co., inc., c1914]
105, [3] p.   22½ cm.
Edited from the original manuscript by L. A. York.

17542　Ruxton, George Frederick Augustus, 1820-1848.
In the old West, by George Frederick Ruxton...

Cleveland and New York, The Macmillan company, 1915.
345 p.   19 cm.

17543 Rye, Edgar.
The quirt and the spur; vanishing shadows of the
Texas frontier, by Edgar Rye. Chicago, W. B. Conkey
company [c1909]
363 p. incl. 10 pl.   front. (port.)   20 cm.

17544 Ryus, William Henry, 1839-
The second William Penn; a true account of incidents
that happened along the old Santa Fe trail in the
sixties. By W. H. Ryus... Kansas City, Mo., Press of
Frank T. Riley publishing co. [c1913]
176 p. incl. front. (port.) illus.   19½ cm.

S

17545 Sabin, Edwin Legrand, 1870-
Kit Carson days (1809-1868) by Edwin L. Sabin;
illustrated by more than one hundred half-tones,
mostly from old and rare sources. Chicago, A. C.
McClurg & co., 1914.
xiv, 669 p.   front., plates, ports., maps, facsims.
21 cm.

17546 Saint-Amant, Pierre C   de.
Voyages en California et dans l'Orégon. Paris,
1854.
52, 651 p.   maps, port., illus.

17547 Die St. Bernard's-Gemeinde zu St. Bernard, Nebraska,
in ihrem Entstehen und Wachsen von 1878-1903. Eine
Festgabe zum Silbernen Jubiläum der Gemeinde gefeiert
am 30. September und 1. Oktober 1903. St. Louis,
Mo., Gedruckt in der Office der "Amerika", 1903.
86 p.   illus.   22 cm.

17548 Saintly falsity. On questions affecting their fanatical
tenets and practises. Should oaths of Mormons be
accepted in the courts? Some strong facts showing
that they should not be. [Salt Lake City, Salt Lake
City Tribune, 1885?]
10 p.   23 cm.

17549 [Sales, Luis] 1745-1807
          Noticias de la provincia de Californias en tres
       cartas de un sacerdote religioso, hijo del Real
       convento de predicadores de Valencia a un amigo suyo.
       Valencia, Por los hermanos de Orga, 1794.
          3 v. in 1.   2 fold. tab.   16 cm.

17550 Salt Lake City. Bureau of Information.
          Utah; its people, resources, attractions and
       institutions, compiled from authentic information
       and the latest reports.   G.A.R. souvenir ed.
       Salt Lake City [n.d.]
          94 p.   illus.   22 cm.

17551 Salt Lake City. Ladies of the Church of Jesus Christ of
       Latter-day Saints.
          "Mormon" women's protest.   An appeal for freedom,
       justice and equal rights... against the tyranny and
       indecency of Federal officials in Utah, and against
       their own disfranchisement without cause.   Full account
       of proceedings at the great mass meeting held in the
       theater, Salt Lake City, Utah, Saturday, March 6, 1886.
       [Salt Lake City, Deseret News print., 1886]
          91 p.   23 cm.

17552 Salter, William, 1821-1910.
          The life of Henry Dodge, from 1782 to 1833.   With
       portrait by George Catlin and maps of the battles of
       the Pecatonica and Wisconsin Heights in the Black
       Hawk war. By William Salter. Burlington, Ia., 1890.
          1 p.l., 76 p.   front.   25 cm.

17553 Salter, William, 1821-1910.
          Memoirs of Joseph W. Pickett, missionary superintendent
       in southern Iowa and in the Rocky mountains for the
       American home missionary society.   By William Salter...
       Burlington, Ia., J. Love; Colorado Springs, Col.,
       Mrs. S. B. Pickett, 1880.
          1 p.l., [5]-150 p.   19½ cm.

17554 San Diego, Calif. Chamber of Commerce.
          Descriptive, historical, commercial, agricultural,
       and other important information relative to the city
       of San Diego, California.   Illustrated with 22
       photographic views.   Containing also a business
       directory of the city.   Published by the Chamber of
       Commerce of the city of San Diego.   [San Diego]
       Printed at the office of the "San Diego daily union",

1874.
50 p.   22 phot. (incl. front.)   22 cm.
"Among the wild flowers of San Diego, by James S.
Lippincott": p. 26-32.

17555   San Francisco. Committee of Vigilance, 1856.
Constitution and address of the Committee of
Vigilance of San Francisco. San Francisco, Morning
globe print, 1856.
8 p.   23 cm.

17556   San Salvador, Agustin Pomposo Fernández de.
Los Jesuitas quitados y restituidos al mundo.
Historia de la antigua California. Mexico, 1816.
213, [11] p.   21 cm.

17557   Sanborn, Kate.
A truthful woman in southern California. New York,
1893.
192 p.   19 cm.

17558   Sandborn, Ruth Ellen.
The United States and the British Northwest,
1865-1870. [Bismarck, State Historical Society of
North Dakota, 1931]
5-41 p.   24 cm.
Reprinted from North Dakota historical quarterly,
v. 6, no. 1, October 1931.

17559   Sanders, Mrs. Sue A   (Pike) 1842-1931.
A journey to, on and from the "golden shore," by
Sue A. Sanders. Delavan, Ill., Times printing office,
1887.
118 p.   20 cm.

17560   Sanford, Mrs. Nettie.
History of Marshall county, Iowa. By Mrs. N. Sanford.
Clinton, Ia., Leslie, McAllaster & co., printers, 1867.
viii, [9]-157, [1] p.   front., plates, ports.
19 cm.

17561   Santleben, August, 1845-
A texas pioneer; early staging and overland freighting
days on the frontiers of Texas and Mexico, by August
Santleben, ed. by I. D. Affleck. New York and
Washington, The Neale publishing company, 1910.
321 p.   21 cm.

17562 Saunders, Charles Francis.
        Under the sky in California, by Charles Francis
        Saunders... illustrated from photographs mainly by
        C. F. and E. H. Saunders. New York, McBride, Nast &
        company, 1913.
        7 p.l., 299 p.   front., plates.   21½ cm.
        Partly reprinted from various periodicals.

17563 Savage, James Woodruff, 1826-
        The discovery of Nebraska. Read before the
        Nebraska historical society April 16, 1880, by James W.
        Savage. [Omaha, E. H. & M. Mortimer, printers, 1880]
        42 p.   20½ cm.

17564 Savage, James Woodruff, 1826-
        A visit to Nebraska in 1662 [Coronado's expedition
        to Quivira] communicated to the Nebraska historical
        society. Boston, 1885.
        25 p.   19 cm.

17565 Sawyer, Eugene Taylor.
        The life and career of Tiburcio Vasquez, the
        California bandit and murderer: containing a full
        and correct account of his many offenses against the
        law from boyhood up, his confessions, capture, trial,
        and execution. To which is appended Judge Collins'
        address to the jury in behalf of the prisoner. By
        Eugene T. Sawyer... [San Francisco, Bacon & company,
        printers, c1875]
        48 p.   ports.   22 cm.

17566 Saxton, Charles.
        The Oregonian; or, History of the Oregon territory:
        containing the laws of Oregon, with a description of
        the political condition of the country; as well as
        its climate, resources, soil, productions, and
        progress in education, with a map... no. I...
        Washington, D. C., U. Ward & son; Oregon City [Ore.]
        G. Abernathy, 1846.
        vi, [7]-48 p.

17567 Schaeffer, L[uther] M[elanchthon]
        Sketches of travels in South America, Mexico and
        California. New York, J. Egbert, printer, 1860.
        247 p.   20 cm.

17568 Schafer, Joseph.
        The acquisition of Oregon Territory. Part 1.

Discovery and exploration. [Eugene, Ore., 1908]
31 p.   20 cm.
Reprinted from the Oregon University bulletin, n.s,,
v. 6, no. 3.

17569   Schafer, Joseph.
Documents relative to Warre and Vavasour's military
reconnoissance in Oregon, 1845-6. Portland, Ore.,
1909.
99 p.   fold. pl.   20 cm.   (Oregon Historical
Society, Quarterly, v. 10, no. 1, March 1909)

17570   Schafer, Joseph.
History of the Pacific northwest. New York, 1905.
321 p.   illus., map, pl., port.   19 cm.

17571   Scharmann, Hermann B
Scharmann's overland journey to California, from
the pages of a pioneer's diary; tr. from the German of
H. B. Scharmann, by Margaret Hoff Zimmermann, A. B.
and Erich W. Zimmermann, Ph. D. [n.p., 1918]
114 p.   front. (port.) illus.   16½ cm.
Reprinted from New-Yorker staats-zeitung, 1852.

17572   Schlagintweit, Robert von, 1833-1885.
Californien. Land und leute. Von Robert von
Schlagintweit... Cöln und Leipzig, E. H. Mayer;
New York, E. Steiger; [etc., etc.] 1871
xvi, 380, [2] p.   illus.   19½ cm.
"Literatur": p. [369]-374.

17573   Schoolcraft, Henry Rowe, 1793-1864.
A memoir of the history and physical geography of
Minnesota, by Henry R. Schoolcraft. St. Paul,
Minnesota Historical Society, 1851.   (In Annals of
the Minnesota Historical Society, 1850-51, p. 144-157)

17574   Schoolcraft, Henry Rowe, 1793-1864.
Scenes and adventures in the semi-Alpine region
of the Ozark mountains of Missouri and Arkansas, which
were first traversed by De Soto, in 1541. Philadelphia, Lippincott, Grambo & co., 1853.
xii, 13-256 p.   3 plates.   21 cm.

17575   Schoonover, Thomas J
The life and times of Gen'l John A. Sutter, by
T. J. Schoonover. Illustrated pocket ed. Sacramento,

D. Johnston & co., printer, 1895.
    4 p.l., 136 p.   front. (port.)   illus.   15 cm.

17576 Schoonover, Thomas J
    The life and times of Gen. John A. Sutter... Rev.
and enl. ed. By T. J. Schoonover. Sacramento, Cal.,
Press of Bullock-Carpenter printing co., 1907.
    2 p.l., ii, [7]-312, iii p.   front. (port.) illus.
21 cm.

17577 Schuyler, Montgomery, 1843-1914.
    Westward the course of empire; "out West" and "back
East" on the first trip of the "Los Angeles limited".
Reprinted, with additions, from the New York Times,
by Montgomery Schuyler. New York and London, G. P.
Putnam's sons, 1906.
    vii p., 2 l., 198 p.   front., 15 pl.   19 cm.

17578 Schwartz, Stephan.
    Twenty-two months a prisoner of war. A narrative
of twenty-two months' imprisonment by the Confederates,
in Texas, through General Twiggs' treachery, dating
from April, 1861, to February, 1863. By Stephan
Schwartz... St. Louis, Mo., A. F. Nelson publishing
co., 1892.
    5 p.l., 17-221 p.   front. (port.) plates.
20 cm.

17579 Scott, Edwin J   b. 1803.
    Random recollections of a long life, 1806 to 1876.
By Edwin J. Scott... Columbia, S. C., C. A. Calvo,
jr., printer, 1884.
    1 p.l., vi, [3]-216 p.   19½ cm.
    Life in South Carolina, principally in Columbia and
Lexington.

17580 Scott, William A
    Repudiation of state debts: a study in the
financial history of Mississippi, Florida, Alabama,
North Carolina, South Carolina, Georgia, Louisiana,
Arkansas, Tennessee, Minnesota, Michigan, and
Virginia. New York [1893]
    10, 325 p.   (Library of edonomics & politics,
no. 2)

17581 Scripps, John Locke, 1818-1866.
    The undeveloped northern portion of the American
continent. A lecture delivered in the course before

Bell's commercial college, February, 1856. Chicago,
"Democratic press" printing house, 1856.
    20 p.   22 cm.

17582   Seegmiller, Emma Carroll ("Emma S. Higbee")
        Personal memories of the United Order of Orderville,
        Utah, by Emma Carroll Seegmiller. Salt Lake City,
        Utah State Historical Society, 1939. (In Utah
        historical quarterly, v. 7, no. 4, October 1939,
        p. 160-200)

17583   Sellards, E   H
        ... Investigation on the Red River made in connection
        with the Oklahoma-Texas boundary suit, by E. M.
        Sellards, B. C. Tharp, and K. T. Hill... Austin,
        University of Texas, 1923.
            172 p.   maps, tables, plates.   24 cm.   (Texas
        University. Bulletin, no. 2327, 15 July 1923)

17584   Seward, William Henry, 1801-1872.
        California, union and freedom. Speech of William H.
        Seward, on the admission of California. Delivered
        in the Senate of the United States, March 11, 1850.
        [Washington] Buell & Blanchard [1850?]
            14 p.   22 cm.

17585   Seyd, Ernest, 1833-1881.
        California and its resources; a work for the
        merchant, the capitalist, and the emigrant... London,
        Trübner and co., 1858.
            2 p.l., 168 p.   col. front., plates (part col.)
        2 fold. maps.   21½ cm.

17586   Shafer, George F
        Cattle ranching in McKenzie County, N. Dak.
        [Bismarck, N.D., State Historical Society of North
        Dakota, 1926]
            55-61 p.   25 cm.
        In North Dakota historical quarterly, v. 1, no. 1,
        Oct. 1926.

17587   Shannon, P[eter] C
        The state of Dakota: how it may be formed.
        Replies to the pamphlet of Hon. Hugh J. Campbell,
        U. S. attorney of Dakota, treating upon the above
        subject. Opinions of courts, jurists and statesmen,
        as to the admission of new states into the Union.
        By P. C. Shannon... Yankton, D. T., Herald printing

house, 1883.
58 p.   22½ cm.

17588   Shasta route. [Brooklyn, N. Y., Southern Pacific co.,
         n.d.]
         [23] pl.   27 x 25 cm.
         Book of views.

17589   The Shasta route in all of its grandeur, a scenic guide
         book from San Francisco, California, to Portland,
         Oregon on the road of a thousand wonders. [Southern
         Pacific Co.] Chicago [n.d.]
         22 plates.   map.   27 cm.

17590   Shaw, D   A
         Eldorado; or, California as seen by a pioneer,
         1850-1900. Los Angeles, California, 1900.
         313 p.   plates, port.

17591   Shaw, Luella, 1886-
         True history of some of the pioneers of Colorado
         [by] Luella Shaw. Hotchkiss, Co., W. S. Coburn,
         J. Patterson and A. K. Shaw, 1909.
         2 p.l., [iii]-vi, [9]-268 p., 1 l.   front.,
         plates, ports.   20½ cm.

17592   Shaw, Pringle.
         Ramblings in California; containing a description
         of the country, life at the mines, state of society,
         & c., interspersed with characteristic anecdotes,
         and sketches from life, being the five years' experience
         of a gold digger. Toronto [1856?]
         239 p.

17593   Shaw, Thomas, 1843-1918.
         Report of trip through central Oregon during the
         fall of 1910. St. Paul, McGill-Warner co., 1911.
         30 p.   23 cm.

17594   Shaw, William.
         Golden dreams and waking realities; being the
         adventures of a gold-seeker in California and the
         Pacific islands... London, Smith, Elder and co., 1851.
         xii, 316 p.   19½ cm.

17595   Sheldon, Addison Erwin.
         History and stories of Nebraska... with maps and

illustrations. Chicago, 1913.
xvi, 306 p.   front. illus., maps, port.   20 cm.

17596   Sheldon, Addison Ervin.
Poems and sketches of Nebraska. With 64 illustrations. Lincoln, 1908.
199 p.   illus., pl., port.   18 cm.

17597   Sheldon, Addison Ervin.
Report on the archives of the state of Nebraska.
American historical association. Annual report for
1910, p. 365-420. Washington, 1912.
Eleventh report of the Public archives commission,
appendix D. [1910]

17598   Sheldon, Addison Ervin.
Semi-centennial history of Nebraska, historical
sketch by A. E. Sheldon, illustrations, state and
county statistics, public buildings and biographical
sketches, by the Lemon publishing company. Lincoln,
Neb., 1904.
376 p.   front. illus., port.   20 cm.

17599   Sheldon, Addison Ervin.
Three articles on a site for the Historical Society
building. From the Sunday State Journal. Lincoln,
Nebraska, July 14, 1907.
13 p.   port. illus.   18 cm.

17600   Sherman, Edwin Allen, 1829-   comp.
The life of the late Rear-Admiral John Drake Sloat,
of the United States navy, who took possession of
California and raised the American flag at Monterey
on July 7th, 1846. Comp. from the most authentic
sources of family history etc. ... By Major Edwin A.
Sherman, secretary of the Sloat monument association
of California... [Enl. monumental ed.] Oakland,
Cal., Carruth & Carruth, printers, 1902.
[369] p.   front., illus., plates, ports., geneal.
tab., coat of arms.   26 cm.

17601   Sherwood, J   Ely.
California: her wealth and resources; with many
interesting facts respecting the climate and people;
the official and other correspondence of the day,
relating to the gold region; Colonel Mason's report,
and all that part of the President's message having
reference to the country in which these vast discoveries

have been made; also, a memorial offered in Congress,
in relation to the proposed railroad to the Pacific
ocean. By J. Ely Sherwood... New York, G. F. Nesbitt,
printer, 1848.
    40 p.   22 cm.

17602   Shinn, Charles Howard, 1852-1924.
        Mining-camps; a study in American frontier government,
by Charles Howard Shinn. New York, C. Scribner's
sons, 1885.
    xi, 316 p.   21 cm.

17603   Shinn, Josiah Hazen, 1849-1917.
        ... History of education in Arkansas... Washington,
Govt. print. off., 1900.
    121 p.   front., plates.   24 cm.   (Contributions
to American educational history, ed. by Herbert B.
Adams.   no. 26)
        U. S. Bureau of education. Circular of information
no. 1, 1900.

17604   Shinn, Josiah Hazen, 1849-1917.
        Pioneers and makers of Arkansas, by Josiah H. Shinn...
[n.p.] Genealogical and historical publishing company
[c1908]
    v, [4], 10-423 p.   24 cm.

17605   Shively, J   M
        Route and distances to Oregon and California, with
a description of watering-places, crossings, dangerous
Indians, etc., etc. Washington, D. C., W. Greer,
printer, 1846.
    15 p.   21 cm.

17606   [Shook, Martha Caroline (Dial)] 1838-
        Along the King's highway; or, The invisible route;
a romance of the southern United States, by John
Cornelius [pseud.]   Illus. by the author.   [San Antonio,
Maverick-Clarke litho. co., c1912]
    506 p.   front., plates.   20 cm.

17607   Shuck, Oscar Tully, ed.
        History of the bench and bar of California...
comprehending the judicial history of the state.
Los Angeles, 1901.
    xxiv, 1152 p.   port.   25 cm.

17608   Shurtliff, Lewis W   , 1835-1922.
        The Salmon River Mission, extract from the journal
        of L. W. Shurtliff, as edited by W. W. Henderson.
        Salt Lake City, Utah State Historical Society, 1932.
        (In Utah historical quarterly, v. 5, no. 1, January
        1932, p. 2-24)

17609   Sibley, Henry Hastings, 1811-1891.
        Address delivered before the Minnesota Historical
        Society, at the sixth anniversary, February 1st,
        1856. By the Hon. H. H. Sibley. St. Paul, Minnesota
        Historical Society, 1856. (In Annals of the
        Minnesota Historical Society, 1856, p. 1-17)

17610   Sibley, Henry Hastings, 1811-1891.
        Description of Minnesota [letter to Henry S. Foote,
        U. S. Senator, 15 Feb. 1850] St. Paul, Minnesota
        Historical Society, 1850. (In Annals of the
        Minnesota Historical Society, 1850, 2d ed., p. 29-32)

17611   Sibley, Henry Hastings, 1811-1891.
        Sketch of the life of Nicollet. Furnished for the
        Minnesota Historical Society. By Hon. Henry H.
        Sibley. St. Paul, Minnesota Historical Society, 1853.
        (In Annals of the Minnesota Historical Society,
        no. IV, 1853, p. 7-11)

17612   Sibley, Henry Hastings, 1811-1891.
        Speech of Henry H. Sibley, of Minnesota, before
        the Committee on Elections of the House of Repre-
        sentatives delivered December 27, 1848. St. Paul,
        Minnesota Historical Society, 1850. (In Annals of
        the Minnesota Historical Society, 1850, 2d ed.,
        p. 58-62)

17613   Silverwood, Francis B
        California welcomes you; the official souvenir
        book of Al Malaikah temple, A. A. O. N. M. S., 1919,
        imperial council meeting, pilgrimage to Indianapolis,
        Indiana, June 10th to 14th. The contents of this
        book were written, borrowed, stolen and comp. by
        "Daddy" Silverwood. [Los Angeles, Printed by
        Western lithographing co., c1919]
        [80] p.   illus. (incl. ports., part col.)
        23½ x 31½ cm.

17614   Simonds, Frederic William, 1853-
        The geography of Texas, physical and political, by

Frederic William Simonds... Boston, New York [etc.]
Ginn & company [cl905]
xix, 237 p. incl. front., illus., maps.   double
map.   19 cm.

17615 Simonin, Louis Laurent, 1830-1886.
Le grand-ouest des États-Unis, par L. Simonin.
Les pionniers et les peaux-rouges: les colons du
Pacifique. Paris, Charpentier, 1865.
ii, 324 p.   19 cm.

17616 Simonin, Louis Laurent, 1830-1886.
... Le mineur de Californie, par L. Simonin...
Paris, L. Hachette et c^{ie}, 1866.
50, [2] p.   15½ cm.   (Conférences populaires
faites à l'Asile imperial de Vincennes...)

17617 Simpson, Arthur J   , ed.
The century in southwest Texas.   San Antonio, Texas,
Southwest publications, 1937.
226, [4] p.   illus.   22 cm.

17618 Simpson, Sir George, 1792-1860.
California: its history, population, climate,
soil, productions, and harbors. From Sir George
Simpson's "Overland journey round the world." An
account of the revolution in California, and conquest
of the country by the United States, 1846-7. By
John T. Hughes. Cincinnati, J. A. & U. P. James, 1848.
105 p.   19½ cm.
"An account of the revolution in California..."
taken from Hughes' "Doniphan's expedition" with
alterations and additions.

17619 Simpson, Howard E
The winter of 1807-1808 at Pembina, North Dakota.
Alexander Henry's Journal of the weather".
[Bismarck, State Historical Society of North Dakota,
1931]
239-347 p.   24 cm.
Reprinted from North Dakota historical quarterly,
v. 5, no. 4, July 1931.

17620 Simpson, James Hervey, 1813-1883.
The shortest route to California illustrated by a
history of explorations of the great basin of Utah
with its topographical and geological character,
and some account of the Indian tribes. Philadelphia,

J. P. Lippincott & co., 1869.
58 p.   front. (map)

17621   Sinclair, William J
        ... The exploration of the Potter Creek Cave, by
        William J. Sinclair. Berkeley, The University press,
        1904.
            cover-title, 27, [1] p.   xiv pl. (partly fold.)
        27 cm.   (University of California publications.
        American archaeology and ethnology.   v. 2, no. 1)

17622   Sinclair, William J
        ... Recent investigations bearing on the question
        of the occurrence of neocene man in the auriferous
        gravels of the Sierra Nevada, by Wm. J. Sinclair.
        Berkeley, The University Press, 1908.
            cover-title, [107]-131 p.   2 pl.   27 cm.
        (University of California.   Publications in American
        archaeology, v. 7, no. 2)

17623   Siringo, Charles A   1855-1928.
        ... A Lone Star cowboy, being fifty years experience
        in the saddle as cowboy, detective and New Mexico
        ranger, on every cow trail in the wooly old West...
        by Chas. A. Siringo...   Santa Fe, N. M., 1919.
            3 p.l., 290 p.   illus. (incl. ports., facsim.)
        20½ cm.
            "This volume is to take the place of 'A Texas cowboy.'"
        - Pref.

17624   Siringo, Charles A   1855-1928.
        A Texas cow-boy; or, Fifteen years on the hurricane
        deck of a Spanish pony. Taken from real life, by
        Charles A. Siringo...   Chicago, Ill., M. Umbdenstock
        & co., 1885.
            2 p.l.,   ix -xii, [13]-316 p. incl. port.   front.
        (port.) illus., col. pl.   20½ cm.

17625   Sketch of Joseph Renville, a "bois brûlé" and early
        trader of Minnesota [signed by N., p. 16] St. Paul,
        Minnesota Historical Society, 1853. (In Annals of
        the Minnesota Historical Society, no. IV, 1853,
        p. 12-16)

17626   Sketches of the inter-mountain states; together with
        biographies of many prominent and progressive citizens
        who have helped in the development and history-making
        of this marvelous region. 1847. 1909. Utah, Idaho,

292

Nevada. Illustrated. Salt Lake City, The Salt Lake
Tribune, 1909.
376 p.   illus. (incl. ports.)   29 cm.

17627 Slater, Milo H
An historical narrative, address... delivered at
the dedication of the monument erected by the state
of Colorado to the memory of Colorado soldiers of the
Federal army who fell during the Civil War, October
9th, 1907. [Denver] 1907.
30 p.   port.   20 cm.

17628 Slaughter, Benjamin Franklin, 1842-1896.
Portions of the diary of Dr. B. F. Slaughter,
Dakota Territory. [Bismarck, State Historical Society
of North Dakota, 1927]
36-40 p.   25 cm.
In North Dakota historical quarterly, v. 1, no. 2,
Jan. 1927.

17629 Smet, Pierre Jean de, 1801-1873.
Reminiscences of Indian habits and character
[by P. J. de Smet, S. J.] Salt Lake City, Utah State
Historical Society, 1932. (In Utah historical
quarterly, v. 5, no. 1, January 1932, p. 25-27)

17630 Smiley, Jerome Constant.
Semi-centennial history of the state of Colorado,
by Jerome C. Smiley [and others] New York, Lewis
Publishing co., 1913.
2 v.   front., ports.   27 cm.

17631 Smith, Ashbel, 1805-1886.
Reminiscences of the Texas republic. Annual address
delivered before the Historical Society of Galveston,
December 15, 1875. With a preliminary notice of the
Historical Society of Galveston. Pub. by the Society.
Galveston, Tex., 1876.
xvi, [17]-82 p.   23½ cm.
Half-title: "Historical Society of Galveston series,
no. 1." No more published of this series.

17632 Smith, J   Alden.
Catalogue of the principal minerals of Colorado,
with annotations on the local peculiarities of several
species. Central City, 1870.
16 p.   20 cm.

17633   Smith, Justin Harvey, 1857-
        The annexation of Texas, by Justin H. Smith...
        New York, The Baker and Taylor co., 1911.
        ix, 496 p.   24 cm.

17634   Smithers, Wilfred Dudley, 1895-
        Pancho Villa's last hangout; on both sides of the
        Rio Grande in the Big Bend country. [Alpine? Tex., n.d.]
        95 p.   illus., maps, facsims.   23 cm.

17635   Snook, J[ames] E
        Colorado history and government, with state constitu-
        tion, by J. E. Snook... Denver, Col, The Herrick
        book and stationery company [1904]
        63, 47 p.   illus. (incl. maps)   20 cm.

17636   Snow, William J
        Ancient mound grains, by Dr. Wm. J. Snow. Salt Lake
        City, Utah State Historical Society, 1941. (In Utah
        historical quarterly, v. 9, nos. 3, 4, July, October
        1941, p. 134-136)

17637   Snow, William J
        Robert Gardner, typical frontiersman and early Utah
        pioneer, by Dr. Wm. J. Snow. Salt Lake City, Utah
        State Historical Society, 1941. (In Utah historical
        quarterly, v. 9, nos. 3, 4, July, October 1941, p. 179-
        183)

17638   Snow, William J
        Utah Indians and the Spanish slave trade, by Dr.
        Wm. J. Snow. Salt Lake City, Utah State Historical
        Society, 1929. (In Utah historical quarterly, v. 2,
        no. 3, July 1929, p. 67-90)

17639   Society of California Pioneers.
        Annual report, 1896-97, 1899, 1900-1915, 1923/1924.
        San Francisco, 1897-1924.
        16 v.   23 cm.

17640   Sons of Colorado; a monthly publication devoted to the
        interests of the society and "for Colorado."
        v. 1-2; June 1906 - May 1908. [Denver, W. C. Bishop]
        1906-08.
        2 v.   illus., pl.   25½ cm.
        W. C. Bishop, editor.
        Superseded by the Trail.

17641   Sorenson, Alfred Rasmus, 1850-
        Early history of Omaha; or, Walks and talks among
        the old settlers; a series of sketches in the shape
        of a connected narrative of the events and incidents
        of early times in Omaha, together with a brief
        mention of the more important events in later years.
        By Alfred Sorenson, city editor of the Omaha Daily
        Bee. Illustrated with numerous engravings, many of
        them being from original sketches drawn especially
        for this work by Charles S. Huntington. Omaha,
        Printed at the office of The Daily Bee, 1876.
        248 p.   illus.   23 cm.

17642   Sources of the history of Oregon, v. 1, pt. 1-6.
        Eugene, Or., 1897-99.
        26, 28, xix, 262 p.   fold. maps.   24½ cm.
        No more published. Superseded by the Quarterly of
        the Oregon historical society.
        Edited by F. G. Young.

17643   Southern California. Bureau of Information.
        Southern California: an authentic description of
        its natural features, resources, and prospects...
        Los Angeles, 1892.
        98 p.   map, plates.

17644   Southern California Panama Expositions Commission.
        Southern California, comprising the counties of
        Imperial, Los Angeles, Orange, Riverside, San Bernardino,
        San Diego, Ventura; issued by Southern California
        Panama expositions commission... [San Diego?]
        Southern California Panama expositions commission
        [c1914]
        263 p.   illus.   26½ cm.

17645   Southern California quarterly, v. 1-   1884-
        [Los Angeles, 1884-   ]
        v. in   illus., plates, ports., maps, facsims.
        24 cm.

17646   South Western Immigration Company.
        ... Texas; her resources and capabilities...
        Austin, Texas, South Western Immigration Company,
        1881.
        255 p.   illus., plates.   22 cm.

17647   Sowell, A[ndrew] J[ackson]
        Early settlers and Indian fighters of southwest

Texas... Austin, Tex., B. C. Jones & co., 1900.
viii, 844 p.   illus., pl., port.   22 cm.

17648 Spears, John Randolph, 1850-
Illustrated sketches of Death Valley and other
borax deserts of the Pacific Coast. By John R.
Spears. Chicago and New York, Rand, McNally &
company, 1892.
226 p. incl. front., illus., map.   20 cm.
(On cover: Globe library, v. 1, no. 175)

17649 Spec, pseud.
Line etchings. A trip from the Missouri river to
the Rocky Mountains, via the Kansas Pacific railway.
St. Louis, 1875.
69 p.   map, plates.   22 cm.

17650 Sprague, John T
Treachery in Texas, the secession of Texas and
the arrest of the United States officers and soldiers
serving in Texas. Read before the New-York historical
society, June 25, 1861. New-York, 1862.
142 p.   21 cm.   (New York historical society.
Discourses, 1862-1866)

17651 Spurr, Josiah Edward.
... Atlas to accompany Monograph xxxi on the
geology of the Aspen district, Colorado. Washington,
1898.
30 sheets.
At head of title: Dept. of the Interior, U.S.
Geological Survey.

17652 A stage ride to Colorado. From Harper's New Monthly
Magazine. July, 1867.
137-150 p.   illus.   22 cm.
Reprinted from Harper's New Monthly Magazine,
July, 1867, p. 137-150.

17653 Stanley, Sir Henry Morton, 1841-1904.
My early travels and adventures in America and
Asia, by Henry M. Stanley... New York, C. Scribner's
sons, 1895.
2 v.   fronts. (ports.)   19½ cm.

17654 Stansbury, Howard, 1806-1863.
An expedition to the valley of the Great Salt Lake
of Utah: including a description of its geography,

natural history, and minerals, and an analysis of
its waters; with an authentic account of the Mormon
settlement. Also a reconnoissance [!] of a new route
through the Rocky mountains, and two large and accura
maps of that region. By Howard Stansbury, captain,
Corps topographical engineers. Philadelphia,
Lippincott, Grambo, 1852.
    487 p.   34 illus. (3 fold.), 10, 9, 4 plates,
fold. map.   25 cm. and atlas of 2 fold. maps.

17655 Starley, James, 1817-1914.
    Journal of James Starley. Salt Lake City, Utah
State Historical Society, 1941. (In Utah historical
quarterly, v. 9, nos. 3, 4, July, October, 1941,
p. 168-178)

17656 State military, first state encampment. Review of the
late state encampment at the Encinal de Alameda.
By an officer of the camp. San Francisco, Charles F.
Robbins & co., 1863.
    47 p.   20 cm.

17657 Statement of the facts connected with the claims of the
creditors of Texas on the government of the United
States. Washington, 1852.
    16 p.   20 cm.

17658 Statement of the Oregon and Washington delegation, in
regard to the war claims of Oregon and Washington.
[Washington, 1860]
    65 p.   20 cm.

17659 Steele, James William, 1840-1905.
    California: brief glimpses of her valleys,
mountains, lakes and famous places. Chicago [n.d.]
    75 p.   illus.   20 cm.

17660 Steele, James William, 1840-1905.
    Colorado the magnificent. [Chicago, n.d.]
    45 p.   illus., plates.   20 cm.

17661 Steele, James William, 1840-1905.
    Colorado via the Burlington route. Omaha [1901]
    71 p.   illus.   22 cm.

17662 Steele, James William, 1840-1905.
    Old Californian days [by] James Steele... Chicago,
Belford-Clarke co., 1889.

viii, 9-227 p. incl. front., illus.   19½ cm.
(On cover: The household library. v. 6, no. 3)

17663 Steele, John, 1821-
Extracts from the journal of John Steele. Salt
Lake City, Utah State Historical Society, 1933.
(In Utah historical quarterly, v. 6, no. 1, January
1933, p. 2-28)

17664 Steele, John, 1832-1905.
In camp and cabin. Mining life and adventure,
in California during 1850 and later. By Rev. John
Steele... Lodi, Wis., J. Steele [c1901]
1 p.l., 81 p.   23½ cm.
"In camp and cabin" is the sequel to "Across the
plains in 1850". - Introd., p. 1.

17665 Steele, William G
The mountains of Oregon. Portland, 1890.
112p.   plates, ports.   20 cm.

17666 Stellmann, Edith Kinney.
Katie of Birdland; an idyl of the aviary in Golden
Gate Park, by Edith Kinney Stellmann... Illustrated
with special camera studies by Louis J. Stellmann.
San Francisco, H. S. Crocker co. [n.d.]
40 p.   illus.   20 cm.

17667 Stensrud, Edward Martinus.
The Lutheran church and California, by E. M. Stensrud.
San Francisco, 1916.
282 p.   illus., maps, ports.   32 cm.

17668 [Stephens, Louis G   ] 1843-
Letters from an Oregon ranch, by "Katharine"
[pseud.] with twelve full-page illustrations from
photographs. Chicago, A. C. McClurg & co., 1905.
212 p.   12 pl. (incl. front.)   23 cm.

17669 Sterne, Simon, 1839-1901.
Argument on Senate bill no. 11, entitled An act to
provide for ascertaining and settling private land
claims in certain states and territories. By Simon
Sterne, on behalf of certain owners of lands in the
territory of New Mexico. May 24, 1886. [Washington?
1886]
cover-title, 50 p.   22 cm.

17670 Stevens, O   A
        Audubon's journey up the Missouri River, 1843,
        by O. A. Stevens. [Bismarck, State Historical
        Society of North Dakota, 1943]
        62-82 p.   illus.   24 cm.
        Reprinted from North Dakota historical quarterly,
        v. 10, no. 2, April 1943.
        Bibliographical footnotes.

17671 Stevens, Thaddeus, 1792-1868.
        Speech on the president's message concerning Texas
        and New Mexico, delivered in the house of represent-
        atives, Aug. 14, 1850. [Washington, 1850]
        [unpaged]   22 cm.

17672 Stevens, Walter Barlow, 1848-
        Through Texas. A series of interesting and
        instructive letters by Walter B. Stevens, special
        correspondent of the St. Louis globe-democrat.
        Illustrated by Armand Welcker.   [St. Louis] 1893.
        112 p.   illus.   21½ cm.

17673 Stewart, Mrs. Elinore (Pruitt) 1878-
        Letters of a woman homesteader; by Elinore Pruitt
        Stewart; with illustrations by N. C. Wyeth.   Boston
        and New York, Houghton Mifflin company, 1914.
        vii, [1] p., 2 l., 3-281, [1] p., 1 l.   front.,
        plates.   19½ cm.
        Descriptive of ranch life in southwestern Wyoming.
        The letters are dated from April, 1909 to November,
        1913, and were printed originally in the Atlantic
        monthly.

17674 Stickney, V   H
        The roundup. [Bismarck, N. D., State Historical
        Society of North Dakota, 1926]
        3-15 p.   25 cm.
        In North Dakota historical quarterly, v. 1, no. 1,
        Oct. 1926.

17675 Stillman, J   D   B
        Seeking the golden fleece; a record of pioneer life
        in California: to which is annexed. Footprints
        of early navigators, other than Spanish, in California;
        with an account of the schooner Dolphin. San Francisco,
        1877.
        352 p.   pl.   21 cm.

17676 Stirling, Patrick James, 1809-1891.
        The Australian and Californian gold discoveries,
        and their probable consequences; or, An inquiry into
        the laws which determine the value and distribution
        of the precious metals: with historical notices of
        the effect of the American mines on European prices
        in the sixteenth, seventeenth, and eighteenth centuries.
        In a series of letters. By Patrick James Stirling...
        Edinburgh, Oliver & Boyd; [etc., etc.] 1853.
        1 p.l., xiii, [1], [13]-279 p.   front. (fold. diagr.)
        19½ cm.

17677 Stoddard, Charles Warren, 1843-1919.
        In the footprints of the padres. San Francisco,
        1902.
        vii, 335 p.   plates.   22 cm.

17678 Stone, Elizabeth Arnold.
        A Washakie anecdotes, by Mrs. Elizabeth Arnold Stone.
        Salt Lake City, Utah State Historical Society, 1930.
        (In Utah historical quarterly, v. 3, no. 2, April 1930,
        p. 56-57)

17679 Stone, Wilbur Fiske, 1833-1920, ed.
        History of Colorado; Wilbur Fiske Stone, editor...
        Chicago, The S. J. Clarke publishing company, 1918-19.
        v.   front., illus., ports.   27½ cm.

17680 [Stone, William Hale] 1875-
        Twenty-four years a cowboy and ranchman in southern
        Texas and old Mexico; desperate fights with the Indians
        and Mexicans, by Will Hale [pseud.]... Hedrick, O. T.,
        W. H. Stone [c1905]
        1 p.l., 5-268 p.   plates.   19½ cm.

17681 Storey, Samuel.
        To the golden land; sketches of a trip to southern
        California. Illustrated. [By] Samuel Storey...
        London, W. Scott, 1889.
        2 p.l., [iii]-vi p., 1 l., [7]-101 p., 1 l.
        front. (map) plates, ports., facsim.   21½ cm.
        "These sketches were... penned... for publication
        in The Newcastle daily chronicle. The Sunderland
        daily echo, and other English newspapers." - Pref.

17682 Stott, Edwin, 1836-1928.
        A sketch of my life, by Edwin Stott. Salt Lake City,
        Utah State Historical Society, 1941. (In Utah his-

torical quarterly, v. 9, nos. 3, 4, July, October
1941, p. 184-189)

17683   Strahorn, Robert E
        The hand-book of Wyoming and guide to the Black
        Hills and Big Horn regions, for citizen, emigrant
        and tourist. By Robert E. Strahorn ("Alter ego")
        Cheyenne. [Chicago, Knight & Leonard, printers] 1877.
        272 p.   illus.   19 cm.

17684   Strong, Frank, 1859-1934.
        The government of the American people, by Frank
        Strong... and Joseph Schafer... [Oregon ed.]
        Boston, New York [etc.] Houghton, Mifflin and
        company, 1901.
            viii, 314, [2] p.   front., pl., maps.   19½ cm.
        "The growth of civil government in Oregon":
        p. [245]-308.

17685   Strong, Thomas Nelson, 1853-
        Cathlamet on the Columbia; recollections of the
        Indian people and short stories of early pioneer days
        in the valley of the lower Columbia River, by Thomas
        Nelson Strong. Portland, Or., The Holly press, 1906.
        119 p.   19 cm.

17686   Strong, William Duncan.
        Arikara and Cheyenne earth lodge sites in North
        and South Dakota, by Wm. Duncan Strong. [Bismarck,
        State Historical Society of North Dakota, 1941]
            158-166 p.   illus., plates.   20 cm.
        Reprinted from North Dakota historical quarterly,
        v. 8, no. 3, April 1941.

17687   [Strubberg, Friedrich Armand] 1808-1889.
        The backwoodsman; or, Life on the Indian frontier,
        ed. by Sir C. F. Lascelles Wraxall, bart.; with illus.
        by Louis Guard, engraved by John Andrew. Boston,
        T.O.H.P. Burnham; New York, O. S. Felt, 1866.
            302 p.   [8] plates.   19½ cm.
        "A translation, without credit to authorship of
        Strubberg [Amerikanische Jagd- und Reiseabenteuer.
        Stuttgart und Augsburg, J. G. Cotta, 1858]" - cf.
        Wagner-Camp, The Plains & the Rockies, nos. 311a
        and 407.

17688   Struble, Isaac S
        Oklahoma. Speech in the house of representatives,

June 3, 1886. Washington, 1886.
87 p.

17689 The struggle of the Mussel Slough settlers for their
homes! An appeal to the people; history of the
land troubles in Tulare and Fresno counties; the
grasping greed of the railroad monopoly. By the
Settlers' committee. Visalia, Delta printing establishment, 1880.
32 p.   18 cm.

17690 Sumner, Helen L
Chronological outline history of Colorado. First
authentic and complete compilation. From Denver
Daily News, April 23, 1903. [Denver, 1903]
12 p.   22 cm.

17691 Svenskarne i Texas i ord och bild, 1838-1918, ett
historiskt-biografiskt arbete samladt och utgivet af
Ernest Severin, redigeradt och utarbetadt af dr. Alf.
L. Scott, pastor T. J. Westerberg; granskadt och
öfversedt af red. J. M. Ojerholm. [Austin, Tex.,
Printed by E. L. Steck, c1919]
2 v.   illus., plates, ports.   27½ cm.

17692 Swanton, John R
... Indian tribes of the lower Mississippi Valley
and adjacent coast of the Gulf of Mexico, by John R.
Swanton. Washington, Govt. print. off., 1911.
vi p., 1 l., 387 p.   illus., fold. map (front.)
24 cm.   (U. S. Bureau of American Ethnology,
Bulletin, 43)

17693 Swasey, William F
The early days and men of California; by W. F.
Swasey, 1891. Oakland, Cal., New York [etc.]
Pacific press publishing company [1891]
x, 9-406 p.   front., plates, port.   23 cm.

17694 Sweet, Alexander Edwin, 1841-1901.
On a Mexican mustang, through Texas, from the Gulf
to the Rio Grande. By Alex. E. Sweet and J. Armoy
Knox... Hartford, Conn., S. S. Scranton & company,
1883.
672 p.   front., illus., plates.   22½ cm.

302

17695　Sweet, George H
　　　　Texas: her early history, climate, soil and
　　　　material resources; with sketches of eastern, central
　　　　and western Texas principal counties and cities...
　　　　or, The immigrants' hand-book of Texas. New York,
　　　　1871.
　　　　　160 p.　　20 cm.

17696　Swett, John, 1830-
　　　　History of the public school system of California.
　　　　By John Swett. San Francisco, A. L. Bancroft and
　　　　company, 1876.
　　　　　246 p., 1 1.　　front., plates.　　23½ cm.

T

17697　Talbot, Ethelbert, bp., 1848-
　　　　My people of the plains, by the Right Reverend
　　　　Ethelbert Talbot... bishop of central Pennsylvania...
　　　　New York and London, Harper & brothers, 1906.
　　　　　xi, [1], 265 p.　　front., plates, ports.　　21½ cm.

17698　Taylor, Bayard, 1825-1878.
　　　　Colorado: a summer trip. New York, G. P. Putnam &
　　　　son, 1867.
　　　　　3 p.l., 185 p.　　19 cm.

17699　Taylor, Bayard, 1825-1878.
　　　　Eldorado, or Adventures in the path of empire:
　　　　comprising a voyage to California, via Panama;　life
　　　　in San Francisco and Monterey;　pictures of the gold
　　　　region and experience of Mexican travel. New York
　　　　[1882]
　　　　　xiv, 444 p.　　pl., front.　　19 cm.

17700　Taylor, Benjamin Franklin, 1819-1887.
　　　　Between the gates. Chicago, S. C. Griggs & co.,
　　　　1878.
　　　　　[1], 292 p.　　front., illus.　　20 cm.

17701　Taylor, Benjamin Franklin, 1819-1887.
　　　　Summer-savory, gleaned from rural nooks in pleasant
　　　　weather. By Benj. F. Taylor... Chicago, S. C. Griggs
　　　　and company, 1879.
　　　　　2 p.l., 3-212 p.　　19½ cm.
　　　　Prose sketches and essays.

17702 [Taylor, Burrell B   ] comp.
       How to get rich in California. A history of the
       progress and present condition of the gold and silver
       mining and other industrial interests of the great
       Pacific state... containing... some brief notices
       of some of California's most successful business men.
       Philadelphia, McMorris & Gans, 1876.
          vi, 7-137 p.   24 cm.

17703 Taylor, Eli F
       Indian reservations in Utah, by Eli F. Taylor,
       Register, U. S. Land Office, Salt Lake City, Utah,
       Salt Lake City, Utah State Historical Society, 1931.
       (In Utah historical quarterly, v. 4, no. 3, January
       1931), p. 29-31)

17704 Taylor, Henry Ryder, 1850-
       History of the Alamo and of the local Franciscan
       missions, by Henry Ryder-Taylor... assisted by Chas.
       H. Stanford. 6th ed. San Antonio, Tex., N. Tengg
       [1908]
          95 p.   illus., ports.   19 cm.

17705 Taylor, Joseph Henry.
       Bloody Knife and Gall, by Joseph Henry Taylor.
       [Bismarck, State Historical Society of North Dakota,
       1930]
          165-173 p.   24 cm.
       Reprinted from North Dakota historical quarterly,
       v. 4, no. 3, April 1930.

17706 Taylor, Joseph Henry.
       Fort Berthold Agency in 1869, by Joseph Henry
       Taylor. [Bismarck, State Historical Society of
       North Dakota, 1930]
          220-226 p.   24 cm.
       Reprinted from North Dakota historical quarterly,
       v. 4, no. 4, July 1930.

17707 Taylor, Joseph Henry.
       Fort Totten Trail, by Joseph Henry Taylor.
       [Bismarck, State Historical Society of North Dakota,
       1930]
          239-246 p.   24 cm.
       Reprinted from North Dakota historical quarterly,
       v. 4, no. 4, July 1930.

17708 Taylor, Joseph Henry.
       Inkpaduta and sons, by Joseph Henry Taylor.
       [Bismarck, State Historical Society of North Dakota,
       1930]
       153-164 p.   24 cm.
       Reprinted from North Dakota historical quarterly,
       v. 4, no. 3, April 1930.

17709 Taylor, Joseph Henry.
       Lonesome Charley, by Joseph Henry Taylor. [Bismarck,
       State Historical Society of North Dakota, 1930]
       227-238 p.   24 cm.
       Reprinted from North Dakota historical quarterly,
       v. 4, no. 4, July 1930.

17710 Taylor, Joseph Henry.
       A romantic encounter, by Joseph Henry Taylor.
       [Bismarck, State Historical Society of North Dakota,
       1930]
       207-219 p.   24 cm.
       Reprinted from North Dakota historical quarterly,
       v. 4, no. 4, July 1930.

17711 Taylor, T   U
       ... The Austin dam, by T. U. Taylor... Austin,
       University of Texas, 1910.
       85 p.   illus., tables.   23cm.   (Texas.
       University. Bulletin, no. 164. Scientific series,
       no. 16. 22 December 1910)

17712 Taylor, William, 1821-
       California life illustrated. By William Taylor,
       of the California conference... 12th thousand.
       New York, For the author, by Carlton & Porter, 1859.
       348 p. incl. front., pl.   20 cm.

17713 Teal, Joseph N
       Oregon's heritage of natural resources, shall they
       be conserved for the people?... delivered at the
       University of Oregon on Commonwealth day, Saturday,
       Feb. 13, 1909. [n.p.] 1909.
       13 p.   20 cm.

17714 Tenney, Edward Payson, 1835-1916.
       The new West as related to the Christian college
       by E. P. Tenney. 3d ed. Cambridge, Printed at the
       Riverside press, 1878.
       106 p.   illus., plates, map, plan.   23 cm.

17715 [Territorial government, 1890, enabling act for
Oklahoma, 1906] (In Thrope, Francis N. The federal
and state constitutions. 1909. v. 5, pp. 2939-2981;
v. 7, pp. 4269-4344)

17716 Terry, James.
Sculptured anthropoid ape heads, found in or near
the valley of the John Day river, a tributary of the
Columbia River, Oregon. New York, 1891.
15 p.   pl.   20 cm.

17717 Tevis, A   H
Beyond the Sierras; or, Observations on the
Pacific coast. Philadelphia, J. B. Lippincott &
co., 1877.
259 p.   front., pl.

17718 Tevis, Lloyd.
California: an address of Mr. Lloyd Tevis
(president of Wells, Fargo & company), San Francisco,
before the American bankers' association, at Niagara
Falls, August 10, 1881. [n.p., 1881]
31 p.   19 cm.

17719 Texan Emigration & Land Co., pub.
A descriptive view of Texas, the beautiful land.
Louisville, Ky., 1870.
19 p.   19 cm.

17720 Texas.
Declaration of the people of Texas in general
convention assembled. San Felipe de Austin, Printed
by Baker and Bordens, 1835.
broadside.   31 x 17 cm.

17721 Texas.
The resources, soil, and climate of Texas. Report
of commissioner of insurance, statistics, and
history. A. W. Spaight, commissioner. Galveston,
A. H. Belo & co., 1882.
x, 360 p.   fold. map.

17722 Texas (Republic) Congress. Senate.
... Secret journals of the Senate, republic of
Texas, 1836-1845; ed. from the original records in
the State library and the Department of state by
Ernest William Winkler, state librarian. [Austin]
Austin printing company, 1911.

337 p.   24 cm.   (In Texas. Library and
historical commission. Biennial report. Austin,
1911. 1st, pt. 2)

17723 Texas. Immigration Bureau.
          Texas the home for the emigrant, from everywhere.
       Houston, 1875.
          43 p.   map.   20 cm.

17724 Texas. Library and Historical Commission.
          Biennial report.
              v.   24½ cm.
          Library has no. 1, 1909/1910 (1911), "accompanied
       by the" secret journals of the Senate, Republic of
       Texas, 1836-1845.

17725 Texas almanac... Galveston, 1857-1910.
              v.   23 cm.
          Library has: 1857-61, 1867-70, 1904-10.

17726 Texas & Pacific Railway, Passenger Dept.
          Texas along the line of the Texas & Pacific Ry.
       Corrected to and reissued, November, 1900. Dallas,
       Tex., 1900.
          152 p.   illus., maps.   22 cm.

17727 Texas Applied Economics Club.
          ... Studies in the land problem in Texas, by members
       of the Texas Applied Economics Club, ed. by Lewis H.
       Haney. Austin, Tex., The University [1915]
          3 p.l., [5]-181 p.   illus. (maps) diagr.   23 cm.
       (Bulletin of the University of Texas. 1915: no. 39.
       July 10, 1915)

17728 Texas as it is, or the main facts in a nut-shell...
       [n.p., n.d.]
          40 p.   20 cm.

17729 Texas Western Railroad Company.
          Charter of the Texas Western Railroad Company, and
       extracts from reports of Col. A. B. Gray and secretary
       of war, on the survey of route, from eastern borders
       of Texas to California... Cincinnati, O., Porter,
       Thral & Chapman, printers, 1855.
          40 p.   fold. map.   22 cm.

17730 Textor, Lucy Elizabeth.
          ... Official relations between the United States

and the Sioux Indians. By Lucy E. Textor, M.A.
Palo Alto, Cal., The University, 1896.
    ix, [11]-162 p. incl. tables.   2 maps (incl. front.)
25 cm.   (Leland Stanford junior university publications.
History and economics, 2)

17731 Thoburn, Joseph Bradfield, 1866-
    A standard history of Oklahoma; an authentic narrative
of its development from the date of the first European
exploration down to the present time, including accounts
of the Indian tribes, both civilized and wild, of the
cattle range, of the land openings and the achievements
of the most recent period, by Joseph B. Thoburn,
assisted by a board of advisory editors... Chicago
and New York, The American historical society, 1916.
    5 v.   front., illus., plates, ports.   27½ cm.

17732 Thom, Adam.
    The claims to the Oregon Territory considered.
London, 1844.
    44 p.   21 cm.

17733 Thomas, William R
    Boreas, Breckenridge and the Blue: over three
mountain ranges, through canons and parks. Denver,
1896.
    30 p.   plates.
    Issued by the passenger department of the South
Park line.

17734 Thomes, William H
    California, as it is and was; a journey overland
from Boston to the golden state and return. Boston,
1887.
    130 p.   19 cm.

17735 Thomes, William H
    On land and sea; or, California in the years 1843,
'44, and '45. Corrected and revised from Ballou's
Monthly Magazine. Illustrated by F. Childe Hassam.
Boston, 1884.
    351 p.   illus.   19 cm.

17736 Thompson, Almon Harris, 1839-1906.
    Diary of Almon Harris Thompson, geographer,
explorations of the Colorado River of the west and
its tributaries, 1871-1875. Salt Lake City, Utah
State Historical Society, 1939. (In Utah historical
quarterly, v. 7, nos. 1-3, p. 2-138)

17737 Thorlaksson, Paul, 1849-1882.
       The founding of the Icelandic settlement in Pembina
       County. An article dictated by the Reverend Paul
       Thorlakson, February 11, 1882. [Ed. by Richard Beck.
       Bismarck, State Historical Society of North Dakota,
       1932]
           150-146 p.   24 cm.
       Reprinted from North Dakota historical quarterly,
       v. 6, no. 2, January 1932.

17738 Those old Spanish gold mines. Salt Lake City, Utah State
       Historical Society, 1941. (In Utah historical
       quarterly, v. 9, nos. 3, 4, July, October, 1941,
       p. 129-131)

17739 Thwaites, Reuben G[old] 1853-1913.
       The Bancroft library. A report submitted to the
       president and regents of the University of California
       upon the Bancroft library, by Reuben G. Thwaites...
       Berkeley, Cal., 1905.
           20 p.   22½ cm.

17740 Tidwell, H   M
       Unitah and Ouray Indian agency, Fort Duchesne,
       Utah, by H. M. Tidwell, superintendent. Salt Lake
       City, Utah State Historical Society, 1931. (In Utah
       historical quarterly, v. 4, no. 3, January 1931, p. 112)

17741 Tiling, Moritz Philipp Georg, 1851-
       History of the German element in Texas from 1820-
       1850, and historical sketches of the German Texas
       sinners' league and Houston turnverein from 1853-1913;
       by Moritz Tiling... 1st ed. Houston, Tex., M. Tiling,
       1913.
           viii, 225 p.   front. (port.)   21 cm.

17742 Tilton, George F
       One hundred miles for one hundred cents, Tilton's
       trolly trip from the sea to the orange groves, over
       the Pacific electric... Los Angeles, 1909.
           [30] p.   pl.   21 cm.
       Book of views.

17743 Tinkham, George Henry, 1849-
       California men and events; time 1769-1890, by
       George H. Tinkham... [Stockton, Cal., Print by the
       Record publishing company, c1915]
           3 p.l., 15-336 p. incl. front., illus., ports.
       22 cm.

17744 Tipton, Thomas W
          Forty years of Nebraska at home and in congress.
       Lincoln, 1902.
          8, 570 p.   port.   19 cm.   (Nebraska state
       historical society. Pub. ser. 2, v. 4 [whole no. 9])

17745 Todd, John, 1800-1873.
          The sunset land; or, The great Pacific slope. By
       Rev. John Todd, D. D. Boston, Lee and Shepard, 1871.
          3 p.l., 9-322 p.   18 cm.

17746 Todd, John, 1818-1894.
          Early settlement and growth of western Iowa; or,
       Reminiscences, by Rev. John Todd, of Tabor, Iowa.
       Des Moines, The Historical department of Iowa, 1906.
          203 p.   front. (port.)   21 cm.
          "The material herewith presented appeared in 'The
       Tabor beacon'... in 1891." - Pref.

17747 Tohill, Louis Arthur.
          Robert Dickson, British fur trader on the upper
       Mississippi, by Louis Arthur Tohill. [Bismarck, State
       Historical Society of North Dakota, 1928-1929]
          5-49, 83-128, 182-203 p.   24 cm.
          Reprinted from North Dakota historical quarterly,
       v. 3, no. 1, October, 1928, no. 2, January 1929, and
       no. 3, April 1929.

17748 Tomlinson, William S
          Kansas in eighteen fifty-eight, being chiefly a
       history of the recent troubles in the territory...
       New York, H. Dayton, 1859.
          xii, 13-304 p.   18½ cm.

17749 Tonge, Thomas.
          All about Colorado for home-seekers, tourists,
       investors, health-seekers, written and comp. by
       Thomas Tonge from latest official reports... Denver,
       T. Tonge, 1913.
          112 p. incl. illus., port., map.   23½ cm.

17750 Torrison, Alfred.
          Fisher's Landing, Minnesota, by Alfred Torrison.
       [Bismarck, State Historical Society of North Dakota,
       1941]
          27-34 p.   24 cm.
          Reprinted from North Dakota historical quarterly,
       v. 9, no. 1, October 1941.

17751 Townsend, John Kirk, 1809-1851.
Sporting excursions in the Rocky mountains, including a journey of the Columbia river, and a visit to the Sandwich islands, Chile, &c. By J. K. Townsend, esq.... London, H. Colburn, 1840.
2 v. fronts. 20 cm.
First edition, Boston, 1839, published under title: Narrative of a journey across the Rocky mountains.

17752 Townshend, Samuel Nugent, 1844-1910.
Colorado: its agriculture, stockfeeding, scenery, and shooting. London, The Field, 1879.
viii, 122 p. 20 cm.

17753 [Treaty, act for admission, constitution] (In Thorpe, Francis N. The federal and state constitutions, 1909. v. 1, pp. 377-462)

17754 Triggs, J   H
History of Cheyenne and northern Wyoming, embracing the gold fields of the Black Hills, Powder river and Big Horn countries... Omaha, Neb., 1876.
131 p. map. 21½ cm.

17755 Triunfo Silver Mining & Commercial Company of Lower California.
Report on the property of the Triunfo silver mining and commercial company of lower California, with some account of the mines of the pininsula and observations on the mode of beneficiating silver ores. Philadelphia, 1866.
80 p. pl., port.

17756 Trowbridge, Mrs. Mary Elizabeth (Day)
Pioneer days; the life-story of Gershom and Elizabeth Day, by M. E. D. Trowbridge, with introduction by Z. Grenell... Philadelphia, American Baptist publication society, 1895.
160 p. front. 19 cm.

17757 Truman, Ben[jamin] C[ummings]
Semi-tropical California: its climate, health-fulness, productiveness, and scenery... by Major Ben. C. Truman. San Francisco, A. L. Bancroft & co., 1874.
204 p. 21 cm.

17758   Truman, Benjamin Cummings.
        Tourists' illustrated guide to the celebrated
        summer and winter resorts of California, adjacent to
        and upon the lines of the Central and Southern Pacific
        railroads... San Francisco, 1883.
        232 p.   illus. pl.   20½ cm.

17759   Tucker, Ephraim W
        A history of Oregon, containing a condensed account
        of the most important voyages and discoveries of the
        Spanish, American, and English navigators on the North
        West coast of America... Buffalo, Printed by A. W.
        Wilgus, 1844.
        84 p.   21 cm.

17760   Tullidge, Edward Wheelock.
        The history of Salt Lake City and its founders. By
        Edward W. Tullidge. Incorporating a brief history of
        the pioneers of Utah... By authority of the City
        council and under supervision of its Committee on
        revision... Salt Lake City, E. W. Tullidge [1886?]
        1 p.l., viii, [3]-896, 172, 36 p.   front., pl.,
        port.   24 cm.
        Another issue of his "History of Salt Lake City"
        1886, with a different title-page.

17761   Tullidge, Edward Wheelock.
        Life of Brigham Young; or, Utah and her founders.
        By Edward W. Tullidge. New York, 1876.
        2 p.l., iv, 458, 81 p.   front. (port.)   22½ cm.

17762   Tullidge, Edward Wheelock.
        Tullidge's histories, (volume II) containing the
        history of all the northern, eastern and western
        counties of Utah; also the counties of southern
        Idaho. With a biographical appendix of representative
        men and founders of the cities and counties; also a
        commercial supplement, historical. Edw. W. Tullidge,
        proprietor and publisher. Salt Lake City, Utah,
        Press of the Juvenile instructor, 1889.
        vi, 440 (i.e. 540) p., 1 l., 372 p.   front.,
        illus., pl., ports.   25 cm.

17763   Tullidge's quarterly magazine. v. 1-3, 1880-1885.
        Salt Lake City.
        3 v. illus., ports.   25 cm.   irregular.
        Contains many biographical sketches and historical
        and descriptive articles regarding Utah, Utah

communities and Mormon faith and history.
Supersedes by Western galaxy.

17764 Turner, Frederick Jackson, 1861-1932.
Rise of the new West, 1819-1829. Gloucester, Mass.,
P. Smith, 1961 [c1906]
xviii, 366 p.   port., maps (part fold. col.)
21 cm.   (The American nation: a history, v. 14)

17765 Turrill, Charles B
California notes... By Charles B. Turrill...
v. 1. San Francisco, E. Bosqui & co., 1876.
1 v.   20 cm.

17766 Tuthill, Franklin.
History of California. San Francisco, 1866.
16, 657 p.   22 cm.

17767 Twiss, Sir Travers.
The Oregon territory; its history and discovery,
including an account of the convention of the Escurial,
also the treaties and negotiations between the United
States and Great Britain held at various times for the
settlement of a boundary line, and an examination of
the whole question in respect to facts and the law
of nations. New York, 1846.
264, 4 p.   19½ cm.

U

17768 Union Pacific Railroad.
Oregon, its wealth and resources, with the
compliments of the passenger department. Second
edition, revised. Chicago, Rand, McNally & co., 1889.
67 p.   map.   22 cm.

17769 Union Pacific Railroad.
Wyoming, its resources and attractions. Ed. 2.
[Omaha, 1903]
114 p.   18 cm.

17770 Union Pacific Railroad. Passenger Department.
Resources and attractions of the Texas Panhandle
for the home seeker, capitalist and tourist... Ed. 3.
St. Louis, 1892.
107 p.   map.   20 cm.

17771   Union Pacific Railroad.
        Utah; a complete and comprehensive description of
        the agricultural and mineral resources, stock raising
        and manufacturing interests. Chicago, etc., 1889-19.
        v.   20 cm.
        Ed. 2, rev. and enl., 1889; Ed. 3, rev. and enl.,
        1890; Ed. 6, rev. and enl., 1893; Ed. 10, 1901.

17772   Union Pacific Railway Company.
        Wealth and resources of Oregon and Washington,
        the Pacific northwest; a complete guide over the local
        lines of the Union Pacific railway... Portland, 1889.
        256 p.   illus. maps.   20 cm.

17773   Union Party. California. Union State Convention.
        Sacramento.
        Proceedings.   1862, 1863.   San Francisco [1863?]
        2 v. in 1.   27 cm.

17774   United Confederate Veterans. Arkansas division.
        Confederate women of Arkansas in the civil war, 1861-
        '65; memorial reminiscences, pub. by the United
        Confederate veterans of Arkansas... Little Rock,
        Ark., H. G. Pugh ptg. co., 1907.
        221 p. incl. pl.   pl., ports.   23½ cm.

17775   U. S. Army. Corps of Engineers.
        ... Report of the exploring expedition from Santa Fé,
        New Mexico, to the junction of the Grand and Green
        rivers of the Great Colorado of the West, in 1859,
        under the command of Capt. J. N. Macomb, Corps of
        topographical engineers... with geological report
        by Prof. J. S. Newberry... Washington, Govt. print.
        off., 1876.
        vii, 152 (i.e. 168) p.   plates (part col.)
        fold. map.   30½ x 25½ cm.

17776   U. S. Army. Corps of Engineers.
        Report upon the reconnaissance of northwestern
        Wyoming, including Yellowstone national park, made
        in the summer of 1873, by William A. Jones, captain
        of engineers, U.S.A. With appendix. Washington,
        Govt. print. office, 1875.
        vi, 331 p.   illus., plates, fold. map, tables
        (1 fold.) diagrs.   23½ cm.

17777   U. S. Army. Military Division of the Missouri.
        Report of an exploration of parts of Wyoming, Idaho,

314

and Montana in August and September, 1882, made by
Lieut. Gen. P. H. Sheridan, commanding the Military
Division of the Missouri, with the itinerary of Col.
Jas. F. Gregory, and a geological and botanical
report by Surgeon W. H. Forwood. Washington, Govt.
print. off., 1882.
69 p.   fold. map, 2 diagr.   25½ cm.

17778 U. S. Census Office. 8th Census, 1860.
United States census of Jackson county, Oregon,
1860. [Portland, Or., Genealogical Forum of Portland,
Oregon, 1960-1961]
60 p.   28 cm.
Published on a current basis with numbers of the
Bulletin of the Genealogical Forum of Portland, Oregon.

17779 U. S. Census Office. 9th Census, 1870.
United States census of Jackson county, Oregon, 1870.
[Portland, Or., Genealogical Forum of Portland, Oregon,
1962-1965]
70 p.   28 cm.
Published on a current basis with numbers of the
Bulletin of the Genealogical Forum of Portland, Oregon.

17780 U. S. Census Office. 10th Census, 1880.
United States census, Jackson County, Oregon, 1880.
[Portland, Or.] Genealogical Forum of Portland, Ore.,
1964.
152 p.   28 cm.

17781 U. S. Congress. House of Representatives.
[Speeches on Oregon, delivered in the house of
representatives, 1844-1845, 1846. Bound in one
volume.]
various pagings.   22 cm.

17782 U. S. Congress. House. Committee on Territories.
Admission of Utah; report of the Committee on
Territories on the admission of Utah as a state, to
the House of Representatives, second session,
fiftieth congress. Washington, 1889.
215 p.   22 cm.

17783 U. S. Congress. House. Committee on Territories.
Admission of Wyoming into the Union; views of the
minority, expressed by Mr. Springer, March 21, 1890.
Washington, D. C., 1890.

36 p.   22 cm.   (U. S. Congress. House. 51st, Congress, 1st sess. House report 39, pt. 2)

17784 U. S. Congress. Senate. Committee on Territories.
       The admission of Utah. Arguments in favor of the
       admission of Utah as a state, made before the Committee
       on territories of the United States Senate...
       February 18, 1888. Washington, Govt. print. off., 1888.
       1 p.l., 71 p.   22 cm.

17785 U. S. Congress. Senate. Committee on Territories.
       Home rule for Utah; arguments made by a delegation
       from Utah, before the Senate Committee on Territories...
       in favor of the passage of... "A bill for the local
       government of Utah territory... Washington, 1892.
       113 p.   22 cm.

17786 U. S. Engineer Department.
       ... Report of explorations across the great basin
       of the territory of Utah for a direct wagon-route from
       Camp Floyd to Genoa, in Carson Valley, in 1859, by
       Captain J. H. Simpson... Washington, Gov't. print.
       off., 1876.
       518 p.   illus., pl., fold. maps, diagr.   25 cm.

17787 U. S. Engineer Department.
       ... Reports of the secretary of war, with recon-
       naissances of routes from San Antonio to El Paso, by
       Brevet Lt. Col. J. E. Johnston; Lieutenant N. H.
       Michler; and Captain S. G. French, of Q'rmaster's
       dept. Also, the report of Capt. R. B. Marcy's route
       from Fort Smith to Santa Fe; and the report of Lieut.
       J. H. Simpson of an expedition into the Navajo country;
       and the report of Lieutenant W. H. C. Whiting's
       reconnaissances of the western frontier of Texas.
       July 24, 1850. Ordered to be printed... Washington,
       Printed at the Union office, 1850.
       250 p.   75 pl. (part col., part fold., incl.
       ports., plans) 2 fold. maps.   22½ cm.   (31st
       Cong., 1st sess. Senate. Ex. doc. 64)

17788 U. S. General Land Office.
       Annual report of the commissioner of the General
       Land Office for the year 1882. Washington, Government
       printing office, 1882.
       707 p.   tables (part fold.)   22 cm.

17789 U. S. Library of Congress.
    California: the centennial of the Gold Rush and
the first State Constitution; [catalog of] an exhibit
in the Library of Congress, Washington, D. C., November
12, 1949 to February 12, 1950. Washington, U. S. Govt.
Print. Off., 1949.
    iv, 97 p.   illus., maps.   26 cm.   (Its State
exhibition catalogs, 10)

17790 U. S. Library of Congress.
    Centennial of the Oregon Territory exhibition,
September 11, 1948-January 11, 1949. An address by
Homer D. Angell on the occasion of the ceremonies
opening the exhibition celebrating the establishment
of the Territory of Oregon, at the Library of Congress,
together with a catalog of the exhibition. Washington,
U. S. Govt. Print. Off., 1948.
    76 p.   plates.   26 cm.
    "The eighth in a series of catalogs of exhibitions
commemorating significant anniversaries in the histories
of the forty-eight United States."

17791 U. S. Library of Congress.
    Centennial of the settlement of Utah, exhibition,
June 7, 1947-August 31, 1947. An address by the Hon.
Arthur V. Watkins, on the occasion of the ceremonies
opening the exhibition commemorating the settlement
of Utah at the Library of Congress, together with a
catalog of the exhibition. Washington, U. S. Govt.
Print. Off., 1947.
    iii, 72 p.   illus., maps.   26 cm.
    "The fifth in a series designed to reflect... the
composition of exhibits commemorative of each of the
48 United States."

17792 U. S. Library of Congress.
    Colorado, the diamond jubilee of statehood;
[catalog of] an exhibition in the Library of Congress,
Washington, D. C., November 14, 1951 to February 14,
1952. Washington, U. S. Govt. Print. Off., 1951.
    iii, 75 p.   illus., map.   26 cm.   (Its State
exhibition catalogs, 14)
    Address delivered Nov. 14, 1951: Colorado - The
growth of the Mountain State, by the Hon. Oscar L.
Chapman.

17793 U. S. Library of Congress.
    Kansas and Nebraska, centennial of the Territories,

1854-1954; an exhibition in the Library of Congress,
Washington, D. C., February 3, 1954 to April 26, 1954.
Published in cooperation with the Kansas Territorial
Centennial Committee and the Nebraska Territorial
Centennial Commission. Washington, 1954.
   vi, 71 p.   illus.   26 cm.   (Its State exhibition
catalogs [17])

17794 U. S. Library of Congress.
   Nevada: the centennial of statehood; an exhibition
in the Library of Congress, Washington, D. C.,
June 23, 1965, to October 31, 1965. Washington, 1965.
   x, 66 p.   illus., facsims., maps, ports.   26 cm.
(Its [State exhibition catalogs] 21)

17795 U. S. Library of Congress.
   Oklahoma, the semicentennial of statehood, 1907-1957.
An exhibition in the Library of Congress, Washington,
D. C., November 13, 1957, to February 15, 1958.
Washington, 1957.
   vii, 70 p.   illus.   26 cm.   (Its [State
exhibition catalogs] 19)

17796 U. S. Library of Congress.
   Texas centennial exhibition, held at the Library of
Congress, Washington, D. C., December 15, 1945 -
April 15, 1946. Washington, U. S. Govt. print. off.,
1946.
   iii, 54 p.   front. (map) plates, port., facsims.
25½ cm.
   "The second in a projected series designed to
reflect... the composition of exhibits commemorative
of each of the 48 United States." - p. [2] of cover.

17797 U. S. Library of Congress. Division of Bibliography.
   ... Wyoming: a bibliographical list, compiled by
Florence S. Hellman... [Washington, D. C., Govt.
print. off.]
   2 p.l., 98 numb. l.   28 cm.

17798 U. S. President, 1849-1850 (Taylor)
   California and New Mexico. Message from the president
of the United States [Zachary Taylor] transmitting
information in answer to a resolution of the house
of the 31st of Dec. 1849, on the subject of California
and New Mexico. Jan. 24, 1850. [Reports from the
State department of the territory of California and
other documents] [Washington, 1850]

976 p.   maps.   22 cm.   (U. S. Congress. House.
31st Congress. 1st sess. House executive document
no. 17)

17799   U. S. President, 1841-1845 (Tyler)
... Message from the President of the United States,
to the two houses of Congress, at the commencement of
the second session of the Twenty-eighth Congress...
Washington, Printed by Gales and Seaton, 1844.
18 p.   23 cm.   (28th Cong., 2d Sess. [Senate]
[Doc. 1]

17800   U. S. Railroad Administration.
California for the tourist. Winter ed. [Chicago,
1919]
60 p.   illus., maps.   21 cm.

17801   U. S. Railroad Administration.
Colorado and Utah Rockies. [Chicago, 1919]
62 p.   illus., maps.   21 cm.

17802   U. S. Railroad Administration.
Texas winter resorts. [Chicago, 1919]
62 p.   illus., maps.   21 cm.

17803   U. S. War Department.
Report of the secretary of war, communicating information in relation to the geology and topography of
California. April 3, 1850... [Part 1] [Washington,
1850]
127 p.   maps.   22 cm.   (U. S. Congress, 31st,
1st sess., Sen. Exec. doc. 47)

17804   U. S. Work Progress Administration, Nebraska.
Nebraska party platforms, 1858-1940. [Lincoln]
1940.
xxviii, 523 p.   25 cm.

17805   Upham, Samuel Curtis, 1819-1885.
Notes of a voyage to California via Cape Horn,
with scenes in El Dorado, in the years 1849-50.
With an appendix containing reminiscences...
Philadelphia, The author, 1878.
xxii, 23-594 p. incl. plates, front., illus.,
plates, port.   21 cm.

17806   Upton, Charles Elmer.
Pioneers of El Dorado, by Charles Elmer Upton...

Placerville, Cal., C. E. Upton, 1906.
3 p.l., [3]-201 p.   front., 5 pl.   21 cm.

17807   Urquhart, David, 1805-1877.
Annexation of the Texas, a case of war between
England and the United States... By D. Urquhart,
esq. London, J. Maynard, 1844.
104 p.   21½ cm.

17808   Utah. Bureau of Statistics.
Report. 1st-8th, 1901-1908/10. Salt Lake City,
1902-11.
8 v. in 4.   23 cm.
Annual, 1901-1906; biennial, 1907-1908 - 1909-1910.
Title varies slightly. Continued by the Report of
the State Bureau of Immigration, Labor and Statistics.

17809   Utah and statehood: objections considered... with a
brief synopsis of the state constitution. By a
resident of Utah. New York, 1888.
11 p.   19 cm.

17810   Utah counties magazine, v. 1-   July 1951-
[Kaysville]
v.   illus., ports.   28 cm.   annual.
Organ of Utah State Association of County Officials.

17811   Utah Federation of Labor.
Directory of the Utah Federation of Labor of Salt
Lake City, and of Ogden, Park City and Mercur labor
unions, for 1899-1900. Containing a list of all
labor organizations in the above named places, the
names of officers, standing committees, etc., time
and place of meeting. [Salt Lake City? 1899?]
144 p.   23 cm.

17812   Utah gazetteer... Salt Lake City, Stenhouse [n.d.]
2 v.   24 cm.

17813   Utah historical quarterly. v. 1-   Jan. 1928-
Salt Lake City, Utah, Board of Control, Utah State
Historical Society [1928-   ]
v.   illus.   23½ cm.
Suspended, October 1933-January 1939. Library has
v. 1-12. List of charter members of the Society:
v. 1, p. 98-99. Editor: January 1928-
J. Cecil Alter.

17814 Utah state gazetteer and business directory, v. 1-
　　　　1900-　　　　Salt Lake City, R. L. Polk, 1900-
　　　　　v.　　24 cm.

17815 Utah statehood. Reasons why it should not be granted.
　　　　Will the American people surrender the territory to
　　　　an unscrupulous and polygamous theocracy? Embracing:
　　　　The Mormon preliminary movement; the Democratic and
　　　　Republican refusal to take part and their reasons
　　　　therefor; Utah commission report; Governor West in
　　　　opposition; review of the proposed Mormon constitution;
　　　　its failure to meet the requirements of the occasion.
　　　　Salt Lake City, Tribune print, 1887.
　　　　　16, 71, [1] p.　　22 cm.

17816 Utah Territorial Liberal Convention, 1892.
　　　　Proceedings of the Territorial liberal convention
　　　　held at Salt Lake City, Utah, Feb. 4th, 1892.
　　　　Stenographically reported by Miss G. T. McMaster.
　　　　Salt Lake City, 1892.
　　　　　65 p.　　20 cm.

V

17817 Van Arman, H　　　M
　　　　The public lands of California. U. S. Land Law,
　　　　for preemption of homesteads, etc. Map of California
　　　　& Nevada, together with other valuable information
　　　　for settlers and preemptors... San Francisco, Cal.
　　　　Dewey & co., 1875.
　　　　　44 p.　　pl.,fold. map.　　22 cm.

17818 Van Dyke, Theodore Strong, 1842-
　　　　Millionaires of a day: an inside history of the
　　　　great Southern California "boom". New York, 1890.
　　　　　208 p.　　20 cm.

17819 Van Dyke, Theodore S[trong] 1842-
　　　　Southern California: its valleys, hills and
　　　　streams; its animals, birds, and fishes; its gardens,
　　　　farms and climate. By Theodore S. Van Dyke...
　　　　New York, Fords, Howard & Hulbert, 1886.
　　　　　1 p.l., v-xii, 13-233 p.　　20½ cm.

17820 Van Ostrand, Ferdinand A　　　, 1848-1873.
　　　　Diary of Ferdinand A. Van Ostrand, edited by

Russell Reid. [Bismarck, State Historical Society
of North Dakota, 1942]
219-242, 3-46, 83-124 p.   front., ports.,
fold. plan.   24 cm.
Reprinted from North Dakota historical quarterly,
v. 9, no. 4, July 1942; v. 10, nos. 1, 2, January,
April, 1943.

17821 Vélez de Escalante, Silvestre, fl. 1768-1779.
Father Escalante's journal with related documents
and maps, by Herbert S. Auerbach. Salt Lake City,
Utah State Historical Society, 1943. (In Utah
historical quarterly, v. 11, nos. 1-4, 1943, p. 1-142)

17822 Venegas, Miguel, 1680-1764?
A natural and civil history of California:
containing an accurate description of that country,
its soil, mountains, harbours, lakes, rivers and seas;
its animals, vegetables, minerals, and famous fishery
for pearls. The customs of the inhabitants, their
religion, government, and manner of living, before
their conversion to the Christian religion by the
missionary Jesuits. Together with accounts of the
several voyages and attempts made for settling
California and taking actual surveys of that country,
its gulf, and coast of the South-sea. Illustrated
with copper plates, and an accurate map of the country
and the adjacent seas. Tr. from the original Spanish
of Miguel Venegas, a Mexican Jesuit, published at
Madrid 1758... London, J. Rivington and J. Fletcher,
1759.
2 v.   fronts., fold. map.   19 cm.

17823 Venegas, Miguel, 1680-1764?
Noticia de la California, y de su conquista temporal,
y espiritual hasta el tiempo presente. Sacada de la
historia manvscrita, formada en Mexico año de 1739
por el padre Miguel Venegas, de la Compañia de Jesus;
y de otras noticias, y relaciones antiguas, y modernas
[por Andrés Marcos Burriel] Madrid, En la imprenta
de la viuda de m. Fernandez, y del Supremo consejo de
la Inquisicion, 1757.
3 v.   4 fold. maps.   21 cm.

17824 Victor, Mrs. Frances (Fuller) 1826-1902.
All over Oregon and Washington. Observations
on the country, its scenery, soil, climate, resources,
and improvements, with an outline of its early history...

Also, hints to immigrants and travelers concerning
routes, the cost of travel, the price of land, etc.
By Mrs. Frances Fuller Victor... San Francisco,
Printed by J. H. Carmany & co., 1872.
vi, [7]-368 p.   28½ cm.

17825 Victor, Mrs. Frances (Fuller) 1826-1902.
Atlantis arisen; or, Talks of a tourist about
Oregon and Washington. By Mrs. Frances Fuller Victor...
Philadelphia, J. B. Lippincott company, 1891.
412 p.   front., illus., plates.   22 cm.

17826 Victor, Mrs. Frances (Fuller) 1826-1902.
The early Indian wars of Oregon, compiled from the
Oregon archives and other original sources. With
muster rolls. By Frances Fuller Victor. Salem,
Or., F. C. Baker, 1894.
xii p., 1 l., 719 p.   23 cm.

17827 Victor, Mrs. Frances (Fuller) 1826-1902.
Studies of the California missions. [n.p., 1882]
Reprinted from The Californian, v. 5, p. 389-405,
514-526.
389-405, 514-526, 15-26 p.   illus.   25 cm.
Reprinted from The Californian, v. 5, p. 389-405,
514-526; v. 6, p. 15-26. May-July, 1882.

17828 Victor, Orville James, 1827-1910.
The Kansas-Nebraska struggle. (In his History of
American conspiracies. [1863] p. 451-520)

17829 Vielé, Teresa (Griffin) "Mrs. E. L. Vielé," 1832-
"Following the drum"? a glimpse of frontier life.
By Mrs. Vielé. New York, Rudd & Carleton, 1859.
256 p.   19 cm.
The writer's husband was a lieutenant in the
1st U. S. infantry at the time, and stationed on the
Texas frontier.

17830 Vischer, Edward.
A trip to the mining regions in the spring of 1859;
"Californischer staatskalender" in the leap year
A.D. 1860... trans. from the German by Ruth Frey
Axe. (In California historical society, Quarterly,
v. 11, p. 224-246, 321-338, Sept. - Dec. 1932)

17831 Vischer, Edward.
Vischer's pictorial of California: landscape,

trees and forest scenes. Grand features of California
scenery, life, traffic and customs. Photographs from
the original drawings. In five series of twelve
numbers each, with a supplement, and contributions
from reliable sources. San Francisco, April, 1870.
[San Francisco] Printed by J. Winterburn & company
[1870]
  5 p.l., 132, iii p.   30½ x 24 cm.   and atlas of
169 phot.   35½ x 32½ cm.

17832 Visscher, William Lightfoot, 1842-1924.
   A thrilling and truthful history of the pony express;
   or, Blazing the westward way, and other sketches and
   incidents of those stirring times [by] William
   Lightfoot Visscher... Chicago, Rand, McNally & co.
   [c1908]
   98 p. incl. front., illus., ports.   25½ cm.

17833 [Vizetelly, Henry] 1820-1894.
   Four months among the gold-finders in Alta California:
   being the diary of an expedition from San Francisco
   to the gold districts. By J. Tyrwhitt Brooks, M.D.
   [pseud.]   London, D. Bogue, 1849.
   xviii, 207 p.   front. (map)   20½ cm.

17834 [Vollmer, Carl Gottfried Wilhelm] d. 1864.
   Californien und das goldfieber. Reisen in dem wilden
   Westen Nord-Amerika leben; und sitten der Goldgräber,
   Mormonen und Indianern. Den Gebildeten des deutschen
   volkes gewidmet von dr. W. F. A. Zimmermann [pseud.]
   Berlin, T. Thiele, 1863.
   4 p.l., 744 p.   front., illus., col. plates.
   23 cm.   (Added t.-p.: Naturwissenschaftliche romane.
   Ein versuch die lehren der naturkunde im gewande der
   unterhaltungslectüre zu verbreiten. Von dr. W. F. A.
   Zimmermann [pseud.] 3 bd.)

W

17835 [Wagner, Henry Raup]
   [Bibliography of printed works in Spanish relating
   to those portions of the United States which formerly
   belonged to Mexico. Santiago de Chile, La Impr.
   Diener, 1917]
   43 p.   23 cm.

17836　Wakon Teepee. Grant of land at the care in Dayton's
　　　　　Bluff. St. Paul, Minnesota Historical Society, 1952.
　　　　　(In Annals of the Minnesota Historical Society, 1852,
　　　　　p. 61-64)

17837　Walker, David.
　　　　　Address on the history and resources of the state
　　　　　of Arkansas at Judges' Hall, Philadelphia, October 16,
　　　　　1876. Philadelphia, 1876.
　　　　　18 p.　　18 cm.

17838　Walker, James Lafayette, 1851-
　　　　　History of the Waco Baptist Association of Texas.
　　　　　By J. L. Walker and C. P. Lumpkin. Waco, Tex.,
　　　　　Byrne-Hill Printing House, 1897.
　　　　　446 p.　　ports.　　25 cm.

17839　Wallace, Lewis, 1827-1905.
　　　　　Lew Wallace; an autobiography... New York and
　　　　　London, Harper & brothers, 1906.
　　　　　2 v.　　fronts., illus., plates, ports., facsims.
　　　　　21½ cm.

17840　Wallace, William Ross, 1865-
　　　　　Echo Park Dam. [Salt Lake City? 1954?]
　　　　　[4] ℓ.　　24 cm.

17841　Ware, Eugene Fitch, 1841-1911.
　　　　　The Indian war of 1864, being a fragment of the
　　　　　early history of Kansas, Nebraska, Colorado and Wyoming.
　　　　　Topeka, Kans., 1911.
　　　　　xi, 601 p.　　illus.,maps, pl., port.　　22 cm.

17842　Warner, Charles Dudley, 1829-1900.
　　　　　Our Italy [southern California], by Charles Dudley
　　　　　Warner... New York, Harper & brothers, 1891.
　　　　　viii, 226 p. incl. front., illus., plates.　　24 cm.

17843　Warren, Eliza (Spalding) 1837-1919.
　　　　　Memoirs of the West; the Spaldings, by Eliza
　　　　　Spalding Warren... [Portland, Or., Press of the Marsh
　　　　　printing company, 1916?]
　　　　　153 p.　　front., plates, ports.　　20 cm.

17844　Warren, F　　　K　　　, ed.
　　　　　California illustrated; including a trip through
　　　　　Yellowstone park.　　Boston [1892]
　　　　　142 p.　　illus., pl.　　21½ cm.

17845 Warren, Gouverneur Kemble, 1830-1882.
Preliminary report of explorations in Nebraska
and Dakota, in the years 1855-56-57. Reprint.
Washington, 1875.
125 p.   map.   22 cm.

17846 Warrum, Noble.
Utah since statehood, historical and biographical.
Noble Warrum, editor, assisted by Hon. Charles W.
Morse for bench and bar, and W. Brown Ewing, M.D.,
for the medical chapter... Chicago-Salt Lake, The
S. J. Clarke publishing company, 1919.
4 v.   plates, ports.   28 cm.

17847 Waters, William Elkanah, 1833-
Life among the Mormons, and a march to their Zion:
to which is added a chapter on the Indians of the
plains and mountains of the West. By an officer of
the U. S. Army... New York, Moorhead, Simpson & Bond,
1868.
xv, 219 p.   front. (port.) plates.   19 cm.

17848 Watkins, Albert.
Outline of Nebraska history. Lincoln, Neb., 1910.
45 p.   21 cm.
A special publication of the Nebraska State Historical
Society.

17849 Webb, William Seward, 1851-
... California and Alaska, and over the Canadian
Pacific railway, by William Seward Webb. New York,
London, G. P. Putnam's sons, 1890.
1 p.l., v-xiv p., 1 l., 150 p.   front., illus.,
plates.   23½ cm.

17850 Webster, Kimball, 1828-1916.
The gold seekers of '49; a personal narrative of the
overland trail and adventures in California and
Oregon from 1849 to 1854. By Kimball Webster, a
New England forty-niner; with an introduction and
biographical sketch by George Waldo Browne; illustrated by Frank Holland and others. Manchester,
N. H., Standard book company, 1917.
1 p.l., 7-240 p.   plates, 2 port. (incl. front.)
20½ cm.

17851 Wedel, Waldo Rudolph, 1908-
... An introduction to Pawnee archeology, by

Waldo Rudolph Wedel. Washington, U. S. Govt. print. off., 1936.
xi, 122 p.   illus., 12 pl. on 6 l., 10 maps on 9 l. (part fold.)   23 cm.   (Smithsonian institution. Bureau of American ethnology. Bulletin 112)

17852 Weise, Arthur James.
The discoveries of America to the year 1525... New York and London, G. P. Putnam's sons, 1884.
xii, 380 p.   illus., fold. maps.   23 cm.

17853 Welch, S   L   , comp.
Southern California illustrated, containing an epitome of the growth and industry of the three southern counties [Los Angeles, San Bernardino, San Diego counties]... Los Angeles, 1886-7.
152 p.   illus. maps, pl.   22 cm.

17854 Welles, C   M
Three years' wanderings of a Connecticut Yankee, in South America, Africa, Australia, and California, with description of the several countries, manners, customs, and conditions of the people... also a detailed account of a voyage around the world... New York, 1859.
358 p.   illus.

17855 Wells, Daniel H   , fl. 1848.
Daniel H. Wells' narrative. Salt Lake City, Utah State Historical Society, 1933. (In Utah historical quarterly, v. 6, no. 4, October 1933, p. 124-132)

17856 Wells, Emmeline Blanche (Woodward), 1828-1921, ed.
Charities and philanthropies. Woman's work in Utah. Edited... for the World's Fair. Salt Lake City, G. Q. Cannon, 1893.
90 p.   illus.   22 cm.
Contains biographical sketches of women physicians in Utah. In large part Mormon in viewpoint.

17857 Wells, William V
Wild life in Oregon. New York, 1856.
588-608 p.   24 cm.
Reprinted from Harper's Monthly Magazine, October, 1856.

17858   Wemett, W   M
Custer's expedition to the Black Hills in 1874.
[Bismarck, State Historical Society of North Dakota,
1932]
292-301 p.   24 cm.
Reprinted from North Dakota historical quarterly,
v. 6, no. 4, July 1932.

17859   Wesley, Edgar B
Some official aspects of the fur trade in the
Northwest, 1815-1825. [Bismarck, State Historical
Society of North Dakota, 1932]
201-209 p.   24 cm.
Reprinted from North Dakota historical quarterly,
v. 6, no. 3, April 1932.

17860   Wesley, Edgar B
A still larger view of the so-called Yellowstone
Expedition. [Bismarck, State Historical Society of
North Dakota, 1931]
219-238 p.   24 cm.
Reprinted from North Dakota historical quarterly,
v. 5, no. 4, July 1931.

17861   Western Texas the Australia of America; or, The place
live. By a six years' resident. Cincinnati,
E. Mendenhall, 1860.
iv, vii, 9-235 p.   20 cm.

17862   Weston, William, comp. and ed.
The Denver, Northwestern and Pacific railway
(Moffat road) and inducements of the country traversed
by its operated and projected line to settlers,
miners, tourists and sportsmen, ed. and comp. by
Mr. W. Weston from his reports made for Mr. D. H.
Moffat, president of the Denver, Northwestern and
Pacific railway company. Denver, Col., Majestic
building, 1905.
127 p.   illus., fold. map, diagr.   23 cm.

17863   Westward march of emigration in the United States,
considered in its bearing upon the near future of
Colorado and New Mexico. March, 1874. Lancaster,
Pa., 1874.
53 p.   20½ cm.

17864   Wetherbee, John, jr.
Brief sketch of Colorado territory and the gold

mines of that region. Boston, 1863.
24 p.   21 cm.

17865 Wetmore, Charles A
       Report of Mission Indians of Southern California
       [by] Chas. A. Wetmore. Washington, Government
       Printing Office, 1875.
       17 p.   21½ cm.

17866 Wharton, William H
       Texas. Address delivered in New York, on Tuesday,
       April 26, 1836. Also, Address of the Honorable
       Stephen F. Austin, delivered in Louisville, Kentucky,
       on the 7th March, 1836... New York, 1836.
       56 p.   19 cm.

17867 Wheeler, Alfred, 1822-1903.
       Land titles in San Francisco, and the laws affecting
       the same, with a synopsis of all grants and sales of
       land within the limits claimed by the city. By
       Alfred Wheeler. San Francisco, Alta California
       steam printing establishment, 1852.
       127, 1 p., 1 l.   fold. map.   27½ cm.

17868 Wheeler, George C
       The ants of North Dakota, by George C. Wheeler and
       Esther W. Wheeler. [Bismarck, State Historical
       Society of North Dakota, 1944]
       231-271 p.   illus.   24 cm.
       Reprinted from North Dakota historical quarterly,
       v. 11, no. 4, October 1944.

17869 Wheelock, Mrs. Irene (Grosvenor)
       Birds of California; an introduction to more than
       three hundred common birds of the state and adjacent
       islands, with a supplementary list of rare migrants,
       accidental visitants, and hypothetical subspecies,
       by Irene Grosvenor Wheelock... with ten full-page
       plates and seventy-eight drawings in the text by
       Bruce Horsfall. Chicago, A. C. McClurg & co., 1904.
       xxviii, 578 p.   col. front., illus. (incl. map)
       9 pl.   19½ cm.

17870 Whitaker, Ozi W
       The missionary jurisdiction of Nevada. [n.p., n.d.]
       8 p.   illus.   20 cm.   (P. E. Church.
       Domestic missions. I)

17871   White, J   M
          The newer Northwest; a description of the health
resorts and mining camps of the Black Hills of South
Dakota and Big Horn mountains in Wyoming. St. Louis,
1894.
          205 p.   20 cm.

17872   [White, William Francis] 1829-1891?
          A picture of pioneer times in California, illus-
trated with anecdotes and stories taken from real life.
By William Grey [pseud.] Author's ed. San Francisco,
Printed by W. M. Hinton & co., 1881.
          vii, 677 p. $22\frac{1}{2}$ cm.

17873   Whitely, Ike.
          Rural life in Texas. Atlanta, Ga., 1891.
          82 p.   illus., pl.   21 cm.

17874   Whitford, William C
          Colorado volunteers in the civil war: the New
Mexico campaign in 1862. Denver, 1906.
          159 p.   illus., maps, pl., port.   21 cm.

17875   Whiting, Lilian, 1859-
          The land of enchantment, from Pike's Peak to the
Pacific, by Lilian Whiting... With illustrations
from photographs. Boston, Little, Brown, and company,
1906.
          xii, 347 p.   front., 31 pl. $22\frac{1}{2}$ cm.

17876   [Whiting, William Henry Chase] 1825-1865.
          Diary of a march from El Paso to San Antonio [Apr. 19-
May 5, 1850]. (In Southern history association.
Publications. Washington, D. C., 1902) v. 6, p. [283]-
294, [389]-399.

17877   Whitney, Ernest.
          Pictures and poems of the Pike's Peak region.
Pictures by W. H. Sanford; poems by Ernest Whitney.
Colorado Springs [1891]
          22 p.   pl.   27 x 25 cm.

17878   Whitney, Joel Parker, 1835-1913.
          Colorado in the United States of America. Schedule
of ores contributed by sundry persons to the Paris
universal exposition of 1867, with some information
about the region and its resources. London, 1867.
          61 p.   maps. $20\frac{1}{2}$ cm.

17879   Whitney, Josiah D
          Geological survey of California. An address
          delivered before the legislature of California, at
          Sacramento... March 12, 1861; to which is appended a
          copy of the act authorizing the survey. San Francisco,
          1861.
            50 p.   22 cm.

17880   Whitney, Orson F
          History of Utah, comprising... chapters on the
          previous history of her founders, accounts of early
          Spanish and American explorations in the Rocky
          mountain region, the advent of the Mormon pioneers,
          the establishment and dissolution of the provisional
          government of the state of Deseret, and the subsequent
          creation and development of the territory. Salt Lake
          City, George Q. Cannon & sons, 1892-98.
            3 v.   23 cm.

17881   Who's who in Colorado and Cheyenne, Wyo. Denver, Col.,
          Geo. V. Richards, 1918-
            v.   23 cm.
          Library has 1918-20.

17882   Who's who in Nevada; brief sketches of men who are making
          history in the Sagebrush state. Pub. by Bessie Beatty.
          Los Angeles, Cal. Home printing company, 1907.
            276 p.   port.   23 cm.

17883   Who's who in the Pacific southwest. A compilation of
          authentic biographical sketches of citizens of Southern
          California and Arizona. Los Angeles, The Times-mirror
          printing & binding house, 1913.
            410 p.   26 cm.

17884   Wier, Jeanne Elizabeth.
          The work of the Western state historical society
          as illustrated by Nevada. In American historical
          association, annual report for 1910, p. 199-208.
          Washington, 1912.

17885   Wight, Samuel F
          Adventures in California and Nicaragua, in rhyme.
          A truthful epic, by Samuel F. Wight. Boston, A. Mudge
          & son, 1860.
            84 p.   24 cm.

17886 Wilber, Charles D
      Great valleys and prairies of Nebraska and the
      Northwest. Ed. 3. Omaha, Neb., 1881.
      8, 382 p.   pl.   21 cm.

17887 Wilder, Marshall P
      California. Boston, 1871.
      31 p.   20 cm.

17888 Wilder, Walter Lawson.
      Robert Wilbur Steele, defender of liberty, by
      Walter Lawson Wilder... Denver, Col., Carson-Harper
      co., 1913.
      5 p.l., [9]-327 p.   front., plates, ports.
      21½ cm.

17889 Will, George Francis, 1884-
      Arikara ceremonials. [Bismarck, State Historical
      Society of North Dakota, 1930]
      247-265 p.   24 cm.
      Reprinted from North Dakota historical quarterly,
      v. 4, no. 4, July 1930.

17890 Will, George Francis, 1884-
      Dr. Melvin Randolph Gilmore, by George F. Will.
      [Bismarck, State Historical Society of North Dakota,
      1941]
      179-183 p.   front. (port.)   24 cm.
      Reprinted from North Dakota historical quarterly,
      v. 8, no. 3, April 1941.

17891 Will, George Francis, 1884-
      Magical and sleight of hand performances by the
      Arikara, by George F. Will. [Bismarck, State
      Historical Society of North Dakota, 1928]
      50-65 p.   24 cm.
      Reprinted from North Dakota historical quarterly,
      v. 3, no. 1, October 1928.

17892 Will, George Francis, 1884-
      The Mandan lodge at Bismarck. [Bismarck, State
      Historical Society of North Dakota, 1930]
      38-48 p.   24 cm.
      Reprinted from North Dakota historical quarterly,
      v. 5, no. 1, October 1930.

17893 Will, George Francis, 1884-
      Upper Missouri River Valley a original culture

in North Dakota, by George F. Will and Thad. C.
Hecker. [Bismarck, State Historical Society of
North Dakota, 1944]
    5-126 p., 17 pl.   24 cm.
Reprinted from North Dakota historical quarterly,
v. 11, nos. 1 and 2, January-April 1944.

17894 Will, George Francis, 1884-
       The value of historical societies in the plains
states, by George F. Will. [Bismarck, State Historical
Society of North Dakota, 1944]
       272-281 p.   24 cm.
       Reprinted from North Dakota historical quarterly,
v. 11, no. 4, October 1944.

17895 Willard, Mrs. Emma (Hart) 1787-1870.
       Last leaves of American history: comprising a
separate history of California. By Emma Willard...
New York, A. S. Barnes & co.; Cincinnati, H. W. Derby
& co., 1853.
       277 p.   front. (map)   19 cm.
       "The account of the Mexican war, herein contained, is
taken from the author's history of 'The republic of
America.'" - Pref.

17896 Willard, James Field.
       The public archives of Colorado. American historical
association. Annual report for 1911, v. 1, p. 365-392.
Washington, 1913.

17897 Willcox, R   N
       Reminiscences of California life. Being an
abridged description of scenes which the author has
passed through in California, and other lands. With
quotations from other authors. A short lecture on
psychic science. An article on church and state:
written by his son, R. P. Willcox. By R. N. Willcox,
Avery, Ohio. [Avery] Willcox print., 1897.
       3 p.l., 5-290 p.   21½ cm.

17898 Willey, Samuel H
       The transition period of California from a province
of Mexico in 1846 to a state of the American union in
1850. San Francisco, 1901.
       12, 160 p.   20 cm.

17899 Williams, Alfred M
       Sam Houston and the war of independence in Texas.

Boston, 1893.
7, 495 p.   maps, port.   19 cm.

17900 Williams, Ellen.
Three years and a half in the army; or, History of
the Second Colorados. By Mrs. Ellen Williams. New
York, Pub. for the author by Fowler & Wells co. [c1885]
2 p.l., 178 p.   front. (port.)   19½ cm.

17901 Williams, Parley L
Personal recollections of Wash-A-Kie, chief of the
Shoshones, by P. L. Williams. Salt Lake City, Utah
State Historical Society, 1928. (In Utah historical
quarterly, v. 1, no. 4, October 1928, p. 100-106)

17902 Williams, Robert Hamilton, b. 1831.
With the border ruffians; memories of the Far West,
1852-1868. Edited by E. W. Williams. New York,
Dutton, 1907.
xviii, 478 p.   illus., ports.   23 cm.

17903 Wills, Mrs. Mary H
A winter in California. By Mary H. Wills.
Norristown, Pennsylvania [M. R. Wills] 1889.
150 p.   19 cm.

17904 Willson, Marcius, 1813-1905.
American history: comprising historical sketches of
the Indian tribes; a description of American antiquities, with an inquiry into their origin and the
origin of the Indian tribes; history of the United
States, with appendices showing its connection with
European history; history of the present British
provinces; history of Mexico; and history of Texas,
brought down to the time of its admission into the
American union. New York, M. H. Newman, 1847.
iv, [5]-688 p.   illus., maps.   21 cm.

17905 Wilmer, Lambert A   1805?-1863.
The life, travels and adventures of Ferdinand de
Soto, discoverer of the Mississippi. By Lambert A.
Wilmer. Steel engravings by John & Saml. Sartain...
The illustrations, designed and engraved on wood,
by J. W. Orr and R. Telfer... Philadelphia, J. T.
Lloyd, 1858.
iv, 532 p. incl. illus., 8 pl.   3 pl., 3 port.
(incl. front.)   23 cm.

17906   Wilson, Harry Leon, 1867-
      The lions of the Lord, a tale of the old West,
    by Harry Leon Wilson... illustrated by Rose Cecil
    O'Neill. Boston, Lothrop publishing company [1903]
    viii, [3], 11-520 p.   front., 5 pl.   20 cm.

17907   Wilson, Jeremiah M
      Admission of Utah. Argument on the admission of
    Utah as a state, made before the committee on
    territories of the United States senate... Feb. 18,
    1888. Washington, D. C., 1888.
      14 p.   23 cm.

17908   Wilson, Obed Gray, 1836-
      My adventures in the Sierras. By Obed G. Wilson.
    Franklin, O., The Editor publishing co., 1902.
      1 p.l., 215 p.   port. $19\frac{1}{2}$ cm.

17909   Winkler, Ernest William, 1875-1960.
      Check list of Texas imprints. With a foreword by
    Thomas W. Streeter. Austin, Texas State Historical
    Association, 1949-63.
      2 v.   ports.   25 cm.
      An expansion of a check list begun by the Historical
    Records Survey for the American imprints inventory
    and continued under the State-Wide Library Project in
    Texas. Vol. 2 edited by Ernest W. Winkler and
    Llerena Friend.

17910   Winter, Nevin Otto, 1869-
      Texas, the marvellous, the state of the six flags,
    including accounts of the Spanish settlement and
    establishment of the Indian missions; the unfortunate
    expedition and death of La Salle; the romance of its
    early settlement and stories of its hardy pioneers...
    and the general development of this marvellous state,
    by Nevin O. Winter... with a map and fifty-four
    plates, of which six are in colour. Boston, The Page
    company, 1916.
      xii, 343 p.   col. front., plates (part col.)
    ports. (1 col.) fold. map.   25 cm.   (On verso of
    half-title: See America first series)

17911   Winthrop, Robert C
      Speech on the annexation of Texas, delivered in
    the house of representatives of the United States,
    Jan. 6, 1845. Washington, 1845.
      16 p.   19 cm.

17912 Wisdom, M   D   , comp.
       Oregon; a booklet on the resources of a wonderful
       state, published by the Oregon commission of the
       Alaska-Yukon-Pacific exposition. [Salem, Ore., 1909]
       96 p.   illus.   18 cm.

17913 Wise, Henry Augustus, 1819-1869.
       Los Gringos: or an inside view of Mexico and
       California, with wanderings in Peru, Chili, and
       Polynesia. London, 1849.
       16, 406 p.   20 cm.

17914 Woelmont, Arnold de, baron.
       Ma vie nomade aux Montagnes rocheuses. Paris,
       Firmin-Didot et c^{ie}, 1878.
       366 p.   front., fold. map.   20 cm.

17915 Wolfe, J   M   , comp.
       Guide, gazetteer and directory of Nebraska railroads...
       a general description of the state... and a collection
       of other valuable miscellaneous information.   Omaha,
       1872.
       160 p.   map.   15 cm.

17916 Wolfe, J   M   , comp.
       Nebraska gazetteer and business directory for 1879-80,
       arranged alphabetically by counties; embracing a general
       description of Nebraska... together with a complete
       classified business directory... Omaha, 1879.
       8, 368 p.   map.   18 cm.

17917 Wolfe, J   M   , comp.
       Souvenir of the Nebraska legislature, 1895-96...
       Omaha, Neb., 1895.
       192 p.   illus., port.   18 cm.

17918 Woman's Literary Club, Colorado Springs.
       The Biennial note-book, presented to the delegates
       to the fourth biennial national convention of the
       General Federation of Women's Clubs, at Denver,
       June 21-27, 1898. By the Woman's Literary Club
       [and others]. Colorado Springs, Chamber of Commerce
       [1898]
       64 p.   illus., ports.   14½ x 21 cm.

17919 Wood, Ruth Kedzie.
       The tourist's California, by Ruth Kedzie Wood...
       with numerous illustrations. New York, Dodd, Mead

336

and company, 1915.
6 p.l., 395 p.   front., plates, fold. map.
19½ cm.

17920 [Wood, Stanley]
With nature in Colorado; a brief resume of the
grandeur of the Rocky mountain region... [Denver,
Carson-Harper printing, 1905]
32 p.   illus.   21½ cm.
Published by the Passenger department of the Denver
& Rio Grande system. Fifth edition.

17921 Wood, William D   1828-
Reminiscences of reconstruction in Texas, and Reminiscences of Texas and Texans fifty years ago. By
W. D. Wood. [n.p.] 1902.
58 p.   23½ cm.

17922 Woodbury, Angus M   , 1886.
A history of southern Utah and its national parks,
by Angus M. Woodberry. Salt Lake City, Utah State
Historical Society, 1944. (In Utah historical
quarterly, v. 12, nos. 3, 4, July, October 1944,
p. 112-222)

17923 Woodbury, Angus M   , 1886-
The route of Jedediah S. Smith in 1826 from the
Great Sale Lake to the Colorado River, by A. M.
Woodbury, park naturalist, Zion National Park, Utah.
Salt Lake City, Utah State Historical Society, 1931.
(In Utah historical quarterly, v. 4, no. 2, April 1931,
p. 34-45)

17924 Woodbury, Levi.
Speech in executive session, on the treaty for the
reannexation of Texas to the United States, delivered
in the senate of the United States, June 4, 1844.
[Washington, 1844]
20 p.   18 cm.

17925 Woodruff, George H
Will County [Illinois] on the Pacific slopes, an
historical sketch. Joliet, Ill., 1885.
103 p.   18 cm.

17926 Woods, Daniel B
Sixteen months at the gold diggings. By Daniel B.

Woods. New York, Harper & bros., 1851.
199 p.   19 cm.

17927   Woods, James.
Recollections of pioneer work in California. San
Francisco, 1878.
260 p.   19 cm.

17928   Woods, Samuel D
Lights and shadows of life on the Pacific coast,
by S. D. Woods. New York and London, Funk & Wagnalls
company, 1910.
4 p.l., 474 p.   front. (port.)   20½ cm.

17929   Woodward, Walter Carleton.
The rise and early history of political parties in
Oregon 1843-1868, by Walter Carleton Woodward...
Portland, Ore., The J. K. Gill company, 1913.
xiii, 276, [1] p.   front., ports.   22½ cm.

17930   Wooten, Dudley G   , ed.
Comprehensive history of Texas, 1685 to 1897.
Dallas, 1898.
2 v.   illus., maps, pl., port.   24 cm.

17931   Wren, Thomas, 1824-1904, ed.
A history of the state of Nevada, its resources
and people; the late Hon. Thomas Wren... editor-in-
chief... New York, Chicago, The Lewis publishing
company, 1904.
760 p.   front., plates, ports.   28 cm.

17932   Wright, Ione William (Tanner) "Mrs. S. J. Wright,"
1861-
San Antonio de Bexar, historical, traditional,
legendary. An epitome of early Texas history, by
Mrs. S. J. Wright... illustrated with drawings by
J. M. Longmire, from rare photographs. Austin, Tex.,
Morgan printing co. [c1916]
7 p.l., 169 p. incl. front., illus.   20 cm.

17933   Wright, Robert Marr, 1840-
Dodge City, the cowboy capital, and the great
Southwest in the days of the wild Indian, the buffalo,
the cowboy, dance halls, gambling halls and bad men,
by Robert M. Wright... [Wichita, Kan., Wichita eagle
press, c1913]
344 p.   col. front., plates, ports.   20½ cm.

17934 Wright, William, 1829-1898.
        History of the big bonanza: an authentic account
    of the discovery, history, and working of the world
    renowned Comstock silver lode of Nevada, including the
    present condition of the various mines situated thereon;
    sketches of the most prominent men interested in them;
    incidents and adventures connected with mining, the
    Indians, and the country; amusing stories, experiences,
    anecdotes, &c., &c., and a full exposition of the
    production of pure silver. By Dan De Quille (William
    Wright)... Hartford, Conn., American publishing
    company; San Francisco, Cal., A. L. Bancroft & co.,
    1877.
        xvi, 17-569 p. incl. illus., plates, ports.   23 cm.

17935 [Wright, William]
        A history of the Comstock silver lode & mines,
    Nevada and the great basin region; Lake Tahoe and the
    high Sierras... The mineral and agricultural resources
    of "Silverland"... By Dan De Quille [pseud.]
    Virginia, Nev., F. Boegle [c1889]
        x, 11-158 p.   18 cm.

17936 Wyeth, Nathaniel Jarvis, 1802-1856.
        ... The correspondence and journals of Captain
    Nathaniel J. Wyeth, 1831-6; a record of two expeditions
    for the occupation of the Oregon country, with maps,
    introduction and index... Ed. by F. G. Young...
    Eugene, Ore., University press, 1899.
        xiv, 262 p.   2 fold. maps.   24½ cm.   (Sources
    of the history of Oregon... v. 1, p. 3-6)

17937 Wyoming. State Historian.
        Wyoming. Its symbols. Its capitol. Its Historical
    Department. Cheyenne, Wyoming Historical Department,
    1922.
        8 unnumb. pages.   23 cm.

                              Y

17938 Yates, Lorenzo Gordin.
        Charm stones, the so-called "plummets" or "sinkers"
    of California. Santa Barbara, 1890.
        13-28 p.   pl.   21 cm.   (Santa Barbara society of
    natural history, Bulletin no. 2)

                              339

17939 Year book for Texas... By C. W. Raines... v. [1]-2;
       1901-[03] Austin, Tex., Gammel-statesman publishing
       company, 1902-03.
         2 v.   front., plates, ports.   23½ cm.

17940 Yeary, Mamie, 1876-   comp.
         Reminiscences of the boys in gray, 1861-1865, comp.
       by Miss Mamie Yeary... Dallas, Tex., For the author
       by Smith & Lamar, publishing house M. E. church,
       South [c1912]
         3 p.l., 904 p.   front., plates (1 col.) ports.
       25½ cm.
         Sketches of several hundred Confederate veterans,
       now residing in Texas, giving particulars of their
       war service.

17941 Yellowstone Highway Association.
         Official route book of the Yellowstone highway
       association in Wyoming and Colorado... [Chicago,
       Wallace press, c1916]
         6, viii, 7-145, [1] p.   illus. (incl. ports.,
       maps) fold. pl., fold. map.   26½ x 13½ cm.

17942 Young, Brigham, 1801-1877.
         Letter from Brigham Young, G.S.L. City, July 11,
       1862 to Elder N. V. Jones, Rocky Ford, Beaver County,
       U.T. Salt Lake City, Utah State Historical Society,
       1931. (In Utah historical quarterly, v. 4, no. 1,
       January 1931, p. 24)

17943 Young, Frederick George, 1858-
         ... Exploration northwestward by F. G. Young...
       also The Hudson's Bay company regime in the Oregon
       country, by Eva Emery Dye, A. M. Pub. with the
       approval of the Regents of the university. Eugene,
       Or., The University, 1898.
         2 p.l., 32 (i.e. 31) p.   illus. (maps)   24½ cm.
       (Semi-centennial history of Oregon. [2-3])

17944 Young, Frederick George, 1858-
         Report on the archives of Oregon. In American
       historical association. Annual report for 1902,
       v. 1, p. 337-355. Washington, 1903.
         Submitted by the Public archives commission to the
       American historical association.

17945 Young, John R
         Reminiscences of John R. Young; extracts from letters

written by John R. Young, pioneer of 1847, to his
grandson, John A. Young, to whom they were submitted.
Salt Lake City, Utah State Historical Society, 1930.
(In Utah historical quarterly, v. 3, no. 3, July 1930,
p. 83-86)